The Livery Collar
in Late Medieval
England and Wales

The Livery Collar
in Late Medieval
England and Wales

Politics, Identity and Affinity

MATTHEW WARD

THE BOYDELL PRESS

© Matthew Ward 2016

All Rights Reserved. Except as permitted under current legislation no part of this work may be photocopied, stored in a retrieval system, published, performed in public, adapted, broadcast, transmitted, recorded or reproduced in any form or by any means, without the prior permission of the copyright owner

The right of Matthew Ward to be identified as the author of this work has been asserted in accordance with sections 77 and 78 of the Copyright, Designs and Patents Act 1988

First published 2016
The Boydell Press, Woodbridge

ISBN 978 1 78327 115 3

The Boydell Press is an imprint of Boydell & Brewer Ltd
PO Box 9, Woodbridge, Suffolk IP12 3DF, UK
and of Boydell & Brewer Inc.
668 Mt Hope Avenue, Rochester, NY 14620–2731, USA
website: www.boydellandbrewer.com

A catalogue record for this book is available
from the British Library

The publisher has no responsibility for the continued existence or accuracy of URLs for external or third-party internet websites referred to in this book, and does not guarantee that any content on such websites is, or will remain, accurate or appropriate

This publication is printed on acid-free paper
Printed and bound in Great Britain by TJ International Ltd.

Dedicated to C.E.J. ('Sedge') Smith

The publishers acknowledge the generous financial support of the Marc Fitch Fund in the production of this volume.

Contents

	List of illustrations	viii
	Acknowledgements	x
	Abbreviations	xi
	Introduction: The Livery Collar and Its Contexts	1
	Part I	17
1	Function, Meaning and Significance	19
2	The Political Milieu	49
3	Visual Culture, Agency and Identities of Association	77
	Part II	97
4	The Appearance of Lancastrian and Yorkist Livery Collars on Church Monuments: Distribution and Motivations	99
5	Livery Collars in Wales and the Edgecote Connection	147
	Conclusion	179
	Appendix 1: Genealogies	187
	Appendix 2: Livery Collars on Church Monuments in England, Wales and Ireland to *c.* 1540	199
	Bibliography	213
	Index	237

Illustrations

Plates – *plates appear between pages 116–117*

Plate 1. Henry VI portrait, unknown artist (*c*. 1540). London, National Portrait Gallery.

Plate 2. Sir John Donne portrait, Donne Triptych, Hans Memling (*c*. 1475). London, The National Gallery

Plate 3. SS dog collar worn by a white greyhound, Henry IV's beast, accompanied by the king's motto *Ma soueraine*; *Statutes of England* (1420s). Merton College, Oxford, MS 297B, fol. 273r. By kind permission of the Warden and Fellows of Merton College

Plate 4. A knight is awarded a collar by the king (*c*. 1458). London, British Library, Additional MS 30946, fol. 82v. © The British Library Board

Plate 5. The Lord Mayor's collar. By kind permission of the Rt Hon. The Lord Mayor of London

Plate 6. John, duke of Bedford portrait, from the *Bedford Hours* (*c*. 1423). British Library, Additional MS 18850, fol. 256v. © The British Library Board

Plate 7. William Herbert and his wife kneel before Edward IV, in John Lydgate's *Troy Book* (*c*. 1461–62). British Library, Royal MS 18 D II, fol. 6. © The British Library Board

Plate 8. Henry VII and his courtiers, from *A Collection of Astrological Treatises* (*c*. 1490). British Library, Arundel 66, fol. 201. © The British Library Board

Plate 9. Tomb of William Herbert and his wife, Tintern Abbey; the *Herbertorum Prosapia*. Cardiff Central Library, Philipps MS, 5:7, p. 145. Courtesy of Cardiff Council Library Service

Plate 10. Military ordinance of Charles the Bold; Master of Fitzwilliam 268 (1475). British Library, Additional MS 36619, fol. 5. © The British Library Board

LIST OF ILLUSTRATIONS IX

Figures

Figure 1. St Mary's, Bury St Edmunds (Suffolk). John Baret (d. 1467). By kind permission of Stiffleaf Photography and St Mary's Church, Bury St Edmunds   32

Figure 2. George, duke of Clarence, from the *Rous Roll*. British Library, Additional MS 48976, fols. 58–61. © The British Library Board   43

Figure 3. St Mary's and St Barlok's, Norbury (Derbyshire). Nicholas Fitzherbert (d. 1473). By kind permission of Norbury PCC   133

Figure 4. All Saints', Sawley (Derbyshire). Roger Bothe (d. 1478). By kind permission of the Reverend Tony Street   136

Figure 5. All Saints', Youlgreave (Derbyshire). Thomas Cockayne (d. 1488). By kind permission of the Reverend Garrie Griffiths   138

Figure 6. All Saints', Kedleston (Derbyshire). John Curzon (d. *c*. 1492) and his wife, Joan. By kind permission of the Churches Conservation Trust   141

Figure 7. All Saints', Mugginton (Derbyshire). Nicholas Kniveton (d. 1500). By kind permission of the Reverend Canon Alan Harper   142

Figure 8. Priory Church of St Mary, Abergavenny (Monmouthshire). Sir William ap Thomas (d. 1445) and his wife, Gwladys. By kind permission of Canon Mark Soady   153

Figure 9. John Carter's drawing of Sir Richard Herbert's tomb effigy (1469). British Library, Additional MS 29938, fol. 74r. © The British Library Board   171

Figure 10. Scolton Manor Museum (Pembrokeshire). Sir Henry Wogan (d. 1475). Under the care of the service at the County Museum, Scolton Manor. © Pembrokeshire Museums Service   174

Maps – *appear with plates between pages 116–117*

Map 1. Geographical distribution of livery collars in England, Wales and Ireland

Map 2. Distribution of livery collars according to type

Acknowledgements

I owe a great debt of gratitude to many individuals for their help and advice. Firstly, I would like to express my sincere thanks to Dr Rob Lutton for his encouragement and help throughout the process of writing the book, and for being a supportive mentor during my PhD studies. Some eighteen months into my research, I was made aware of C.E.J. Smith's list of livery collars, compiled in his years of retirement. From the moment I contacted him, C.E.J. kindly made himself available to offer advice and enthusiasm. His help and knowledge of the livery collar, and his offer to share his list of collars with me, were greatly appreciated. I would also like to thank Dr Ross Balzaretti, Dr Gwilym Dodd, Dr Richard Goddard, Dr Gabriele Neher and Professor Tony Pollard for their support, ideas and comments on draft chapters of the book. For their expert knowledge of the history of Derbyshire I must express my gratitude to Margaret O'Sullivan and Philip Riden, and Jennie Pegram for sharing her thoughts on the Pole family of Radbourne. Equally, I would like to acknowledge Dr Rhianydd Biebrach and Professor Ralph Griffiths for their expertise on Welsh history and church monuments during the Wars of the Roses, and for offering their thoughts on a draft of the Wales case study. I owe a great debt of gratitude to Nicholas Fitzherbert, Sir Richard FitzHerbert and Lord Stafford for allowing me to access the Fitzherbert family documents. For their generous thoughts on church monuments I would like to thank Sally Badham MBE, Philip Lankester and Geoffrey Wheeler. I must also express my appreciation to a multitude of incumbents, churchwardens, archivists and librarians who have provided friendly assistance and interest on my site visits. I would like to thank Dr Hector Orengo for his assistance in producing the maps. Dr Rob Kinsey and Caroline Palmer at Boydell and Brewer have always been on hand to answer my queries. Their keenness on the project from its inception has been cherished. Last, but by no means least, my thanks go to my parents, who have endured countless informal lectures on the livery collar over the past few years.

Matthew Ward

Abbreviations

Cal. Inq. Misc.	*Calendar of Inquisitions Miscellaneous, Chancery, Preserved in the Public Record Office*, 7 vols (London, 1916–68)
CChR	*Calendar of Charter Rolls Preserved in the Public Record Office*, 6 vols (London, 1903–27)
CCR	*Calendar of Close Rolls Preserved in the Public Record Office, 1441–85*, 6 vols (London, 1933–54)
CFR	*Calendar of Fine Rolls Preserved in the Public Record Office, 1452–1509*, 4 vols (London, 1911–62)
CIPM	*Calendar of Inquisitions Post Mortem and Other Analogous Documents Preserved in the Public Record Office, Henry VII*, 3 vols (London, 1898–1955)
CPR	*Calendar of Patent Rolls Preserved in the Public Record Office, 1370–1509*, 25 vols (London, 1895–1916)
DAJ	*Derbyshire Archaeological Journal*
Derbyshire Gentry	S.M. Wright, *The Derbyshire Gentry in the Fifteenth Century*, Derbyshire Record Society, 8 (Chesterfield, 1983)
DRO	Derbyshire Record Office, Matlock
Dunham	W.H. Dunham, *Lord Hastings' Indentured Retainers 1461–1483*, Transactions of the Connecticut Academy of Arts and Sciences, 39 (1955, reprinted 1970)
English Church Monuments	N. Saul, *English Church Monuments in the Middle Ages: History and Representation* (Oxford, 2009)
Every MSS	Sir Edward Every Deeds, Derby Local Studies Library
Friar	S. Friar, 'Livery Collars on Late-Medieval English Church Monuments: A Survey of the South-Western Counties and Some Suggestions for Further Study', University of Southampton, unpublished MPhil dissertation (2000)
Harleian 433	R. Horrox and P.W. Hammond (eds), *British Library Harleian Manuscript 433: Register of Grants for the Reigns of Edward V and Richard III*, 4 vols (Upminster and London, 1979–83)

Heraldry	P. Coss and M. Keen (eds), *Heraldry, Pageantry and Social Display in Medieval England* (Woodbridge, 2002)
'The Herberts'	D.H. Thomas, 'The Herberts of Raglan as Supporters of the House of York in the Second Half of the Fifteenth Century', University of Wales, unpublished MA thesis (1967)
HP	*Herbertorum Prosapia*, Cardiff Central Library, Philipps MS, 5:7
Jeayes	I.H. Jeayes, *Descriptive Catalogue of Derbyshire Charters in the Public and Private Libraries and Muniment Rooms* (London and Derby, 1906)
John Vale's Book	M.L. Kekewich, C. Richmond, A.F. Sutton, L. Visser-Fuchs and J.L. Watts (eds), *The Politics of Fifteenth-Century England: John Vale's Book* (Stroud, 1995)
LRO	Lichfield Record Office
'Livery Collar'	C.E.J. Smith, 'The Livery Collar', *Coat of Arms*, 8 (1990), 238–53
Monumental Industry	S. Badham and S. Oosterwijk (eds), *Monumental Industry: The Production of Tomb Monuments in England and Wales in the Long Fourteenth Century* (Donington, 2010)
Mundy MS	Derby Local Studies Library, A900
NLW	National Library of Wales, Aberystwyth
PL	J. Gairdner (ed.), *The Paston Letters A.D. 1422–1509*, Complete Library edn, 6 vols (London, 1904)
PROME	C. Given-Wilson *et al.* (eds), *The Parliament Rolls of Medieval England, 1275–1504* (Leicester, 2005)
SRO	Stafford Record Office
Statutes of the Realm	A. Luders (ed.), *The Statutes of the Realm*, 11 vols (London, 1810–25)
Swynnerton MSS	A family history compiled in 1829, in the possession of Lord Stafford, at Swynnerton Park
Test. Ebor.	J. Raine and J.W. Clay (eds), *Testamenta Eboracensia, or, Wills registered at York*, Surtees Society, 6 vols (London, 1836–1902)
TMBS	*Transactions of the Monumental Brass Society*
TNA	The National Archives, London
VCH Derbys.	W. Page (ed.), *The Victoria County History of the County of Derby*, 2 vols (London, 1905–7)

Introduction

The Livery Collar and Its Contexts

> The maner of ynglonde was whan the kyng Nobilitatyd eny personne, to geve hym a certen baage or lyuery wyth hys Fee, whyche lyuery was a collar wyth letters of S made off golde or syluer.

John Blount's translation of Nicholas Upton's *De Studio Militari*, dating from c. 1500, is one of an abundance of references to the livery collar from the fifteenth and sixteenth centuries, albeit in this case not an entirely accurate interpretation of to whom the collar was given.[1] The collar found its way into literary sources, correspondence and royal ordinances, was the object of legislation, was referred to in petitions to the king, and was depicted in manuscript illustrations and on church monuments, sculpture and stained glass. Quite simply, it had a pervasive presence. If one considers the three hundred and more depictions of livery collars on extant church monuments and in stained glass from the fourteenth and fifteenth centuries, it is clear that the number of recipients of the item reached well into the hundreds, and probably the thousands. Despite this, the collar's very ubiquity has led to its being somewhat overlooked when it appears in the sources; it is forever present, but seemingly only on the periphery. The present study investigates the cultural and political meaning and utility of the livery collar during the fifteenth century, with a particular emphasis on the second half of the century, the period associated with the Wars of the Roses in England.

The livery collar was a band of leather or velvet decorated with devices usually composed of silver, silver-gilt or gold, and was worn about the neck. The more prestigious examples were produced entirely of precious metal and resembled a necklace. Many collars terminated in pendants which depicted an armorial device or, less commonly, an annulet, trefoil or cross, again usually made of metal. Part of the late medieval system of livery, the collar was the most prestigious item, being awarded to those of the rank of esquire or wealthy merchant and above. The more common badges, robes and caps were given to those

---

[1] Oxford, Bodleian Library, MS.Eng.misc.d.227, fol. 32; BL, Additional MS 30946. There is no evidence that a livery collar was given to every individual who was ennobled by the king. Those of a lower rank were also recipients.

further down the social spectrum. When it was introduced in the late fourteenth century the collar was given by leaders of baronial as well as royal affinities, but as a result of legislation in the early fifteenth century it increasingly became the preserve of the royal family. It was frequently referred to as the 'king's livery', and was awarded to household servants and perhaps to officers in the localities such as sheriffs, and to those who had demonstrated their loyalty on the battlefield. In addition it was conferred on foreign dignitaries and royalty; examples can be found in Italy and Belgium. The livery collar witnessed its apogee in the fifteenth century, when complaints over the perceived evils of livery and maintenance were at their loudest. Although it continued to be distributed under the Tudors, it increasingly came to represent insignia of office and was worn by high-ranking government officials, the judiciary and the royal heralds. Indeed, the heralds are still entitled to wear their livery collars today.

During the second half of the fifteenth century there were two types of collar. The Lancastrian collar of *esses*, or 'SS', was introduced in the late fourteenth century and is worn by Henry VI in a sixteenth-century portrait (Plate 1). This collar was revived by Henry Tudor on his accession to the throne in 1485. The Yorkist collar of alternate suns and roses, or more rarely roses set within suns, often referred to as *roses-en-soleil*, was introduced in *c.* 1461 and is depicted around the necks of Sir John and Lady Donne in Hans Memling's Donne Triptych (Plate 2). A total of three livery collars have survived the passage of time and are still with us today. Two examples in the Victoria and Albert Museum date from the early sixteenth century, and a collar discovered in the Thames in 1983, dating from the late fifteenth century, is held in the Museum of London.[2]

The collar was an artefact which held deep cultural significance for contemporaries. It provides the historian with an efficacious vehicle for exploring the understanding of royal authority, and the construction and expression of political and other forms of shared identity during the fifteenth century. The period provides the ideal context for examining the nature of political conviction and expression: the existence of 'opposing' Lancastrian and Yorkist collars during a period of instability and controversy over the function, or apparent malfunction, of bastard feudalism would appear to give the collar particular political pertinence. Collars and their wearers are here placed in their wider contexts in order to reach conclusions about the significance the item held for contemporaries. This book follows two broad strands: the motivations behind the donor who distributed the livery collar; and the motivations of those who wore them and chose to have them depicted on their memorials. Were the aims of the donor realised? Were the motivations of donor and recipient broadly similar, or were there tensions, with some recipients placing their own interpretations

---

[2] B. Spencer, 'Fifteenth-Century Collar of SS and Hoard of False Dice with Their Container, from the Museum of London', *Antiquaries Journal*, 65 (1985), 449–51.

on the collar? Were all collar wearers politically active supporters of the two respective regimes?

Perhaps not surprisingly, there has been little written specifically on the livery collar. Much of the interest has come from the antiquaries of the nineteenth and early twentieth centuries, who were more often than not fascinated by the Lancastrian SS collar and the elusive meaning behind the *esses*. It was this particular collar which was therefore their primary concern. An art-historical stylistic analysis of the collar's forms over a chronological period was also a favoured pursuit. Subsequent studies have in the main followed this approach, with livery collars frequently being treated as concomitant to other major topics. The occasional article devoted to the collar has appeared, which has built on the earlier work, or placed the artefact within the contexts of archaeology or jewellery.[3] A useful introductory article on the livery collar was published by C.E.J. Smith in 1990, and his unpublished catalogue of collars begun in 1992 has been indispensable to the present author. Stephen Friar's unpublished dissertation exploring the appearance of the livery collar on church monuments in the south-west of England has been equally informative. The provenance and meaning of the SS collar, alongside the meaning of the Yorkist suns and roses collar, will be addressed in this study, as will the form of the collar. My principal aim is to attempt to understand what the item meant to contemporaries, and to reach conclusions as to how it was understood and 'read'.

A study of an artefact which pervaded an array of cultural forms and whose presence spanned well over 150 years has necessarily drawn on several strands of literature. Material and visual culture studies have informed much of the work. The growing body of research from scholars of church monuments has also been valuable; the livery collar is portrayed in abundance on tomb effigies and monumental brasses from the late medieval period. In addition, the historiography of the Wars of the Roses has been invaluable, particularly in helping to place the collar within its political contexts.

---

[3] G.F. Beltz, 'Notices Relating to the Ancient "Collars of the King's Livery", and, in Particular, Those which are still Denominated "Collars of SS"', *Retrospective Review*, 16 (1828), 500–10; J. Gough Nichols, 'On Collars of the Royal Livery', *Gentleman's Magazine*, 18 (February, 1842), 157–61; 18 (March, 1842), 250–8; 18 (April, 1842), 378–80; 18 (May, 1842), 477–85; 18 (October, 1842), 353–60; 18 (December, 1842), 595–7; E. Foss, 'Hackington, or St. Stephen's, Canterbury. Collar of SS', *Archaeologia Cantiana*, 1 (1858), 73–93; G. Scharf, 'A Note upon Collars', *Archaeologia*, 39 (1863), 265–71; A. Hartshorne, 'Notes on Collars of SS', *Archaeological Journal*, 39 (1882), 376–83; W.K. Skeat, 'Souvent Me Souvient', *Christ's College Magazine* (Michaelmas Term, 1905), 1–5; A.P. Purey-Cust, *The Collar of SS, A History and Conjecture* (Leeds, 1910); C.K. Jenkins, 'Collars of SS: A Quest', *Apollo*, 49 (1949), 60–2; L. James, 'York and Lancaster, a Study of Collars', *TMBS*, 10 (1968), 454–7; R.W. Lightbown, *Mediaeval European Jewellery* (London, 1992), pp. 245–50; D. Fletcher, 'The Lancastrian Collar of Esses: Its Origins and Transformations down the Centuries', in J.L. Gillespie (ed.), *The Age of Richard II* (Stroud and New York, 1997), pp. 191–204; I. Mortimer, *The Fears of Henry IV* (London, 2008), pp. 384–7.

Used alongside documentary evidence, traditionally the staple of the historian, objects, artefacts and works of art can provide greater insight and depth to research, improving our comprehension of the topic by informing us of the social and psychological assumptions of the audience.[4] Of particular relevance to the present study is the use of material and visual culture to construct social identity, articulate political messages and values, and indicate allegiance to, or membership of, a group. During the medieval period, low levels of literacy meant that ruling regimes would frequently propagate their messages through media other than the written word, such as on sculpture and in painting. We should however be careful not to assume that objects are simply mirrors of a given society. Their intended message is not infrequently interpreted and responded to differently by varying audiences. This is particularly true when one considers the political control of images and objects. Although they often signify social privilege and control, objects can transcend cultural boundaries, making them difficult to control. The meanings of objects can be multifarious, and can change over time as each generation places its own values and assumptions on them. The role of constructivism, originally the focus of philosophy, has been an influence on cultural historians in this respect. It is the period specificity, the focus on the wider context of the objects, and the analysis of the tension between object and audience which the historian can offer to the study of material and visual culture.[5]

The field of cultural history has benefited from the concepts of several other disciplines over recent decades, notably art history, literary studies, anthropology and sociology. The art historian's traditional emphasis on style, form and aesthetics can be paired with a consideration of the social and cultural contexts in which the object was produced. The mid-twentieth century witnessed an accompanying 'visual turn' alongside the 'linguistic turn', with art historians attempting to place visual artefacts in their social contexts. Several ideas were applied from literary theory, not least visual hermeneutics, an interpretative method used for texts and works of art. The alliance between the two disciplines of art history and literary studies was encapsulated in the Warburg Institute, which moved to London in 1933. The philosophy of the institute has encouraged a synthesis between art-historical and historical practices. The disciplines share similar goals: both are interested in 'texts', and both agree that the works of sculptors and artists tell us a great deal about how they perceived their world.[6]

---

[4] R. Grassby, 'Material Culture and Cultural History', *Journal of Interdisciplinary History*, 35 (2005), 591–603.

[5] L. Jordanova, *The Look of the Past: Visual and Material Evidence in Historical Practice* (Cambridge, 2012), pp. 1–13; D. Freeberg, *The Power of Images: Studies in the History of Theory and Response* (Chicago and London, 1989).

[6] P. Erickson and C. Hulse, 'Introduction', in P. Erickson and C. Hulse (eds), *Early Modern Visual Culture: Representation, Race, and Empire in Renaissance England* (Philadelphia, 2000), pp. 1–14.

From the 1960s cultural historians have benefited from the influence of anthropology and sociology, resulting in the emergence of the field of historical anthropology. Scholars now talk of 'cultures' in their plurality, with 'elite', 'popular', 'print' and 'court' culture being subjected to historical enquiry. In addition, and influenced by Clifford Geertz and his interpretative method of 'thick description', historians have taken up the anthropologist's interest in symbols and symbolism, with the symbolic, rather than physical, characteristics of objects and actions the focus of attention.[7] This has permitted historians to take a fresh perspective when considering the use of objects to display power. Although the anthropological turn encouraged the historian to take into consideration mass culture and the role of symbolic action in addition to objects and artefacts as symbols, more recently scholars have revisited 'high' culture and its relationship with politics. Studies of the symbols of aristocratic and monarchical power, such as regalia, architecture and ceremony, have been undertaken in an attempt to assess their efficacy. The effectiveness of the facilitating and controlling abilities of institutions such as the monarchy in determining the use and interpretation of images and objects, in relation to the agency of the 'responder', has also been an area of interest.[8] A related concern has been the role of communities, as opposed to the individual, in interpreting culture, and investigating the political assumptions of groups.

A distinction has been made between 'object-centred' and 'object-driven' approaches to studying material culture. The former, favoured by art historians, focuses on the physical attributes and aesthetic qualities of the artefact, while the latter places the artefact in its historical context and uses it as evidence for analysing social relationships.[9] Although object analysis is an important element, not all material cultural studies require this approach; the existence of the artefact in itself allows the researcher to ask questions which require the analysis of other related evidence.[10] This is not infrequently the approach adopted by historians, and is the approach adopted here.

From the late fourteenth century, the collar began to appear in abundance on tomb effigies and monumental brasses. Extant examples of collars on church monuments provide the historian with the most abundant source of contemporary depictions. There were two primary motivations behind commissioning a church monument in late medieval England: sacred and secular. The intrinsic

---

[7] C. Geertz, *The Interpretation of Cultures* (New York, 1973); R. Chartier, *Cultural History: Between Practices and Representations*, trans. L.G. Cochrane (Cambridge, 1988), pp. 95–111.
[8] P. Burke, *The Fabrication of Louis XIV* (New Haven, CT, and London, 1992); J.A. Walker and S. Chaplin, *Visual Culture: An Introduction* (Manchester and New York, 1997), p. 94.
[9] B. Herman, *The Stolen House* (Charlottesville, VA, and London, 1992), pp. 4–12.
[10] J.D. Prown, *Art as Evidence: Writings on Art and Material Culture* (New Haven, CT, and London, 2001), p. 69.

importance of the doctrine of purgatory in life, death and commemoration cannot be overlooked.[11] The form and content of monuments reflected a concern to elicit prayers from the living to ease the commemorated through their purgatorial pains. Religious symbolism such as depictions of angels, saints and the Holy Trinity abounded on tombs and memorial brasses. The increasing popularity of inscriptions by the fifteenth century is also testament to concerns over the afterlife. They invariably began with the phrase '*Orate pro anima*' (pray for the soul of), followed by the name of the deceased and the day on which they had died. But those who were commemorated by a tomb or brass were also prompted by other concerns: the desire to depict one's social station, to articulate one's identity and social, cultural and political affiliations through secular discourse. It is this area with which the present study is concerned.

The use of secular imagery on monuments began well before the fifteenth century. Secular iconography was a prominent feature in European ecclesiastical buildings by the thirteenth century, with political imagery appearing on corbels and misericords, for example.[12] From the twelfth century, founders' tombs had been erected to celebrate the role of the commemorated in establishing the religious house in which they rested. In the following century, the church sanctioned the erection of intramural monuments for the laity, at least for those who had honoured their church. Influenced by the dynastic royal mausoleums at St-Denis in Paris and Westminster Abbey, nobles and knights followed the lead and tombs began to fill church and monastery, celebrating status, lineage and associations. It was not only the form and content of the monument which was important; the location of burial and funerary monument was a primary concern and reflected the social hierarchy. The very wealthy were buried in the chancel, with the slightly less affluent buried elsewhere in the church, such as in family or fraternity chapels. Memorial brasses were available for those who either favoured that particular medium, or were unable to afford a tomb and effigy. Heraldry began to appear on English monuments to the aristocracy in the thirteenth century, and this was soon followed by a proliferation of monuments commemorating the nobility, knights, gentry and wealthy merchants, a period when secular badges also appeared. By the end of the fourteenth century livery collars were being portrayed on tomb effigies and on memorial brasses. They were to be a burgeoning presence on monuments during the following hundred years.[13]

---

[11] C. Burgess, '"A Fond Thing Vainly Invented": An Essay on Purgatory and Pious Motive in Late Medieval England', in S.J. Wright (ed.), *Parish, Church and People: Local Studies in Lay Religion, 1350–1750* (London, 1988), pp. 56–84.

[12] P. Lindley, 'Introduction: Secular Sculpture 1300–1550', in P. Lindley and T. Frangenberg (eds), *Secular Sculpture 1300–1550* (Stamford, 2000), pp. 1–9.

[13] S. Badham, 'Status and Salvation: The Design of Medieval English Brasses and Incised Slabs', *TMBS*, 15 (1996), 413–65; A. Martindale, 'Patrons and Minders: The Intrusion of the

As the antiquary John Weever stipulated in the 1630s, 'sepulchres should be made according to the qualitie and degree of the person deceased, that by the Tombe every one might bee discerned of what ranke hee was living'.[14] In order for spectators to acknowledge the worldly rank of the deceased, it was crucial that monuments attracted the attention. This they clearly did, as testified with more than a hint of sarcasm in the *Creed of Piers Plowman*:

Tombes upon tabernacles
Tylde opon lofte, [raised high]
Housed in hornes,
Harde set abouten,
Of armede alabaustre
Clad for the nones, [decorated appropriately]
Maad opon marbel
In many manner wyse,
Knyghtes in ther conisante [cognizance]
Clad for the nones;
Alle it semed seyntes
Y-sacred opon erthe.[15]

To put it rather crudely, a monument had to be both a physical and visual obstruction. High tombs with effigies, some including canopies, were commonplace by the fifteenth century and were a conspicuous presence in churches, the eastern ends of which could be filled with an abundance of examples crowded around the high altar. These highly visible tombs served as mnemonic devices for prayers, and as proud representations of the honour and prestige of the deceased and their family. They were carefully positioned, deliberately obstructing the sight lines of both clergy and laity, and usually visible from the nave, altars and chapels in order to afford them a central role in the liturgy of the church.[16] Although brasses were less physically obtrusive (this may well have been a reason for their introduction), their bright metallic gleam would have been no less of an attraction. This, alongside the use of polychromy, jewels, gilding and coloured enamel

---

Secular into Sacred Spaces in the Late Middle Ages', in D. Wood (ed.), *The Church and The Arts* (Oxford, 1995), pp. 143–78; R. Dinn, '"Monuments Answerable to Mens Worth": Burial Patterns, Social Status and Gender in Late Medieval Bury St Edmunds', *Journal of Ecclesiastical History*, 46 (1995), 237–55; N. Rogers, '"Hic Iacet ...": The Location of Monuments in Late Medieval Parish Churches', in C. Burgess and E. Duffy (eds), *The Parish in Late Medieval England: Proceedings of the 2002 Harlaxton Symposium*, Harlaxton Medieval Studies, 14 (Donington, 2006), pp. 261–81.

[14] J. Weever, *Ancient Funerall Monuments* (London, 1631), p. 10.
[15] T. Wright (ed.), *The Vision and Creed of Piers Plowman*, 2 vols (London, 1856), ii, pp. 461–2.
[16] S. Roffey, *The Medieval Chantry Chapel: An Archaeology* (Woodbridge, 2007), p. 106.

served to catch the eye. Witness a Venetian visitor describing the tomb of St Thomas of Canterbury:

> This, notwithstanding its great size, is entirely covered over with plates of pure gold; but the gold is scarcely visible from the variety of precious stones with which it is studded, such as sapphires, diamonds, rubies, balas-rubies, and emeralds; and on every side that the eye turns, something more beautiful than the other appears.[17]

The account goes on to describe the effect of the sunlight illuminating the tomb decoration. Light shining on church monuments through stained glass, the angle of the sun's rays accentuating different aspects of the tomb, added to their magnificence. The same effect would be produced by the movement of candles and tapers around the tomb. The gilt and silver-gilt livery collars worn by tomb effigies, usually achieved by applying oil gilding (several layers of yellow oil and gold leaf),[18] would have played an integral part in the spectacle. Indeed, one of the few details of the collars that Richard Symonds noted on church monuments in the seventeenth century was their colour.[19] In some cases it appears that a metal collar was once affixed to tomb effigies. The effigy of Margaret Holland, duchess of Clarence (d. 1439), in Canterbury Cathedral, has double holes on the right of her neck, a double hole on her breastbone and two single holes on the left side of her neck, suggesting that a collar, in this instance of SS, was once present; this is confirmed by an engraving by Wenceslaus Hollar made in the 1630s. The effigy of Sir Reginald Cobham (d. 1446) at St Peter's and St Paul's, Lingfield (Surrey), features similar holes.[20] 'Elite' objects such as the livery collar were intricately produced to attract the light through their colours, textures, incised lines and relief work, in order to elicit a response. The use of gold and silver or silver-gilt also reflected the power and authority of the collar's donor.

It was not only the striking, shimmering appearance of these metals which attracted the attention. Their symbolic significance would also have been fully appreciated. Gold appeals to the senses through its gleam, and its pliability makes it easy to work. Along with silver, it retains something of its 'nobility' due to its untarnishable colour and brightness. Its rarity and aesthetic appearance

---

[17] C.A. Sneyd (ed. and trans.), *A Relation, or rather True Account, of the Island of England ... about the Year 1500* (London, 1847), p. 30.
[18] Traces of which still survive on the 'choker' collar on the effigy of Joan Nevill (d. 1462) at Arundel: A. Brodrick and J. Darrah, 'The Fifteenth Century Polychromed Limestone Effigies of William Fitzalan, 9th Earl of Arundel, and His Wife, Joan Nevill, in the Fitzalan Chapel, Arundel', *Church Monuments*, 1 (1986), 65–94, at 71.
[19] BL, Harleian MS 944, fols. 18v–25v.
[20] J. Barker, 'Monuments and Marriage in Late Medieval England: Origins, Function and Reception of Double Tombs', Courtauld Institute of Art, unpublished PhD thesis, 2 vols (2015), i, pp. 194–5; N. Saul, *Death, Art and Memory in Medieval England: The Cobham Family and Their Monuments, 1300–1500* (Oxford, 2001), p. 178.

make it a perfect symbol, used to legitimise secular and religious hierarchy and authority.[21] There was therefore something of a 'visual privilege' in being associated with such an artefact; indeed this is reflected today by the SS collar worn by the Lord Mayor of London (see Plate 5). A livery collar, both depicted on a church monument and worn by the living, would have appealed to the senses of sight and, for the more curious, touch.

It is important to bear in mind that the medieval tomb and its environment was a *Gesamtkunstwerk*, a total piece of art in which the tomb interacted with other monuments and church fittings, painted wall panels and stained glass. Indeed a direct relationship between tomb and glass was in some cases deliberately sought after.[22] Livery collars can be found in examples of contemporary stained glass, such as the Yorkist collars worn by the figures of Sir William Chamberlain (d. 1462) and Sir Robert Wingfield (d. 1481), first and second husbands of Anne Harling (d. 1498), at St Peter's and St Paul's, East Harling (Norfolk).[23] Here, the glass was designed to interact with the tomb of Anne and her first husband, and although the brass has now disappeared, it is not inconceivable that both tomb and glass would have featured livery collars, an example of accentuating the message through two types of media. This may well have been the case with other tomb–glass combinations, the disappearance of one or both commemorative media hindering firmer conclusions.

Earlier antiquarian interest in church monuments is reflected in the works of John Weever, Richard Gough and Charles Alfred Stothard, all of which are still used today, not least for their excellent engravings. The studies of post-Renaissance sculpture, medieval monuments and alabaster tombs by Esdaile, Crossley and Gardner in the first half of the twentieth century presented a stylistic and aesthetic appreciation of monuments, with a focus on chronological development of forms, an approach that was broadly followed for several decades. Lawrence Stone's influential study of medieval sculpture pioneered an art-historical approach to the study of church architecture and sculpture, predicated on the development of style from pre-Conquest sculpture, through the Romanesque and Decorated periods, and on to the late Gothic style.[24] A key historiographical

---

[21] P.S. Wells, *Image and Response in Early Europe* (London, 2008), p. 45; G. Clark, *Symbols of Excellence: Precious Materials as Expressions of Status* (Cambridge, 1986), pp. 50–97.

[22] S. Badham and S. Oosterwijk, 'Introduction', in *Monumental Industry*, p. 8; J. Luxford, 'The Hastings Brass at Elsing: A Contextual Analysis', *TMBS*, 18 (2011), 193–211.

[23] D. King, 'The Indent of John Aylward: Glass and Brass at East Harling', *TMBS*, 18 (2011), 251–67.

[24] R. Gough, *Sepulchral Monuments of Great Britain*, 2 vols (London, 1786–96); C.A. Stothard, *The Monumental Effigies of Great Britain* (London, 1817–32); K. Esdaile, *English Monumental Sculpture since the Renaissance* (London, 1927); F. Crossley, *English Church Monuments 1150–1550* (London, 1921); A. Gardner, *Alabaster Tombs of the Pre-Reformation Period in England* (Cambridge, 1940); L. Stone, *Sculpture in Britain: The Middle Ages* (Harmondsworth, 1955); B. Kemp, *English Church Monuments* (London, 1980); M. Duffy, *Royal Tombs of Medieval England*

development came with Erwin Panofsky's study of tomb design from ancient Egypt to the Renaissance, highlighting continuities and changes in the style of monuments over the *longue durée*.²⁵ Several of his observations have since formed the bedrock of research into church monuments, not least his distinction in attitudes between the 'retrospective' tombs of the Greeks, to the 'prospective' tombs of the medieval period, when Christian doctrine – centring on the importance of achieving salvation – encouraged an approach which looked forward to the Last Judgment, rather than glorified the past of the individual. Panofsky traces the development from the sculptured tomb slabs of the eleventh century through to the use of ever higher reliefs, which culminated with the introduction of the three-dimensional effigial tomb during the twelfth century. The next logical step was to place the effigy on top of a tomb, and to add an extravagant canopy. This 'elevation' of the tomb during the Middle Ages accompanied an increasing desire to represent status on memorials.

From the 1980s scholars have been increasingly adept at placing church monuments within their historical contexts, through discussing how contemporary attitudes and eschatological beliefs were reflected in tomb design. Paul Binski's influential *Medieval Death* is a broad investigation into attitudes towards death and dying in the medieval period, with the focus on images as 'visual texts', and their relationship with 'representations'.²⁶ Work by early modern scholars such as Nigel Llewellyn has applied a socio-historical methodology to the study of tombs from the sixteenth century onwards. Consequently, viewing monuments as 'symbols' is now a favoured approach. Influenced by the Warburg school, Llewellyn and others have sought a critical interpretation of all visual (and literary) artefacts through attempting to understand them in relation to their social and cultural meanings and uses, in contrast to the traditional art-historical approach which places emphasis on the aesthetic credentials of fine art.²⁷ Scholars from other disciplines have enriched our understanding of church monuments. An interest in the links between the tomb and medieval concepts of memory and mnemonics has resulted in some thought-provoking studies.²⁸ Jonathan Finch's study of monuments in Norfolk applied an archaeological

---

(Stroud, 2003); P. Lindley, *Tomb Destruction and Scholarship: Medieval Monuments in Early Modern England* (Donington, 2007). Other studies have focused their attention on a region or location: P.E. Routh, *Medieval Effigial Alabaster Tombs in Yorkshire* (Ipswich, 1976); S.M. Bond (ed.), *The Monuments of St. George's Chapel, Windsor Castle* (Windsor, 1958). For brasses see H. Haines, *Manual of Monumental Brasses*, 2 vols (London, 1861); J. Bertram (ed.), *Monumental Brasses as Art and History* (Stroud, 1996).

25 E. Panofsky, *Tomb Sculpture: Its Changing Aspects from Ancient Egypt to Bernini* (London, 1964).
26 P. Binski, *Medieval Death: Ritual and Representation* (London, 1996).
27 N. Llewellyn, *The Art of Death: Visual Culture in the English Death Ritual c. 1500–c. 1800* (London, 1991); Erickson and Hulse, 'Introduction'.
28 E.g., E.V. del Alamo and C.S. Pendergast (eds), *Memory and the Medieval Tomb* (Aldershot, 2000).

methodology, eschewing analysis of style and placing the tombs within the county's material culture.[29] There has been an accompanying revival of interest in the use of visual culture in social and secular display during the medieval period, which has encouraged historians to examine the role of church monuments in expressing status and secular identity.[30] For scholars of monuments dating from the Wars of the Roses period, Hampton's county guide is a welcome addition to the historiography, although it is not comprehensive.[31]

Nigel Saul's *English Church Monuments in the Middle Ages* is the first comprehensive study of its kind for some decades, and has gathered various historiographical strands together. He addresses the dual religious and secular purpose of the medieval tomb and, referring to the 'social body' theory of Nigel Llewellyn, reminds us that one of the primary functions of the monument was to take the place of the deceased and preserve their memory in the community. By the fifteenth century, the patron class for monuments had increased substantially, with lawyers and merchants now having a clear professional identity which was reflected in their memorials. The use of distinguishing marks by the new sub-knightly classes conferred on them a level of dignity, in the same way that heraldry and other secular symbols reflected the dignity and honour of the knightly class. The increasing complexity of English society resulted in confusion over funerary dress code. The more levels in society, the more the boundaries were blurred. The depiction of the deceased in armour – once the preserve of knights who had undertaken military duties – could now be used by those who had never fought, nor intended to fight. The 'social realities' of the deceased were thus glossed over, as more patrons wished to depict their acquired gentle status.[32] Wider kinship ties and associations were also depicted, thus expressing individual and group identity. It is the desire to reflect the social body in tomb effigy and memorial brass which is applicable to the present study. The need to place oneself in a social or political group after death should not be overlooked. The desire to put in stone one's social role and station, and to attempt to cement one's family within their current social situation, was of high importance.

In a particularly useful study of medieval tombs and group identity, Pamela King analysed the appearance of cadaver tombs commemorating individuals associated with the Lancastrian court.[33] King suggests that the group were delib-

---

[29] J. Finch, *Church Monuments in Norfolk before 1850: An Archaeology of Commemoration*, British Archaeological Reports, 317 (Oxford, 2000).
[30] See M. Keen, 'Introduction', in *Heraldry*, pp. 1–16; B. and M. Gittos, 'Motivation and Choice: The Selection of Medieval Secular Effigies', in *ibid.*, pp. 143–67.
[31] W.E. Hampton, *Memorials of the Wars of the Roses* (Upminster, 1979).
[32] *English Church Monuments*, p. 237.
[33] P. King, 'The English Cadaver Tomb in the Late Fifteenth Century: Some Indications of a Lancastrian Connection', in J.H.M. Taylor (ed.), *Dies Illa, Death in the Middle Ages: Proceedings of the 1983 Manchester Colloquium* (Liverpool, 1984), pp. 45–57.

erately copying their associates when choosing to opt for such a monument. Other studies have addressed the use of similar types of monument, or similar iconographical features on them, by groups of kin or associates.[34] At the broadest level, the choice by knights and magnates to represent themselves in a similar fashion on tomb effigies, as physically fit soldiers dressed in armour, proudly displaying their associations through heraldry, illustrated their shared gentle identity and evoked the 'symbolic boundary' between aristocrats and non-aristocrats. Take, for example, the effigy complete with what is probably the first representation of a Yorkist livery collar on an extant tomb, thought to represent Richard Neville, earl of Salisbury (d. 1460) at St Mary's, Burghfield (Berkshire), which is depicted in the same fashion as a knight.[35] The most notable recent study of tombs and the expression of group identity is Saul's examination of the Cobham family's commissioning of a succession of memorial brasses to create an illusion of continuity of lineage. In addition, a number of unpublished theses have recently contributed to the field by relating church monuments and burial locations to the construction of familial identity.[36]

The period associated with the Wars of the Roses in England, traditionally taken as 1455 (the first battle of St Albans) to 1485 (the battle of Bosworth), but often extended back to 1450 and forward to 1500, is a distinct epoch still worthy of study in its own right.[37] Many historiographical trends have developed over the huge corpus of material written on the subject. The humanist-inspired literature of the sixteenth century was in many ways testament to the success of the propaganda of the civil wars. For Thomas More, Edward Hall and their contemporaries the

---

[34] See S. Badham, 'Patterns of Patronage: Brasses to the Cromwell–Bourchier Kinship Group', *TMBS*, 17 (2007), 423–52; B.J. Harris, 'Defining Themselves: English Aristocratic Women, 1450–1550', *Journal of British Studies*, 49 (2010), 734–52.

[35] D. Westerhof, *Death and the Noble Body in Medieval England* (Woodbridge, 2008), pp. 73–4; P. Routh, 'Richard Neville, Earl of Salisbury: The Burghfield Effigy', *The Ricardian*, 6 (1984), 417–23; M. Duffy, 'Two Fifteenth-Century Effigies in Burghfield Church and the Montagu Mausoleum at Bisham (Berkshire)', *Church Monuments*, 25 (2010), 58–84. There are, however, examples of magnates distinguishing themselves from their social inferiors with the addition of a robe and coronet, such as John de la Pole, duke of Suffolk (d. 1491) at St Andrew's church, Wingfield (Suffolk). This may be an example of the increasing anxiety of magnates to set themselves apart from their social inferiors.

[36] R.C. Kinsey, 'Legal Service, Careerism and Social Advancement in Late Medieval England: The Thorpes of Northamptonshire, *c.* 1200–1391', University of York, unpublished PhD thesis (2009); K. Wilson-Lee, '"Their Final Blazon": Burial and Commemoration among the North Midland Nobility and Gentry, *c.* 1200–1536', University of London, unpublished PhD thesis, 2 vols (2009); K. Wilson-Lee, 'Dynasty and Strategies of Commemoration: Knightly Families in Late-Medieval and Early Modern Derbyshire, Part 1', *Church Monuments*, 25 (2010), 85–104; K. Wilson-Lee, 'Dynasty and Strategies of Commemoration: Knightly Families in Late-Medieval and Early Modern Derbyshire, Part 2', *Church Monuments*, 26 (2011), 27–43.

[37] M.A. Hicks, *The Wars of the Roses* (New Haven, CT, and London, 2010), p. 11.

wars were the result of the regicide of Richard II and subsequent monarchs, with divinely sanctioned peace only arriving through the marriage of Henry Tudor to Elizabeth of York in 1486. The fifteenth century was seen as a bloody period of struggle which enveloped the country in chaos and moral degeneracy.[38] Subsequent writers did little to appraise the conclusions made by the Tudor historians, with Charles Plummer blaming the negative effects of bastard feudalism, in particular the behaviour of the 'overmighty' nobility, for the troubles.[39] It was K.B. McFarlane who offered a new paradigm: he could not see anything intrinsically wrong with the structure of fifteenth-century society; bastard feudalism was not evil; it was the weakness of the monarchy under the personal rule of Henry VI which was the principal problem.[40] Subsequent writers have argued that the wars had only a limited impact on society at large, the level of chaos not being as high as was once thought, with actual fighting lasting only twelve to thirteen weeks.[41] Recent interest has focused on ideology, the constitution and the nature of governance, economic trends, regional studies, the influence of Burgundy and France, and the relationships between the gentry, nobility and king, the result being that scholars are now more inclined to ascertain what the wars meant to contemporaries, to ask 'what the Wars were all about' for those who lived through them.[42]

Several recent studies have addressed the understanding of royal authority, the political thinking and cultural assumptions of landed society, and the manifestation of group identities during the latter half of the fifteenth century. Without denying the destabilising role played by the magnates' pursuit of political power, it is suggested that principles were far from lacking among the populace, and to some extent they prompted the actions and attitudes of all levels of society. A shared set of political premises, not least a belief in the duty and loyalty owed to the king and the need to maintain the 'common weal', was supplicated by political commentators such as Sir John Fortescue. The disastrous personal rule of Henry VI was followed by a slow recovery of the monarchy's authority and honour; the same mistakes could not, it was said, be made again. Carpenter has suggested that after 1450 it was the gentry who provided a core of political stability. Deeper links between the crown and the gentry developed

---

[38] A.J. Pollard, *The Wars of the Roses*, 2nd edn (Basingstoke, 2001), p. 8; E. Hall, *The Union of the Two Noble Families of Lancaster and York* (Menston, 1970).
[39] John Fortescue, *The Governance of England*, ed. C. Plummer (Oxford, 1885), p. 16.
[40] K.B. McFarlane, 'Bastard Feudalism', *Bulletin of the Institute of Historical Research*, 20 (1945), 161–80; C. Carpenter, *The Wars of the Roses: Politics and the Constitution in England, c. 1437–1509* (Cambridge, 1997), pp. 16–17, 263.
[41] J.R. Lander, *Crown and Nobility, 1450–1509* (London, 1976).
[42] J.L. Watts, *Henry VI and the Politics of Kingship* (Cambridge, 1996); Pollard, *Wars of the Roses*; Carpenter, *Wars of the Roses*; A.J. Pollard, 'Introduction: Society, Politics and the Wars of the Roses', in A.J. Pollard (ed.), *The Wars of Roses* (Basingstoke, 1995), pp. 1–19; R. Horrox, *Richard III: A Study of Service* (Cambridge, 1989); Hicks, *Wars of the Roses*, p. x.

under Edward IV, particularly after his restoration to the throne in 1471, serving to extend the crown's authority.[43] Perhaps the swift replacement of Lancastrian by Yorkist collars on church monuments after 1460, and the equally brisk move to depicting the Tudor SS collar after 1485, are evidence of the need to acknowledge allegiance to the crown, albeit in some cases tacitly.

Regional and county studies have proliferated over the last two decades, serving to emphasise differences in the ways the wars affected the localities.[44] Many have addressed the question of whether a sense of local identity developed during the period, and whether the concept of the 'county community', emphasising the political independence of the local gentry at the expense of power from above, is applicable to late medieval England.[45] Carpenter sees the county of Warwickshire as being geographically split along a north/south axis in the fifteenth century. Earlier in the century the county was also split between the east and west, due principally to the influence of Richard Beauchamp, earl of Warwick (d. 1439). In Warwickshire, at least, the county was therefore an artificial creation, thoughts echoed by Pollard who postulates that an identification of a county community in Leicestershire and Nottinghamshire may simply be an illusion.[46] That said, it should be stressed that in certain circumstances the gentry could appeal to a county mentality, particularly in times of political instability. In the shire session on 15 July 1494, amid growing tension in the county, Henry Willoughby pleaded with those present: 'Sires remembre we are neybours and warrewykshire men and this mater hath ben inquered of afore this tyme and the matter of trouth founden and if ye fynde eny more or othirwise then hath ben aforetyme founden ye shall cause warre amonges us duryng oure lifes.'[47]

If there was no feeling of a 'community' in a given shire, who then did the local gentry turn to for stability, leadership and support? For the first four decades of the fifteenth century the powerful influence of Richard Beauchamp was felt across Warwickshire. His leadership abilities cemented the local gentry together, and peace and stability were the rule. However, from the 1450s things began to change. The new earl, Richard Neville, may have been the kingmaker, but he failed to live up to his reputation in Warwickshire. Through bad leadership and a

---

[43] J.L. Watts, 'Polemic and Politics in the 1450s', in *John Vale's Book*, pp. 3–42; Carpenter, *Wars of the Roses*, p. 263–5.

[44] Including N. Saul, *Knights and Esquires: The Gloucestershire Gentry in the Fourteenth Century* (Oxford, 1981); *Derbyshire Gentry*; S. Payling, *Political Society in Lancastrian England: The Greater Gentry of Nottinghamshire* (Oxford, 1991).

[45] C. Carpenter, 'Gentry and Community in Medieval England', *Journal of British Studies*, 33 (1994), 340–80; S. Walker, 'Communities of the County in Later Medieval England', in M.J. Braddick (ed.), *Political Culture in Later Medieval England: Essays by Simon Walker* (Manchester, 2006), pp. 68–80.

[46] C. Carpenter, *Locality and Polity: A Study of Warwickshire Landed Society, 1401–1499* (Cambridge, 1992); Pollard, 'Introduction', pp. 8–9.

[47] Carpenter, *Locality and Polity*, p. 580.

commitment to the national political stage, the 'umbilical cord' tying the nobility to the gentry was broken.[48] In response, the gentry were forced to develop their own networks and power bases. The pattern was to change, however. As *de facto* earl of Warwick, Edward IV began to assert effective leadership. His interventionist approach, aided by his lieutenant, William, Lord Hastings, was effective, creating a stability in the shire which had not been witnessed for years.

Pollard argues that, although there was no regional identity in the north-east of England until the eighteenth century, there were distinct, close-knit groups of local gentry during the second half of the fifteenth century whose ties were manifested through co-witnessing deeds, arbitration and intermarriage. This was particularly true of the Nevilles' Middleham affinity, centring on the honour of Richmond. Although disputes inevitably arose, gentry families such as the Conyers and Metcalfes were associated over several generations by family service to their lord, shared values and mutual material interests.[49] In the north-east it was the magnate power of the Nevilles (and their heir the duke of Gloucester) and the Percys which helped form common gentry identities. It was only after 1483 when the Middleham estates were annexed to the crown that royal authority began to strengthen. In areas with little magnate influence the gentry were left to fend for themselves. If there was a strong crown presence in a given area, they would naturally be inclined to look to the king for leadership and employment.

The two local case studies here utilise a similar approach to those of Pollard and Carpenter, at least with regards to the application of source material. Where available, wills, deeds, enfeoffments, land charters, in addition to central government records and sources of national significance such as chronicles, are used in order to draw out any associations between the individuals and their families. This study, however, diverges from other research into localities and regions in one important respect. Here the starting point for identifying connections is the appearance of a livery collar on church monuments to a group of individuals. The aforementioned sources are therefore used to prove or disprove the existence of connections between the members of the group.

The book is divided into two parts, each following a broad methodological approach. The first three chapters investigate the various late medieval contexts in which the collar existed and functioned, while the final two chapters comprise case studies examining the utility of the item on church monuments. Chapter 1 introduces the livery collar and places it within its historical context. It appraises the collar's significance from its inception in England in the late fourteenth

---

[48] Carpenter, *Locality and Polity*, p. 611.
[49] A.J. Pollard, 'The Richmondshire Community of Gentry', in C. Ross (ed.), *Patronage, Pedigree and Power in Later Medieval England* (Gloucester, 1979), pp. 37–59; A.J. Pollard, *North-Eastern England during the Wars of the Roses: Lay Society, War and Politics 1450–1500* (Oxford, 1990).

century, and discusses its subsequent development as a political and cultural artefact. The iconographical functions and meanings of the collar are examined, as is its value in both monetary and symbolic senses. In addition, the chapter attempts to provide some answers to the question of who was entitled to wear a livery collar. The following chapter places the livery collar within its political contexts. Through positioning the item within the wider political culture of landed society in fifteenth-century England, a more nuanced picture of the item's political resonance can be developed. Especial consideration is given to contemporary attitudes towards the authority of the king, and legislative attempts to bring the collar under royal control. Chapter 3 places the livery collar within a discussion of the methods through which group identities were constructed and maintained by contemporaries, and the ways in which royal power and dignity were symbolically expressed. It utilises anthropological models and semiotics theory to help understand the collar's symbolic resonance as a royal symbol. After a consideration of the geographical distribution of livery collars, two case studies then analyse the appearance of the collar on church monuments in Derbyshire and Wales, examining a variety of motives and investigating local geographical, tenurial and kinship contexts. The approach in both case studies is principally prosopographical: the appearance of collars on memorials is used as a basis for illuminating connections between the commemorated and their families.

My approach has been deliberately interdisciplinary, utilising not only visual, material and literary sources, but also broadly adopting approaches used predominantly by sociologists and anthropologists, and subsequently by historians. But the starting point has always been a seemingly simple yet ubiquitous piece of medieval material culture. By clarifying the ways in which contemporaries understood the livery collar, and by modifying the ways in which historians interpret the item, this book aims to contribute to our understanding of the interaction of late medieval politics, society and culture.

Part I

1

Function, Meaning and Significance

Qui gerit S tandem turmam comitatur eandem
Nobilis ille quidem probus et juvenis fuit idem
Sic quasi de celis interfuit ille fidelis.[1]

'Qui gerit S': he who wears the S. Thus is Henry Bolingbroke, earl of Derby, described by John Gower in his *Cronica Tripertita*, a metrical chronicle written at the close of the fourteenth century as a sequel to *Vox Clamantis*. The poem proceeds to compare the device, and by association the individual it represents, to a heavenly gift. For Gower, the collar of SS was clearly the most widely recognised means of identifying the earl. For the next century and a half the livery collar would attract similar attention from many a commentator, chronicler and artisan. Its authority, its potency as a royal symbol and what it represented clearly mattered.

In early January 1400, after parliament had ruled that all livery collars save those of the king were no longer to be worn, Raulyn Govely, an esquire of John Holland, earl of Huntingdon, refused to remove his lord's collar while he was still living. This political act of defiance did not last long; the earl was beheaded soon after for his involvement in the Epiphany Rising against Henry IV.[2] Against the demands of several of the king's representatives, Govely adamantly stated that no individual would convince him to remove his collar. The artefact demonstrably represented a close bond between Govely and his lord, a bond which would only be broken by death. In the intervening centuries the SS collar in particular has attracted antiquarians and historians, principally concerned with its stylistic development and the allusive, and elusive, meaning of the 'S'. The 150 years after the collar's introduction in England in the late fourteenth century witnessed the item's epoch. The livery collar developed into a salient and abundant artefact, treasured by its recipients. It would become a significant aspect of the gift-giving

---

[1] 'He who wears the S I see in the same company / Noble is he forsooth that same illustrious youth / As though from heaven that faithful one had been given': BL, Harley MS 6291, fols. 134v–149v; G.C. Macaulay, *The Complete Works of John Gower*, 4 vols (Oxford, 1899–1902), iv, p. 315.
[2] *Cal. Inq. Misc. 1399–1422*, p. 54.

milieu of the fifteenth-century aristocracy and would find its way into the ceremonial of the highest echelons of society. It was more than an eye-catching piece of finery: its symbolic value was not lost on contemporaries.

Development of the livery collar

From its inception, the design of the livery collar was intended to signify possession and ownership, that of the lord over the servant. This is most obvious when one considers the earliest form of the SS collar, a strap of leather, velvet or silk onto which were affixed several letters 'S', the ends terminating in a buckle or clasp and pendant. An example of this embryonic collar could be found in the stained glass surrounding the arms of John of Gaunt, once situated near his tomb in Old St Paul's, as drawn by Nicholas Charles in c. 1605.[3] A similar collar is worn by Sir William Bagot (d. 1407) and his wife Margaret on their brass at St John the Baptist's, Baginton (Warwickshire). Bagot was a retainer of Gaunt and a close confidant of Henry Bolingbroke. Allusion to the dog collar was presumably the intention, the similarity with illustrations of hound collars dating from the period is striking. Indeed, a curious play on the dog collar parallel exists in a manuscript illustration of a white greyhound – Henry IV's beast – wearing an SS collar in Merton College, Oxford (Plate 3). The message was simple: the collar worn by the individual signified the service they provided to their lord. It was frequently depicted on tomb effigies and monumental brasses, but the same message could be portrayed symbolically. There are several examples at home and abroad of a livery collar encircling an individual's coat of arms.[4]

A collar was used by successive kings from Henry IV to Henry VIII to surround their signets, visually combining two symbols of royal authority. The physical act of encircling a neck, or indeed a coat of arms, with a collar graphically symbolised the relationship between the individual and lord. But just as the relationship between lord and servant was in reality one of reciprocity and mutual aid, the collar could also be utilised to portray multi-faceted forms of possession and ownership: it could signify the lord's 'ownership' of the individual and, tactfully positioned, could emphasise the individual's possession of the collar. Petrus Christus's 1446 portrait of Edward Grimston, held in the National Gallery in London, shows him playing with his delicate SS collar between his fingers, simultaneously affirming his possession of the item and appealing to the tactility of such a prestigious piece of jewellery. Similarly, a painting showing Louis, duke of Orléans (d. 1407), being presented with a manuscript by Christine de Pisan depicts one of the courtiers touching his collar of the duke's Order

---

[3] BL, Lansdowne MS 874, fol. 115v.
[4] Such as the brass representation of a suns and roses collar surrounding the incised slab shield of Joos de Bul (d. 1488), formerly in the Hôpital St Josse in Bruges.

of the Porcupine with one hand and pointing to the manuscript with the other, thus affirming the duke's ownership of the book.[5] A collar could also be used to make a subtle political statement. Around the hart's head crest on the tomb of Ralph Grene (d. 1418) at St Peter's, Lowick (Northamptonshire), is depicted an SS collar. This could be a comment on the deposition of Richard II, whose badges included the white hart, by Henry IV, whose badge became the SS collar.[6] Grene successfully switched his allegiance from Richard to Henry, although tellingly he did not choose to depict the collar on his tomb effigy. Perhaps this was a step too far for an individual who had enjoyed close connections with the deposed king.

The wearing of a gold chain or collar about the neck as a sign of rank or prestige has ancient precedents. Worn by the Egyptians and Romans, the item has a long antiquity. But it was in the latter half of the fourteenth century that the livery collar emerged in England. It developed from the custom of distributing robes to mark followers or clients, which began in the twelfth century and evolved into a system of matching livery with a particular lord during the early fourteenth century.[7] From this developed other forms of livery, the most common being badges and hats, given to retainers in return for military, legal or domestic aid.[8] The collar became the most prestigious livery device, and can be witnessed in contemporary records and accounts from the reign of Richard II.

Although the creation of the collar of SS is frequently ascribed to Henry Bolingbroke, earl of Derby, it may in fact have been introduced by his father, John of Gaunt. In addition to the collar represented in Old St Paul's, six collars of the livery of the duke of Lancaster are mentioned in an inventory of the mercer William Caly in 1375.[9] On his return from Spain in 1389 Gaunt was observed wearing his own livery collar which, as we shall see, was donned by Richard II. What is not clear is whether these were SS collars. Henry, earl of Derby, did, however, begin to distribute the SS collar during the lifetime of his father. His accounts for 1391–92 refer specifically to: 'I coler auri facto pro domino Henrico Lancastrie, Comiti Derb. Cum xvij literis de S. ad modum plumarum' (one collar of gold of Henry Lancaster, earl of Derby, with seventeen letters of S in the form of feathers). Another entry records a collar of *esses* and flowers of *souveyne vous de moys*, the forget-me-not, a phrase used by Henry as his motto.[10] In preparation

---

[5] BL, Harley MS 4431, fol. 95. This collar comprised a gold chain with a badge of a porcupine standing on green enamelled turf. The order was established in 1394.
[6] H. Stanford London, *Royal Beasts* (East Knoyle, 1956), pp. 35, 60.
[7] F. Lachaud, 'Liveries of Robes in England, c. 1200–c. 1330', *English Historical Review*, 111 (1996), 279–98.
[8] For extant examples of badges see B. Spencer, *Pilgrim Souvenirs and Secular Badges* (London, 1998), pp. 278–98.
[9] TNA, C 131/193/43.
[10] TNA, DL 28/1/3, fols. 14–15v; DL 28/1/6, fol. 22v.

for Henry's expedition to the Holy Land in 1392 several collars were purchased in various forms, and in the first year of his reign 192 collars were distributed by his receiver-general, of which ninety-one were silver-gilt, eighty-one were silver and the remaining were of a lesser metal. Although none were explicitly described as SS collars it is likely that they were.[11] During the first ten years of Henry's reign dozens more collars were purchased through the exchequer, some for the personal use of the king, and some to be sent to European courts.[12] Here we have a case of the use of the collar *en masse* to aid the new dynasty's accession, through creating a visually coherent affinity at home and abroad: a practice which would be repeated by subsequent monarchs.

The livery collar was a fresh innovation; wearers would immediately be distinguished from retainers of other lords wearing the more common livery badges.[13] The distribution of the item has been described as 'a spectacular but hopeful means of collecting members of an affinity',[14] although it should be noted that, although this may have been the case with Henry IV's mass distribution of collars, they may have been given to existing retainers in order to create a visual, as well as psychological, coherence to the affinity. The SS collar was adopted by both Henry's son Henry V, as exemplified on their statues on the choir screen at York Minster,[15] and his grandson Henry VI, as portrayed in his painting in the National Portrait Gallery, London (Plate 1). Despite all three Lancastrian kings being depicted wearing their SS collars, it is questionable whether they would have worn them in life. As collars of livery, it would seem unnecessary for the king to don one himself, although, as will be shown, they certainly wore collars given by other rulers. The York Minster sculptures, in particular, should therefore be interpreted as a piece of Lancastrian propaganda, stressing continuity, and advertising and explicitly associating the rulers with the regime's most important identifying badge. The figures are represented in their full regalia, the collar's inclusion suggesting that it was afforded the same importance as the other emblems of royal dignity: the crown, sword and sceptre.

---

[11] L. Toulmin-Smith, *Expeditions to Prussia and the Holy Land made by Henry, Earl of Derby In the Years 1390–1 and 1392–3*, Camden Society, New Series, 52 (London, 1894), pp. 112, 240, 280, 287; TNA, DL 28/4/1, fol. 18v.

[12] TNA, E 403/571, mem. 3 (eight collars to be sent to his sister and nephew in Portugal); E 403/582, mem. 8 (a silver-gilt collar and five silver collars to be sent to the Bohemian court); J. Lutkin, 'Luxury and Display in Silver and Gold at the Court of Henry IV', in L. Clark (ed.), *The Fifteenth Century, IX: English and Continental Perspectives* (Woodbridge, 2010), pp. 155–78, at 163–5.

[13] S. Walker, *The Lancastrian Affinity, 1361–1399* (Oxford, 1990), pp. 94–5.

[14] P.S. Lewis, 'Decayed and Non-Feudalism in Later Medieval France', *Bulletin of the Institute of Historical Research*, 37 (1964), 175.

[15] The accompanying statue of Henry VI is a replacement dating from 1810: R. Marks, 'Yorkist–Lancastrian Political and Genealogical Propaganda in the Visual Arts', *Family History*, 12 (1982), 149–66, at 153–4.

From the evidence of depictions on church monuments, the livery collar became more elaborate during the early decades of the fifteenth century. The strap collar was gradually replaced, with examples made entirely of metal becoming popular, the letters 'S' often joined together. Pendants began to appear more frequently and took a variety of forms, from simple clasps of metal, to pieces of jewellery (Robert, Lord Hungerford's collar in Salisbury Cathedral features a pendant of nine pearls), or badges such as the Lancastrian swan device. Examples of the later, more intricate SS collar can be seen on the effigies of Sir Richard Vernon (d. 1451) and his wife Benedicta at St Bartholomew's, Tong (Shropshire), and Sir Humphrey Stafford (d. 1450) at St John the Baptist's, Bromsgrove (Worcestershire). By the middle of the fifteenth century, numbers of the SS livery collar on church monuments had proliferated: there are well over one hundred extant examples from this period in England and Wales.

With the accession of Edward IV in 1461 a new collar was introduced, that of alternate suns and white roses, or *roses-en-soleil*, roses set within suns. There are impressive examples of the Yorkist collar on extant tomb effigies and brasses, including Sir Robert Harcourt (d. 1470) at St Michael's, Stanton Harcourt (Oxfordshire), and James, Lord Berkeley (d. 1463) and his son at St Mary's, Berkeley (Gloucestershire). The pendant badge is more common on Yorkist collars than their Lancastrian counterparts. More often than not, the white lion of March badge used by Edward IV is appended to the collar. There is one example of the boar badge of Richard III as a pendant to a livery collar, that on the tomb effigy of Ralph Fitzherbert (d. 1484) at St Mary's and St Barlok's, Norbury (Derbyshire). The wooden effigy of Ralph Neville, earl of Westmorland (d. 1484) at St Brandon's, Brancepeth (County Durham) also featured the boar badge, although sadly this was destroyed by fire in the 1990s.[16]

There is evidence of earlier collars associated with the house of York. In an inventory from November 1399 of the valuables belonging to Edward III, Richard II and other members of the royal family, a collar of the duke of York is referred to as comprising 'vii linkettz et vi faucons blancz': seven fetterlocks and six white falcons, the falcon and fetterlock being badges of the dukes of York.[17] It is not certain whether these were distributed as livery collars, or if this was the personal collar of the duke. There are no examples of such collars on church monuments, although the fetterlock badge does appear on tombs, such as the brass commemorating Sir Simon Felbrigge (d. 1443) at St Margaret's, Felbrigg (Norfolk).[18] This particular brass also features the white hart badge used by Richard II. Felbrigge was Richard's standard-bearer, although he was created a knight of the Garter by Henry V in 1415. The inclusion of such a seemingly

---

[16] An illustration of the effigy can be found in Stothard's *Monumental Effigies*, p. 100.
[17] TNA, E 101/335/5, mem. 5.
[18] H.W. Macklin, *The Brasses of England* (London, 1907), pp. 153–4.

politically sensitive badge can be partly explained by the fact that Henry V had solemnly reburied Richard in Westminster Abbey in 1413, seeking to rectify his father's misdeeds. Another collar, that of white roses (without suns) was apparently used by Edward IV's father Richard, duke of York (d. 1460). An inventory dating from 1466 refers to a collar of 'a white rose' of the duke of York: 'unum monile distissimum vocata anglice a white rose nuper domini ducis Eboracum.' This is echoed by an expensive collar bought by the duke of York and given to Sir John Fastolf, but again there is little evidence that this was given to followers as a livery collar. A number of tomb effigies appear to be wearing collars of florets, such as that of William, Lord Lovell (1455) at St. Kenelm's, Minster Lovell (Oxfordshire). Could this be an example of one of the duke's early 'Yorkist' collars, the florets representing white roses, or does it have some other, possibly religious, significance? Later collars 'of roses' which do not mention suns, such as that bequeathed by Joan Methley in 1480, may simply be an example of the term used to describe a suns and roses collar.[19]

After the defeat of Richard III in 1485 Henry VII swiftly reintroduced the SS collar, which would frequently be paired with the Tudor rose. No doubt the visual association with the Lancastrian regime was too good an opportunity to miss. At first it appears the Tudor collar remained in a similar form to that used by the Lancastrians and Yorkists: a reasonably thin collar extending down to the chest, such as that worn by John Curzon (d. c. 1492) at All Saints', Kedleston (Derbyshire) (see Figure 6). By the early sixteenth century collars had become broader and more ostentatious, and presumably more costly to produce. Two excellent examples can be found on the effigies of Sir John Cheney (d. 1499) at Salisbury Cathedral and Richard Vernon (d. 1517) at St Bartholomew's, Tong. Typical of the Tudor collar, these examples are long, extending down to waist level, with a portcullis and double rose pendant on the effigy of Cheney and a double rose pendant on Vernon's collar.[20] It is likely that the large 'coler of Essis' donned by Nicholas Vaux during the marriage festivities of Prince Arthur and Katherine of Aragon in 1501, worth a staggering £800 of nobles, would have born a likeness to these collars.[21] During the mid-sixteenth century the collar evolved to denote a badge of office rather than livery; a collar was frequently given to members of the judiciary, for example. Perhaps the most recognisable example of these later collars can be found on the portrait of Sir Thomas More, wearing

---

[19] A. Hartshorne, 'The Gold Chains, the Pendants, the Paternosters and the Zones of the Middle Ages, the Renaissance, and Later Times', *Archaeological Journal*, 66 (1909), 77–102, at 83; *PL*, ii, p. 280; *Test. Ebor.*, iii, p. 219.

[20] The portcullis was the badge of the Beaufort family. Henry VII's mother was Margaret Beaufort, countess of Richmond and Derby (d. 1509).

[21] A.H. Thomas and I.D. Thornley (eds), *The Great Chronicle of London* (London, 1938), pp. 311–12. The noble was a measurement used to calculate Tower weight, a system for weighing precious metals. One noble was worth 6s. 8d. and weighed 108g.

his in right of his position as chancellor to Henry VIII. Fittingly, it is at this juncture that collars slowly begin to disappear from tomb effigies, coinciding with the point when they ceased to be given out as a form of livery. There are, however, impressive examples of later collars on the tomb effigies of judges dating from the later sixteenth century, such as that worn by Richard Harper (d. 1577), justice of the Common Pleas, at St. James's, Swarkestone (Derbyshire), and the long collar depicted on the effigy of Sir Robert Broke (d. 1558), chief justice of the Common Pleas, at All Saints', Claverley (Shropshire). The collar was still being used into the seventeenth century. In 1649 an inventory of the contents of the Jewel House in the Tower of London listed three SS collars, one weighing 35½ ounces at a value of £3 per ounce.[22] The livery collar has not completely disappeared. The SS collar is still worn by the lord chief justice, the kings of arms, the serjeants at arms, the lord mayor of London and other mayors. Additionally, the eagle-eyed will be able to spot the SS collars worn by the royal heralds at state ceremonies such as the opening of parliament.

Manufacturers and monetary value

By the fifteenth century the responsibility for the storage and upkeep of jewellery had been transferred from the Great Wardrobe to the Jewel House at Westminster.[23] The livery collar was considered an item of jewellery and occasional references to them can be found in connection with the king's jewellers and goldsmiths, such as Marcellus Maures, a goldsmith from Utrecht, who began supplying the royal court by 1480,[24] Edward Ellesmere, treasurer of the chamber and master of the jewels to Queen Margaret of Anjou,[25] and John van Delf, one of Henry VII's goldsmiths.[26] Other ad hoc work by goldsmiths for the royal court can occasionally be glimpsed. In 1407 John Cotton was fined 3s. 4d. for faulty workmanship 'dez colers appelez "S"' by the goldsmiths' Mistery in London. As they were probably intended for the court it was prudent that unsatisfactory items were kept in custody. In the accounts for 1441–42, Henry Luton, 'Dutchman', paid 2s. for defect in the workmanship of collars for Humphrey,

---

[22] 'Livery Collar', p. 251.
[23] A.F. Sutton and P.W. Hammond (eds), *The Coronation of Richard III: The Extant Documents* (Gloucester and New York, 1983), p. 47.
[24] N.H. Nicolas, *Privy Purse Expenses of Elizabeth of York: Wardrobe Accounts of Edward the Fourth* (London, 1830), p. 119.
[25] Gold SS collars for Thomas Wood, under-treasurer of England, are listed in his accounts of 1452–53: TNA, E 101/410/11, mems. 1–3; A.R. Myers, 'The Jewels of Queen Margaret of Anjou', *Bulletin of the John Rylands Library*, 42 (1959), 113–31.
[26] He provided a gold collar worth £30 for the king in 1502: S. Bentley, *Excerpta Historica, or, Illustrations of English History* (London, 1831), p. 127.

duke of Gloucester.[27] In an inventory of Henry VIII's moveable goods compiled in September 1547, several minutely described collars are listed as being stored in the king's secret jewel house in the Tower, and in a coffer in another secret jewel house in the gallery at Westminster.[28] The fact that they were kept in a private location, stored in a separate coffer away from public view but easily accessible to the king, reflects not only the impressive monetary value of such items, but also their worth as prestigious items of royal authority and dignity.

In an intensely hierarchical society it is not surprising that the composition of a collar reflected the recipient's status, or indeed the donor's estimations of them. Therefore those of knightly status or above were usually awarded a gold or silver-gilt collar, and those of the rank of esquire silver collars, as confirmed in John Hall's will of 1483 in which he left his curate Thomas Laundey 'my silver livery collar with designs of roses made for the King's esquires'.[29] Gabriel Tetzel's account of Leo of Rozmital's visit to England in 1465–67 recorded their attendance at Edward IV's court, at which 'the king admitted my lord and all his attendants to his fellowship. The knights received a gold [badge], and those who were not knights a silver one, which he himself hung about our necks.'[30] The gradation was reflected in tomb effigies, some of which retain traces of their original polychromy, such as the gold suns and roses on the collar of Sir William Gascoigne (d. 1461–65) at All Saints', Harewood (Yorkshire).[31] Antiquarian church notes confirm the use of now lost polychromy on effigies. In 1645 Richard Symonds described the 'fairely gilt' SS collars on the effigies of members of the Mathew family in Llandaff Cathedral.[32] If tomb effigies were on the whole idealised images of the deceased, eschewing portraiture in favour of placing the commemorated within their role and position in society, this is plausible evidence that their livery collar at least was a more realistic portrayal.

However, there is evidence that this strict hierarchy was not always adhered to. It is possible that some esquires may have worn collars befitting a higher rank. In the 1478 ordinances for the household of Edward IV it was stipulated that every lord, knight and esquire within the household should wear livery

---

[27] L. Jefferson (ed.), *Wardens' Accounts and Court Minute Books of the Goldsmiths' Mistery of London 1334–1446* (Woodbridge, 2003), pp. 333, 521.

[28] D. Starkey (ed.), *The Inventory of King Henry VIII* (London, 1998), pp. 68, 80.

[29] 'colerium meum argenti signis rosarum pro armigeris regiis': TNA, PROB 11/7, fol. 109v; L. Boatwright, M. Habberjam and P. Hammond (eds), *The Logge Register of PCC Wills, 1479 to 1486*, 2 vols (Knaphill, 2008), i, no. 173.

[30] M. Letts (ed.), *The Travels of Leo of Rozmital through Germany, Flanders, England, France, Spain, Portugal and Italy, 1465–1467* (Cambridge, 1957), p. 45.

[31] P. Routh and R. Knowles, *The Medieval Monuments of Harewood* (Wakefield, 1983), p. 67.

[32] BL, Harley MS 911, fols. 67r–69v. Collars were not, however, always either gold or silver. Some could be composed of both, such as the 'coler de S deauratis in parte argenti et in parte auri', mentioned in the 1463 will of Euphemia Langton: *Test. Ebor.*, ii, p. 258.

collars 'as to them apperteyneth'.[33] In the 1533 Act for Reformation of Excess in Apparel it was specified that 'no man oneless he be a knight weare any color of Gold ... named a color of S'.[34] Evidently Edward IV's previous attempts to control who wore what type of collar were not entirely effective. It is important to stress, however, that there is no evidence that collars given as bequests were worn by those not entitled to one. If this were the case, it would be expected that cases would have been brought before King's Bench, as they were for the illegal wearing of less prestigious livery badges and robes. I have not yet found any litigation concerning the illegal wearing of livery collars. It is more likely that bequeathed collars were either kept as heirlooms or given as gifts to churches, or the silver and gold components were sold. The responsibility for passing on collars apparently lay with the king. Robert Waterton (d. 1424), an esquire of the body to Henry IV, had his SS collar removed by the king to give to another individual: this was replaced by another, similar collar. If an individual who had been awarded a collar happened to mislay the item, it was expected that they should pay for a replacement, this being the case with Richard Whittington in 1402 who was forced to pay the exchequer £8 for losing his SS collar.[35] It is perhaps helpful to view the way collars were treated in the same manner as medals are viewed today. They are frequently passed down as heirlooms, occasionally given away, but seldom worn by those not entitled to wear them. On the rare occasions that this has occurred, it has been a matter of controversy.

The monetary value of a livery collar, and indeed its weight, also mirrored the recipient's standing in society. The cost of a collar could vary tremendously. For those below the highest social ranks, a livery collar could be valued at several pounds, such as Sir Thomas Charleton's Yorkist collar of gold with roses and a white enamelled lion pendant, weighing 8 ounces and valued at £8.[36] In his will of 1456 Sir Edmund Ingoldesthorpe ordered his gold collar to be sold for £5, with the money going to Richard Cawdrey who was yet to be paid for its manufacture.[37] It is striking that Ingoldesthorpe did not simply return the collar. Cawdrey may of course have simply not wanted a secondhand item, or perhaps in this instance the act of giving a collar to one who had not originally been entitled to it was deemed inappropriate. The collar was, after all, a personal item.

For those individuals acting as high-ranking representatives for the king, a more expensive example was required. Richard III ordered William Daubeney,

---

[33] A.R. Myers (ed.), *The Household of Edward IV: The Black Book and the Ordinance of 1478* (Manchester, 1959), p. 205.

[34] *Statutes of the Realm*, 24 Henry VIII c.13. Also see TNA, E 36/113.

[35] 'pro ponder argenti unius Colerii facti cum Esses rollati et dati Roberto de Waterton eo quod dominus dederat colerium ipsius Roberti alio armigero': Beltz, 'Notices', p. 507; A.B. Steel, *The Receipt of the Exchequer 1377–1485* (Cambridge, 1954), p. 87.

[36] 1466 inventory of goods: London, Westminster Abbey Muniments, 6646, 6625.

[37] TNA, PROB 11/4, fols. 53r–54r.

clerk of the king's jewels, to deliver a collar worth £30 to Thomas Barrett, bishop of Annaghdown in Ireland, destined for the earl of Desmond. It was to be handed over in a ceremony appropriate for an item which represented the king's authority: 'the said Bisshop shalle deliver unto his said Cousyne in most convenient place and honnorable presence the kings lyvree that is to wite a Color of gold of his devise.'[38] This is not the first instance where the word 'collar' is given a capital; perhaps a further indication of its significance. At the higher end of the spectrum, vast amounts of money could be spent on livery collars, reflecting the recipient's social standing. In 1489 the 'coller of gold of Kyng Edwardes lyverey', once owned by the king's trusted companion William, Lord Hastings (d. 1483), was valued at £40.[39] The collar had been pledged, but was now returned to Hastings's heir Edward.

At the apex of society, it would seem natural that a personal livery collar for a king or queen would attract the highest price. At their marriage ceremony in 1403 Henry IV gave his bride Joan of Navarre a gold SS collar worked with jewels and his motto *soveignez*, worth £385 6s. 8d, paid for by the royal chamber. The collar, probably made by the London goldsmith Christopher Tildesley, was an expensive piece of jewellery befitting a royal bride, but in addition it served to advertise, as it were, the king's livery badge. It appears that Henry IV, keen to not only distribute his SS livery collars to others, but also to publicly exhibit his personal collars, used them to conceal his insecurities over his usurpation in a visual sense. He certainly favoured expensive collars. In January 1408 he paid Drugo Barantyn an extortionate £550 for a gold collar garnished with precious stones.[40] Finally, there is the aforementioned white rose collar given by the duke of York to Sir John Fastolf for repayment of a loan, priced at 4,000 marks.[41] Its price could, of course, have been deliberately inflated, but it is another reflection of the place a livery collar could have in the hearts of lords and their servants. The collar did not, however, simply have monetary value. The act of giving and receiving the item was also charged with symbolic resonance.

Gift giving, diplomacy and the removal of the collar

After the execution of Sir William Stanley in February 1495 for his involvement in the Perkin Warbeck conspiracy, his residence, Holt Castle, was seized by the crown. Among the contents of his treasure house were found the components

---

[38] *Harleian 433*, iii, pp. 109–11.
[39] Historical Manuscripts Commission, *Report on the MSS of the late Reginald Rawdon Hastings, Esq., The Manor House, Ashby de la Zouche*, 4 vols (1928–42), i, p. 305.
[40] TNA, E 403/594, mem. 11; F. Devon, *Issue Rolls of the Exchequer; being a Collection of Payments Made out of His Majesty's Revenue, from King Henry III to King Henry VI inclusive* (London, 1837), pp. 305, 307.
[41] *PL*, ii, p. 280.

of a Yorkist suns and roses collar, some of which were broken.[42] The find was of course politically profitable for the Tudor regime, open to any evidence of his lingering Yorkist sympathies. Stanley may well have retained the collar simply for its fiscal value, but it is not implausible that it had sentimental worth. Perhaps he could not force himself to part with an item which symbolised his intimacy with Edward IV. He had, after all, been steward of the household to Edward's son, the prince of Wales. Sadly, the state of the collar when discovered reflected the Yorkist regime: broken and disjointed. For some individuals, the livery collar did have political value and intrinsic meaning, and was a tangible link to the donor as an individual, as well as to the royal authority which the collar represented. The collar linked donor and recipient through the act of giving and receiving, and the ways in which testators bequeathed collars reflected the ways in which they interacted with the item in life.

Certain aspects of anthropological theory concerning the reciprocal nature of gift giving may help inform a late medieval paradigm, particularly when focusing on the collar as a gift from the sovereign. Conceived by Lévi-Strauss, Mauss and Morgan, and developed by later social anthropologists, gift theory has a rich literature.[43] For anthropologists, the 'gift' defines the personal relationships forged through the exchange of items. The salient point here is that those exchanging gifts form a qualitative social relationship through the transaction. This can be juxtaposed with commodity exchange or trade, which establishes a relationship between the objects transacted. Gift exchange therefore stimulates personal interaction between donor and recipient, the nature and intensity of the bond determined by the differing social status of the transactors: the original gift is usually conferred by one of superior rank. The donor gives the gift in return for the personal relationship, thus placing the recipient in a position of subordination. The ideal outcome is one of mutual indebtedness.[44]

England during the Wars of the Roses was not, however, the perfect context in which to achieve this ideal. The donor's principal motive in giving a livery collar was the loyalty and adherence of the recipient. The 'counter-gift' was therefore intangible: it could only be hoped for, and was far from being guaranteed. As regards a counter-gift of enduring political conviction, the collar may not have been entirely effective. Although there were of course individuals whose lasting loyalty could be relied upon, the gentry and nobility of the late fifteenth century were notoriously pragmatic in their approach to dynastic politics. The success

---

[42] 'The garnisshing of colier golde. White roses and the Sonne broken': TNA, E 154/2/5, fol. 13v; I. Arthurson, *The Perkin Warbeck Conspiracy 1491–1499* (Stroud, 1994), p. 93.
[43] M. Mauss, *The Gift* (London, 1925); C. Lévi-Strauss, *The Elementary Structures of Kinship* (London, 1949).
[44] C.A. Gregory, *Gifts and Commodities* (London, 1982), pp. 1–9, 15–24, 41–70; M. Strathern, 'Qualified Value: The Perspective of Gift Exchange', in C. Humphrey and S. Hugh-Jones (eds), *Barter, Exchange and Value, An Anthropological Approach* (Cambridge, 1992), pp. 174–5.

of the gift depended on the personality and individual situation of each recipient. However, the collar could have been a more successful gift in terms of the recipient's acknowledgement of pride in royal service – whether that was for the Lancastrian or Yorkist king – the counter-gift being manifested in the recipient's choice to depict their collar on their memorial. The crown in the second half of the fifteenth century may well have been conscious of the success (or otherwise) of the earlier distribution of badges and collars, notably by Richard II and Henry IV. Although it may not have been the individual's primary motive in including the item on their memorial, the number of extant examples on church monuments and in stained glass is testament to the efficacy of effigial depictions of livery collars in displaying royal authority.

Although interpreting allegiance or loyalty as a form of counter-gift may be a step too far for some anthropologists who, on the whole, have been reluctant to discuss intangible counter-gifts, the model postulated above is not entirely inconsistent with the theory. Offer's discussion of the 'economy of regard', whereby the grant of the gift is driven by the donor's desire for regard, is applicable here. In order to satisfy regard, the counter-gift does not have to be tangible. It can, at the very least, simply be a grant of attention.[45] Anxiety over losing regard provides a stimulus to continued gift giving although, crucially, Offer maintains that in some circumstances not all gifts are successful in sustaining bonds.[46]

The act of being decorated with a livery collar by the king amid regal ceremony, kneeling before him and his royal banner, loaded the collar with deep significance (Plate 4). Before Henry IV's coronation Richard Beauchamp, the future earl of Warwick (d. 1439), was made a knight of the Bath and awarded an SS collar by Henry amid similar solemnity. The occasion was recorded for posterity in the Beauchamp Pageant, a posthumous series of illustrations charting the major events of Beauchamp's life.[47] Livery collars were included among the largesse distributed on occasions such as New Year, when they were given to existing supporters or foreign dignitaries. The act of gift giving was a royal virtue and generous patronage reflected the donor's wealth, generosity and worship.[48] Although the collar was technically a gift, it differed from other similar items in significant ways. Although most gifts were given with the expectation of something in return, wearing a livery collar would benefit not only the recipient, who received a prestigious item, but also the ruling regime. What better way to advertise royal authority than to have one's servants wearing one's badge? The

---

[45] A. Offer, 'Between the Gift and the Market: The Economy of Regard', *Economic History Review*, 50 (1997), 450–76, at 451–4.
[46] Offer, 'Between the Gift and the Market', 453.
[47] V. Dillon and W.H. St John Hope (eds), *Pageant of the Birth Life and Death of Richard Beauchamp Earl of Warwick K.G. 1389–1439* (London, 1914), plate III.
[48] M. Hayward, *Dress at the Court of King Henry VIII* (Leeds, 2007), pp. 121–4.

bestowal of a collar was expected to engender a degree of reciprocity, the gift accompanied by the expectation of the recipient's loyalty.

The collar could be an efficacious recruitment aid, and there appears to have been no age limit as regards who was targeted. In 1452–53 the infant son of Sir Robert Harcourt, a member of Margaret of Anjou's household, was given a collar 'de tissewe cum esses argenti', worth 6s. 8d.[49] Although it was essentially a plaything, wearing it would prepare the boy for expected loyal service later in life. Things did not, however, go according to plan. Sir Robert became an early adherent of Edward IV, and was made a knight of the Garter in 1462. Collars could also be given as wedding gifts, with not only the monetary but also the symbolic and sentimental value of the item reflecting the esteem the recipient held for the giver. In January 1467 John Howard, the future duke of Norfolk (d. 1485), lavished a variety of gifts on his new bride Margaret, including 'a coler of goolde with xxxiiij. roses and sonnes set on a corse of blak sylke with an hanger [pendant] of goolde garnyshed with a saphyre'.[50] Perhaps in this context the collar was also given in expectation of loyalty, or faithfulness, this time to the husband, its acceptance confirming the wife had entered her husband's 'affinity'.

When it came to bequests, collars found a variety of recipients. On occasion it was given as a guarantee or recompense for an unpaid loan, as was the case with Thomas Dalby, a canon of York Minster, in c. 1500, who pledged a gold 'colare cum le esses' for £100 he had taken from the common chest. In his interminable 1463 will John Baret (d. 1467), a wealthy merchant from Bury St Edmunds, wished his collars to be sold to pay for prayers:

> I wil bothe my colers of silvir, the Kyng's lyfre, be sold, and the money disposid in almesse for Edmund Tabowre soule and his frendys, to recompense broke silvir I had of his to oon of the colerys and othir things with othir stuff by syde wich I took to my owne vse.[51]

Although Baret seems principally concerned with the monetary value of his collars, the fact that they were also given in exchange for alms tangibly connected the item with the care of his acquaintances' souls, the spiritual association suggesting a more significant role for the collar. A collar does not, unsurprisingly, feature on his cadaver effigy in St Mary's, Bury St Edmunds, but an SS collar does appear on the small figure sculpture of Baret on the side of the tomb chest, holding a scroll bearing the word 'me' from his motto 'Grace me Governe'. The message here could not be more graphic: this was a portrait of Baret as in life, as he wished to be remembered (Figure 1).[52] It appears that he therefore wore the

---

[49] TNA, E 101/410/11, mem. 3.
[50] *PL*, iv, p. 263.
[51] S. Tymms (ed.), *Wills and Inventories from the Register of the Commissary of Bury St. Edmunds and the Archdeacon of Sudbury*, Camden Society, Original Series, 49 (London, 1850), p. 41.
[52] The roof of his chapel is also decorated with SS collars surrounding his initials.

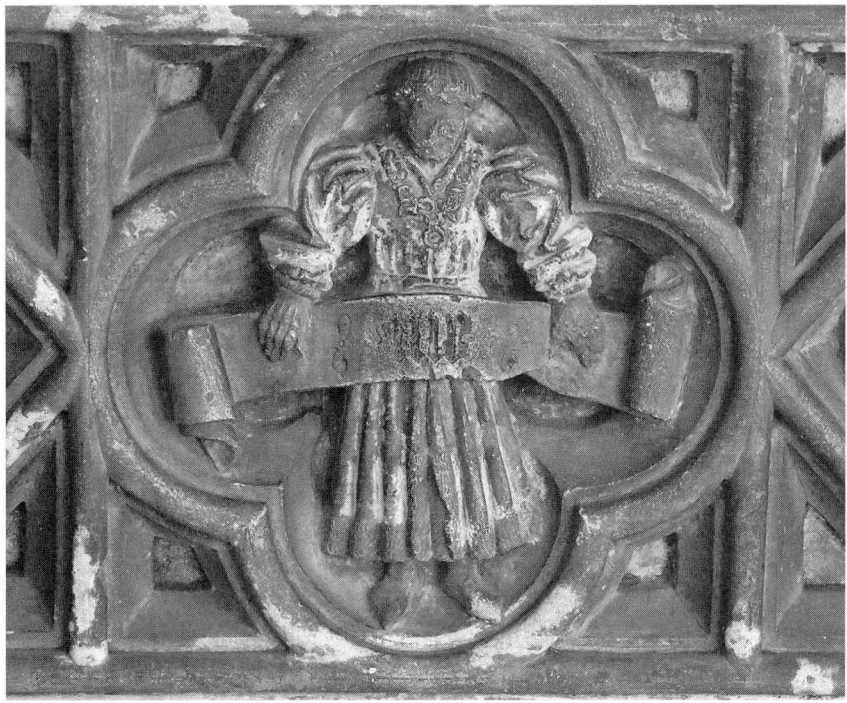

Figure 1. St Mary's, Bury St Edmunds (Suffolk). John Baret (d. 1467).

collar which is represented on his sculpture, perhaps one of the collars referred to in his will.

A collar could also be used to perpetuate the donor's memory, in both a spiritual and secular sense. Sir John Aleyn, mayor of London, had this in mind when making his will in 1545:

> I will that the Lorde mayre of London for the tyme being shal have my Collo[r] of SS to use and occupie yerely at and uppon principall and festivall dayes and the same ... to hym and his successours mayres for the same effecte. So that the same mayre and his successours come yerely to myne obytte in the mercers chapel in London.[53]

Not only did Aleyn benefit from the grateful prayers of his successors, but the bequest ensured that his name would be perpetually linked with the gift. The collar, kept at the Mansion House, is still used today by the lord mayor (Plate 5).

More frequently, a collar was bequeathed to a family member, often as an heirloom, highlighting the importance of the item as a memorandum of the royal service of the testator and the pride and honour which it had bestowed

---

[53] TNA, PROB 11/31, fol. 2v. He was buried in the Mercers' Chapel.

on their family. The continuing presence of the individual's collar within their kin would also encourage commemoration; their memory would live on. Henry Fotherby of Lincoln left his collar 'of the lord King Henry the Sixth' to his son John in February 1471, and in 1482 Sir Richard Roos bequeathed his 'collar of golde of the kings lyverey' and other items of jewellery 'that I was wont to were' to his nephew, Sir Henry Roos.[54] Occasionally there is evidence that a collar was passed down several generations, such as Thomas Reresbie's collar, left to him by his father, and then bequeathed to his son Lionel.[55] One can imagine the family showing off such a collar to neighbours and kin, accompanied by the story of when, why and to whom it was awarded.

The livery collar not only reflected the relationship between worldly individuals and their ownership, as it were, of each other. It could also reflect the bonds between living and celestial individuals, as was the case with William Swayne who in 1484 left his 'colour of silver of the kinges lyverey' for the making of St Osmond's shrine in Salisbury Cathedral. Five years previously his son Henry, who predeceased him, also left a livery collar – possibly the same one – for the same purpose,[56] an expression of family solidarity through shared devotion to a saint for whom the family obviously held close affection. In 1463 Euphemia Langton left her SS collar, along with a gold necklace and an alabaster figure of the Virgin Mary, to the altar of the Virgin in Elmet church (North Yorkshire). Judging by the opulent bequests, the church was evidently a favoured place of worship.[57]

Occasionally we can glean more, the donation of a collar being inlaid with a deeper, more symbolic value than its cash worth or as a stimulus for saintly intercession. In 1499 Henry VII presented a rich collar of twenty-five *esses*, two portcullises, a double 'R' and a red rose to Norwich Cathedral to adorn an image of the Holy Trinity.[58] The gift was not only a pious statement of favour from the king; it definitively united the most powerful and evocative of religious images with a potent symbol of Henry's authority, an item incorporating the very essence of his royal dignity and honour. As the collar was intended to 'adorn' the image, which was likely a sculpture, it is probable that it was hung around it in some way. This act added to the symbolism: not only was the king, represented by his collar, being physically 'united' with the Holy Trinity (there is even a hint that he was claiming 'ownership' of the image), but a degree of heavenly

---

[54] Lincoln Cathedral Library, Dean and Chapter, A/2/35, fol. 131v. The description of Henry VI as king coincides with the period between October 1470 and April 1471 when he was restored to the throne; Boatwright, Habberjam and Hammond (eds), *Logge Register*, i, no. 38.

[55] *Test. Ebor.*, vi, p. 181.

[56] TNA, PROB 11/7, fol. 3; PROB 11/7, fols. 153v–155; Boatwright, Habberjam and Hammond (eds), *Logge Register*, ii, no. 268; i, no. 5.

[57] See n. 32 above.

[58] Norwich, Norfolk Record Office, Norwich Sacrist's Register, DCN 40/11, fol 111r.

intercession was transmitted to the king through physical contact with his collar. The timing of this gift is also noteworthy. Not long after the Cornish rebellion, the standoff at Blackheath in 1497 and the execution of the earl of Warwick in 1499, the king's political position now appeared more secure. Perhaps he was expressing his personal thanks for divine intervention.

In the royal courts of Europe the collar could be used for diplomatic purposes. The act of giving or wearing a collar was politically efficacious and utilised to great effect, with the medium of art regularly recording the act for posterity. We have previously witnessed Henry IV ordering a plenitude of collars for use at home and abroad during the first years of his reign. The practice was continued by his successors. A manuscript illustration from *c.* 1470 shows Edward IV being presented with a book, the king dressed in full regalia and wearing the collar of the Order of the Golden Fleece.[59] The order was established by Philip the Good, duke of Burgundy in 1430. Edward had forged an alliance with the dukedom, and his sister Margaret married Philip's son, Charles the Bold, in 1468. Charles was made a knight of the Garter the following year, shortly after Edward's investiture into the Order of the Golden Fleece.[60] After the death of duke Charles in 1477, Edward ceased to wear his collar. When quizzed by the Burgundian ambassadors as to the reason, he stated that he would wait until the uncertain state of the Anglo-Burgundian alliance was clearer. On one occasion he is reported to have declared that he now wore the collar beneath his clothes, a diplomatic answer indeed, explaining why the collar was no longer on show whilst suggesting that the collar, and with it his affection for the regime, remained quite literally close to his heart.[61]

Examples of English livery collars can be found on tombs and in stained glass across Europe. In the Hôpital St Josse in Bruges is an incised slab with a canted shield commemorating Joos de Bul (d. 1488) and his wife Katherine. Around the shield was originally a brass replica of a collar of suns and roses with a lion pendant, recording de Bul's connections with Edward IV.[62]

One incident which highlights the significance and potentially contentious nature of a king wearing another's collar concerns Richard II. In the parliament of 1394 the earl of Arundel complained that the king's decision to wear the collar of John of Gaunt was detrimental to his honour, as was the fact that members of the king's retinue were also wearing it. Obviously a king should only wear the

---

[59] BL, Royal 15 E IV, fol. 14, from Jean de Waurin's *Chronique d'Angleterre*.
[60] C.L. Scofield, *The Life and Reign of Edward the Fourth*, 2 vols (London, 1923), i, pp. 462–3, 484–5.
[61] L. Visser-Fuchs, 'The Garters and the Garter Achievements of Charles the Bold, Duke of Burgundy', *The Ricardian*, 23 (2013), 1–19, at 9.
[62] The brass collar is now held in the Musée des Hospices Civils in Bruges: W.J. Hemp, 'A Late Fifteenth Century Incised Slab at Bruges with a Collar of Suns and Roses in Brass', *TMBS*, 6 (1913), 320–5; *CPR 1467–77*, p. 19.

collar of an equal, and as regards Richard's retinue, just who was their lord, the king or Gaunt? Richard's answer was that he had personally taken the collar from Gaunt's neck and 'would wear it as a sign of the great love and whole-heartedness between them, as he had done with the liveries of his other uncles'. He added that it was also his decision that his retinue wore Gaunt's livery collar.[63] Here we return to the significance of the livery collar as an expression of the donor's ownership over the recipient. Evidently Richard either misunderstood this, or was attempting to use it in a different context, something which confused, and perhaps instilled jealousy among contemporaries. The king was evidently attempting to show solidarity through wearing his uncles' livery collars.

Wearing a collar to express the 'love' between rulers became commonplace. Jean Froissart reported that Henry IV wore 'aboute his neck the lyverie of France' at his coronation.[64] This act may also have been a subtle means of reminding the French of the English claim to their throne. A similar motive probably lay behind a collar of SS and broomcods made for the young Henry VI in 1426.[65] Another SS collar, possibly a personal collar of Henry V, was given to Emperor Sigismund in 1416 on his admission into the Order of the Garter. He was an enthusiastic recipient, noted to have worn it in a procession in Constance the following year. A further batch of twenty-four silver-gilt and sixty silver collars were sent to him in 1434, for mass distribution to the knights and esquires of Basle, at the emperor's and the English ambassador's discretion.[66] A similar group distribution of collars symbolised the close connection between the Lancastrian court and the Gonzaga dynasty of Mantua. In 1436 Henry VI granted Gianfrancesco Gonzaga permission to distribute fifty gold SS collars to his most prominent men. Gianfrancesco had been given a similar collar some thirty years previously. A mural in the Palazzo Ducale in Mantua depicts a tournament scene. The border is created by a line of SS collars with swan pendants and marigold flowers, the combination of the Lancastrian and Gonzaga badges symbolising their alliance. The SS collar is also featured on some of the horses' caparisons.[67] Perhaps the scene depicts the tournament at which the collars were officially distributed; although the frieze is incomplete, there may have originally been fifty collars in the border, representing those distributed. In 1426 John, duke of Bedford sent two gold collars of his livery to Paolo Guinigi and his son Ladislas, rulers of Lucca, delivered

---

[63] *PROME*, Richard II, Parliament of January to March 1394, mem. 6.
[64] J. Jolliffe (ed. and trans.), *Froissart's Chronicles* (London, 1967), p. 416. This collar was composed of broomcods.
[65] TNA, E 404/42/306.
[66] T. Rymer, *Foedera conventiones, literae, et cujuscunque generis acta publica, inter reges Angliae*, 20 vols (London, 1704–35), ix, pp. 435–6; N.H. Nicolas (ed.), *Proceedings and Ordinances of the Privy Council of England*, 7 vols (London, 1834–37), iv, p. cxvii.
[67] I. Toesca, 'Lancaster and Gonzaga: The Collar of SS at Mantua', in D. Chambers and J. Martineau (eds), *Splendours of the Gonzaga* (London, 1981), pp. 1–2.

by the earl of Salisbury and intended to win their support against France.⁶⁸ The collars were probably similar to that of alternate roots and *esses* with an eagle pendant, worn by Bedford in his portrait in the *Bedford Hours* (Plate 6). Although a Guinigi agent, Jacopo Bernardini, lent money for the English military cause in France, this was the limit of the gifts' effectiveness. In 1432 the seigneur de Châteauvillain, another recipient of one of Bedford's collars, returned his. The reasons appear to have been political, as Châteauvillain had switched his allegiance from Burgundy to Charles VII of France. The act, which contravened his oath on receiving the collar, immensely angered Bedford.⁶⁹

Just as the livery collar could be given as a gift, it could just as easily be returned for political reasons. Similarly, political motivations could result in a collar being taken away, the forceful nature of the removal being used in narratives to underline the symbolism of the act; it was considered a physical insult not only to the collar wearer, but also to the donor. In early January 1400 Thomas Holland, earl of Kent visited Isabella, the queen of the recently deposed Richard II, to whom the earl had remained loyal. Declaring that Richard was still alive at Pontefract, he ripped off the SS collars worn by Henry IV's servants who were attending Isabella: 'to cause his speech the better to be believed he took awaie the king's cognizances from them that ware the same as the collars from their necks ... and throwing them awaie, said that such cognizances were no longer to be borne.'⁷⁰ Not only was the act highly politically charged, but the aggressive manner in which it was undertaken heightened its significance. Livery collars were regarded as potent symbols of royal power and dignity and, as we shall see, even viewed as physical embodiments of the essence of the king's dignity.

Iconography

The elusive meaning of the 'S' has fascinated scholars since the nineteenth century, and a multitude of suggestions have been postulated. These include *Saint Simplicius*, *signum* (badge or sign), *souveignez* (remember), *soverayne* (sovereign), *seneschallus* (steward) and *sanctus* (saint). Other more imaginative suggestions have included the 'S' representing a bridle bit or a swan.⁷¹ None are implausible, although the only two suggestions which can be corroborated with evidence are *souveignez* and *soverayne*.⁷² As we have seen, the phrase *souveyne vous de moi* was favoured by Henry IV, with the forget-me-not flower appearing on items of

---

⁶⁸ J. Stratford, *The Bedford Inventories* (London, 1993), pp. 101–3.
⁶⁹ Stratford, *Bedford Inventories*, p. 102.
⁷⁰ J.H. Wylie, *History of England under Henry the Fourth*, 4 vols (London, 1884–98), i, p. 97.
⁷¹ See Gough Nichols, 'Collars of the Royal Livery'; Hartshorne, 'Notes on Collars of SS'; Foss, 'Hackington, or St. Stephen's, Canterbury'; Skeat, 'Souvent Me Souvient'; Scharf, 'A Note upon Collars'; Jenkins, 'Collars of SS'.
⁷² Mortimer, *Fears of Henry IV*, p. 385.

clothing, and SS collars, worn by the king. The word *Soverayne* appears several times on the tester of Henry's tomb at Canterbury Cathedral, which also features SS collars encircling heraldic shields bearing the royal arms and the arms of Navarre. The word was also included on Henry's seal as duke of Lancaster, and Henry's son John, duke of Bedford, adopted *Sovereigne* as his motto.[73]

However, perhaps the antiquaries of the nineteenth century and subsequent scholars have misunderstood the meaning of the 'S', chiefly through attempting to ascertain which one particular meaning should be attributed to it. An alternative suggestion is that the letter was deliberately chosen because of the multiplicity of meanings which it signified for contemporaries, meanings which have multiplied as each successive generation has sought its own interpretation. It is striking that no 'official' explanation of the 'S' exists, opening up the possibility that no one meaning was ever intended. There is evidence to support this theory. An illuminated frontispiece to a Sarum Breviary dating from *c*. 1420–30, now held in St John's College, Oxford, features a shield of the Five Wounds of Christ surrounded by a gold collar of nineteen *esses*, each letter forming the start of a word. The following inscription is written at the bottom of the page: 'O qui cuncta regis miles fortissime vere collarium regis es dignum dignus habere' ('O that among all things of the king, most brave knight, certainly you are worthy to have the worthy collar of the king').[74] Notwithstanding this phrase, which neatly sums up the importance of the livery collar and the explicit connection it had with the king, the illumination reveals several additional meanings of the 'S', suggesting that, at least for the individual who commissioned the breviary and in all likelihood received the collar, the 'S' represented a variety of words of both secular and religious pertinence. An additional clue to the multiplicity of meanings attached to the 'S' lies in the *Tirant lo Blanc*, a romance written by Joanot Martorell, a Venetian knight who visited England in 1438. In the manuscript Martorell describes the device's significance, listing saintliness, sagacity, sapience, 'and many other noble words' as its principal meanings, adding that no other letter in the alphabet has such lofty significance.[75]

When compared to the SS collar, the two components of the Yorkist collar, suns and roses, have received less scholarly attention. This is surprising, as contemporaries would have accorded no less significance to its meaning than to the Lancastrian equivalent. Indeed, as the Yorkist collar was introduced as a rival to

---

[73] Duffy, *Royal Tombs*, pp. 199–206.

[74] N. Morgan, 'An SS Collar in the Devotional Context of the Shield of the Five Wounds', in J. Stratford (ed.), *The Lancastrian Court: Proceedings of the 2001 Harlaxton Symposium*, Harlaxton Medieval Studies, XIII (Donington, 2003), pp. 147–62. The words are: *Salve Salvator, Spes, Sol, Sapiencia, Splendor, Salve, Sola Salus, Salve Scola, Summa, Salvus, Sanctifica, Servo, Salvans, Sub Sanguine*, and *Sanus*.

[75] Joanot Martorell and Marti Joan de Galba, *Tirant lo Blanc*, ed. and trans. D.H. Rosenthal (New York and London, 1984), pp. 127–8.

its predecessor, its meaning and significance were undoubtedly of paramount importance.

For centuries religion and politics, on the face of it diametrically opposed, have in fact interacted. Religious ceremony has served to define and legitimise political institutions, leading some to describe religious practice as an 'idiom of political expression'.[76] During the late medieval period ruling regimes utilised the visual arts to bolster their identity through appropriating religious symbolism. The Yorkists were particularly astute at this, their propaganda frequently being channelled through religious themes.[77] This was no more so than in their principal emblems: the white rose, the sun, and the combination of the two, the *rose-en-soleil*. These devices abounded in monumental art and architecture,[78] on jewellery and clothing,[79] in manuscripts and paintings,[80] and of course on tomb effigies and brasses in the form of the suns and roses livery collar. In addition to providing an aesthetically pleasing combination, the sun and rose were intrinsically associated in contemporary verse; the rose withers without the sun.[81] Due to the religious and secular contexts in which these badges were used, we should be wary of interpreting every white rose, sun or *rose-en-soleil* as Yorkist. In some cases their appearance was perhaps intended to convey a religious rather than secular meaning. This may have been the case with the brass of Canon John Byrkhede (d. 1468), in St Mary's, Harrow-on-the-Hill (Middlesex), on which a *rose-en-soleil* appears on the morse of his processional vestment. The depiction of the Virgin on the head of his orphrey suggests that the *rose-en-soleil* was a Marian symbol. Equally, the fifteenth-century stained glass in St Lawrence's, Diddington (Huntingdonshire), depicting Saints Katherine and Margaret with *roses-en-soleil* in the borders, does not appear to have any Yorkist connotations. A nuanced reading of such examples is therefore required. It may have been the case that the majority of such depictions were indeed acknowledging both religious and political contexts. The multiplicity of meanings would have certainly appealed to the late medieval mind, and served to increase the potency and effectiveness of their use.

Legend has it that Edward IV adopted the sun in splendour motif after his victory at Mortimer's Cross in February 1461, during which three suns appeared in the sky, an example of the rare meteorological phenomenon known as

---

[76] R. Firth, 'Spiritual Aroma: Religion and Politics', *American Anthropologist*, 83 (1981), 582–601.
[77] Marks, 'Political and Genealogical Propaganda', 154.
[78] Examples can be found in the stained glass of the east window of Holy Trinity Collegiate Church, Tattershall.
[79] For examples of extant Yorkist badges see Spencer, *Pilgrim Souvenirs*, pp. 295–7.
[80] The *rose-en-soleil* features in several of Edward IV's manuscripts: BL, Royal 19 E V, fols. 32, 196; Royal 14 E IV, fol. 244v.
[81] H. Walther, *Initia carminum ac versuum Medii Aevi posterioris Latinorum*, 5 vols (Göttingen, 1959), v, no. 32540.

a parhelion.[82] Edward was not, however, the first English king to adopt a sun motif, as Richard II had used 'the sonne shyning' (a sunburst through a cloud) as one of his badges. Henry IV may have sparingly used the red *rose-en-soleil*, and it possible that the badge was earlier adopted by Edward III.[83] But the use of sun iconography goes back much further, having classical precedents. The concept of the divinity of the king has existed since antiquity, and the sun device had been linked with the sacerdotal function of the king, seen as the *Christomimesis*, or the imitation of Christ on earth, for centuries before the accession of Edward IV. The Hellenistic device of a circle of the sun's rays was adopted by Rome in the third century as one aspect of the deification of the ruler and the cult of kingship. Thereafter, the emperor would be referred to as *Sol Invictus*, the unconquered sun. Although subsequent concepts of kingship developed in the west did not adhere so vigorously to the notion of the king as the sun, the two were frequently tied.[84] Gian Galeazzo Visconti (d. 1402) adopted a white dove set within a radiating sun as his device, which was worn as a necklace by his followers. The sun was not infrequently connected with the rose. A bust at Paestum depicts a rose growing out of a crown in the form of a sundial worn by a goddess.[85] The Christian church adopted the sun symbol, which frequently surrounded depictions of the Virgin and Christ in art.[86] A sixteenth-century sermon also linked the two: 'And as in the morning the rose opens, receiving the dew from heaven and the sun, so Mary's soul did open and receive Christ the heavenly dew.'[87]

As with the sun emblem, the rose has a long history dating back to classical antiquity and beyond.[88] The cultural meanings associated with the rose developed in Rome, where it was closely linked to Venus, Bacchus and Aphrodite, the flower symbolising love, drinking and death. The healing and cleansing powers of the flower were discussed by Pliny, roses featured on the standards of the empire's legions, and rose chaplets and wreaths became increasingly popular as an 'orgy of rose worship' flourished. The *Rosalia*, the festival of the rose during

---

[82] The event was immortalised by William Shakespeare in Act II, Scene 1 of *Henry VI, Part III*, and illustrated in BL, Harley MS 7353. Also see J. Gairdner (ed.), *The Historical Collections of a Citizen of London in the Fifteenth Century*, Camden Society, New Series, 17 (London, 1876), p. 211.
[83] M. Biddle, B. Clayre and M. Morris, 'The Setting of the Round Table: Winchester Castle and the Great Hall', in M. Biddle (ed.), *King Arthur's Round Table: An Archaeological Investigation* (Woodbridge, 2000), pp. 59–101, at 78–9; M. Biddle, 'The Hanging of the Round Table', in *ibid.*, pp. 393–424, at 414–17.
[84] S. Bertelli, *The King's Body: Sacred Rituals of Power in Medieval and Early Modern Europe* (University Park, PA, 2001), pp. 6, 10–13.
[85] E. Wilkins, *The Rose-Garden Game* (London, 1969), p. 111.
[86] R.W. Jones, *Bloodied Banners: Martial Display on the Medieval Battlefield* (Woodbridge, 2010), p. 24; BL, Additional MS 31835, fol. 24.
[87] Quoted in Wilkins, *Rose-Garden Game*, p. 113.
[88] For this paragraph, see J. Potter, *The Rose, A True History* (London, 2010), pp 6–50.

which the flower was venerated, developed from the second century, and the flower became increasingly connected with debauchery. Nero was obsessed with roses, and Marcus Aurelius Antoninus was reported to have smothered his guests with rose petals showered on them from a reversible ceiling.

The flower has a long history in England as both a decorative and heraldic emblem.[89] Henry III's queen, Eleanor of Provence, is said to have introduced the golden rose badge to England, which was inherited by Edward I. There is tangential evidence that the rose was used as a badge by subsequent royals, including John of Gaunt and Henry IV, although the colour is not specified and it may have simply been a decorative device. The white rose was adopted by the house of York, probably through their Mortimer descent, from at least the 1430s.[90] The 1399 list of royal jewels included a collar of white roses and mascles which may have been an early collar of the house of York. If not a livery collar, it is likely that it was associated with the family.[91] Richard, duke of York's seals included roses, but again we cannot be certain of their colour. It appears that the duke may have used a form of white rose livery collar such as the example given to Sir John Fastolf. Edward IV, dubbed the 'Rose of Rouen' after his place of birth, was definitively associated with the white rose. After the Towton campaign of 1461 he was referred to as 'thys fayre white ros and herbe, the Erle of Marche', and in other verses of the period he is dubbed the white rose.[92] Edward's seals depicted roses, suns or a *rose-en-soleil*, and a pedigree roll compiled for the king includes several examples, alongside the falcon and fetterlock badge.[93] His white *rose-en-soleil* badge is most famously depicted alongside a portrait of the king in the window of the north-west transept of Canterbury Cathedral, dating from c. 1482.

Contrary to popular belief, there is no evidence that the red rose was associated with the house of Lancaster until after the accession of Henry VII, when it was adopted as one of his badges.[94] It was the Croyland continuator who first mentioned the red rose of Henry as avenging the boar of Richard III.[95] With the inception of the Tudor red and white rose, symbolising the union of Lancaster

---

[89] See M.P. Siddons, *Heraldic Badges in England and Wales*, 4 vols (Woodbridge, 2009), ii, pp. 211–26; S. Anglo, *Images of Tudor Kingship* (London, 1992), pp. 74–9.

[90] A list of the badges and lordships of the house of York dating from c. 1460 associates the white rose with Clifford castle, acquired after the marriage of Richard, earl of Cambridge (d. 1415) to Maud, daughter of Thomas, Lord Clifford: Bodleian Library, Digby MS 82.

[91] TNA, E 101/411/9, mem. 4.

[92] T. Wright, *Political Poems and Songs Relating to English History*, 2 vols (London, 1859–61), ii, pp. 269–82; J. Gairdner (ed.), 'Gregory's Chronicle, 1461–1469', in Gairdner (ed.), *Historical Collections*, p. 215; R.H. Robbins (ed.), *Historical Poems of the Fourteenth and Fifteenth Centuries* (New York, 1959), no. 92.

[93] Free Library of Philadelphia, MS Lewis, E 210.

[94] J. Ashdown-Hill, 'The Red Rose of Lancaster?' *The Ricardian*, 10 (1996), 406–20.

[95] N. Pronay and J. Cox (eds), *The Crowland Chronicle Continuations 1459–1486* (London, 1986), p. 184.

and York with the marriage of Henry VII to Elizabeth of York in 1486, it became convenient for Tudor writers such as Edward Hall to integrate a 'red rose of Lancaster' into their narratives. The badge was therefore very much a product of the Tudor propaganda machine. The golden rose of Eleanor of Provence was now transformed into a red rose by her son Edmund, earl of Lancaster, and Henry IV was given a red rose badge in *Writhe's Garter Book*, a heraldic manuscript dating from c. 1488.[96] The concept of the union of the red and white roses is epitomised in an extant book of motets, the beginning of which includes a picture of a red, white and Tudor rose tree enclosing a poem celebrating Henry VIII, the embodiment of the union of both roses.[97] The Yorkist white rose and sun were not, however, abandoned immediately after the accession of Henry VII, perhaps in a prudent move so as not to completely alienate himself from past supporters of his father-in-law, Edward IV, many of whom had helped him to the throne. At Henry's marriage to Elizabeth of York, her badges of the sun and white rose were displayed in abundance, and the queen was referred to as 'þe lyly-whiȝte rose' in a ballad dating from the same period,[98] the allusion to the Virgin being particularly apt for the matriarch of the Tudor dynasty. The careful integration of Elizabeth into the Tudor historical narrative was completed during the reign of her son Henry VIII, her badge now being represented as a rose branch springing from a sunburst, bearing a red and white *rose-en-soleil*: the white rose was not now illustrated in isolation. Perhaps the intention was to nullify any lingering political associations it had with the house of York.

Virginia Henderson has discussed the red rose's multivalent symbolism, proposing that it was adopted by Henry VII predominantly for its Marian and Christological associations, the political importance of the symbol being superimposed by the regime.[99] However, the white rose was equally, and in some contexts more, associated with the Virgin. It should therefore be acknowledged that one of the motivations behind the emblem being adopted by the house of York, and promulgated by Edward IV alongside the sun device, was its religious resonance. The Virgin was a favoured saint of many royals, not least due to her association with fertility, birth and nurturing lineage, and Marian references can be found in political images and narratives of the fifteenth century.[100] Along-

---

[96] See A. Wagner, N. Barker and A. Payne (eds), *Medieval Pageant: Writhe's Garter Book: The Ceremony of the Bath and the Earldom of Salisbury Roll* (London, 1993).
[97] BL, Royal 11 E 11, fol. 2r.
[98] Robbins, *Historical Poems*, no. 34.
[99] V.K. Henderson, 'Retrieving the "Crown in the Hawthorn Bush": The Origins of the Badges of Henry VII', in D. Biggs, S.D. Michalove and A. Compton Reeves (eds), *Traditions and Transformations in Late Medieval England* (Leiden, 2001), pp. 237–59.
[100] M. Rubin, 'Religious Symbols and Political Culture in Fifteenth-Century England', in L. Clark and C. Carpenter (eds), *The Fifteenth Century, IV: Political Culture in Late Medieval Britain* (Woodbridge, 2004), pp. 97–110, at pp. 106–7.

side St Anne, the Virgin was a focus of Yorkist religious devotion. Both Edward IV and his mother Cecily, duchess of York (d. 1495), committed their souls to the Virgin in their respective wills, and images of the saint were depicted in the north clerestory windows in the Yorkist mausoleum at Fotheringhay, probably at Cecily's instigation.[101] Edward further demonstrated his favouritism by making the Virgin the joint patron saint of the Order of the Garter in 1469.

The Christian church was at first reticent to encourage the use of the emblem but the rose was eventually adopted and soon came to represent the Virgin, the mystical rose. It was Bernard of Clairvaux who promulgated the Marian association, principally through his sermons on the Song of Songs: 'Mary was a white rose by reason of her virginity, a red rose by reason of her charity; white in her body, red in her soul; white in cultivating virtue, red in treading down vice.'[102] The virtues represented by the white rose, in particular purity and its association with paradise, were no doubt one of the reasons why it was adopted by the house of York. By the fifteenth century the link between roses and prayers for the Virgin was firmly established. *Aves* were transformed into roses for the Virgin, which she wore as a chaplet. A popular story connected with *Our Lady's Psalter* recalled how the Virgin appeared before a monk, whose prayers turned into white and red roses which she collected together to form a wreath.[103] The rosary was frequently depicted in art as three sets of five rings each containing ten roses, representing ten *Aves*. The first set, the 'white rosary' recalled the birth of Jesus, with the second and third sets, the 'red' and 'golden' rosaries, representing his later life and death.[104] The rosary devotion was intrinsically linked to the prayer beads which represented it. There is a visual similarity between the beads and the livery collar, not least when one considers that beads could be worn around the neck. Examples include the Langdale rosary (*c.* 1500), which is comparable to the suns and roses collar held by the duke of Clarence in the *Rous Roll* (Figure 2). When one considers the fact that the beads represented roses, and the Yorkist collar comprised suns and roses, there may have been a symbolic link between the two.

It is not difficult to understand why such powerful and commonplace symbols as the sun and white rose were utilised by the Yorkists. The effect of wearing

---

[101] Bentley, *Excerpta Historica*, pp. 366–79; TNA, PROB 11/10, fols. 195r–196v; R. Marks, 'The Glazing of Fotheringhay Church and College', *Journal of the British Archaeological Association*, 131 (1978), 79–109.
[102] Potter, *The Rose*, p. 83; N. Morgan, 'The Monograms, Arms and Badges of the Virgin Mary in Late Medieval England', in J. Cherry and A. Payne (eds), *Signs and Symbols: Proceedings of the 2006 Harlaxton Symposium*, Harlaxton Medieval Studies, XVIII (Donington, 2009), pp. 53–63, at p. 54; B. Seward, *The Symbolic Rose* (New York, 1960), pp. 43–8.
[103] Wilkins, *Rose-Garden Game*, pp. 165–73.
[104] A. Winston-Allen, *Stories of the Rose: The Making of the Rosary in the Middle Ages* (University Park, PA, 1997), pp. 34–8.

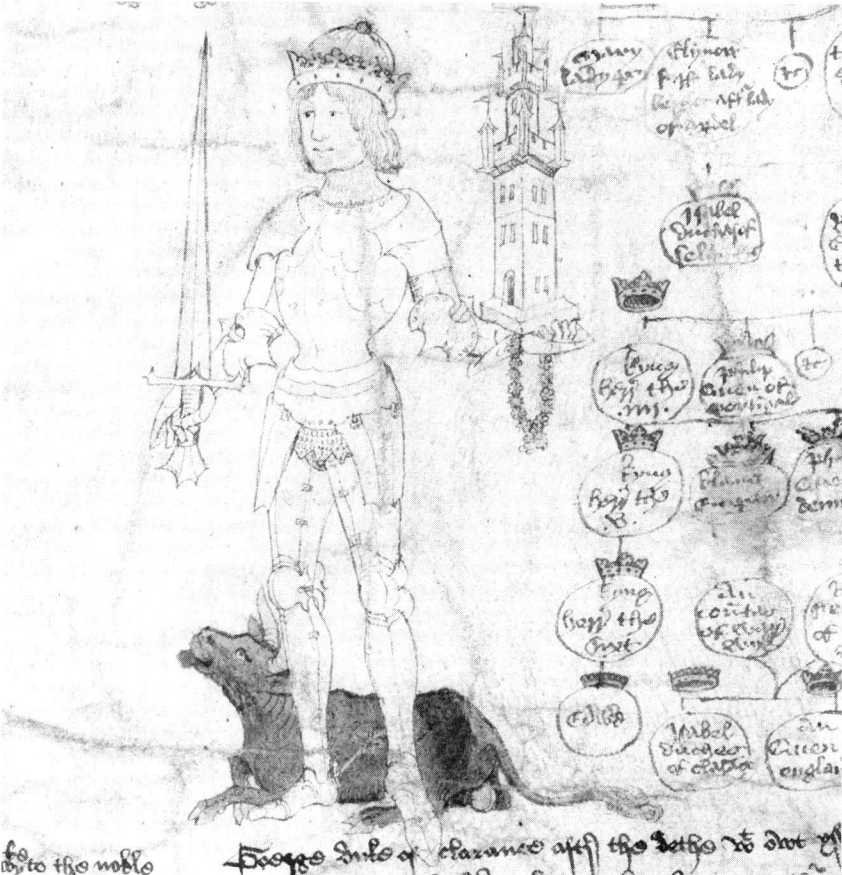

Figure 2. George, duke of Clarence, from the *Rous Roll*.

a collar composed of suns and roses would have been profound. Such an interplay of religious, secular and political implications was abundant during the late medieval period. The collar was a sign of the relationship between the wearer and the king, but it would have served at the very least as a visual reminder of the Yorkists' Marian piety and, by implication, of the Virgin's patronage of the regime.

Who wore the livery collar?

Put simply, there is no definitive answer to this question. If one considers the 391 extant collars on church monuments, in addition to the examples depicted in stained glass, it is to be assumed that hundreds of individuals wore a livery collar. Alongside royal household servants and courtiers, the collar was also given to individuals outside the household who undertook governmental duties, perhaps including sheriffs, and notable foreigners and their diplomats, such as the Belgian knight Jean Chabot of Emæl (d. 1496), depicted wearing his SS collar whilst presenting a book to Henry VII in a copy of the *Livre de physique* (c. 1494).[105] Members of the nobility who can be considered supporters of Lancaster or York would also have been recipients. It may also have been distributed to those who had served the regime on the battlefield. In some cases we can be certain that a recipient was given their collar personally by the king, as was the case with John Eylestone, sheriff and mayor of Lincoln.[106] More generally, the collar may also have been given as a gift or reward for service or favour. John Leventhorpe's brass (1433) at St Mary's, Sawbridgeworth (Hertfordshire), depicts an SS collar, probably due to his prominence as an administrator for the duchy of Lancaster. Thomas Colte (d. 1471), an adviser to Edward IV, wears a Yorkist collar on his brass at St Peter's, Roydon (Essex). But there are exceptions. Prominent government officials whose monuments do not feature a collar include John Throckmorton (1445) at St John the Baptist's, Fladbury (Worcestershire), and Sir William Pecche (1487) at St Botolph's, Lullingstone (Kent).[107] I would argue that the absence of a collar on such a memorial was a consequence of either the individual's or their family's choice – choices that were made for a variety of reasons. They may well have received a livery collar during their lifetime. Conversely, there are examples of individuals whose effigies wear collars, but who do not appear to have been members of the royal household, as was the case with several tombs of the Derbyshire gentry. They may of course have been awarded a collar for other reasons, although the lack of extant household accounts from the 1470s and 1480s must be taken into consideration.

Within the royal household we can be more certain that servants of the rank of esquire and above were given a livery collar. Legislation in 1401 stipulated that dukes, earls, barons, bannerets and the king's sons were permitted to wear the king's livery collar, in addition to 'certain other knights and esquires'.[108] This suggests that collars were also given to individuals outside the royal household. The 1478 ordinance for the household of Edward IV stated that:

> Euery lorde, knyght, and squyer, aswele squyers for the body as other within the household, were daily a coler of the kinges lyuerye aboute their nekkes as to

---

[105] BL, Royal 19 A V, fol. 1v.
[106] As attested in his will of 1492: 'meum colerium quod Edwardus Rex quartus michi dedit', bequeathed to the Clerks' Guild in Lincoln: Lincoln, Lincolnshire Archives Office, Corporation of Lincoln Registers, I [The White Book], L1/3/1, fol. 87. I am grateful to Dr Anne F. Sutton for providing this reference.
[107] James, 'York and Lancaster', 454–7.
[108] *PROME*, Henry IV, Parliament of January to March 1401, mem. 2.

theym apperteyneth, and that none of the said squyers faille herof, vpon payne of loosing a weekes wages.¹⁰⁹

The rule alludes to the fact that collars had been distributed to the above groups for some time, although evidently not all the king's esquires had been wearing their collars when required.¹¹⁰ There are several plausible reasons why this was so, beyond the simple conclusion that some were choosing not to wear them. Perhaps they had simply forgotten, or perhaps they were unsure as to when and where they should wear their collars due to the lack of precise regulations. The 1478 ordinance sought to rectify this by establishing a set of rules to allow for consistent collar-wearing among household staff. They were now expected to display their collars when they themselves were on display, thus creating a visually distinct group.¹¹¹ Whether these individuals chose to depict their collars on their monuments was still, of course, a matter of choice. This was, however, the case with John Gower and Robert Waterton. Gower (d. 1408), 'esquire', received a livery collar from Henry, earl of Derby in 1393, costing 26s. 8d.¹¹² It is probable that this is the collar, complete with a swan pendant, featured on his tomb effigy in Southwark Cathedral. As we have seen, Gower became an intimate of Henry IV to whom he dedicated his *Confessio Amantis*. We have witnessed Waterton receiving at least two collars: Henry's wardrobe accounts for 1396–97 record that a collar of *esses* was given to him to replace the collar that the king had given to another esquire. His alabaster tomb effigy, in the Waterton Chapel at St Oswald's, Methley (West Yorkshire), wears a collar of alternate reversed *esses* and crowns.¹¹³ We also know that Sir Thomas Charleton received a Yorkist collar, probably due to his position of knight of the body to Edward IV, although he has no extant monument.¹¹⁴

As regards women whose monuments depict a livery collar, the traditional supposition which saw ladies as appendages of their husbands should be revised. It may be true that some women did have livery collars depicted on their memorials in right of their husbands, but there are examples of those who were probably awarded a collar for their own royal service. Margaret Holland, duchess of

---

¹⁰⁹ Myers, *Black Book*, p. 217.
¹¹⁰ In 1681 Sir Henry St George, Clarenceux king of arms, left instructions regarding to whom the title of esquire should be given, stating that they are made thus by the king placing a collar of SS about their necks: J. Bedells (ed.), *The Visitation of the County of Huntingdon 1684 made by Sir Henry St. George, Knight, Clarenceux King of Arms*, Harleian Society, New Series, 13 (London, 2000).
¹¹¹ J. Watts, 'Looking for the State in Later Medieval England', in *Heraldry*, p. 267.
¹¹² 'Liverez a Richard Dancastre pour un Coler a luy doné par monseigneur le Conte de Derby par cause d'une autre Coler doné par monditseigneur a un Esquier John Gower, vynt et sys soldz oyt deniers': TNA, DL 41/424.
¹¹³ Routh, *Alabaster Tombs in Yorkshire*, pp. 75–9.
¹¹⁴ *Harleian 433*, iii, pp. 109, 111.

Clarence, whose tomb effigy in Canterbury Cathedral once wore a metal livery collar, was likely awarded the artefact in right of her prominent place in the Lancastrian court. Elizabeth Donne, wife of Sir John Donne, is depicted along with her husband wearing a collar of suns and roses with a white lion pendant in Hans Memling's Donne Triptych. As she was one of Queen Elizabeth Woodville's gentlewomen, receiving a £10 annuity, it is likely that she received a collar in this capacity.[115] The same can be said of Margaret, wife of Nicholas Gaynesford (d. 1498), whose brass at All Saints', Carshalton (Surrey), survives. Although her husband has no collar, Margaret is depicted in a 'choker' collar of suns and roses. According to the tomb inscription, she served in the households of both Elizabeth Woodville and her daughter Elizabeth of York.[116]

Conclusions

The significance of the livery collar for various levels of late medieval society should not be underemphasised. The numbers of extant collars on church monuments, very nearly 400, is likely to be the tip of the iceberg, particularly if we take into consideration those individuals who were awarded the item but chose not to depict it on their memorial. The 150 years from 1400 was the epoch in which the livery collar was most prevalent. After the middle of the sixteenth century it slowly disappeared from church monuments, probably as the collar was increasingly awarded only to members of the judiciary.

The livery collar served a variety of functions. It was an expensive piece of jewellery, with costs varying according to the rank of the recipient. The composition of the collar, whether it was a solid piece of gold or silver, or a leather strap with metal appendages, reflected the status of the recipient. The collar also had immense symbolic significance. As a gift from the sovereign it was intrinsically connected to royal authority, and was given frequently as a reward, to serve a diplomatic purpose or in the expectation of service and loyalty. As bequests to kin, associates or saints, collars constituted a noteworthy contribution to commemorative practices. It supported the identity construction of individuals and groups, both donors and recipients.

Just as the collar had a variety of functions, it too had a variety of meanings, both secular and religious. As far as the Lancastrian 'S' is concerned, it may have originally had one salient meaning, yet the meanings of the device quickly proliferated, interpreted in various ways from group to group, and individual to individual. For this reason it is not implausible that it was chosen deliberately by Henry Bolingbroke for inclusion on his collar: it could mean all things to all

---

[115] A.R. Myers, 'The Household of Queen Elizabeth Woodville, 1466–7', *Bulletin of the John Rylands Library*, 50 (1967–68), 207–35, 443–81, at 451–2.

[116] M. Stephenson, *A List of Monumental Brasses in the British Isles* (London, 1926), p. 481.

men. Although historians should be careful of over-interpreting symbols whose meanings may have been well known, but now elude us,[117] it is clear that the dual religious and secular symbolism of the sun and the rose was one of the reasons why the devices were chosen as the components of Yorkist livery collar, perhaps in an effort to match the multiplicity of meanings inherent in the Lancastrian 'S'.

Another important facet of the collar's role was its political significance. During the fifteenth century, and particularly during the Wars of the Roses, there were uniquely two collars: one for Lancaster and one for York. It is therefore important to examine the collar within its political contexts.

---

[117] C. Grössinger, 'Questioning Signs and Symbols: Their Meaning and Interpretation', in Cherry and Payne (eds), *Signs and Symbols*, pp. 180–91.

2

The Political Milieu

The term 'political culture' has been in vogue since it was coined by political scientists in the mid-1950s. It envelopes the activities, beliefs and actions of the political community, and their relation to the structures of power.[1] A key aspect of fifteenth-century political culture was the attitudes of the political community, particularly the landed classes, towards the authority and sovereignty of the king. In the 'profoundly visual culture' of late medieval England,[2] the particularly ubiquitous problem of the use and abuse of livery was a major focus of concern. Although the collar was the most prestigious form of livery, it is necessary to examine it within the greater context of complaints surrounding livery and the associated abuse of maintenance, in the form of robes and badges, which provided the focus of attention for a succession of ordinances and statutes from the middle of the fourteenth century, laws which permitted the crown to increase its monopoly over the livery system as the fifteenth century progressed. The result was hundreds of Lancastrian and Yorkist royal livery collars displayed on church monuments and in stained glass across the realm, and a striking visual display of crown presence in the localities.

It was Quentin Skinner and the 'Cambridge School' of intellectual historians who emphasised the importance of understanding political history through the ideas and principles of contemporaries. A series of accepted principles provided a boundary for political actions and discourse, and a forum in which political ideas were formulated.[3] One accepted principle was loyalty to the king, and acceptance of his authority and sovereign power. Things were not, of course, as straightforward as this, and if there was a shared political language and a

---

[1] C. Carpenter, 'Introduction: Political Culture, Politics and Cultural History', in Clark and Carpenter (eds), *Fifteenth Century*, IV, pp. 1–19; G. Gendzel, 'Political Culture: Genealogy of a Concept', *Journal of Interdisciplinary History*, 28 (1997), 225–50.

[2] Keen, 'Introduction', p. 2.

[3] Q.R.D. Skinner, 'The Principles and Practice of Opposition: The Case of Bolingbroke vs. Walpole', in N. McKendrick (ed.), *Historical Perspectives: Studies in English Thought and Society in Honour of J.H. Plumb* (London, 1974), pp. 93–128; Skinner, *The Foundations of Modern Political Thought*, 2 vols (Cambridge, 1978), i, pp. ix–xv.

set of shared assumptions, their meanings and articulation differed in various political spheres.[4]

Dogs in collars

If one of the purposes of the livery collar was to provide a striking visible sign with which to attract attention, then it was successful. Collars and other insignia such as badges were subject to scrutiny from contemporaries from the late fourteenth century. Writers and magnates alike would draw attention to the use, or indeed misuse, of livery. The wearing of 'Signe, Lyverey or Token', as such ensigns were increasingly referred to,[5] would also come under criticism from the parliamentary Commons. Paradoxically, they themselves were often the wearers of the very signs they were attacking. Within the wider context of a variety of forms of livery and badges, the issue of what the collar represented, and its connection to the bastard feudal malpractice of livery and maintenance, were key issues for debate. The collar was nothing if not controversial.

On the afternoon of 20 February 1377, Sir Thomas Swinton, a Scotsman and household knight of John of Gaunt, was riding through the streets of London flaunting the duke's collar, evidently to the dismay of the populace.[6] This was presumably the collar of SS, given by Gaunt to members of his affinity from the early 1370s, and perhaps the earliest form of livery collar.[7] Swinton's actions were not prudent, to say the least. He was abruptly thrown down from his horse and his collar was violently torn from his neck by the enraged citizens. Had it not been for the swift intercession of the mayor, he could well have been killed. Hearing news of this event, other retainers of Gaunt swiftly took the decision to hide their own collars from view. These individuals, who had hitherto proudly displayed their collars, which had apparently bestowed on them the riches of heaven and earth, were now forced to conceal them to avoid being lynched.[8] It seems that Swinton was unlucky. Evidently it did not appear to matter who he was as an individual (although being a Scot may not have helped his cause), for he was attacked for wearing an ensign that represented the duke, or at least his affinity to the duke. The events of that day must be placed in the wider context of

---

[4] G.L. Harriss, 'The Dimensions of Politics', in R.H. Britnell and A.J. Pollard (eds), *The McFarlane Legacy, Studies in Late Medieval Politics and Society* (Stroud and New York, 1995), pp. 1–20.
[5] *PROME*, Edward IV, Parliament of June 1467 to June 1468, mem. 39.
[6] E.M. Thompson (ed.), *Chronicon Angliae ab anno domini 1328 usque ad annum 1388* (London, 1874), p. 125; N. Saul, *Richard II* (New Haven, CT, 1999), p. 437. Walsingham is probably referring to Sir John Swinton: Walker, *Lancastrian Affinity*, pp. 12, 282.
[7] Lightbown, *Mediaeval European Jewellery*, p. 246. Sir John Swynford (1371) in St Andrew's Church, Spratton (Northamptonshire), wears the earliest extant example of an SS collar: A. Hartshorne, *The Recumbent Monumental Effigies in Northamptonshire* (London, 1876), pp. 33–4.
[8] Thompson (ed.), *Chronicon Angliae*, p. 125.

February 1377, when the atmosphere in London was tense and hatred for Gaunt had reached new heights.⁹ The previous day, Gaunt had introduced a bill in parliament that proposed to shift the reins of authority in London from the mayor to a captain appointed by the royal court. It also authorised the marshal of England, Gaunt's associate Henry Percy, to make arrests in London as he did in the rest of the country. The Londoners, seeing their liberties threatened, were livid, and set out to find Gaunt and his followers. The same day John Wyclif, Gaunt's clerk, appeared before convocation in the Lady Chapel at St Paul's to answer charges of heresy. Gaunt, Percy and a host of their supporters were on hand. The meeting quickly turned into a slanging match between Gaunt and Percy, and the bishop of London, William Courtenay.¹⁰ Amid rioting, Gaunt and Percy managed to escape up the Thames to Kennington. Courtenay arrived at Gaunt's palace of the Savoy just in time to save it from being destroyed by the populace, who were apparently intent on killing the duke, 'had thei not be lettid be her bischop'.¹¹ In the absence of the duke, they proceeded to attack any symbol representing him in the city. Wherever they found his arms they reversed them, implying that he was a traitor.¹² The duke's collar was apparently just as potent and tangible a representation of Gaunt as his coat of arms, and evidently the Londoners were more than aware that it was the badge of the duke. The recipient of an SS collar, normally expecting to reap political as well as psychological benefits,¹³ and gaining what was virtually an element of ennoblement by wearing it, was for a short period wearing a liability. Anyone wearing the collar was potentially in danger that day. It appears that the power derived from wearing the device was not enough to overbear the Londoners, at least for a short period.

The chroniclers were not the only individuals who commented on the appearance of the collar in London. William Langland was also to address the situation. The 'Rat Parliament' passage in the prologue to Langland's *The Vision of Piers Plowman* elucidates the scene in London in the mid-1370s. A rat describes the situation:

'I haue ysein segges [dogs],' quod he 'in the cite of London
Beren biȝes [necklaces] ful briȝte abouten here neckes,
And some colers of crafty werk; vncoupled thei wended
Bothe in wareine and in waste where hem leue lyketh;
And otherwhile thei aren ells-where as I here telle.'¹⁴

⁹ J. Dahmus, *William Courtenay Archbishop of Canterbury, 1381–1396* (London, 1966), pp. 31–43.
¹⁰ Thompson (ed.), *Chronicon Angliae*, pp. 119–21.
¹¹ F.C. Hingeston (ed.), *The Chronicle of England by John Capgrave*, Rolls Series (London, 1858), p. 232.
¹² V.H. Galbraith (ed.), *The Anonimalle Chronicle 1333 to 1381*, Rolls Series (Manchester, 1927), pp. 102–3; Thompson (ed.), *Chronicon Angliae*, p. 125.
¹³ J.M.W. Bean, *From Lord to Patron* (Manchester, 1989), p. 82.
¹⁴ W.W. Skeat (ed.), *The Vision of William concerning Piers the Plowman in Three Parallel Texts*, 2 vols (Oxford, 1886), ii, pp. 14–15; B. Prol. 158–64.

In the C-text the author revises the wording:

> 'Ich haue yseie grete syres in cytees and in tounes
> Bere by3es of bry3t gold al aboute hure neckes,
> And colers of crafty werke bothe kny3tes and squiers.'[15]

The change in the text reflects the changes in circumstance in which the collars were being worn. It is traditionally thought that the B-text was written during the period between the Good Parliament of 1376 and the Bad Parliament of the following year, although it could have been written after both, with the purpose of highlighting the author's exacerbation at the Commons' failure to carry through the good work of 1376 in the following year.[16] In this version, the problem appears to be concentrated in and around the capital, where the men, alluded to as dogs, are uncoupled and allowed to roam wherever they wish, outside the confines of the royal household.[17] It is probable that Langland is making reference to the presence of Gaunt and his retainers, including Swinton, in London during the period between the Good Parliament and the Peasants' Revolt of 1381. Gaunt's affinity cannot, it appears, be kept on a leash and under control. They are left to lord over and terrorise the populace under the ownership, or protection, of their master. It is plausible that the 'segges' referred to may also have included the retainers of Gaunt's son Henry, earl of Derby.[18] It will be recalled that the earl had adopted the collar of SS by the early 1390s. Henry is known to have used collars of other devices, perhaps featuring Lancastrian badges such as the swan and the fox's brush, in the previous decade.[19] In this context, however, the collar referred to may be that of a link of white greyhounds, another of the earl's devices. The earl's use of a collar of greyhounds was commented on by Adam of Usk who, when referring to the earl's usurpation of Richard II in 1399, stated that Henry became known as 'the dog, because of his livery of linked collars of

---

[15] C. Passus I. 176–79. The individuals are described wearing not only fine collars, but also necklaces. Presumably these too are livery. If this is the case, we have an indication that the thinner, more delicate livery necklaces (also referred to as collars), as depicted in Edward Grimston's portrait, were used in the fourteenth century.

[16] J.A.W. Bennett, 'The Date of the B-Text of Piers Plowman', *Medium Ævum*, 12 (1943), 55–64; A. Gross, 'Langland's Rats: A Moralist's Vision of Parliament', *Parliamentary History*, 9 (1990), 286–301, at 290; G. Dodd, 'A Parliament Full of Rats? *Piers Plowman* and the Good Parliament of 1376', *Historical Research*, 79 (2006), 21–49.

[17] For the Rat Parliament and collars see K.E. Kennedy, 'Retaining Men (and a Retaining Woman) in *Piers Plowman*', *Yearbook of Langland Studies*, 20 (2006), 191–214, at 208–14.

[18] Ibid., 211.

[19] J.R. Planché, 'On the Badges of the House of Lancaster', *Journal of the British Archaeological Association*, 6 (1851), 374–93.

greyhounds ... and because he drove utterly from the kingdom countless numbers of harts'. The white hart was the badge adopted by Richard.[20]

The more generalised handling of the passage in the C-text, written later in the 1380s, refers directly to the changes in retaining policy adopted by Gaunt and Richard II, changes which were to cause anxiety in the Commons. Those in positions of authority were now not only retaining knights, but also those from lower down the social spectrum, the esquires. It appears the problem was no longer confined to London, as they were to be seen wearing their collars (now made of bright gold) in towns and cities across the kingdom. By calling them 'grete syres' the author may be sarcastically referring to the perceived empowering effect that wearing such a device could lend to the wearer – another cause of anxiety. The Commons became increasingly concerned with eradicating the evils of maintenance, in particular the problem of retainers harassing and extorting their communities under the auspices of their lord's authority.[21] To some of those present at the Rat Parliament, the only answer to the worsening problems was to attempt to collar the cat. The fable of the rats and mice trying to bell the bullying cat had earlier precedents and would have been familiar to contemporaries.[22] Traditionally the cat has been interpreted as Gaunt. More recently it has been suggested that the meaning of the Rat Parliament passage evolves from the B to the C recensions, reflecting changes in contemporaries' attitudes towards maintenance. The identification of the cat may also be attributed to several individuals throughout the recensions: Gaunt, Henry Bolingbroke and Richard II.[23] The rodents (the Commons gentry) complain of the domineering presence of a 'cat of a courte', who 'lauȝte hem at his wille, And pleyde with hem perilouslych and possed hem aboute'.[24] A rat proposes that they appease the cat by offering him livery, an intriguing reversal of the accepted practice of the lord giving his household retainers his livery, and perhaps also an allusion to the frowned-upon practice of lesser gentry retaining their own men.[25] Several suggestions are then proposed to control the cat. The rodents could attempt to attach a bell 'of briȝt syluer' to the cat's collar, a reference to the pendants worn on livery collars, but this is considered too dangerous. A mouse then suggests feeding the cat venison in order to distract his attention away from them. Any attempt to kill the cat would be fruitless, as there are many more to take his place: 'Thouȝ we culled

---

[20] C. Given-Wilson (ed. and trans.), *The Chronicle of Adam Usk, 1377–1421* (Oxford, 1997), p. 53; H. Stanford London, 'The Greyhound as Royal Beast', *Archaeologia*, 97 (1959), 139–63, at 55.
[21] *Statutes of the Realm*, 1 Richard II c.3, 1 Richard II c.7, 8 Richard II c.2.
[22] M.A. Devlin (ed.), *The Sermons of Thomas Brinton, Bishop of Rochester (1373–1389)*, Camden Society, 3rd Series, 85–6 (London, 1954), p. 317.
[23] Kennedy, 'Retaining Men', 208–9.
[24] B. Prol. 149–50.
[25] Kennedy, 'Retaining Men', 209.

the catte, ʒut sholde ther come another'.²⁶ By the C recension, changing attitudes are reflected in the rodents' acceptance of their role as retainers, despite their continuing hostility towards maintenance. The mouse suggests that the best policy is to 'soffren and sigge nouht and so is the beste'.²⁷ If the cat in the C-text does represent Richard, then the suggestion is that the Commons had at least begrudgingly accepted his authority, and their position. Without the bell to control him, he was free to act as he wished, and to develop his own affinity. Indeed, this is what he attempted to do, but the Commons were not finished yet. A flurry of petitions and legislation attempting to control livery and maintenance began to appear during his reign.

Legislation

Richard's reign witnessed a proliferation of parliamentary condemnation of the wearing of badges and its perceived link to the evils of livery and maintenance. Concomitantly badges, or 'signes' as they were usually referred to, began to attract the interest of writers of political verse. From the late fourteenth century some badges were worn around the neck and were referred to as collars. Indeed, collars became a more prestigious hybrid of the badge.

In 1377 a statute focused on the distribution of livery of hats, and in an angry rebuke to parliament in 1384 John of Gaunt defended the lords' ability to control their own retinues, in the face of fresh criticism of the uncontrollable behaviour of liveried retainers.[28] The matter resurfaced in 1390 when the king issued an ordinance permitting the distribution of livery of cloth to secular peers, their knights and esquires retained for life, and their household servants only.[29] The legislation was not effective. Petitions continued throughout the reign complaining of lords distributing 'livery of signes' to their retinues, particularly those below the rank of esquire, 'in order to have power to perform their false treasons'.[30] The retainers, emboldened by their lords' badges, and inflated with 'insolent arrogance', were left to oppress their localities under their lords' protection.[31] In his revised version of *Confessio Amantis*, John Gower lamented Richard's half-hearted

---

[26] B. Prol. 185.
[27] C. Passus I. 210.
[28] *PROME*, Richard II, Parliament of October to November 1377, mem. 12.
[29] See A.R. Myers (ed.), *English Historical Documents: 1327–1485* (1969), no. 655; R.L. Storey, 'Liveries and Commissions of the Peace 1388–90', in F.R.H. Du Boulay and C.M. Barron (eds), *The Reign of Richard II: Essays in Honour of May McKisack* (London, 1971), pp. 143–7; N. Saul, 'The Commons and the Abolition of Badges', *Parliamentary History*, 9 (1990), 302–3.
[30] *PROME*, Richard II, Parliament of January to February 1393, mem. 1.
[31] L.C. Hector and B.F. Harvey (eds), *The Westminster Chronicle, 1381–1394* (Oxford, 1982), p. 354.

attempts to control the problems. The knightly retinues were serving only their self-interests, to the detriment of the common weal.[32]

The Commons petitioners probably had their own interests at heart. Perhaps their principal concern was a perceived challenge to their established pre-eminence in their own 'countries'. Condemnation of those below the rank of esquire suggests that their anxieties focused on those 'second kings' in the shires, individuals such as William Chorlegh, Lancastrian steward for Penwortham (Lancashire), accused of a series of oppressions and extortions, who donned their lord's livery and acted above the law. They were tempted to act above their station, and this was not going to be permitted by those above them in the pecking order.[33] The problems over the distribution of livery robes continued throughout the fifteenth century. In 1481 Robert Hawtmount of Watlington (Oxfordshire), a tenant of Edward, prince of Wales, complained to the prince's council that a John Abrey was committing robberies, acts of felony and other 'great extortions' in the shire whilst wearing the prince's white and green livery robes.[34]

Amid the tensions earlier in the century, the king had plans for creating an affinity of his own. From 1390 Richard began a recruitment drive, with over eighty knights being retained, most of them for life.[35] Prior to introducing his infamous white hart badge, Richard had unsuccessfully attempted to adopt other insignia. In 1387 he sent one of his sergeants at arms into East Anglia to distribute badges of silver and gilt crowns to the local gentry, in return for their armed support when required. This was not a success, and the individual was arrested.[36] It was at the Smithfield tournament in October 1390 that Richard introduced the white hart badge.[37] His propensity for using visual imagery to promote his regal and sacerdotal qualities can be seen on his tomb at Westminster, in Westminster Hall, and on the Wilton Diptych, where the attendant angels and the king himself wear his badge. The king is also depicted with a collar of broomcods around his neck, emphasising his Plantagenet ancestry.[38] What was at first a reasonably successful attempt to create a personal, loyal affinity – something successfully implemented by later monarchs – soon backfired. After 1397 the king began recruiting lesser gentry, focusing his attentions on Cheshire, where he created a personal bodyguard of 311 archers devoted to his safety day and night, in addi-

[32] Macaulay (ed.), *John Gower*, ii, pp. 469–71.
[33] S. Walker, 'Lordship and Lawlessness in the Palatinate of Lancaster, 1370–1400', *Journal of British Studies*, 28 (1989), 336–9; *CPR 1370–74*, p. 107; Saul, 'Abolition of Badges', 313.
[34] TNA, SC 8/344/E1306.
[35] C. Given-Wilson, *The Royal Household and the King's Affinity: Service, Politics and Finance in England 1360–1413* (New Haven, CT, and London, 1986), p. 214.
[36] Hector and Harvey (eds), *Westminster Chronicle*, pp. 187, 355–9.
[37] G.B. Stow (ed.), *Historia Vitae et Regni Ricardi Secundi* (Philadelphia, PA, 1977), pp. 131–2.
[38] See D. Gordon, *The Wilton Diptych* (London, 1993). For an exploration of Richard's use of visual media, see A. Goodman and J. Gillespie (eds), *Richard II: The Art of Kingship* (Oxford and New York, 1999).

tion to a wider affinity of between 700 and 2,000 men.[39] The Cheshire affinity was despised, and was a political miscalculation, not least because the band of men had been recruited in such a concentrated geographical area that it could hardly be seen to be in the realm's interests. The badge of the white hart came to represent not the power and majesty of the king – its intended purpose – but the inflated attitudes of the king and of those who wore it. By limiting the recipients of his badge to a select band of followers, Richard had alienated the hearts of his subjects. The author of *Richard the Redeless* sums this up:

> For on that ye merkyd ye myssed ten schore
> Of homeliche hertis that the harme hente.[40]

He then proceeds to criticise the king's retinue, and exposes the signs as empty and meaningless, now that what they represented – the king – no longer demanded respect:

> Thane was it foly in feith, as me thynketh,
> To sette siluer in signes that of nought serued.
> But moche now me merueilith and well may I in soothe,
> Of youre large leuery to leodis aboute,
> That ye goodliche gaf but if gile letted,
> As hertis y-heedyd and hornyd of kynde
> No lede of youre lond but as a liege aughte.[41]

Richard had failed to 'control' the badge, as befitting his royal dignity. Adam of Usk proposed that it was ultimately the formation of the Cheshire retinue that caused the king's downfall, and he was possibly correct.[42] It is left to Gower, with further allusions to badges, to illustrate Richard's demise. Referring to the Ovidian story of Actaeon beholding the naked Diana, he describes how the protagonist is turned into 'the likenese … of an Hert', which is put to the chase and torn apart by 'his oghne houndes', the greyhound of course representing Henry Bolingbroke.[43]

During the first years of Henry IV's reign further attempts at restricting the distribution of badges were undertaken. In October 1399 a statute prohibited

---

[39] R.R. Davies, 'Richard II and the Principality of Chester 1397–9', in Du Boulay and Barron (eds), *The Reign of Richard II*, p. 273; Given-Wilson, *The Royal Household*, pp. 222–3.

[40] H. Barr (ed.), *The Piers Plowman Tradition* (London, 1993), pp. 101–33; Passus Two, ll. 42–3; H. Castor, *The King, the Crown, and the Duchy of Lancaster* (Oxford, 2000), pp. 13–16.

[41] Passus Two, ll. 44–50. Also see T. Ostrom, '"And He Honoured that Hit Hade Euermore After": The Influence of Richard II's Livery System on *Sir Gawain and the Green Knight*', University of Florida, unpublished MA dissertation (2003), pp. 45–8.

[42] Given-Wilson (ed. and trans.), *Chronicle of Adam Usk*, pp. 48–9, sentiments reflected by Walsingham in the *Annales Ricardi Secundi*: C. Given-Wilson (ed. and trans.), *Chronicles of the Revolution, 1397–1400* (Manchester, 1993), pp. 73–4.

[43] A.W. Astell, *Political Allegory in Late Medieval England* (Ithaca, NY, and London, 1999), p. 92.

lords from giving out livery badges, with the king being excepted.[44] He was permitted to give his livery to all lords, and to knights and esquires who were in his household or who were his life retainers. They were to wear the livery only in the king's presence. Presumably the items of jewellery taken from Eleanor Welle and delivered to the king in 1406, including a gold collar of the livery of the duke of Norfolk, and another collar of the livery of 'Bromcoddes', were technically now forbidden from being distributed to followers.[45] The king may have had political as well as monetary gain in mind when receiving them, particularly as his predecessor had favoured the broomcod collar. A small number of other 'private' collars appearing on effigies and brasses from the late fourteenth century would also have been deemed illegal to distribute,[46] although it should be stressed that it would not have been illegal to wear one's own family collar. That said, private collars such as these all but disappear from church monuments after the early fifteenth century.

In 1401 the Commons attempted once more to outlaw all livery badges, with the significant exception being that of the king, called 'le Coler'. This is the first explicit reference to the livery collar in legislation, and suggests that it was now seen as a separate entity from other badges. The royal livery was becoming a more prestigious item, worthy of different treatment. Henry was also granted more concessions: his knights and esquires could wear his livery when travelling to and from his household; those of a superior rank were allowed to wear his livery throughout the realm; and his son, Prince Henry, was permitted to use a swan pendant on his SS collars.[47] Efforts were made to enforce the legislation: Raulyn Govely was brought to task for refusing to remove his lord's livery collar.[48] Civic officials were also encouraged to outlaw the giving of livery, which was seen as particularly divisive in close-knit urban communities, although

---

[44] *PROME*, Henry IV, Parliament of October to November 1399, mem. 14.

[45] *CPR 1405–8*, p. 277.

[46] For example, a collar of ragged staffs with a dog pendant set within a crown on a now lost brass (*c.* 1390) once in St Mary's and St Andrew's, Mildenhall (Suffolk). This may have been an example of the collar of John, duke of Brittany. Sir Thomas Markenfield's tomb effigy at Ripon Cathedral, dating from the late fourteenth century, wears a collar of park palings with a front enclosure housing a hart. Lightbown suggests that the collar could be a cloak strap. The emparked stag was a badge of Henry Bolingbroke, and the white hart was Richard II's primary cognizance. Ralph Neville, earl of Westmorland, and his sons wear similar collars in a manuscript illumination in a Book of Hours (*c.* 1427) now held in the Bibliothèque Nationale, Paris: P. Sheppard Routh and R. Knowles, 'The Markenfield Collar', *Yorkshire Archaeological Journal*, 62 (1990), 133–40; Lightbown, *Mediaeval European Jewellery*, p. 250. Thomas, Lord Berkeley's brass (1417) at St Mary's, Wotton-under-Edge (Gloucestershire), features a collar of seated mermaids, the family badge. However, this is more likely a decorative feature added to the camail.

[47] *PROME*, Henry IV, Parliament of January to March 1401, mems. 1–2; Given-Wilson, *The Royal Household*, pp. 240–1.

[48] See above, p. 19.

many officials continued to receive annuities from their local lords.[49] It appears that, in general, the statutes were reasonably successful in achieving their goals, although not everyone was willing to adhere. Janico Dartasso, one of Richard II's retainers, refused to remove his master's badge when ordered to by Henry, evidence of the strong loyalty evinced by the wearing of a lord's livery, even if this lord was apparently dead.[50] In 1461 the Yorkist government confirmed a statute of 1429 permitting lords to give livery, on the king's bequest, 'to raise people for the king's aid'.[51] A 1468 statute targeted life retaining by peers, and was the first act to distinguish between 'Signe, Lyverey or Token'.[52] In a further example of royal concessions, a statute of 1475 allowed Prince Edward, then aged four, to retain and give out his livery and sign at his pleasure.[53]

This succession of acts can be interpreted as an attempt by the king to secure for the royal livery badge – the collar – a distinction from other livery badges. In this regard the attempts were successful, demonstrated by the exemption of the king's 'Coler' from the 1401 legislation. If the Commons had wanted to curtail the use of the king's livery, as was probably the case, they did not achieve their goal. The events of 1468 in particular have been interpreted as an attempt by Edward IV to bolster the king's authority, and this was probably the motive behind many of the statutes.[54] Indeed, the wording of the 1468 statute makes it clear that it was in fact a personal statement of the king's intent rather than a Commons petition. Although the sporadic reappearance of statutes in the fifteenth century, and the existence of surviving base metal badges, suggest that problems of illegal distribution of livery continued, it is telling that the livery collar is not mentioned, the reason being that they were permitted and were under the control of the king. By 1401 the Lancastrian livery collar of SS had been transformed into the royal livery collar. Subsequent acts served to maintain the distinction and authority of the royal livery. The process was augmented by Henry VII with a further statute of 1504, and licences issued by signet letter to those requesting retinues.[55] As in 1468, some 'illegal' retaining could be allowed, indeed licences had been granted throughout the fifteenth century: in 1454 the duke of York was given permission to grant the king's livery, probably in the form of collars, to eighty of his

---

[49] R. Horrox, 'Urban Patronage and Patrons in the Fifteenth Century', in R.A. Griffiths (ed.), *Patronage, the Crown and the Provinces in Later Medieval England* (Gloucester, 1981), pp. 145–66.
[50] Given-Wilson, *The Royal Household*, p. 225.
[51] PROME, Edward IV, Parliament of November 1461 to May 1462, mem. 17.
[52] PROME, Edward IV, Parliament of June 1467 to June 1468, mem. 39; M. Hicks, 'The 1468 Statute of Livery', *Historical Research*, 64 (1991), 15–28.
[53] PROME, Edward IV, Parliament of October 1472 to March 1475, Third Roll, mem. 5.
[54] Bean, *Lord to Patron*, pp. 216, 225.
[55] A. Cameron, 'The Giving of Livery and Retaining in Henry VII's reign', *Renaissance and Modern Studies*, 18 (1974), 17–35.

followers. Given the king's approval, retinues had in fact become a weapon of royal authority.[56]

'Might I but know thee by thy household badge.' Thus Lord Clifford addresses the earl of Warwick in Act V, Scene 1 of *Henry VI, Part II*. The earliest badge to be recorded was the swan, used by the de Bohuns at the beginning of the fourteenth century, and adopted by the Lancastrians after the marriage of Henry Bolingbroke to Mary de Bohun in 1381. It was distributed to ladies in the court of Henry IV, and is depicted on the brasses of Joan Peryent (d. 1415) at St John's, Digswell (Hertfordshire), and Eleanor de Bohun, duchess of Gloucester, in Westminster Abbey.[57] A continuing Lancastrian attachment to the badge can be seen through Margaret of Anjou's distribution of it on behalf of her son, Prince Edward, to retainers in Cheshire in the late 1450s.[58] It is likely that the widespread use of badges had been developing from the beginning of the reign of Edward III.[59] By the end of the fourteenth century badges and their more prestigious hybrid, the collar, were linked inextricably with the retinue, being the visible expression of one's connection to a lord.[60] Because of increasing regulation, they were usually given only to household members, legal advisers and those retained in their lord's service. Probably as a result of the recent livery legislation which had targeted the dukes of Norfolk and Suffolk, in 1469 John Paston noted that he and two associates were given 'no gownys at thys seson', and consequently chose not to serve Norfolk.[61] Badges could be manufactured swiftly and distributed wholesale when widespread support was required. Early in 1454 the duke of Buckingham apparently intended to produce 2,000 badges of his cognizance of 'bendes with knottes',[62] and in 1483 Richard III ordered 13,000 cloth boar badges for the investiture of his son as the prince of Wales, an incident that no doubt prompted the antiquary John Rous to comment that, during that turbulent summer, he had not witnessed so many men wearing the same badge since the days of the Kingmaker.[63] There are many examples in contemporary literature of

---

[56] Nicolas (ed.), *Privy Council*, vi, p. 209; Bean, *Lord to Patron*, p. 217.
[57] J.A. Goodall, 'Heraldry Depicted on Brasses', in Bertram (ed.), *Monumental Brasses*, p. 51; M. Norris, *Monumental Brasses: The Craft* (London, 1978), Figure 173.
[58] J.S. Davies, *An English Chronicle of the Reigns of Richard II, Henry IV, Henry V, and Henry VI*, Camden Society, 1st Series, 64 (1856), pp. 79–80.
[59] A.R. Wagner, 'The Swan Badge and the Swan Knight', *Archaeologia*, 97 (1959), 127–38; Hector and Harvey (eds), *Westminster Chronicle*, p. 357.
[60] Bean, *Lord to Patron*, p. 21; D. Starkey, 'The Age of the Household: Politics, Society and the Arts, c. 1350–c. 1550', in S. Medcalf (ed.), *The Later Middle Ages* (London, 1981), pp. 264–8.
[61] N. Davis (ed.), *Paston Letters and Papers of the Fifteenth Century*, 2 vols (1971–76), i, p. 545; Hicks, '1468 Statute', 23–4.
[62] i.e. the Stafford knot: *PL*, ii, p. 297.
[63] G.L. Harriss, 'The King and His Subjects', in R. Horrox (ed.), *Fifteenth-Century Attitudes: Perceptions of Society in Late Medieval England* (Cambridge, 1994), p. 21; *Harleian* 433, ii, p. 42; T. Hearne (ed.), *Historia Regum Angliae* (Oxford, 1745), p. 216.

allusions to individuals through their personal cognizances and heraldic devices. A poem dating from c. 1449, lamenting the English disasters in France, refers to several magnates through their devices:

> The Rote is ded, the Swanne is goone,
> The firy Cressett hath lost his light ...
> The castelle is wonne where care begowne,
> The Portecolys is leyde adowne ...
> The White Lion is leyde to slepe,
> Thorouȝ the envy of the Ape clogge;
> And he is bownden that oure dore shuld kepe,
> That is Talbott oure goode dogge.[64]

A lord's badge was particularly useful on the battlefield, but on occasion it could be more of a hindrance than an aid. In the mist at the battle of Barnet in 1471, the earl of Warwick's troops mistook the earl of Oxford's badge of a silver star for the Yorkist sunburst, and proceeded to attack their allies, turning the course of the battle.[65] In the not uncommon event that an individual belonged to the affinities of several lords, one would suppose that this would create a degree of confusion, but this was not so. On the battlefield, a soldier could effectively only be part of one retinue. Off the battlefield, it appears that an order of precedence was adopted. During the duke of Gloucester's usurpation in 1483, a contingent from York took the decision to wear their city badge until they reached Pontefract, and from there they added Gloucester's boar badge.[66]

During a period of fluid allegiances, it was of course possible that one's lord, and therefore badge, could change. This was the case with those serving in the Calais garrison in 1470, shortly after Henry VI had been restored to the throne with the support of Richard Neville, earl of Warwick, once Edward IV's closest ally. The diplomat Philippe de Commines noted that John, Lord Wenlock, hitherto a staunch Yorkist, had swiftly replaced his white rose badge with a gold hat badge of the Nevilles' ragged staff. The rank and file were wearing similar cloth badges.[67] Interestingly, they were not wearing a Lancastrian device; perhaps that

---

[64] Wright (ed.), *Political Poems*, ii, pp. 221–5. The 'Rote' is John, duke of Bedford (d. 1435), the 'Swanne' is Humphrey, duke of Gloucester (d. 1447), who took the Lancastrian badge of the swan as his cognizance. The 'Cressett' is John Holland, duke of Exeter (d. 1447), the 'Portecolys' is Edmund Beaufort, earl (later duke) of Somerset. The 'White Lion' refers to John Mowbray, duke of Norfolk (d. 1432), the 'Ape clogge' is the much maligned duke of Suffolk, killed in 1450 (he was also commonly referred to as Jack Napes due to his device). The 'goode dogge' is John Talbot, earl of Shrewsbury, whose device was a dog.

[65] J.O. Halliwell (ed.), *A Chronicle of the First Thirteen Years of the Reign of King Edward the Fourth, by John Warkworth*, Camden Society, 1st Series, 10 (London, 1839), p. 16.

[66] D.M. Palliser, 'Richard III and York', in R. Horrox (ed.), *Richard III and the North* (Hull, 1986), p. 72.

[67] B. de Mandrot (ed.), *Mémoires de Philippe de Commynes*, 2 vols (Paris, 1901–3), i, pp. 212–13.

was considered a step too far. After the duke of Clarence's reconciliation with his brother, Edward IV, in 1471, James Gresham reported to John Paston that the duke's men 'have the Gorget on their breests, and the Rose over it'.[68] The gorget was one of Clarence's badges, with the white rose being Edward's principal badge. In the volatile atmosphere surrounding Edward's return to England in the spring of 1471, badges were being utilised to make an explicit visual statement not only of the new-found affection between the brothers, but also of the allegiance of those wearing them. They were Clarence's men, but the fact that Edward's badge was placed 'over' Clarence's, with the rose either obscuring the gorget or positioned above it, meant that an order of precedence was made so the soldiers knew who they were really fighting for. Of course, the white rose was a generic badge of the house of York, not just Edward; consequently those who wore it were fighting for both dynasty and king. It is of course unlikely that in normal circumstances individuals would have worn a mass of badges, in a similar manner to pilgrims, but the circumstances of late fifteenth-century England were not necessarily normal.

With the help of legislation, particular personal badges were transformed into royal badges, in the form of the SS collar and then the collar of suns and roses. With the accession of the Yorkist dynasty came a proliferation of royal servants, administrators and messengers, and an expansion of the royal household centred on the knights of the body. The crown badge was adopted for yeomen of the crown and sergeants at arms. Badges were now being used as a governmental device, with the SS collar slowly evolving into an official crown symbol under the Tudors. An act of 1487 stipulated that royal tenants were to wear only the king's 'livery and sign'.[69] Those not lucky, or worthy, enough to receive a collar from the king were given his badge of the red rose. The bastard feudal device had been utilised by the crown as a device for propaganda.[70]

Bastard feudalism

It is now accepted that bastard feudalism was not the evil that Plummer once thought.[71] It was integral to society, woven into its fabric, and was not in itself to blame for the lawlessness and civil war of the second half of the fifteenth century. Even though livery and maintenance were not deemed acceptable, most retaining was. It was actively sought after by lords and prospective servants alike. It was natural for a society, in an age of deference, to look upwards for support,

---

[68] *PL*, v, pp. 96–7.
[69] *Statutes of the Realm*, 3 Henry VII c. 15.
[70] Watts, 'Looking for the State', pp. 266–7; Starkey, 'Age of the Household', pp. 264–76.
[71] See Fortescue, *Governance*, p. 16.

protection, patronage, and for the chance to improve one's prospects for social advancement.[72]

The first example of a contract for service (as opposed to the traditional tenurial relationship between lord and vassal) dates from at least the thirteenth century, a century which also witnessed the first problems over the giving of livery. In 1218 a robber from Yorkshire was accused by Lady Stenton of clothing his conspirators in livery 'as if he had been a great lord'.[73] The problems over livery and maintenance had not abated by the fifteenth century. Livery, the 'visible expression of service',[74] was linked to the malpractice of maintenance. Many localised issues were brought to the attention of the courts, one example being Sir Edward Stanley's indictment for distributing the eagle's foot badge of his kinsman, the earl of Derby, throughout Lancashire in the 1490s.[75] As was so often the case during the second half of the century, some localised incidents would quickly take on a national significance. During his family's feud with the Nevilles in 1453, Lord Egremont was accused of illegally giving his red and black livery robes to several yeomen. The duke of Exeter's involvement in the feud escalated to the extent that, at Spofforth on 21 May 1454, he offered to give the red and white livery of the duchy of Lancaster to anyone who would join him, in a flagrant, and not untypical, disregard of royal authority.[76] Wearing the livery robes of a lord formally identified the individual with him. Different colours were used by individual lords: the retainers of Richard, duke of York, wore his livery of blue and white, whilst the followers of his son, the duke of Clarence, wore green. From the middle of the fourteenth century badges were used in addition to, and sometimes as a replacement for, livery robes. At the first battle of St Albans in 1455, the protagonists wore their lords' badges so 'that every man myghte knowe his owne feleschippe by hys lyverey'. In addition the Lancastrians donned the livery of Prince Edward, 'a bende of crymesyn and blacke with esteryge [ostrich] ys fetherys'.[77] By the onset of civil war in the 1450s, robes and badges had become

---

[72] C. Carpenter, 'The Beauchamp Affinity: A Study of Bastard Feudalism at Work', *English Historical Review*, 95 (1980), 514; J.G. Bellamy, *Bastard Feudalism and the Law* (1989), p. 7; Hicks, '1468 Statute', 15; P. Coss, 'An Age of Deference', in R. Horrox and W.M. Ormrod (eds), *A Social History of England 1200–1500* (Cambridge, 2006), pp. 31–73.

[73] S.D. Lloyd, 'The Lord Edward's Crusade, 1270–2: Its Setting and Significance', in J. Gillingham and J.C. Holt (eds), *War and Governance in the Middle Ages: Essays in Honour of J.O. Prestwich* (Woodbridge, 1984), pp. 120–33; P.R. Coss, 'Bastard Feudalism Revised', *Past & Present*, 125 (1989), 32–4; D.M. Stenton, *Rolls of the Justices in Eyre for Yorkshire in 3 Henry III*, Selden Society, 56 (1937), p. xxxviii.

[74] Horrox, *Richard III*, pp. 6–7.

[75] TNA, KB 9/434, mems. 27, 28, 38, 435; mems. 9–11.

[76] R.A. Griffiths, 'Local Rivalry and National Politics: The Percies, the Nevilles, and the Duke of Exeter, 1452–55', *Speculum*, 43 (1968), 602, 615.

[77] M. Hicks, *Bastard Feudalism* (London and New York, 1995), pp. 63–5; Gairdner (ed.), 'Gregory's Chronicle', p. 212.

a ubiquitous feature across the realm, leading Thomas Billing, an acquaintance of the Pastons, to accuse lords of spending 'alle the good they have on men and lewery gownys'.[78]

In the localities it was the baronial affinity which was expected to provide the basis of political authority, although this was not always possible. In areas such as Nottinghamshire and Derbyshire, where there was no strong baronial presence during the period, the prominent local gentry took it upon themselves to provide leadership. Under an effective monarch these affinities could be used to the benefit of the crown. Ultimately, the loyalty of the lord was needed, and indeed expected.[79] In the same way that a member of the gentry would bring their own servants into their lord's affinity, as made explicit in the 1476 indenture between the duke of Gloucester and Lady Scrope on behalf of her son Thomas,[80] the lord himself would bring his affinity to the king. The most impressive retinue of the late medieval period was that of John of Gaunt. His 200 and more knights and esquires, retained primarily for military purposes, not least to promote his aspirations as the king of Castile and Leon, were unprecedented and formed the core of the political retinue which brought his son to the throne in 1399.[81] The incentives for joining Gaunt were multiple: a level of prestige was attached to becoming a member of the most powerful of affinities, and he also offered high fees.[82] It was, however, important for the lord to control his retinue, and even for Gaunt this was not easy, despite his claim to the contrary in 1384. The accusation that Gaunt was an oppressor who lorded over his estates without due regard for law and order was not entirely accurate. In actuality, it was nigh on impossible for him to control all his squabbling retainers and secure effective local authority even in Lancashire.[83] Indeed, no lord could have a monopoly of control in the provinces, where authority lay between the crown, the magnates and the local gentry.[84] A successful lord (whether king, magnate, or gentry) would skilfully maintain the equilibrium, thus building on his reputation as a 'good lord'.

Good lordship could be advantageous for the local gentry. Indeed the relationship between lord and retainer was one of mutual convenience and profit. A good lord offered a central point of focus in his 'country', and could open up links to the wider political stage.[85] He offered support and protection, not least

---

[78] *PL*, ii, p. 330.
[79] Pollard, 'Introduction', pp. 6–10.
[80] L.C. Attreed, 'An Indenture between Richard Duke of Gloucester and the Scrope Family of Masham and Upsall', *Speculum*, 58 (1983), 1025.
[81] T.B. Pugh, 'The Magnates, Knights and Gentry', in S.B. Chrimes, C.D. Ross and R.A. Griffiths (eds), *Fifteenth Century England 1399–1509* (Manchester, 1972), pp. 107–8.
[82] Walker, *Lancastrian Affinity*, pp. 9–10, 36, 257, 260.
[83] Walker, 'Lordship and Lawlessness', 325–48.
[84] G. Harriss, 'Political Society and the Growth of Government in Late Medieval England', *Past & Present*, 138 (1993), 32; Walker, 'Lordship and Lawlessness', 327.
[85] Carpenter, *Locality and Polity*, pp. 281–346.

in legal disputes, and was a source of patronage and profit in the form of annuities and offices. Many individuals, in particular lawyers, developed links with several lords. There was not, in theory, any question of divided allegiances; one could have a multitude of masters, but an order of precedence would have to be adhered to.[86] Sir Sampson Meverell's tomb inscription in Tideswell church, Derbyshire, celebrated his service to various lords:

> he came to the service of the noble John Montagu, earl of Salisbury, the which ordained the said Sampson to be a captain of divers worshipful places in France; and after the death of the said earl, he came to the service of John duke of Bedford and so being in his service, he was at XI great battles in France within the space of two years ... and after that he abode under the service of John Stafford, archbishop of Canterbury.[87]

To avoid confusion, Meverell evidently chose to serve one lord at a time. Those higher up the social scale were also retained by many. John Howard, created duke of Norfolk in 1483, was retained by several masters: he was the king's carver and chamberlain to John Mowbray, duke of Norfolk, in the early 1460s, in addition to acting as steward for the duchess of York at Clare, and for the dowager duchess of Suffolk at Harwich. He was also given livery robes by the earl of Warwick and the duke of Clarence.[88] But retainers did not have it all their own way, as their lords' expectations had to be met. Sir William Skipwith had his annuity cancelled by the duke of York for not fighting for him at the first battle of St Albans.[89] In 1478 Lord Strange advised Sir William Stonor, who had recently requested that he become one of Strange's feed men, to be on good behaviour: 'I woll not be ovirmastred.'[90] The belief that the gentry could pick and choose their lords at a whim with little respect for loyalty and deference is not entirely accurate. There was not a 'free market' in political loyalties.[91]

Examples of effective good lords included Richard Beauchamp, earl of Warwick, and Richard, duke of Gloucester. Beauchamp's Warwickshire affinity provided a force of coherence in the region, the earl's firm grip on local government ensuring the good rule of the shire. For some members of the affinity, such as Thomas Porter, the earl opened the door to crown patronage. As a result of his success, the earl gained 'worship', an enhanced reputation which in turn attracted more followers. Conversely, a lack of worship could have a negative impact on

---

[86] Walker, *Lancastrian Affinity*, p. 103.
[87] J.M.J. Fletcher, 'Sir Sampson Meverell of Tideswell, 1388–1462', *DAJ*, 30 (1908), 1–22.
[88] A. Crawford, *Yorkist Lord: John Howard, Duke of Norfolk, c. 1425–1485* (London and New York, 2010), pp. 30, 145.
[89] *CPR 1452–61*, pp. 552–3.
[90] C.L. Kingsford (ed.), *The Stonor Letters and Papers 1290–1483*, Camden Society, 3rd Series, 29–30, 2 vols (London, 1919), ii, p. 70.
[91] R. Horrox, 'Personalities and Politics', in Pollard (ed.), *Wars of the Roses*, p. 95.

one's fortunes. In 1468 Thomas Stonor expressed his relief that his adversary, Richard Fortescue, had been shamed due to his conspicuous lack of worship.[92] The larger his retinue, and the more men seen wearing his livery, the further the lord's worship was enhanced, and worship clearly mattered. In October of 1465 the duke of Norfolk wrote to John Paston, requesting his attendance on him in London and asking 'that ye doo warne our ffeede men and servaunts, suche as be nye too yow, that they be ther thann in owr leverey'.[93] In January 1471 the duke of Suffolk failed to appear at court as his affinity had been greatly reduced due to the Christmas period.[94] Liveried retainers, in essence the physical manifestation of their lords' power, and evidently seen as a barometer of his worship, were clearly fundamental in an age of spectacle and outward display.

The crown could benefit from a good lord. A trustworthy and competent magnate could effectively run a region for the king.[95] During the 1470s Edward IV allowed his brother, the duke of Gloucester, to develop a large retinue based around the lordship of Middleham, in effect delegating royal authority in the region to the duke. Gloucester retained the earls of Northumberland and Westmorland, and the Lords Scrope of Bolton and Masham, Dacre, Greystoke and Neville, en route to becoming the 'Lord of the North'. There was, of course, a potential problem in placing such power in the hands of one man. Unfortunately, and unknowingly for Edward, his brother would become the archetypal 'overmighty subject', using the affinity to take the throne in 1483.[96] A lord who failed to fulfil his duties could be a threat, even if he was of royal blood. The duke of Clarence's rule of the north Midlands in the 1470s proved to be ineffective, much to the frustration of the king. With the loss of Tutbury honour in 1474 to William, Lord Hastings – another favourite given the opportunity to build up a retinue on behalf of the king – Clarence's authority was dealt a serious blow. The king steadily took over his retinue, with his brother's own household servants, Roger Harewell and John Tapton, betraying him before his death in 1478.[97] Henry VI was not as decisive, allowing William de la Pole and his servants, Sir Thomas Tuddenham and John Heydon, to dominate and oppress East Anglia unchecked during the 1440s, through manipulating their positions at court.[98] The Pastons were particularly affected. In April of 1449 Margaret Paston noted

---

[92] Carpenter, 'Beauchamp'; Kingsford (ed.), *Stonor Letters*, i, p. 97.
[93] *PL*, iv, pp. 200–1.
[94] Kingsford (ed.), *Stonor Letters*, i, p. 117.
[95] Carpenter, 'Beauchamp', 514–32; K.B. McFarlane, *The Nobility of Later Medieval England* (Oxford, 1973), pp. 113–14.
[96] C. Ross, *Edward IV* (London, 1974), pp. 424–6.
[97] C. Carpenter, 'The Duke of Clarence and the Midlands: A Study in the Interplay of Local and National Politics', *Midland History*, 11 (1986), 23–48; M. Hicks, *False, Fleeting, Perjur'd Clarence: George, Duke of Clarence 1449–78* (Gloucester, 1980), pp. 151–2.
[98] R.L. Storey, *The End of the House of Lancaster* (Stroud, 1986), p. 54.

that a claimant to their manor of Oxnead 'hath my lord of Suffolkes good lordschip, and he wol ben his good lord in that mater'.[99] For those being retained, good lordship meant obtaining the support of one's lord in the courts. According to the Commons the duke had failed in his primary responsibilities, conserving the peace and upholding justice.[100] He had failed to carry out his duties as king's representative in the region.

How important was loyalty and cohesion to an affinity? Certainly for a retainer, fidelity to one's lord was expected and could benefit his own reputation. The lord would in turn benefit from an affinity which was united in shared honour and common profit.[101] For the gentry in particular, pragmatism often appeared to be the best policy, and there are many who swapped sides, such as Sir John Barre (d. 1483), who in 1459 switched his allegiance to the Lancastrians despite having received an annuity of £20 from the duke of York since the 1430s.[102] There were, however, examples of loyalty to a particular estate or lordship, as demonstrated by the Richmondshire community of gentry, whose sense of duty to the lords of Middleham became an important factor in both local and national politics.[103] Up to the reign of Henry V, and after 1471 when the duke of Gloucester reimposed active, personal lordship, the tenants of the honour of Pontefract also demonstrated a degree of loyalty to their lord as duke and then king.[104] Though the 'cohesive and exclusive' honour of the early medieval period was now the exception rather than the norm, a degree of cohesion may have been sustained through loyalty and continuity of service to an honour, particularly if there was effective, personal lordship, and the distribution of its manors formed a geographically compact estate.[105] This may have been the case with the gentry of south Derbyshire, whose connection to the duchy honour of Tutbury (and thus to the crown) up to and beyond the Yorkist accession in 1461, generated a unity expressed through the depiction of livery collars on church monuments in the area into the sixteenth century.

Personal and/or local considerations and practicalities often dictated the degree of loyalty, particularly if this was expected to be translated into military support. Although many would prudently choose to sit still and do nothing,

---

[99] *PL*, ii, p. 100.
[100] *PROME*, Henry VI, Parliament of November 1449 to June 1450, mem. 18.
[101] M.H. Keen, 'Brotherhood in Arms', *History*, xlvii (1962), 14–17; G.L. Harriss, 'Introduction', in K.B. McFarlane, *England in the Fifteenth Century: Collected Essays* (London, 1981), p. xviii.
[102] *CPR 1452–61*, p. 548.
[103] Pollard, 'Richmondshire Community', pp. 37–59.
[104] S. Rose, 'A Twelfth-Century Honour in a Fifteenth-Century World: The Honour of Pontefract', in Clark (ed.), *Fifteenth Century*, IX, pp. 38–57.
[105] D. Crouch, D.A. Carpenter and P. Coss, 'Debate: Bastard Feudalism Revised', *Past & Present*, 131 (1991), 185–8.

as one chronicler put it,[106] there were still those who proved to be loyal servants to a political cause or dynasty, as the Beaufort family and their supporters demonstrated, even after offers of reconciliation from Edward IV.[107] But it must be stressed that they were refusing to reconcile themselves to a king who, in their eyes, had usurped the throne. Sir Thomas Tresham, when attainted for his opposition to Edward at Towton in 1461, cited his lifelong loyalty through his service to Henry VI, something he 'durst not disobey',[108] a loyalty which clearly impressed the new king: he was subsequently pardoned.

The distribution of badges and collars was intended to instil a sense of unity and group identity among a lord's affinity. We have witnessed Henry Bolingbroke acquiring 200 collars of his livery, made of silver and silver-gilt, to distribute to his retinue on his arrival in England in 1399. The livery collar of SS, and the Yorkist equivalent of alternate suns and roses, could therefore be utilised as a symbol of honour, pride, fidelity and comradeship.[109] The prestige associated with receiving such an expensive item must surely have impressed contemporaries. There are examples of family mausolea where the same collar is portrayed on monuments to several generations, for example the array of Vernon tombs at Tong and the Cockayne chapel in St Oswald's church, Ashbourne (Derbyshire).

When considering the power of magnate affinities versus an independent county community of gentry in the fifteenth century, both propositions are acceptable and are not necessarily mutually exclusive. In Warwickshire in the first half of the fifteenth century, an area with a powerful magnate presence, Richard Beauchamp proved successful in working with the local gentry to his advantage, whilst the gentry themselves benefited from his patronage and connections. A successful affinity had to satisfy the interests of king, magnates and gentry.[110]

The authority of the crown

There is a conspicuous absence of individuals wearing their lords' badges and personal livery collars on church monuments from the early decades of the fifteenth century onwards. This was accompanied by a gradual decline in complaints over illegal distribution of livery in parliament. Although there are

---

[106] J. Bruce (ed.), *Historie of the Arrivall of King Edward IV*, Camden Society, 1st Series, 1 (1838), pp. 20–1.
[107] M.A. Hicks, 'Edward IV, the Duke of Somerset and Lancastrian Loyalism in the North', *Northern History*, 20 (1984), 23–37; M. Mercer, 'Lancastrian Loyalism in the South-West: The Case for the Beauforts', *Southern History*, 19 (1997), 42–60.
[108] PROME, Edward IV, Parliament of June 1467 to June 1468, mem. 29. Unfortunately his unswerving sense of obedience to the Lancastrians led to his death in 1471.
[109] Walker, *Lancastrian Affinity*, pp. 94–5.
[110] Ibid., pp. 3–4.

examples of individuals wearing their personal badges, this was not considered an issue as there is no implication that they were being distributed illegally to others. Examples include the Stafford knot on the tomb of the earl of Wiltshire (d. 1499) at St Peter's, Lowick (Northamptonshire), who also wears an SS collar, and Richard Willoughby's whelk shell badge on his brass at St Leonard's, Wollaton (Nottinghamshire). In neither case is the badge being worn by the commemorated.[111] Although problems continued to arise intermittently throughout the century, the 1390 ordinance and the statutes from 1399 to 1401 were evidently effective, at least with regard to the livery collar. The abundance of royal livery collars of SS and suns and roses on monuments is likely to be a consequence of the crown's tightening grip over the livery system, a system which it came to dominate by the end of the century. It can be seen as a tangible and visible reflection of the crown's attempts to increase its presence and authority in the localities.[112] It is important not to dismiss the political significance of a livery collar; however, it is equally important not to overstress this in some cases. Although it is axiomatic that, in a period of civil war, a proportion of examples do represent political allegiance to Lancaster or York, it must be stressed that livery collars were essentially distributed for service to the crown, whether it was in the hands of Lancaster or York. It may be that, in some cases, it was this service to the crown that meant most to contemporaries. There are countless examples of individuals, particularly among the gentry, who were willing to support both Lancaster and York, depending on who was in the ascendancy. Equally, there are many whose pragmatism ensured they quickly reconciled themselves with the Tudor regime in 1485. The inscription on the tomb of Sir Marmaduke Constable (d. 1518) in St Oswald's, Flamborough (Yorkshire), lists his offices and achievements under Edward IV and Henry VII, but fails to mention his duties as knight of the body to Richard III, to whom he was a loyal servant.[113]

The king was, after all, the 'good lord of all good lords'.[114] Crown service could reap financial rewards and facilitate a rise in a family's fortunes. It could, of course, prove to be a poisoned chalice. The earl of Warwick's jealousy of parvenus such as the Herberts of Raglan, who benefited enormously from King Edward's patronage, resulted in their annihilation at the battle of Edgecote in 1469. The role of patronage and service in the late medieval polity, the central focus of historians following the Namier tradition, has been challenged by those suggesting

---

[111] University of Nottingham, Manuscripts and Special Collections, Middleton Collection, Mi 5/168/34; N. Saul, 'The Contract for the Brass of Richard Willoughby (d. 1471) at Wollaton (Notts.)', *Nottingham Medieval Studies*, 50 (2006), 166–93.

[112] During the reign of Edward IV the king's badges and livery were omnipresent: A.F. Sutton and L. Visser-Fuchs, *The Royal Funerals of the House of York at Windsor* (Bury St Edmunds, 2005), pp. 75–92.

[113] K. Dockray, 'Sir Marmaduke Constable of Flamborough', *The Ricardian*, 5 (1979–81), 265–6.

[114] McFarlane, *Nobility*, p. 119.

that principle was just as important to contemporaries. It is true that political allegiance could be induced through effective crown patronage at the centre and in the regions, with local offices awarded to loyal servants, but there were shared accepted principles, perhaps the most important being loyalty and respect for the monarch. Patronage and principle were not incompatible.[115] Literature such as the *De Re Militari*, popular with nobility and gentry alike, stressed their partnership with the king in the governance of the realm.[116] Political society shared assumptions, ideas and prejudices with the sovereign. The aristocracy, despite underlying tensions which could bubble to the surface, saw it as their duty to support their king and uphold his authority, which of course served their own interests.[117] Writers of political verse such as John Gower, Thomas Hoccleve and John Lydgate skilfully employed rhetoric to refer to political events and assumptions in order to reach various levels of audience.[118] All levels of society shared an acceptance that the king was their leader.

The king enjoyed sovereign power at the heart of the polity, and no constitutional procedure was able to remove him.[119] He was under no man, although he was subject to God and the law, both of which justified his power and existence. As *rex et sacerdos* he was ordained by God to exercise his authority on earth. The numerous 'Mirrors for Princes' read by the aristocracy and gentry stressed the importance of preserving and exercising the king's independent will.[120] Of the body politic, in which all sections of society were compared to a part of the anatomy, the king frequently represented the head, as explained in *The Descryuyng of Mannes Membres*. All parts of the body politic were required for it to function, yet without the head it was useless.[121]

The king's rule was personal, and he was expected to protect his people in return for their loyalty, as Edmund Dudley succinctly noted whilst awaiting execution in 1510: 'god hath ordeyned ther prince to protecte them and thei to obey ther prince.'[122] Dudley may have been writing in the hope that he would be

---

[115] E. Powell, 'After "After McFarlane": The Poverty of Patronage and the Case for Constitutional History', in D.J. Clayton, R.G. Davies and P. McNiven (eds), *Trade, Devotion and Governance: Papers in Late-Medieval History* (Stroud, 1994), pp. 1–16; Pollard, 'Introduction', pp. 11–12.

[116] F. Vegetius Renatus, *Knyghthode and Bataile*, ed. R. Dybosky and Z.M. Arend, Early English Text Society, Original Series, 201 (London, 1936).

[117] M. Hicks, *English Political Culture in the Fifteenth Century* (London and New York, 2002), p. 36; J.L. Watts, 'Ideas, Principles and Politics', in Pollard (ed.), *Wars of the Roses*, pp. 110–33.

[118] Astell, *Political Allegory*, pp. 4–6.

[119] Watts, *Politics of Kingship*, p. 17.

[120] Harriss, 'The King and His Subjects', pp. 13–14; Hicks, *English Political Culture*, pp. 21–7; R.R. Steele (ed.), *Three Prose Versions of the Secreta Secretorum*, Early English Text Society, Extra Series, 74 (London, 1898), pp. 16, 209; R. Radulescu, 'Literature', in R. Radulescu and A. Truelove (eds), *Gentry Culture in Late Medieval England* (Manchester and New York, 2005), pp. 100–18.

[121] V.J. Scattergood, *Politics and Poetry in the Fifteenth Century* (London, 1971), pp. 268–9.

[122] Edmund Dudley, *The Tree of Commonwealth*, ed. D.M. Brodie (Cambridge, 1948), p. 31.

spared the death penalty, but his views were shared by political thinkers of the epoch. Sir John Fortescue echoed the sentiments in his *Governance of England*. Though the king was the supreme temporal figure in the land, and his people should sustain his estate, his duties were to protect the realm and ensure that justice prevailed.[123] There was, to some extent, a degree of reciprocity between the king and his subjects. They did not, of course, have the power to dethrone their sovereign, but the concept of a fair and just ruler was used to justify rebellion, and the support of the commoners was frequently sought by the magnates, not least for their manpower during civil war. The earl of Warwick was particularly astute at winning the support of the commoners by pandering to the public weal, something which was said to have instilled jealousy in his erstwhile ally, Edward IV.[124] As they were reminded in their 'mirrors', the leaders of society had a responsibility to listen to the voice of their subjects: 'Loose not the loue of alle þe commynalte.'[125] Their duty was to govern responsibly.

Yet the body could not live without its head. The king was supreme, and his subjects were expected to be loyal. Indeed the 'ineradicable authority' of the English monarchy meant that popular opposition was not likely to succeed.[126] It was the king who was lord of all, and in return for his good rule, his subjects were expected to love and 'drede' him. Bishop Russell noted that 'Drede is the begynnyng of wyse demenynge', and connected the respect the populace had for their sovereign with his own particular form of justice, 'so terrible and precise in processe that alle the pertees and persones adioignaunt quake and tremble for fere'.[127] For Russell, at least, the king's justice meant tough justice. Deference – obedience and 'love' – was the accepted norm of behaviour. This would apply to a lord and a king, and being obedient to both could prove difficult. Despite receiving several letters from the duke of Clarence asking for his assistance before the battles of Barnet and Tewkesbury in 1471, Henry Vernon used a variety of excuses to avoid committing himself. Typically of many gentry during the period, he chose to eschew involvement in politically sensitive issues.[128] His lord had proved to be a volatile figure over the previous months, and Vernon was perhaps not entirely sure who he would be fighting for by joining him. At least by avoiding involvement, Vernon's loyalty to the king would not be openly

---

[123] Fortescue, *Governance*, pp. 116, 127.
[124] *Philippe de Commynes: The Reign of Louis XI 1461–83*, ed. and trans. M. Jones (London, 1972), p. 195.
[125] Robbins (ed.), *Historical Poems*, p. 85.
[126] Watts, *Politics of Kingship*, p. 127.
[127] 'Tractatus de Regimine Principum ad Regem Henricum Sextum', in J.P. Genet (ed.), *Four English Political Tracts of the Later Middle Ages*, Camden Society, 4th Series, 18 (London, 1977), p. 72; Watts, *Politics of Kingship*, pp. 29, 59, 61; S.B. Chrimes, *English Constitutional Ideas in the Fifteenth Century* (Cambridge, 1936), pp. 171–3.
[128] Historical Manuscripts Commission, *The Manuscripts of His Grace the Duke of Rutland, K.G. preserved at Belvoir Castle*, 4 vols (London, 1888–1905), p. 188.

questioned. It was this loyalty to the king which was frequently expressed, the extent of sincerity being open to question, although Skinner would argue that sincerity did not really matter. What did matter was to justify one's actions publicly. As one of the accepted principles of political society, loyalty to the king had to be expressed.[129] As it had done in 1381, opposition to the government therefore focused its attention on the king's 'evil councillors', something stressed by those involved in the Cade rebellion of 1450. Despite calling for the destruction of the duke of Suffolk, they remained true liegemen of the king:

> Desiring of our saide soveraigne lorde and of all the trewe lordis of his counsel he to take inne all his demaynes that he may reigne like a king roiall according as he is borne oure trewe christen king anoynted.[130]

The same sentiments were echoed by the petition of Robin of Redesdale in 1469.[131] The grievances expressed by Cade were fundamental to the duke of York during the early 1450s. He constantly reiterated their principal points: he was the king's 'trewe liegeman and humble subgiet', he was merely petitioning the king and did not seek to replace him, and he wanted the 'traitors' in the royal council (now led by the duke of Somerset) removed.[132] In 1459 the *Somnium Vigilantis*, issued in support of the attainder of the Yorkists, reiterated the importance of obedience to the king, 'to whom alle honoure and dredfulnesse be du with lauly subjeccioun ... with fayithfull and voluntarie honoure'.[133] The defence of the common weal was now overshadowed by a more vigorous assertion of royal authority. After the duke of York claimed the throne in 1460, the majority of the lords remained loyal to Henry VI until the Lancastrian cause was irrevocably lost at Towton a year later.[134] The weak and ineffectual personal rule of the king had ultimately stretched loyalty to the limit. With the head of state now unable to rule effectively he was replaced, with the expectation that royal authority would once again be capably asserted. This did not, of course, bring an end to the fighting, although it is significant that the earl of Warwick and the duke of Clarence still thought it necessary to stress their 'fervente zeele, love and affeccion' for the crown and the common weal during their rebellion in 1470.[135] Although addressing the Commons of England, it was still evidently necessary to stress

---

[129] Skinner, 'Principles and Practice of Opposition', pp. 93–128.
[130] I.M.W. Harvey, *Jack Cade's Rebellion of 1450* (Oxford, 1991), pp. 82–4.
[131] C. Richmond and M.L. Kekewich, 'The Search for Stability, 1461–1483', in *John Vale's Book*, pp. 44–5.
[132] BL, Harley MS 545, fols. 134v–136; J. Stow, *The Annales or Generall Chronicle of England* (London, 1600), pp. 658–61; *John Vale's Book*, pp. 185–95.
[133] J.P. Gibson, 'A Defence of the Proscription of the Yorkists in 1459', *English Historical Review*, 26 (1911), 512–25.
[134] Watts, *Politics of Kingship*, p. 39; Pugh, 'Magnates, Knights and Gentry', p. 90.
[135] *John Vale's Book*, pp. 218–20.

obedience to the 'crown', although they astutely avoided reference to the 'king', whether Henry or Edward.

The livery collars featured on church monuments, stained glass and in works of art from the fifteenth century overwhelmingly depict the royal collars of the Lancastrian (and later Tudor) SS and the Yorkist suns and roses. Evidently the majority of those individuals who chose to have them depicted on their memorials saw royal service as important enough to be commemorated for posterity. Royal service is often mentioned on epitaphs; the antiquary John Weever noted many examples in the seventeenth century.[136] Royal servants were wont to remember their past masters in their wills, and some, such as Nicholas Southworth, asked to be laid to rest near to their lord, 'in the colege of Wyndesour be side my old maister King Edward'. In his will, Jacques Blondell asked for prayers for Edward IV and his queen, and Henry VI's queen, Margaret of Anjou, all of whom he had served during his career.[137] Service was a defining characteristic of gentry status and, as the fifteenth century progressed, service took on a more domestic feel.[138] Holding office from a lord or the king, as a household servant, lawyer or counsellor, or working in local government positions as a sheriff or justice of the peace, gave members of the gentry a place in society and offered opportunities to climb the social ladder.[139] Malory's *Morte Darthur* stressed the importance of 'jantyllmannys servyse' as a marker of gentility and dignity,[140] and the highest degree of dignity would be derived from serving the king. Blondell noted that his service to various royal masters had improved his living 'better thenne I coud deserve'. The king would also offer the biggest benefits; crown patronage was sought after most. A popular ballad recounting the bestowing of a livery collar by Edward IV describes (perhaps with a hint of irony) the effect of such a gift:

> A coller a coller our King gan call
> Lo here I make thee the best Esquir
> in all the North Countrie.[141]

Magnate service was of course sought after, and local offices would, more often than not, be provided by the local lord. But in areas with little magnate influence,

---

[136] Weever, *Ancient Funerall Monuments*, pp. 269, 324, 326, 397, 482, 515, 542.
[137] TNA, PROB 11/8, fol. 154v; Horrox, *Richard III*, p. 25; TNA, PROB 11/11, fol. 93v.
[138] SS collars on monuments from earlier in the fifteenth century may have carried a more militaristic significance, with many of the wearers having fought in France.
[139] Fleming, 'Politics', in Radulescu and Truelove (eds), *Gentry Culture*, pp. 52–6.
[140] E. Vinaver and P.J.C. Field (eds), *The Works of Sir Thomas Malory*, 3rd edn (Oxford, 1990), pp. 375, 682–3.
[141] John Danter, *A Merrie Pleasant and Delectable Historie betweene King Edward the Fourth and a Tanner of Tamworth* (London, 1596).

the greater gentry would serve as crown agents.[142] Nearer the centre, the splendour and majesty of the king's household, the heart of social life and source of lavish patronage, could rub off on those attached to it.[143] King's servants could, of course, be despised, but they did carry with them a degree of their master's authority. In a letter to John Paston, John Pampynge thought it necessary to note that 'Wymondham is here … and the King's livery about his neck'.[144] The collar attracted the attention, and immediately the link between the wearer and the king had been made; Wymondham was identified and authenticated through the king's collar.[145] It was important for the king's presence to be felt in the localities, and this was given a visual dimension with the royal livery collar, whether it was on a messenger arriving at the door, or on a tomb effigy or memorial brass in the parish church. In the latter instance, the effect was of course more permanent, and would be seen regularly by the community.

The appearance of the livery collar on monuments may therefore be linked with the efforts of the crown to extend its influence in the localities, first attempted by Richard II in East Anglia and Cheshire, but more successfully implemented by the Yorkists alongside their expansion of the royal household into the provinces, a process continued (some may say completed) by the Tudors.[146] Several hundred knights, esquires and gentlemen, wearing the king's livery, were used to undertake royal duties in the provinces. Edward IV was particularly astute in bringing local gentry into royal governance, and he realised the need for a working partnership in the regions. The *Black Book* of 1478 stressed that his esquires should 'be of sondry sheres, by whome hit may be knowe the disposicion of the cuntries'. They were explicitly instructed to wear the king's livery collar, 'for the more glory and in worshipp this honorable housholdʾ.[147] In the autumn of 1468 the king was already sending his household yeomen into various counties to seek out and arrest troublemakers,[148] and the Croyland chronicler later commented on the success of Edward's policy of distributing his loyal servants throughout the realm after his return to power in 1471.[149] We have witnessed contemporaries commenting on the ubiquitous presence of Edward's badges and livery in the shires. Although the relationship between the crown and the provinces may well

---

[142] Fleming, 'Politics', p. 56; *Derbyshire Gentry*, pp. 60–145.
[143] Given-Wilson, *The Royal Household*, pp. 258–60.
[144] H.S. Bennet, *The Pastons and Their England* (Cambridge, 1932), p. 29.
[145] Friar, p. 45.
[146] R. Virgoe, 'The Crown and Local Government: East Anglia under Richard II', in Du Boulay and Barron (eds), *The Reign of Richard II*, pp. 218–41; Ross, *Edward IV*, pp. 322–3; D.A.L. Morgan, 'The King's Affinity in the Polity of Yorkist England', *Transactions of the Royal Historical Society*, 23 (1973), 1–25; E.F. Jacob, *The Fifteenth Century, 1399–1485* (Oxford, 1961), p. 645; Starkey, 'The Age of the Household', pp. 264–87.
[147] Myers, *Black Book*, p. 127.
[148] T. Stapleton (ed.), *Plumpton Correspondence*, Camden Society, 1st Series, 4 (1839), p. 20.
[149] H.T. Riley (ed.), *Ingulph's Chronicle of the Abbey of Croyland* (London, 1854), p. 480.

have been 'direct, immediate and crucial',[150] the relationship could not be one sided. It was crucial for the monarch to understand that the connection between centre and shire needed to be equal. Successful governance resulted from a dialogue between the king and the political community, where mutual benefits were fully realised.[151] Ignoring the often delicate balance of power in the localities, and demonstrating a particularly partisan attitude, could result in the alienation of the locals, something which precipitated the conflict between Thomas Courtenay, earl of Devon, and William, Lord Bonville, in the 1450s. Courtenay, feeling that his rightful place in his 'country' had been denied by the king, resorted to armed conflict as a last resort. The lack of support from the court had stretched his loyalty to the limit.[152] Henry VII's failure to reward his loyal supporters in the south-west with adequate patronage after they had fought for him at Bosworth in 1485 resulted in their unexpected involvement in the 1497 rebellion.[153] Despite the symbols of his authority being visible throughout the realm, the king was not omnipresent, and had to trust his agents to implement his policies and exercise his authority. For some, this trust had to be won. Indeed, in some instances the giving of a livery collar could well have been an attempt to win favour or secure services.

Conclusions

For many, it was service to the king that was commemorated on their tombs,[154] and not politically sensitive allegiances. Particularly for high-profile figures, the volatile situation in England during the Wars of the Roses could dictate the extent to which one's political persuasions were depicted on a tomb. There are of course exceptions to the rule. The brass commemorating John Sacheverell in St Matthew's, Morley (Derbyshire), records his death fighting for Richard III at Bosworth in 1485. The brass, however, dates from c. 1525, so perhaps the passage of time had made his link with the 'tyrant' less sensitive. There are examples of Yorkist livery collars on church monuments which were evidently erected after the Tudor accession to the throne, one example being the tomb effigy of Sir Henry Pierrepont (d. 1499), at St Edmund's, Holme Pierrepont (Nottinghamshire).

---

[150] Griffiths, 'Introduction', in Griffiths (ed.), *Patronage, The Crown and the Provinces*, p. 10.
[151] Harriss, 'Political Society', 28–57; J.B. Gillingham, 'Crisis or Continuity? The Structure of Royal Authority in England, 1369–1422', in R. Schneider (ed.), *Das spätmittelalterliche Königtum im europäischen Vergleich* (Sigmaringen, 1987), pp. 59–80.
[152] M. Cherry, 'The Courtenay Earls of Devon: The Formation and Disintegration of a Late-Medieval Aristocratic Affinity', *Southern History*, 1 (1979), 71–97.
[153] D. Luckett, 'Patronage, Violence and Revolt in the Reign of Henry VII', in R.E. Archer (ed.), *Crown, Government and People in the Fifteenth Century* (Stroud and New York, 1995), pp. 145–60.
[154] Or in the case of John Manners (d. 1492), service to the Kingmaker: BL, Harley MS 3607, fol. 17.

The reasons for this particular instance may include the fact that he had no heir to face any potential repercussions.[155] Richard Clervaux of Croft, a member of the Richmondshire community of gentry, clearly felt it best to be a loyal subject to the king, whether Lancastrian, Yorkist or Tudor. As the epitaph on his tomb at Croft elucidated, he began his career as a Lancastrian, became a supporter of the house of York and then served the Tudor dynasty, perhaps as early as 1487 when other members of his community were hesitating to shed their Yorkist sympathies.[156] His reconciliation to the Tudor regime was expressed through the depiction of an SS collar surrounding the coats of arms which once adorned the sides of the tomb.

The amount of attention given to livery from the late fourteenth century points to a realisation among contemporaries not only of the potential danger, but also of the benefits of distributing and wearing robes, badges or collars. The collar certainly polarised opinion. Wearing the item could bestow an immense sense of pride on the recipient, although this could overspill into arrogance, leading some to oppress their neighbourhoods under the supposed protection of their lord. But the collar also reflected the current 'character' of the donor, even if their reputation was on the wane. As was the case with Thomas Swinton, it was viewed as such a tangible link to the recipient's lord that it could be torn from the recipient's neck, an act which is reminiscent of other symbolic actions, such as the reversal of heraldic arms.

But if controlled, in both a legislative and symbolic sense, the livery collar could be a useful tool for any lord, especially for the king. It could be utilised as a symbol of his authority, a 'cut above' badges. The extent to which successive statutes were successful in restricting the livery collar to members of the royal family and favoured followers can be judged by the virtual monopoly of royal livery collars on tombs and monuments from the fifteenth century. Although complaints over the illegal distribution of other forms of livery, such as badges and robes, continued as the century progressed, the lack of references to problems over the distribution of collars suggests the separate trajectory of the collar from other livery had been successfully established by the crown. Whilst being mindful of the political statements that some collars undoubtedly were (there may also have been political reasons for choosing *not* to represent a collar on one's memorial), I have attempted to demonstrate that a significant proportion of those who depicted them on their memorials did so primarily to express their past service to the king, whoever he was and whichever regime he represented. Reaping the benefits of the prestige associated with royal service was at least an important

---

[155] M. Ward, 'The Life and Death of Sir Henry Pierrepont, 1430–1499: A Search for Identity and Memorial', *The Ricardian*, 20 (2010), 80–93.
[156] A.J. Pollard, 'Richard Clervaux of Croft: A North Riding Squire in the Fifteenth Century', *Yorkshire Archaeological Journal*, 50 (1978), 166–9.

facet in the vast majority of examples. It is therefore not surprising that, in the instances where livery collars are mentioned in wills, it is usually stipulated that they are collars 'of the king's livery'.[157] In 1485 the Croyland chronicler lamented the attainder of those who had served their king at Bosworth. Perhaps the king was listening. In 1497 Henry VII declared that henceforth no individual who fought for the king could subsequently be attainted for treason.[158] It is important to reflect that livery collars would have served as a visible expression of the authority and presence of the king across his realm, from Ireland to Northumberland, from Cornwall to Kent.

Whilst this chapter has focused on the links between the livery collar and the crown, and the motivations behind the use of the item, there is another side to the story: the motivations which lay behind individuals choosing to depict them on their memorials. The expression of political conviction and demonstration of royal service may well have been important motivating factors, and were no doubt the primary reasons why collars were distributed. Their appearance on tombs for this reason would certainly have served as a useful tool of visual propaganda for the respective regime. But other factors should be considered. Where geographically clustered groups of 'collared' tombs appear, perhaps the item was being interpreted and utilised in additional ways. Another salient facet of the livery collar's utility was in the construction and articulation of shared identities, in particular its relation to those who were awarded a collar: landed society.

---

[157] LRO, B/A/1/13, fols. 245v–248v (Anne Kniveton, 1488); TNA, PROB 11/8, fols. 162v–163r (Thomas Fetherston, 1489); TNA, PROB 11/11, fol. 250r (Edward Stafford, earl of Wiltshire, 1499).
[158] Riley (ed.), *Croyland*, pp. 511–12; Morgan, 'The King's Affinity', 8.

3

Visual Culture, Agency and Identities of Association

Concepts of the construction and expression of identities continue to be utilised by sociologists, anthropologists and historians alike. Scholars of late medieval communities, whether they were peasant villagers or gentry networks, have appropriated the concept in their work. The importance of articulating one's identity during life and formulating an identity for the afterlife cannot be denied, particularly for those whose income permitted some form of commemoration. As with many visual artefacts, the livery collar could be appropriated to represent a variety of identities, associations and networks, some of which overlapped. For example, the item played no small part in the expression of the collective identity of its recipients; it was also a symbol of the king and royal dignity. In order to fully comprehend the collar's role in constructing identities, it is advantageous to view the item as a cultural rather than an exclusively political or economic entity. Regarding the collar in this manner is particularly appropriate when one considers that historians have in recent times been encouraged to view social groups themselves as cultures, focusing on the agency of individuals in addition to institutions.[1] It is therefore necessary to examine the cultural identities of groups, and the use of visual and material culture in the form of the livery collar, to formulate these identities, whether they were implicit or explicit.[2]

If one of the principal intentions of depicting a collar on a memorial was to associate with like-minded individuals whose monuments also featured the artefact, then the patron's agency was required to make the decision: one would expect that the choice would have been made by the individual commemorated, their family or executors. It is therefore also necessary to examine the process of commissioning church monuments to ascertain whether the stimulus for depicting a collar on a monument came primarily from the patron or the workshop.

---

[1] K. Mertes, 'Aristocracy', in Horrox (ed.), *Fifteenth Century Attitudes*, pp. 42–60; R. Radulescu, 'Introduction', in Radulescu and Truelove (eds), *Gentry Culture*, pp. 1–4.

[2] See T. Tolley, 'Visual Culture', in Radulescu and Truelove (eds), *Gentry Culture*, p. 167; D. Youngs, 'Cultural Networks', in *ibid.*, p. 127.

Semiotics

Aspects of semiotics theory can help provide a framework for understanding the ways in which a collar was employed. Originally developed as a linguistic model by Saussure, who appropriated a structuralist methodology to analyse the use of signs in language, the study was elaborated to encompass images, gestures, sounds and objects: 'a sign is everything which can be taken as significantly substituting for something else.'[3] Two strands dominate the field: the Saussurean dyadic model with its 'signifier' (the form which the sign takes, in this case the livery collar), and the 'signified' (the concept which it represents, principally the king and royal authority); and Peirce's semiotic model of the 'representamen' (the form which the sign takes), 'interpretant' (the sense made of the sign), and the 'object' (to which the sign refers). The interaction between the three is termed 'semiosis'. It is Saussure's simpler model of signifier and signified which is usually referred to today. The process of signification, the interpretative response of the addressee to the sign, is of tantamount importance here. 'Nothing is a sign unless it is interpreted',[4] and the livery collar as a sign could be interpreted differently by individuals in various contexts. One further term is applicable: the 'symbol', another less complicated and more frequently used term for the form which the sign takes. The symbol does not physically resemble the signified, but refers to it. The relationship must therefore be learned. As with national flags or political symbols and slogans, there is scope for variant interpretations.[5] This was frequently the case with medieval badges. Many had an elusive quality, utilising emblems and symbols (perhaps deliberately) which may not have been entirely understood by a cross-section of society; take for example the abundance of meanings apportioned to the Lancastrian SS device. Although their primary role – association with the individual or group they represented – was usually readily understood, the elements within the sign, frequently containing veiled visual or textual messages pertinent only to the upper echelons of society, were open to a multitude of interpretations and understandings. This 'negotiability' of badges opened up a potentially vast array of shared meanings between donor and recipient, thus providing more scope for common ground between them.[6] It should not be forgotten that this could, of course, open up the possibility for

---

[3] R. Barthes, *Elements of Semiology*, trans. A. Lavers and C. Smith (London, 1967), p. 9; U. Eco, *A Theory of Semiotics* (Bloomington, IN, 1976), p. 7.

[4] C.S. Peirce, *Collected Writings*, ed. C. Hartshorne, P. Weiss and A.W. Burks, 8 vols (Cambridge, 1931–58), ii, pp. 172, 228.

[5] C.K. Ogden and I.A. Richards, *The Meaning of Meaning* (London, 1923), p. 14; Peirce, *Collected Writings*, ii, p. 249.

[6] C.W. Bynum, *Christian Materiality: An Essay on Religion in Late Medieval Europe* (New York, 2011), pp. 11, 19.

misinterpretation on behalf of the recipient.[7] Finally, some semioticians have proposed that the physical properties of the symbol are crucial interpretative factors.[8] This too is applicable to the livery collar, which predominantly took the form of the Lancastrian SS or Yorkist suns and roses, and whose composition varied from silver to silver-gilt or gold, depending on the rank of the recipient, or indeed their estimation in the eyes of the donor.

The king's collar

Livery collars were regarded as potent symbols of royal power and majesty, even as physical embodiments of the king's dignity and honour. Livery collars would, as it were, translate a proportion of that essence to the wearer. 'It was accepted that the signifying image was worthy of the honour of the signified',[9] and honour was particularly due to the most potent of secular signs: the images, seals and banners of the king, including his royal livery. The maltreatment of such images was considered a personal insult to the king's dignity. In 1450 William Tresham was murdered, and his son Thomas wounded, by supporters of Lord Grey of Ruthin at Thorplandclose in Northamptonshire. The resulting petition to the king singled out the victims' livery collars among several items which were stolen, as the petitioners put it, 'ayenst youre peas, your corone and your dignite'.[10] Although the livery collar would not elicit the same response as the great seal, with individuals doffing their caps in its presence, an appropriate level of decorum was required. They represented a certain 'presence-in-absence' of the king's essence.[11] Initially serving as personal devices to distinguish lords and their retinues, certain badges slowly came to be associated with the crown, the most significant of which was the livery collar. As we have seen, those permitted to distribute a collar were restricted to members of the royal family after the legislation of 1401, thus initiating the process of the conversion of the SS collar from a personal device used by John of Gaunt and Henry Bolingbroke, to a badge associated with the crown. Although the process was slow and not infrequently abused,[12] the collar, in addition to the less omnipresent crown device worn by yeomen of the crown, had become a crown symbol by the late fifteenth century. In a process begun by Edward IV, the 'signs of kings became the signs of

---

[7] Jones, *Bloodied Banners*, pp. 8–9.
[8] V.N. Voloshinov, *Marxism and the Philosophy of Language* (New York, 1973), pp. 10–11.
[9] M. Aston, 'The Use of Images', in R. Marks and P. Williamson (eds), *Gothic: Art for England 1400–1547* (London, 2003), p. 69.
[10] *PROME*, Henry VI, Parliament of November to December 1450, mems. 2–3.
[11] Aston, 'The Use of Images', p. 74.
[12] Although complaints focused on the illegal distribution of other forms of livery such as robes and badges.

kingship' under Henry VII.[13] Alongside the Tudor rose, the SS collar had been transformed into an official crown badge, graphically distributed throughout the kingdom on the personages of royal agents and administrators.

Although it seems natural today to describe the livery collar as a symbol, contemporaries, for whom the distinction between representation and presentation was not as definite, may have interpreted the collar as something more powerful and tangible.[14] Caroline Walker Bynum has discussed the materiality of late medieval holy images and objects, arguing that they went beyond simply signifying what they represented by, in a sense, becoming what they represented. For contemporaries, relics *were* saints; the matter which constituted the image was, in a sense, living.[15] Though we must, of course, be cautious when appropriating concepts of the materiality and animation of religious images to those of a secular nature, it can be argued that royal badges such as the livery collar had a similar effect on contemporaries. Although they would not have been regarded as having the same potential for animation as some statues of the Virgin, we should interpret them as did contemporaries: powerful representations of the dignity and honour of the king, representations which appeared to a degree to contain his essence. Any abuse of the symbol was considered an insult to the king's authority and majesty.

Although this would at first appear to somewhat undermine the theory that the livery collar served as a symbol of the king, rather than actually 'being' the king or at least aspects of his essence, both Bynum's model and that provided by semiotics theorists are applicable. The Tresham case demonstrates that, to an extent, the livery collar did appear to be treated by contemporaries as an extension of the king's dignity and honour. Utilising semiotics theory and viewing the collar as a symbol allow for the agency of the recipient and a greater variety of interpretations of the artefact.

Agency and workshop

The present study is underpinned by one important premise: the vast majority of livery collars on tomb effigies and memorial brasses and in stained glass were requested by the individual or the deceased's family or executors. When attempting to interpret the appearance of collars on memorials, it is important to keep in mind that we are considering conscious choices by the individual or family to include a collar. The role of the agency of those who commissioned the memorials ought not to be underemphasised. There is however a possibility that collars were added as a 'stock item' by a workshop. Unfortunately, of the fifteen

---

[13] Watts, 'Looking for the State', p. 267.
[14] Aston, 'The Use of Images', p. 69; Bynum, *Christian Materiality*, p. 117.
[15] Bynum, *Christian Materiality*, pp. 22–65, 104–21, 280–6.

extant tomb contracts dating before 1540, none refer to the inclusion of a collar on a memorial.[16] That said, there is evidence to suggest that livery collars were indeed requested.

The dominant alabaster workshop during the first half of the fifteenth century was that run by Thomas Prentys and Robert Sutton at Chellaston in Derbyshire. An often-quoted contract for one of their tombs survives, that for Ralph Grene and his wife Katherine, at Lowick, made in 1419.[17] Colin Ryde has identified a feature common to a group of alabaster tombs which were evidently made at the Chellaston workshop: figures of angels holding shields set within the tomb panels. The distribution of the workshop's output appears not to have been confined to Derbyshire or indeed the East Midlands; the tomb of Sir William ap Thomas (d. 1445) and his wife, at the Priory Church of St Mary, Abergavenny (Monmouthshire), also shows close comparisons to this group.[18] Here we have a pattern used by the same workshop over a durable period. Of the set of nine primary tombs listed by Ryde, although the majority feature the livery collar of SS, the effigies of Ralph Grene at Lowick, Sir William Gascoigne (d. 1419) at Harewood, and an unidentified effigy at St Mary's, Lutterworth (Leicestershire), do not.[19] Several of the Derbyshire alabaster effigies included in the present study, dating from the second half of the century, also feature standing angels.[20] These may or may not come from a later generation of the Chellaston workshop. Although the majority feature a livery collar, that of Richard Barley at St John

---

[16] *English Church Monuments*, pp. 100–3; N. Saul, J. Mackman and C. Whittick, 'Grave Stuff: Litigation with a London Tomb-Maker in 1421', *Historical Research*, 84 (2011), 572–85; 'An Agreement for the Construction of a Tomb in Wollaton Church, 1515', in J.H. Hodson, P.A. Kennedy and V.W. Walker (eds), *A Nottinghamshire Miscellany* (Nottingham, 1962), pp. 1–2; J. Blair, 'Henry Lakenham, Marbler of London, and a Tomb Contract of 1376', *Antiquaries Journal*, 60 (1980), 66–74; S. Badham, 'Monumental Brasses: The Development of the York Workshops in the Fourteenth and Fifteenth Centuries', in C. Wilson (ed.), *Medieval Art and Architecture in the East Riding of Yorkshire*, British Archaeological Association Conference for the Year 1983, 9 (Leeds, 1989), pp. 165–85, at p. 168; Saul, 'Contract'; R.F. Scott, 'On the Contracts for the Tomb of the Lady Margaret Beaufort, Countess of Richmond and Derby', *Archaeologia*, 66 (1915), 365–76; J.C. Cox, 'Derbyshire Monuments to the Family of Foljambe', in his *Memorials of Old Derbyshire* (London, 1907), p. 108; G.M. Bark, 'A London Alabasterer in 1421', *Antiquaries Journal*, 29 (1949), 89–91; J. Bayliss, 'An Indenture for Two Alabaster Effigies', *Church Monuments*, 16 (2001), 22–9.

[17] Crossley, *English Church Monuments*, p. 30; S. Badham and S. Oosterwijk, '"Cest endenture fait parentre": English Tomb Contracts of the Long Fourteenth Century', in *Monumental Industry*, pp. 217–18.

[18] C. Ryde, 'Chellaston Standing Angels with Shields at Aston on Trent: Their Wider Distribution 1400–1450', *DAJ*, 113 (1993), 69–90.

[19] The latter two are depicted in civilian dress.

[20] John Bradbourne, Ashbourne; Richard Barley, Dronfield; John Rolleston, Swarkestone; Nicholas Montgomery, Cubley; John Curzon, Kedleston; Thomas Cockayne, Youlgreave. The tombs of Thomas Frauncys at Repton, Ralph Pole at Radbourne, and the Fitzherberts at Norbury have collars, but no standing angels on the tomb chests. See Chapter 4.

the Baptist's, Dronfield, and the incised slab to John Rolleston (d. 1482) and his wife at St James's, Swarkestone, have no collar. Although the Fitzherbert tombs at Norbury do not feature standing angels, the sleeping bedesman at the feet of Ralph Fitzherbert is a characteristic shared with other effigies which also include a livery collar, including Sir Richard Herbert's tomb at Abergavenny (1469) and the Mathew tombs in Llandaff Cathedral, suggesting another workshop pattern.[21] However, once again not all effigies from this group feature collars, an exception being Sir John Strelley (d. 1501) at All Saints', Strelley (Nottinghamshire). It should also be noted that, even with those tombs which feature standing angels, the collars are depicted differently, opening up the possibility that they may have been copied from those owned by the commemorated person, or at least from extant examples.

The assertion here is that, although the livery collar was certainly part of the workshop's repertoire (we should recognise that we are probably talking about several workshops here), it would be added on order. Indeed, it is accepted that various additional elements could be appended to a set tomb pattern depending on personal preference and cost. These could be negotiated during the tomb's manufacture.[22] They need not necessarily have been put in writing, and could have been agreed verbally with the workshop. In his 1437 will, Richard Beauchamp, earl of Warwick, referred to the erection of his chapel and tomb, the particulars of which were 'knowen wel', and several patterns and a drawing, or 'portraicture' of the tomb were given to the workshop by his executors.[23] Edmund Wighton's will of 1485 asked that his executors erect his tomb 'like as I have declarid to them by mouthe'.[24]

It should be kept in mind that there are other forms of collared memorial in Derbyshire which came from other workshops. There is no evidence to suggest that the incised slab at St Lawrence's, Barlow, was produced by the same workshop as the alabaster effigies mentioned above. What of the brasses? The Bothe brasses at All Saints', Sawley and the Kniveton brass at All Saints', Mugginton, are evidently a product of the same workshop, London 'D', which operated for the majority of the fifteenth century. Again we have a variation of collared and non-collared examples from this workshop. Although the two Sawley examples are remarkably similar and were probably commissioned at the same time, the father's figure does not wear a livery collar. Other non-collared examples from the same workshop include Ralph Eyre at St Michael's and All Angels', Hathersage (1493), and Thomas Stathum at St Matthew's, Morley (1470), whilst the

---

[21] A similar bedesman can be seen on the tomb to Edward Redman and his wife (*c.* 1510) at Harewood: Routh and Knowles, *Medieval Monuments of Harewood*, p. 65.

[22] Ryde, 'Chellaston Standing Angels', 81.

[23] TNA, PROB 11/1, fol. 146r; W. Dugdale, *The Antiquities of Warwickshire* (London, 1656), pp. 354–5.

[24] Boatwright, Habberjam and Hammond (eds), *Logge Register*, ii, no. 279.

brass to Thomas Clarell (1471) at St Mary's, Lillingstone Lovell (Buckinghamshire), does have a collar.[25]

Now to turn to evidence which augments the theory that collars on memorials were commissioned. Firstly, it should be ascertained whether those individuals whose effigies include a collar actually owned a collar. We are restricted here by a lack of evidence; although there are several examples which confirm that individuals at least owned a livery collar, whether this was the same collar featured on their tomb effigies is a matter of conjecture. We have witnessed John Gower and Robert Waterton being awarded collars which were probably depicted on their tomb effigies, and John Baret's tomb sculpture features a 'self-portrait' of him wearing his SS collar; it will be recalled that he bequeathed two livery collars in his will. The same is true of Edward Stafford, earl of Wiltshire (d. 1499), who left his collar to his cousin the earl of Shrewsbury in his will; Stafford's effigy at Lowick features an SS collar.[26] In 1509 Sir John Darell left his SS collar to his wife; a collar fitting the description is depicted on his effigy in St Mary's, Little Chart (Kent).[27]

There is one definite example of a testator requesting a livery collar on their memorial. In 1489 Thomas Fetherston asked for 'a picture after my persone in Laton to be gravid and fast sett in the seid stone with a coler of Esses of King Henry is livery a bought my nekk'.[28] In 1494 Sir Edmund Mountford requested that his monument record his service to Henry VI and Jasper Tudor, duke of Bedford.[29] Although there is no specific mention of a livery collar in this will, it is possible that Mountford envisioned an SS collar on his (now lost) effigy.

There is therefore a strong case for arguing that the appearance of a collar would not simply have been added as a workshop stock item, or by an individual artisan. Similarly, the appearance of idiosyncrasies on tombs, such as the knight on the tomb chest of Nicholas Fitzherbert at Norbury, shown in a long gown with a *cross-patté* on his shoulder, and the small livery collars featured on two of the other weepers, or the fox looking at itself in a mirror on the Kniveton brass at Mugginton, must have been added by request. In his 1466 contract with James Reames for his brass at Wollaton, Richard Willoughby specifically asked that whelk shells be included on his memorial, which they duly were.[30] Finally, it

---

[25] Stephenson, *List of Monumental Brasses*, p. 45. In this instance the civilian figure is depicted in a suns and roses collar.
[26] TNA, PROB 11/11, fol. 250r ('I wil my lord and cousin of Shrewisbury have my Coler of the kingis livere').
[27] TNA, PROB 11/16, fol. 189r ('I bequeth to Dame Anne my wif my coler of gold of Esses').
[28] TNA, PROB 11/8, fols. 162v–163r.
[29] J.R.H. Weaver (ed.), *Some Oxfordshire Wills Proved in the Prerogative Court of Canterbury, 1393–1510* (1958), p. 48.
[30] University of Nottingham, Manuscripts and Special Collections, Middleton Collection, Mi 5/168/34; Saul, 'Contract', 166–93.

should be noted that the intricate carving of many livery collars on tomb effigies would have required time and therefore money, suggesting that they would not have simply been added by the workshop without consultation.

Collective identity

In 1860 Jacob Burckhardt famously declared that during the Middle Ages, 'man was conscious of himself only as a member of a race, people, party, family, or corporation – only through some general category'.[31] The possibilities for self-expression and individualism were simply not available until the sixteenth century, as one was first and foremost a member of a group. This statement has both influenced and been challenged by historians ever since. Indeed, the debate as to whether members of medieval society saw themselves essentially as members of groups or as individuals is on-going. A useful concept to employ when considering medieval identities is the 'social self'. Originally used by George H. Mead, the term discourages the historian from adopting the notion of the individual 'versus' the community, by considering the individual within the community.[32] The 'self', it is suggested, was constructed in society; the social group was equally important as the individual.[33] One's behaviour was therefore a means of identity construction, as identity can only be formed and articulated within social spaces.[34] The creation of identity was thus 'the result of a complex interplay between personal and social forces, or between the individual and the community'.[35] The notion that the individual was able to mould their various identities within the social milieu – within groups – informs this chapter. The decision to depict the livery collar on a memorial, taken by an individual in the first instance, whether by the commemorated or a relative, placed the deceased and perhaps their immediate family within a group. Whether the visual device was used to place the commemorated within a relatively small, localised context of like-minded acquaintances, within a larger group of Lancastrian or Yorkist servants or supporters with the emphasis on political association, or within a broader 'elite' class, where their gentility was enhanced through the intimate association with a royal symbol, was determined by the individual or their family. Indeed, it is not implausible that in some cases the meaning behind the depiction of such

---

[31] J. Burckhardt, *The Civilization of the Renaissance in Italy*, 6th edn (London, 1960), p. 81.
[32] G.H. Mead, *Mind, Self and Society*, ed. Charles Morris (Chicago, 1934), pp. 178–86; D.G. Shaw, *Necessary Conjunctions: The Social Self in Medieval England* (New York and Basingstoke, 2005), p. 3.
[33] Shaw, *Necessary Conjunctions*, pp. 3, 4, 9, 12, 15, 19.
[34] R.C. Trexler, 'Introduction', in Trexler (ed.), *Persons in Groups: Social Behaviour as Identity Formation in Medieval and Renaissance Europe* (Binghamton, NY, 1985), p. 4.
[35] M. Rubin, 'Identities', in Horrox and Ormrod (eds), *Social History of England*, p. 412.

a device could be multi-layered and was intended to perform all of the above functions.

It is not possible to talk of an individual's single identity. There was a multiplicity of medieval identities an individual could choose to associate with – religious, social, ethnic, national, professional, familial, political – that evolved, were accumulated and were negotiated over a lifespan. These identities were pronounced through various associations and affinities, voluntary and involuntary, some of which could be adjusted according to circumstances.[36] Indeed, members of late medieval landed society were particularly prone to switching their allegiances as and when it suited. Contemporaries were aware of the variety of social associations they were part of. The thirteenth-century friar John of Wales described the array of categories each person could belong to according to gender, age group, social status, religion, prosperity, and so on.[37] Identity formation was relational, manifested through connections with others, and could be made more explicit when defined against the 'other'. The 'boundary', the differentiation made between one group and another, is thus a significant factor for creating and strengthening identities.[38] This is usually articulated through social interaction, but it is suggested here that it could also be achieved through symbolism, with an obvious 'other' available where Lancastrian and Yorkist livery collars were juxtaposed. Through the visual representation of the Yorkist badge of the *rose-en-soleil*, for example, in some circumstances one could explicitly identify oneself against the other, the Lancastrian device of SS.

Identities were expressed through a variety of features: through both written and visual media such as literature, prayers, wills, clothes, and on various forms of architecture.[39] One's identities could also be formulated through actions and connections. Both individual and group identities could be forged through religious participation, with fraternities such as the Corpus Christi guilds allowing for associations to be formed, often between members of landed society.[40] Kinship ties were another important sphere in which identities were articulated. As is made clear on the many extant examples of funerary sculpture in churches and cathedrals, familial bonds – particularly if one was associated to an honourable 'name' – were considered important, dynastic identity being perpetuated

---

[36] Rubin, 'Identities', p. 383; M. Rubin, 'Small Groups: Identity and Solidarity in the Late Middle Ages', in J. Kermode (ed.), *Enterprise and Individuals in Fifteenth Century England* (Stroud, 1991), p. 141; D. Woolf and N.L. Jones, 'Introduction', in Jones and Woolf (eds), *Local Identities in Late Medieval and Early Modern England* (Basingstoke and New York, 2007), pp. 1–18.

[37] J. Swanson, *John of Wales: A Study of the Works and Ideas of a Thirteenth Century Friar* (Cambridge, 1989), pp. 142–58.

[38] A.P. Cohen, *The Symbolic Construction of Community* (London and New York, 1985), p. 12.

[39] F. Barth (ed.), *Ethnic Groups and Boundaries: The Social Organization of Culture Difference*, 2nd edn (Long Grove, IL, 1998), p. 14.

[40] Rubin, 'Small Groups', p. 140.

through the use of heraldic insignia on a variety of memorials. The visual representation of estate could also be made explicit on monuments; inscriptions advertising the fact that the deceased had been a knight (*miles*) were common. Names (determining ethnicity such as 'Welsh', and more abstract terms such as names of social classes) could therefore be used to construct collective identities, and inform the historian of the self-perception of the individuals and groups concerned.[41] National and, perhaps more importantly for our period, regional and local identities were also relevant to medieval society, particularly for those whose horizons did not extend beyond their place of origin. Indeed, geographical constructions such as liberties could act to bolster the feeling of unity within a locality or region, with all residents living under the control of a single ecclesiastical or secular lord.[42] The work of Rees Davies and Susan Reynolds has highlighted the importance of ethnicity and lay collective action on medieval identity construction, with 'collectives' and 'solidarities' being formed by all levels of the laity. The traditional emphasis on vertical authority and royal and seigneurial power has been challenged by Reynolds, who stresses the impact of horizontal ties on medieval society which could transcend hierarchical divides themselves, for example with lords and peasants reacting together against oppression.[43]

It is worth briefly revisiting the concept of the 'community' at this juncture. The notion of the medieval cohesive community has been questioned by several historians. Though there were opportunities to enter into communal ventures such as guilds and royal and noble retinues, one must be careful not to overuse or misapply the term.[44] One has only to consider the debate over the existence of the 'county community' in late medieval England to understand the difficulty the term has caused for some historians, although the term has been used to describe liberties, for example. As regards the present study, the term 'community' does not suffice on its own to describe localised, or indeed national groups of individuals who share a common badge of identity. Other terms such as affinity have therefore been used where more applicable.

---

[41] R.R. Davies, 'Presidential Address: The Peoples of Britain and Ireland, 1100–1400: II. Names, Boundaries and Regnal Solidarities', *Transactions of the Royal Historical Society*, 6th series, 5 (1995), 1–20.

[42] K. Stringer, 'States, Liberties and Communities in Medieval Britain and Ireland (*c.* 1100–1400)', in M. Prestwich (ed.), *Liberties and Identities in the Medieval British Isles* (Woodbridge, 2008), pp. 5–36. For loyalty to a particular lordship see M. Devine, 'The Lordship of Richmond in the Later Middle Ages', in Prestwich, (ed.), *Liberties and Identities*, pp. 98–110; Pollard, 'Richmondshire Community', pp. 37–59.

[43] P. Stafford, J.L. Nelson and J. Martindale, 'Introduction', in Stafford, Nelson and Martindale (eds), *Law, Laity and Solidarities: Essays in Honour of Susan Reynolds* (Manchester, 2001), pp. 1–11; S. Reynolds, *Kingdoms and Communities in Western Europ. 900–1300* (Oxford, 1984).

[44] J.C. Calhoun, 'Community: Towards a Variable Conceptualization for Comparative Research', *Social History*, 5 (1980), 105–29; Carpenter, 'Gentry and Community'; Walker, 'Communities of the County'.

Royal service

The choice to place the livery collar on their memorial, at a time when such secular imagery was not abundant on monuments, served to enhance the dignity of the deceased and their family. A liveried retainer was regarded as a gentleman, the wearing of livery robes being one of the ways to express their *gentilesse*.[45] Livery, whether in the form of robes or badges and collars, derived a degree of authority and worship from a more prestigious individual or dynasty, bolstered the status of the wearer, marked their political identity through association and displayed their prestigious associations. It enabled some to 'acquire' gentility. Traditional interests and pursuits, such as hunting, knowledge of chivalry, military activity, governance and prudence, upholding justice, keeping the laws of God and advancing the common weal, were still regarded as the defining characteristics of *gentilesse* and *noblesse*. Despite protestations from individuals such as William of Worcester, who particularly lamented gentlemen who wasted their talents by pursuing a career in law and bureaucracy, by the fifteenth century it was widely accepted that magnate and royal service was one of the elements which engendered gentility and nobility. This was particularly pertinent for those who did not inherit their status through blood.[46] Naturally, one's honour would be enhanced all the more if the decision was taken to depict the king's livery on one's monument, thus celebrating past royal service. It was as if the dignity of the king had to some extent rubbed off on the wearer of his livery, all the more so if the livery was his collar. At the same time it acted to advertise the honour and worship of the master. A 'symbolic unity' was created.[47] Contemporaries accepted that a king's esquire was in some cases more distinguished than a conventional esquire.[48] The enhanced honour bestowed on an individual who wore a royal livery collar is neatly summed up in a 1436 case from the Year Books. It was argued that, even though an individual was a sergeant of the kitchen in the royal household and should technically be described as a cook, as he wore the king's livery collar he should also be styled a gentleman. Indeed, Chief Justice Inyn declared that individuals serving in the king's household would be affronted at being described simply by their occupation.[49] Evidently it was royal

---

[45] R.L. Storey, 'Gentleman-Bureaucrats', in C.H. Clough (ed.), *Profession, Vocation and Culture in Later Medieval England* (Liverpool, 1982), pp. 90–109; E. Acheson, *A Gentry Community, Leicestershire in the Fifteenth Century, c. 1422–c. 1485* (Cambridge, 1992), p. 30; F.R.H. Du Boulay, *An Age of Ambition, English Society in the Late Middle Ages* (London, 1970), pp. 65–75.
[46] J.G. Nichols (ed.), *The Boke of Noblesse* (London, 1860), pp. 76–7; 'The Book of St Albans', in E.F. Jacob, *Essays in Later Medieval History* (Manchester, 1968), pp. 195–213, at p. 208; *English Church Monuments*, pp. 166, 234, 237, 259.
[47] Shaw, *Necessary Conjunctions*, p. 152.
[48] Horrox, *Richard III*, pp. 7–11.
[49] G. Sawbridge, W. Rawlins and S. Roycroft, *La premiere part des ans du Roy Henry le VI* (London, 1679), 14 Henry VI, no. 51; Storey, 'Gentleman-Bureaucrats', p. 92.

service, represented by his livery collar – explicitly highlighted by the judges – which transformed a cook into a gentleman.[50]

The wearing of a livery collar could, in some contexts, signify a more tangible association, being used to exhibit personal identification between the recipient and donor. We have witnessed Richard II wearing the collar of John of Gaunt to disclose the 'good love' between them, and the broomcod collar of his father-in-law, Charles VI of France, along with his own personal device of the white hart, was likely included in the Wilton Diptych for similar effect. The depiction of a livery collar on a tomb signified a tangible, personal relationship with the king or dynasty. Although the association between donor and recipient was in most cases less commensurate than that between royal princes, it still represented a degree of attachment between the commemorated and the king. As will be demonstrated, in some cases it did not necessarily matter which particular king.

A shared culture

During the past decade historians have considered the cultural aspects of the aristocracy in its broadest sense: all those of gentle status.[51] In a society defined through the three estates, those of the status of esquire and above constituted the fighting order; the magnates, gentry and, from the twelfth century, the bourgeoisie, were all part of a privileged social class. The system of social honour extended beyond the peerage to all landowners, all of whom appropriated the term 'gentility', which was in some contexts equated with 'nobility' when defined as a set of assumptions as opposed to a group.[52] Though an internal hierarchy existed, the gentry and nobility shared common values, interests, traditions, assumptions, beliefs and behaviour which provided the context for a 'common world'.[53] There were many opportunities to interact on a personal level too. Although local government was more immediately relevant to the county gentry than their peers, together the gentry and nobility ruled the shires through the county bench and the county courts. Contact with individuals higher up the social spectrum was available on other local commissions of array and *oyer* and *terminer*, and more regular contact was on hand for those who sought to undertake estate administration, legal duties and military service in a lord's retinue.

---

[50] M. Keen, *Origins of the English Gentleman* (Stroud, 2002), p. 139.

[51] Keen, *Origins*; J. Denton, 'Image, Identity and Gentility: The Woodford Experience', in L. Clark (ed.), *The Fifteenth Century, V: 'Of Mice and Men': Image, Belief and Regulation in Late Medieval England* (Woodbridge, 2005), pp. 1–18. For problems over definition see J. Powis, *Aristocracy* (Oxford, 1984), pp. 6–14.

[52] J. Scott, *The Upper Classes: Property and Privilege in Britain* (London and Basingstoke, 1982), pp. 4–30; A.J. Duggan, 'Introduction', in Duggan (ed.), *Nobles and Nobility in Medieval Europe: Concepts, Origins, Transformations* (Woodbridge, 2000), pp. 1–14.

[53] Mertes, 'Aristocracy', pp. 42–3.

The wider political stage was another arena in which the gentry could interact with the nobility. Particularly under Edward IV, the gentry were encouraged to involve themselves more with the royal court, where the cultural tastes of their superiors were digested and introduced into their localities.

So, despite the peerage essentially being set apart from the gentry, as manifested in the two houses of parliament, both lords and non-lords shared the attribute of gentility. The principal differences between them were predominantly of scale, not of interests or ideologies. In 1465 Henry Beaufort, late duke of Somerset, was accused of neglecting the 'gentilnes and the noble honour that oweth to be grounded in every gentilman', by turning his back on the king's grace and rebelling at Hexham the previous year.[54] Maurice Keen has talked of a process of acculturation between the 'squirearchy' and gentry, and those above them in the social hierarchy. All emulated their superiors' interests, conduct and lifestyles. As John Trevisa noted in the fourteenth century, 'a yeman arraieth hym as a squyer, a squyer as a knyghte, a knighte as a duke and a duke as a kyng'.[55] By the fifteenth century, a group consciousness had developed between lords and non-lords.[56] If resources allowed, those of a lower status could match or even better their superiors. Take for example residences such as Wingfield Manor and Haddon Hall in Derbyshire, erected by powerful magnate and local gentry respectively. Wingfield, constructed in the mid-fifteenth century and home to Ralph, Lord Cromwell, is no bigger than Haddon, built by the Vernon family in the fourteenth century, and augmented in the fifteenth. Houses, alongside a multitude of other cultural pursuits and interests, are examples of the shared social and political outlooks of those who shared gentle status.[57] Although tastes were not infrequently popularised from the aristocracy downwards, there was, in reality, a two-way process of cultural diffusion: in addition to imitating the assumptions and activities of social superiors, the elites were not averse to adopting the cultural tastes of their inferiors.[58]

Take, for example, literature. Through a generally competent level of literacy, gentlemen were able to 'learn' gentility. The reading habits of the county gentry mirrored those of the nobility and peerage, with a shared interest in chivalric and romance literature, histories, courtesy books and treatises on hunting and

---

[54] D.A.L. Morgan, 'The Individual Style of the English Gentleman', in M. Jones (ed.), *Gentry and Lesser Nobility in Late Medieval Europe* (Gloucester, 1986), pp. 15–35, at p. 16; *PROME*, Edward IV, Parliament of April 1463 to March 1465, mem. 11.
[55] C. Babington and J.R. Lumby (eds), *Polychronicon Ranulphi Higden Monachi Cestrensis, together with the English translation by John Trevisa*, 9 vols (1865–86), ii, p. 171.
[56] Keen, *Origins*, pp. 22, 80–1, 102, 131–7, 163–5.
[57] A. Emery, 'Late-Medieval Houses as an Expression of Social Status', *Historical Research*, 78 (2005), 140–61, at 145.
[58] G. Duby, 'The Diffusion of Cultural Patterns in Feudal Society', *Past & Present*, 39 (1968), 3–10; P. Coss, 'Aspects of Cultural Diffusion in Medieval England: The Early Romances, Local Society and Robin Hood', *Past & Present*, 108 (1985), 35–79.

good governance, all of which could be applied to the disparate social contexts of gentry and peer. British history such as the *Brut*, advice manuals such as Thomas Hoccleve's *Regement of Princes* and Vegetius's *De Re Militari*, Arthurian romance such as Malory's *Morte Darthur*, and 'mirrors' primarily written for royals, such as versions of the *Secreta Secretorum* and *The Booke of the Ordre of Chevalrye or Knyghthode*, printed by Caxton in 1484, made their way into the manuscript collections of the gentry, nobility and peerage.[59] Printers such as Caxton and Shirley addressed a broad readership, encompassing all those of gentle status. The *St Albans Chronicles*, printed by Caxton in 1480 and containing advice on a range of pursuits applicable to lord and non-lord alike, including hawking, hunting and heraldry, were written 'at the request of dyvers gentylmen'.[60] Similarity in tastes encouraged reading networks of a diverse membership, often through and between households. John Paston II is known to have shared books with fellow gentry and those above, including the earl of Arran.[61]

As with literature, the gentry's use of visual and material culture such as church monuments differed little from that of the nobility. Resources may have dictated the scale of the commission, but members of the aristocracy such as Henry Bourchier, earl of Essex (d. 1483), could favour the less expensive memorial brass (albeit a fine example), whereas the Fitzherbert family of Derbyshire opted for the more extravagant alabaster tomb and effigy. The medium of monument was not entirely dictated by monetary resources, however. Local trends in monument style, and what message the commemorated wished to communicate, may have, in some cases, been more influential factors. Of the various identities represented through late medieval church monuments and other church fittings, such as stained glass, perhaps the most fundamental was the identity of a member of landed society. Through the use of visual cues such as dress and jewellery, and of course livery collars, gentlemen were able to maintain their cultural dominance.[62] Perhaps livery collars can therefore be regarded as examples of cultural capital. This concept, developed by Pierre Bourdieu, refers to material and symbolic goods that are considered worthy of acquisition in order to promote one's social mobility and prestige. Cultural capital, along with social and economic capital, is distributed by the dominant classes in order to maintain their autonomous position at the apex of society. Bourdieu subdivided cultural capital into three spheres: 'embodied', the consciously and sub-consciously inherited properties of one's character and disposition, usually acquired through the family; 'institutionalised', referring to institutional recognition; and 'objectified',

---

[59] R. Radulescu, 'Literature', pp. 100–18; Nichols (ed.), *Boke of Noblesse*, p. liv.
[60] 'Book of St Albans', pp. 196–208.
[61] Coss, 'Cultural Diffusion', 55.
[62] T. Reuter, 'Nobles and Others: The Social and Cultural Expression of Power Relations in the Middle Ages', in Duggan (ed.), *Nobles and Nobility*, pp. 85–98.

physical objects which are frequently appropriated for their symbolic worth.⁶³ The livery collar would therefore fall into the last category. Although the item had tangible, occasionally exorbitant, monetary value, the components were chosen primarily to reflect the symbolic value of the artefact.

Through the use of distinguishing marks, and through their associations and actions, members of landed society were able to assert their identity and superior status over the commoners, in life and in death. By being depicted in armour and using a rich array of heraldry, and indeed through the proclamation of service to the king by placing a livery collar on their effigies, individuals were using their prosperity to help attain 'exclusionary closure'; their superiority and exclusivity over those who were not of gentle status were visually affirmed.⁶⁴ Particularly after the Black Death, greater social mobility provided more opportunities for those not of gentle birth to enter the landed classes. As a result, the stratification within landed society became more complex. Anxieties were heightened as some individuals began to utilise the trappings of the wealthy, anxieties which resulted in the sumptuary regulation of the fourteenth and fifteenth centuries.⁶⁵ The rise of lawyers and other parvenus, who advertised their new-found gentility on their tombs to the extent that some depicted themselves as members of the second estate, caused consternation. The use of heraldry and the depiction of livery collars may have helped those within the gentle ranks to reassert their status over such intruders. Paradoxically, the same trappings could be used by those very intruders from lower down the social spectrum who wished to pronounce their arrival on the scene, and to enhance their dignity. It is indeed the case that individuals of relatively low status (although the evidence suggests that the majority were from armigerous families) did choose to depict their livery collars on their memorial brasses, which were less costly than tombs but still affordable only to those with a reasonable degree of disposable income. Equally, those individuals or families who were facing some crisis of identity, such as the extinction of the male line, may have used such trappings on their monuments in an attempt to hide their insecurities.⁶⁶ So when talking of a 'gentle' identity represented on monuments, it is equally applicable to talk of social identity – the

---

⁶³ P. Bourdieu, 'The Forms of Capital', in J.G. Richardson (ed.), *Handbook of Theory and Research for the Sociology of Education* (New York, 1986), pp. 241–58. Also see P. Bourdieu, *Outline of a Theory of Practice* (New York, 1977).

⁶⁴ S.H. Rigby, *English Society in the Later Middle Ages: Class, Status and Gender* (Basingstoke and London, 1995), pp. 1–14; R. Murphy, *Social Closure: The Theory of Monopolization and Exclusion* (Oxford 1988). Also see P. Coss, 'Knighthood, Heraldry and Social Exclusion in Edwardian England', in *Heraldry*, pp. 39–68.

⁶⁵ M.T. Rosenthal, 'Cultures of Clothing in Later Medieval and Early Modern Europe', *Journal of Medieval and Early Modern Studies*, 39 (2009), 459–81.

⁶⁶ B. and M. Gittos, 'Motivation and Choice'.

role of the deceased in society – being exhibited. They were making a statement about their social roles in life and their social and cultural capital.[67]

Art historians of Renaissance Italy have studied the ways in which material representation was used to construct identities.[68] Whilst the historian must be sensitive to the differences between the Italian city states of the sixteenth century and fifteenth-century England, not least in architectural style, from the late Middle Ages there was a pan-European elite culture, in which the English landed classes played no small part. Influences and ideas permeated geographical boundaries through an interactive court culture. The Yorkist regime under Edward IV had strong political and cultural ties with the Burgundian court, for example. Art historians use terms to describe the ways in which elite families used material and visual culture to legitimise and enhance their authority and identity. These have been appropriated by medieval historians exploring how individuals projected themselves to wider society through the use of various representational means, such as language, public behaviour and choice of attire.[69] 'Visual controls' were imposed by the families through imagery on buildings, furniture, paintings and sculpture, and through the use of colour, heraldic symbolism, and badges and collars. The cultural pre-eminence of a dynasty was articulated, and the political allegiance of the wearer of such imagery was made explicit, through these visual signs of affiliation. In actuality, the strenuous efforts of some dynasties to legitimise their authority hid their insecurities. The impression of control through such projects did not reflect the reality of tension between the court and the wider community. In order for this type of self-fashioning to be successful, the viewer's response was crucial.[70] For those connected to the court, such visible association provided them with a source of cultural capital which served to maintain their standing.[71] Many of the visual and political references in such imagery would be understood only by those close to the court; the significance would have to be explained to visitors. In this way, the exclusive identity of the dynasty would be upheld.

---

[67] For the social body, see Llewellyn, *The Art of Death*, pp. 47–9. The term 'social identity' here carries a different nuance to that used by social psychologists: J.E. Stets and P.J. Burke, 'Identity Theory and Social Identity Theory', *Social Psychology Quarterly*, 63 (2000), 224–37, esp. 224–6.

[68] See A. Patterson, '"The Face Divine": Identity and the Portrait from Locke to Chaucer', in S. McKee (ed.), *Crossing Boundaries: Issues of Cultural and Individual Identity in the Middle Ages and the Renaissance* (Turnhout, 1999), pp. 155–86.

[69] S. Crane, *The Performance of Self: Ritual, Clothing and Identity during the Hundred Years War* (Philadelphia, PA, 2002).

[70] E.S. Welch, *Art and Identity in Renaissance Milan* (New Haven, CT, and London, 1995), pp. 6–7.

[71] S.J. Campbell, 'Introduction', in Campbell (ed.), *Artists at Court: Image-Making and Identity, 1300–1550* (Boston, 2004), p. 10; W. de Clercq, J. Dumolyn and J. Haemers, '"Vivre Noblement": Material Culture and Elite Identity in Late Medieval Flanders', *Journal of Interdisciplinary History*, 38 (2007), 1–31.

The livery collar was a mark of gentility and honourable service, and an example of an artefact used to portray a shared gentle culture. A collar served the same purpose as the wearing of a lord's arms and livery on an individual's clothing: it represented an association with a superior and an association with others who wore it. By the early fifteenth century, the livery collar represented an association with the king. It was awarded to individuals from many levels of society, from esquire and merchant to prince, although the constitution of the collar depended on rank: esquires typically received leather collars with silver components, while those of knightly status or above were given collars composed of silver-gilt or gold. The addition of precious jewels and pearls would signify a higher rank. The inventory of the goods of Henry Bowet, archbishop of York (d. 1423), lists two collars of gold valued at £40, several of silver-gilt and a total of fifty-four collars of silver, presumably SS collars given by the king to be distributed according to rank.[72] Although some collars were evidently given for service in battle or for diplomatic purposes, at least on the more exalted stage of the princely courts of Europe, on a fundamental level the majority of collars signified the same thing: royal service, or some form of association with the king. In this respect the collar was a visual representation of a shared identity. This is undoubtedly one of the ways in which the king would have wished the collar to have been interpreted. However, it will be demonstrated that groups could appropriate them for their own ends when choosing to include collars on their church monuments.

Fictive kinship

Kinship terminology and symbolism are frequently employed in hierarchical societies. This was particularly true for late medieval society, when seigneurial relationships were often described in familial terms. One only has to examine contemporary correspondence to find an abundance of examples of a lord addressing servants as his 'welbelovid Frendis'. 'Trust' was another common term adopted when addressing family members, servants and acquaintances alike. The relationship was two way, with servants addressing their masters in a similar idiom.[73] In reality, of course, the use of such language was frequently nothing more than the application of a common gentlemanly etiquette. The relationship between some who addressed one another in such terms could be far from cordial. But even in these cases we have another example of a social group adopting similar modes of address in order to define themselves as superior to those below them in the social spectrum: it was another means of seeking social closure. In other cases, the use of such language, particularly when employed by members of a group such as a household or a lord's retinue, at least refers to

[72] *Test. Ebor.*, iii, p. 77.
[73] *PL*, pp. 4, 5, 121, 296.

the way in which the individuals perceived themselves, and the way in which they wished to be perceived by others.[74] Put simply, it served as a social bonding mechanism, and referred to the support and protection such a bond was expected to elicit. Late medieval understandings of 'family' and 'affinity' extended beyond blood ties to include servants, third cousins, godparents, and even followers and friends. The Latin *famulus* was originally used to denote a servant or retainer; this developed into *familia*, although the term retained its emphasis on a servant group. Other religious and secular affinities such as chivalric orders would also employ affective terminology. The household, and perhaps to a lesser extent the retinue, was frequently interpreted as a family, and in some circumstances an association between lord and servant could be as earnest and affective as those engendered within a family unit.[75]

Theorists have approached the definition and role of kinship in broad terms, proposing that we should think of kinship not only in biological or genealogical contexts, but also social. In various societies the distinctions between biological and social kinship become blurred, with 'relatedness' constructed through social statements and practices as much as through family ties. Broader socio-economic and political contexts can therefore be used by groups to nurture and express their relatedness.[76] Is it possible to apply this concept to late medieval society, in particular to suggest that the visual statement of wearing a livery collar, and the representation of the item on funerary monuments, helped to produce a consciousness of relatedness among the individuals and families concerned? Firstly, to use the term fictive kinship may be too strong in this context. We must ask ourselves at what level of grouping would this be applicable? When considering all those individuals who were awarded a collar, and those who opted to place them on their memorials as a homogenous group, the most appropriate interpretation would be to view the use of the collar as a means of identifying with a broader 'class' of gentility, a group who all shared a connection to the king in some form. However, on a more localised level, it will become apparent that many of those collared individuals *were* in fact kin. This is indeed one of the most striking patterns revealed through researching the appearance of livery collars on memorials.

It is therefore informative to draw out the distinction between conceptual or 'imagined' communities,[77] and actual communities. In the broadest sense, all collar wearers would have shared a common bond, and perhaps identified

---

[74] J. Bestard-Camps, *What's In a Relative? Household and Family in Formentera*, trans. R. Pitt (Oxford and New York, 1991), p. xv.

[75] Powis, *Aristocracy*, pp. 51–3; I. Davis, 'Introduction', in I. Davis, M. Müller and S. Rees Jones (eds), *Love, Marriage, and Family Ties in the Later Middle Ages* (Turnhout, 2003), pp. 1–13.

[76] J. Carsten, 'Introduction: Cultures of Relatedness', in Carsten (ed.), *Cultures of Relatedness: New Approaches to the Study of Kinship* (Cambridge, 2000), pp. 1–36.

[77] Cohen, *Symbolic Construction*, pp. 18–21.

themselves as part of a wider symbolic 'community' comprising fellow recipients. As there were both Lancastrian and Yorkist collars during the period associated with the Wars of the Roses, which in some cases primarily served to denote the political conviction of the recipient, this assumption should be more nuanced. For those individuals who had remained loyal to one particular regime, and therefore placed political meaning on their livery collar, it would have been difficult to have felt a degree of association with wearers of the opposing regime's collar. But for those who placed more of an emphasis on the fact that they were wearing the royal livery collar, perhaps there was a common association in the king. On a more localised level, and in particular concerning those individuals who depicted the item on their memorials, many were in fact closely related by blood or marriage. To view collar wearers as something akin to 'fictive kin' at least helps us to comprehend some of the motives at play. These individuals and their families were concerned with being portrayed as part of a group.

Conclusion

Gerd Althoff has stressed the importance of non-verbal forms of communication in expressing bonds: a ceremony, gesture or visual cue could all express association with others.[78] This chapter has sought to place the livery collar in the context of identity construction, in particular the formation of identities of association. In attempting to elucidate how the collar was read by late medieval society, it has proposed that the artefact was used to construct group identities, whether it was the larger group of all collar wearers, or smaller groups where the various individuals had a greater level of personal contact. This was applicable both during life and in a commemorative context. If one collar wearer came into contact with another there would have been an immediate sense of concordance, both individuals being linked through a degree of affinity to the king, perhaps in some cases through a member of the aristocracy. A group of collar wearers would have felt a degree of solidarity, or at least similarity, if they were undertaking royal duties. We have previously witnessed a correspondent of the Pastons noting that one of his visitors was wearing the king's livery. Several individuals wearing the livery collar would have served to enhance the impact. On the battlefield the effects would surely have been more profound, perhaps eliciting a consciousness of 'brotherhood' during the fight.[79] But livery collars could also be utilised to construct identities after the death of an individual, through their depiction on church monuments and in stained glass.

---

[78] G. Althoff, *Family, Friends and Followers: Political and Social Bonds in Early Medieval Europe*, trans. C. Carroll (Cambridge, 2004), pp. 162–3.
[79] See below, Chapter 5.

Part II

4

The Appearance of Lancastrian and Yorkist Livery Collars on Church Monuments

Distribution and Motivations

When analysing the distribution of livery collars which appear on memorials, it should be kept in mind that there were originally many more monuments across the country. Antiquarian notes and physical traces remind us that churches were once filled with tombs and memorial brasses. In the county of Cambridgeshire there are 163 extant brasses, although records show that a minimum of 582 have been lost over the centuries.[1] Indents on church pavements, such as those at Holy Trinity Church, Blythburgh (Suffolk), indicate where a proliferation of brasses once lay. The principal reasons for their disappearance are religious: the Reformations in England and Scotland and the ravages of the English Civil War witnessed the destruction of many examples. Some seem to have disappeared before the early modern period: the tomb of Catherine of Valois was broken up and her remains moved to make room for Henry VII's chapel at Westminster Abbey. The queen's coffin was left to languish next to her husband Henry V's tomb, and was still there in the eighteenth century. There were also cases of tomb effigies being commandeered and altered to commemorate other individuals during the late medieval period, and instances of brasses being turned over, the blank reverses being reused. Other tombs were simply neglected, their materials being used in building works.[2] As there were once many more monuments, it would be safe to assume that so too were there more examples featuring livery collars. William Dugdale recorded several brasses, now lost, commemorating members of the Hugford family at All Saints', Emscote (Warwickshire), in his *Book of Monuments*, compiled in 1640–41 in anticipation of the outbreak of the Civil War. They appear to be wearing collars of hearts, although it is conceivable that Dugdale may have mistaken them for Yorkist collars of suns and roses.[3] However, it should be stressed that any conclusions to be drawn regarding the

---

[1] N. Rogers, 'Cambridgeshire Brasses', in C. Hicks (ed.), *Cambridgeshire Churches* (Stamford, 1997), pp. 303–19.
[2] Lindley, *Tomb Destruction and Scholarship*, pp. 6–7.
[3] BL, Additional MS 71474, fol. 42.

distribution of collars on church monuments can only be made from the evidence of extant examples.

As can be seen on Map 1 and 2, examples of collars on church monuments extend across England and Wales and over the Irish Sea. They stretch north into Northumbria, south-west into Cornwall, and there are two examples of what appear to be Yorkist collars in Ireland. The effigies of Sir Roland FitzEustace (1482) at St Audeon's (Dublin) and that thought to commemorate James Bermingham in the Church of Ireland, Lusk (County Dublin), both feature rather idiosyncratic collars of suns and roses, although the armour on the latter dates from the seventeenth century.[4] There are examples of English livery collars further afield. The aforementioned incised slab commemorating Joos de Bul in Bruges included a brass Yorkist collar. In Italy there are several examples of the SS collar on memorials, such as that represented on a monument commemorating a member of the Della Croce family in St Eustorgio's (Milan). In the Church of S. Maria delle Grazie, near Mantua, can be found the monument of Baldesar Castiglione (d. 1529), above which an SS collar surrounds his arms. Castiglione, perhaps best known for his authorship of *The Book of the Courtier*, was given such a collar by Henry VII on his visit to England in 1506.[5]

The two maps show collared tombs dating from their inception in England in the late fourteenth century (it will be recalled that the earliest extant example is that on the effigy of Sir John Swynford (1371) at Spratton) until c. 1540. As we have seen, livery collars continued to appear on tomb effigies and brasses after that date. By the end of the sixteenth century there are fewer church monuments featuring livery collars, although those depicting the collar of the Order of the Garter did continue to be commissioned. Map 1 illustrates the geographical spread of livery collars on church monuments, and includes their representation in other media such as stained glass and other forms of sculpture. It should be noted that several locations have more than one relevant monument; examples include Abergavenny, with collars depicted on the tomb effigies of Sir William ap Thomas, Sir Richard Herbert (d. 1469) and Richard Herbert of Ewyas (d. 1510), and the assortment of tombs dating from the late fifteenth to early sixteenth centuries commemorating members of the Savage family at St Michael's, Macclesfield (Cheshire). These instances are no doubt an illustration of a family penchant for depicting the artefact on their memorials. The number of monuments featuring collars in such locations has not been illustrated: they are still represented by one circle. There are, therefore, more collars than appears on the maps.

The first point of note is that livery collars were depicted on church monuments across England and into Wales. Almost every English county has at least

[4] J. Hunt, *Irish Medieval Figure Sculpture, 1200–1600*, 2 vols (Dublin, 1974), ii, pp. 138–9, 146.
[5] J.R. Woodhouse, *Baldesar Castiglione: A Reassessment of* The Courtier (Edinburgh, 1978), p. 37.

one surviving example, with some, such as Northumberland, providing only one. As would be expected, the further one moves away from the south-east and the Midlands, the fewer examples can be found. There are notably fewer collared monuments in Wales and Cornwall: further inland the examples appear to be reasonably evenly spread. This follows a general trend for the appearance of medieval church monuments. Effigial tombs can be found more abundantly the nearer one gets to within reasonable travelling distance of the homes of the major workshops, the most notable during our period being those in London, Chellaston and Burton-on-Trent. That is not to say that monuments were not transported to far-flung locations. Indeed, it is possible that the tombs at Abergavenny were products of a Midland workshop. An apparent lack of interest in representing livery collars on monuments in the far north of England may be a reflection of a comparable lack of interest in affirming social status on tombs when compared to the south. In areas such as Cornwall, the problem of transporting monuments long distances over poor communications routes may also help to explain the relative lack of examples.[6]

There is a discernible south-east/north-west split when one compares the collar's appearance on tomb effigies with those in brass: representations on brasses are more abundant in the south-east and the east of England, although by no means confined to these areas. Again, this is not particularly surprising. The trend appears to broadly follow the geography of monumental brass workshops, the most prominent of which, during the fifteenth century, were based in the urban centres of London (whose workshops dominated the trade), Norwich, Cambridge, Bury St Edmunds and York, with another later workshop based in Coventry.[7] The appearance of brasses in the south-east and east of England may also reflect the tastes of those with the disposable income to afford such a memorial and/or be an illustration of the influence of continental tastes for the medium.

Of particular interest is the appearance of clusters of collars: a density of monuments featuring the artefact which lie within close geographical proximity. There are several noticeable groups of collars in England. A note of caution is however required, as some apparent clusters may in fact be deceiving. Take, for example, the group of collared monuments in the East Riding, clustered north of Hull, towards the east coast. Although they are all located within a radius of approximately 30 miles, chronologically they span a long period dating from the 1380s to the early sixteenth century. In these instances it is perhaps not

---

[6] *English Church Monuments*, p. 44.
[7] For the organisation of the monumental brass workshops, see J.P.C. Kent, 'Monumental Brasses: A New Classification of Military Effigies, c. 1360–c. 1485', *Journal of the British Archaeological Association*, 12 (1949), 70–97; M. Norris, 'An Analysis of Style in Monumental Brasses', in Bertram (ed.), *Monumental Brasses*, pp. 103–31.

appropriate to view the monuments as clusters. More appropriate are groups of monuments whose dates of production encompass a shorter timescale. This is the case in the south of Derbyshire, which has a collection of Yorkist and Tudor SS collars appearing on monuments dating from c. 1465 to 1490. A similar group can be found in north Somerset and Gloucestershire, where a total of ten monuments dating from the mid-1440s to the 1490s have livery collars: examples of SS and Yorkist collars are also portrayed here. All are located within four miles of each other, within a ten-mile radius.[8] It is striking that these monuments are situated so closely together. It would be tempting to suggest that this was due to the influence of a local workshop, although the collars appear on both tomb effigies and brasses, and there does not appear to be a discernible workshop pattern or design. It should also be recalled that collars appeared on memorials at the behest of those commissioning them; it is unlikely that workshops would have added a livery collar without one being requested. There are, however, kinship links between those commemorated in the north Somerset and Gloucestershire group. For example, two expertly carved monuments at St Mary's, Yatton (Somerset), commemorate Sir Richard Newton (d. 1449) and his second wife Emmota, and Sir John Newton (d. 1488) and his wife Isabel. Both Sir Richard and Sir John wear SS collars.

As regards the depiction of collars in stained glass, there appears to be a belt of examples stretching from Norfolk to Somerset, with others found in the north Midlands. As is the case with church monuments, it is likely that there were many more examples across England and indeed in Wales.

Map 2 depicts collars according to type: Lancastrian (L); Yorkist (Y); probable Yorkist (Y?); and 'Other' (O). These last are, in the main, collars which have been damaged. The majority no doubt once featured a Lancastrian or Yorkist collar, although the ravages of time make it impossible to positively identify them today. It is plausible that some collars on brasses have been deliberately abraded by the families of the commemorated, perhaps many years after they had been produced, in an attempt to extinguish unwanted references to past connections and political allegiances.

It would be expected that the presence of SS collars on monuments would outnumber Yorkist suns and roses collars. This is indeed the case, although the latter is by no means under-represented. The Lancastrian SS collar was in circulation for at least eighty years before the Yorkist collar was introduced in c. 1461. There are a small number of SS collars on monuments dating from the Yorkist period, John Baret's tomb at Bury St Edmund's being one such example. As we have seen, Henry Tudor was quick to reintroduce the SS collar in 1485, after which it saw a renaissance, appearing on church monuments well into the sixteenth century. Suns and roses collars begin to appear from the beginning of

---

[8] See Friar, p. 143.

the Yorkist period, and disappear swiftly after 1485 although, as was the case with their Lancastrian counterparts, there are a small number of examples dating from the 1490s, such as that on the alabaster effigy of Sir Henry Pierrepont at Holme Pierrepont.

As a general rule of thumb, Lancastrian collars predominate in the Midlands, with Yorkist collars appearing with more frequency in the south of England, below the River Trent. Should it be expected that livery collars representing the two royal houses would be more abundant in areas where their support was traditionally at its strongest? This is of course dependent on the variety of motives which were at play when an individual or their family chose to place a collar on a memorial. That said, it would perhaps be logical to assume that in areas where Lancastrian support was at its most concentrated, for example, there would be more SS collars on church monuments. This would be a more likely occurrence during the period prior to the 1430s, when the Lancastrian affinity – concentrated around the duchy of Lancaster estates – slowly began to break down. Until that date the core support for the first two Lancastrian kings, particularly Henry IV, came from the duchy affinity. Members of the affinity were frequently drawn on to fill royal household roles, and those in receipt of duchy annuities were expected to provide military service: this they did at the battle of Shrewsbury in 1403 and in Henry V's French campaigns. The largest and most valuable duchy honours were in the north of England at Lancaster, Pontefract and Tutbury. Other significant estates were to be found at Knaresborough, Tickhill, Bolingbroke, Leicester and Kidwelly. The county palatine of Lancaster provided the core of the Lancastrian affinity, particularly up to and during the reign of Henry IV.[9] However, the only extant example of an SS collar in Lancashire is that on the tomb effigy of Thomas Stanley, earl of Derby (d. 1504), originally located at Burscough Priory and now at Ormskirk. More collars can be found in Cheshire, with six dating from before the 1430s.[10] In Yorkshire, the two Waterton effigies at Methley and the Hatfield brasses at All Saints', Owston (c. 1417), are located within a reasonably short distance of Pontefract. Indeed, Sir Robert Waterton worked for the duchy in his capacity of constable of Pontefract Castle.[11] We also know that he received two SS livery collars. Robert Hatfield (d. 1417) served as controller of the household for John of Gaunt. To the north, at St Peter's and St Paul's, Pickering, can be found the effigies of Sir David Rowcliffe (d. 1407), who succeeded his father Sir Richard as steward of Pickering, and his wife Margaret.

---

[9] Castor, *The King, the Crown, and the Duchy*, p. 28; R. Somerville, *History of the Duchy of Lancaster*, 2 vols (London, 1953–70), i, p. 240.

[10] Two Mainwearing effigies at St Lawrence's, Over Peover, dating from *c.* 1410; two Lovell effigies at St Michael's and All Angels', Mottram in Longendale (*c.* 1408); another Mainwearing effigy at St Mary's, Acton (1399); and the effigy commemorating Sir Robert Foulshurst at St Bertoline's, Barthomley (1389).

[11] Somerville, *History of the Duchy*, i, p. 515.

To the west of Pickering, the SS collar on Sir John Marmion's tomb effigy at St Nicholas's, West Tanfield, dating from *c*. 1386, may also have reflected his duchy service as steward of Knaresborough. He also served as chamberlain to John of Gaunt.[12] A later group of livery collars clustered around Tutbury, perhaps surprisingly including those of Yorkist suns and roses, is examined below.

There is not, therefore, any particular concentration of SS collars dating from *c*. 1380–1430 in areas where the principal Lancastrian estates lay, although a not insignificant number of individuals commemorated wearing SS collars from those areas were associated with duchy service. The most notable lack of collars comes from Lancashire, a county where one would expect to have a reasonable concentration of collars from the period. There may, of course, have originally been more examples in the county, although if this were the case, there appears to have been a more pronounced rate of destruction of collared memorials there when compared to other counties. A number of SS collars can be found in Northamptonshire, where the castle at Higham Ferrers provided a link to the duchy, although those from the period do not represent individuals who had any clear-cut connections with the duchy. A significant proportion date from the sixteenth century.[13]

What of the York estates? Richard, duke of York, held land in over twenty counties. His principal lordships were the Mortimer lands inherited from his mother Anne, lying in the east of Wales and the Marches and stretching into Shropshire, where Ludlow Castle provided his principal residence. The York lands also extended north into the West Riding, with the castle at Sandal near Wakefield providing a focus, and there was a further concentration of estates in East Anglia, notably along the Norfolk/Suffolk border. The castle at Fotheringhay in Northamptonshire was another favoured residence of York's family, and provided another administrative centre alongside Ludlow.[14] In the West Riding there is no cluster of Yorkist collars, although the effigy of Sir John Saville (1481) at St Michael's and All Angels', Thornhill, is located some five miles to the west of Sandal Castle. In the east of England the search for Yorkist livery collars is more fruitful. Examples can be found on the Bourchier brasses at St Mary's, Little Easton,[15] the Colte brasses at Roydon and the effigy of Ann Tyrell (1482) at St Mary Magdalene's and St Mary the Virgin's, Wethersfield, all in Essex; the brass of Sir John Say (1478) at St Augustine's, Broxbourne (Hertfordshire); and the Jankyn Smith brass at Bury St Edmunds and the brass of Sir Gilbert Debenham

---

[12] *Ibid.*, pp. 364, 378, 372, 364.

[13] There is one indirect link: Edmund, son of Sir Richard Knightly of Upton, whose effigy at St Michael's, Upton, features an SS collar, served as attorney general to the duchy in the 1520s: *ibid.*, p. 407.

[14] P.A. Johnson, *Duke Richard of York 1411–1460* (Oxford, 1988), pp. 6–15.

[15] Commemorating Henry Bourchier, earl of Essex (d. 1483), and his wife Isabel, sister of the duke of York. Not surprisingly, Bourchier was a member of the Yorkist elite.

(c. 1493) at All Saints', Holbrook, both in Suffolk. In addition, a brass commemorates Sir Anthony Grey (1480) in St Alban's Cathedral. A number of Yorkist collars are located on tombs in the south of Wales and near to the Mortimer lordships in the Marches: these will be the subject of closer scrutiny later.

A small number of individuals depicted wearing Yorkist collars on monuments located within or near the major York estates were associated with Richard, duke of York, as a servant or annuitant. There are, however, limitations when attempting to link the appearance of Yorkist collars with the duke of York. He died in 1460, before the introduction of the suns and roses collar by his son, Edward IV. Many recipients of Yorkist collars may not, therefore, have served the duke, although there are examples of individuals or their heirs who served the duke and went on to serve Edward IV in some capacity, William Hastings being a high-profile and successful example. In these cases, the individuals concerned continued to serve in their capacities on the York estates – their lord now being the king – and many went on to serve in the royal household. As was the case with the Lancastrians, magnate service transferred to royal service for many: we should bear in mind that, in the fifteenth century, the majority of livery collars were awarded for royal service of some kind. The Say family were associated with the duke of York through John Say's service as seneschal of Hitchin (Hertfordshire) during the 1450s. Sir John Saville, buried at Thornhill, was the duke's seneschal of Wakefield, and John Smith 'the younger' was made receiver of all the lands of the duke of York and the earl of March in July of 1461. This may be the same Jankyn Smith buried at Bury St Edmunds; alternatively, it could be either his father or son, both of whom were also called Jankyn/John.[16] Finally, William Browning (d. 1467), whose effigy in St Mary's, Melbury Sampford (Dorset), wears a suns and roses collar, was the duke's surveyor and receiver in Dorset and Somerset.[17] All memorials date from the 1460s to the 1480s. It would therefore be assumed that their service was easily transferred to Duke Richard's son, Edward IV, after the former's death; we know this was the case with Jankyn Smith.

This brief enquiry has not revealed any conspicuous clusters of livery collars near the significant Lancaster or York estates. Our conclusions may be somewhat hampered by the disappearance of tombs and brasses over time: more extant examples may well have highlighted discernible trends. However, from the evidence that survives, the maps show a reasonably even spread of Lancastrian and Yorkist collars. When contemplating the appearance of groups of collars on church monuments – indeed all collars on monuments – we should be aware that the choice to depict the artefact was the result of a number of factors and objectives. Some decisions may have been made due to the local context,

---

[16] See M. Statham and S. Badham, 'Jankyn Smith of Bury St. Edmunds and His Brass', *TMBS*, 18 (2011), 227–50.

[17] Johnson, *Richard of York*, pp. 229, 238.

for example. Patrons of church monuments and stained glass were well aware of their neighbours' commissions. We should also bear in mind that the multifarious motivations for placing a collar on a memorial may have differed from the reasons why the individual was originally given their collar. It is to these motivations that we now turn.

Livery collars on church monuments to the Derbyshire gentry

The county of Derbyshire has left us one of the greatest legacies with regards to depictions of livery collars on church monuments from the period associated with the Wars of the Roses. A total of eleven collars can be found on tomb effigies and memorial brasses from c. 1465 to 1500. This can be compared to neighbouring Leicestershire, which has no extant examples from the period, and Nottinghamshire, which has only two.[18] Eight of the monuments in Derbyshire feature a collar of the Yorkist device of alternating suns and roses and the remaining three represent the SS collar, revived by Henry Tudor after his victory at Bosworth in 1485. The inclusion of livery collars on tombs in the county tallies with the national picture: the appearance of the Yorkist collar soon after 1461 following an extended period of the use of the Lancastrian collar, followed by a swift introduction of the Tudor SS collar after 1485.

What motivations lay behind the choice to depict a livery collar on a memorial? The obvious interpretation would be to express Yorkist or Lancastrian (or after 1485, Tudor) political allegiance, yet there were other factors specific to Derbyshire. Firstly, the gentry whose monuments feature a collar were linked through geographical proximity; the majority are located in the south-west of the county, clustered within a radius of approximately twelve miles. Save for the tombs at Sawley, Barlow and Youlgreave, there is little more than five miles separating each church. The families were therefore well known to one another and were, in effect, neighbours. The individuals were also brought together through strong ties of affinity to the duchy of Lancaster's Tutbury honour, whose pervasive presence was felt throughout the county during the late medieval period. It is not insignificant that the locations of the majority of the monuments form an umbrella to the north and east of Tutbury Castle, home of the honour, and centre point of royal power in the area. Many gentry were also retained by William, Lord Hastings, during the 1470s. A further, and perhaps most significant, consideration must be kinship ties: every one of the individuals commemorated was closely related to at least one other individual. It appears that they, or their families, were consciously choosing to adopt the collar as a group symbol, a durable declaration of their affinity.

---

[18] Sir Henry Pierrepont at Holme Pierrepont, and a mutilated effigy at St Anne's, Sutton Bonington, thought to represent Thomas Staunton (d. c. 1486).

The individuals to be examined are:

Nicholas Fitzherbert (d. 1473), St Mary's and St Barlok's, Norbury
Ralph Fitzherbert (d. 1484), St Mary's and St Barlok's, Norbury
Roger Bothe II (d. 1478), All Saints', Sawley
John Bradbourne (d. 1488), St Oswald's, Ashbourne
Robert Barley (d. 1467), St Lawrence's, Barlow
Thomas Cockayne (d. 1488), All Saints', Youlgreave
Thomas Fraunceys (d. 1482), St Wystan's, Repton
Nicholas Montgomery (d. 1465), St Andrew's, Cubley

Ralph Pole, (d. 1492), St Andrew's, Radbourne
John Curzon III, (d. c. 1492), All Saints', Kedleston
Nicholas Kniveton, (d. 1500), All Saints', Mugginton

The first group feature the Yorkist collar of suns and roses, the second the Lancastrian SS collar. In addition, the tombs of Sir Henry Vernon (d. 1515), at Tong, Sir Henry Pierrepont (d. 1499) at Holme Pierrepont, and Sir John Savage IV (d. 1495) at Macclesfield will be considered, as they shared strong tenurial and kinship ties with those listed above. Two earlier tombs, those of Sir John Cockayne (d. 1438) at Ashbourne and Sir Richard Vernon (d. 1451) at Tong will also be addressed as they can be interpreted as precedents for the above tombs.

The families had a long association with the county, some holding lands there since the Conquest. The wealthier knightly families such as the Vernons, the Curzons and the Montgomerys had enjoyed a privileged position within the county for a substantial time. Other families developed close tenurial ties with these wealthier families; for example, the Fitzherberts were under-tenants to the Montgomerys in several of their estates.[19] If one takes the list compiled by Susan Wright of the thirty-two most prominent knightly families in the county in the fifteenth century, then all the individuals concerned were members of the political and landed elite.[20] This distinct group developed their ties through intermarriage and through filling major local offices such as sheriff or justices. Peter Pole of Radbourne was almost ever present on the bench until 1450, after which his son Ralph and John Curzon of Kedleston carried out much of the work until the early 1460s. During the latter part of the century, John and William Bothe regularly sat on the bench, frequently alongside Nicholas Fitzherbert. Some also served further afield by representing their shire in parliament.[21]

---

[19] D. and S. Lysons, *Derbyshire* (London, 1817), p. 94.
[20] *Derbyshire Gentry*, appendix 2.
[21] G. Turbutt, *A History of Derbyshire*, 4 vols (Cardiff, 1999), ii, p. 661; *Derbyshire Gentry*, appendix 9a.

The Derbyshire gentry also developed a close affinity with the duchy of Lancaster, in the hands of the king from 1399, through their association with the Tutbury honour. They were certainly loyal to their Lancastrian lords, playing an influential part in the coup of 1399, fighting for Henry IV at Shrewsbury in 1403, and for Henry V at Agincourt in 1415, where members of the Cockayne and Fitzherbert families were present.[22] Both kings rewarded the loyalty of their Derbyshire supporters with local offices. Consequently many of the special commissions in the period 1400 to 1420 were dominated by their duchy servants.[23] This cohesive network, centred on south-west Derbyshire and east Staffordshire, can still be observed into the 1440s, although it had begun to wane, chiefly due to the weakness of Henry VI. Although the retinues of local magnates such as Henry, Lord Grey, and Humphrey Stafford, created duke of Buckingham in 1444, kept some members of the gentry network together, they were not successful in creating an effective affinity.[24] Troubles came to a head when members of the Derbyshire gentry attacked the property of Walter Blount in 1454. Led by the Longford family, the attackers, apparently numbering over 1,000, raised the Lancastrian standards and ransacked Elvaston Hall, with the accusation that Blount had 'gone to serve traytors', referring to his support for Richard Neville, earl of Warwick, and Richard, duke of York.[25] A reconciliation was eventually achieved and by 1460, when Buckingham and another local Lancastrian magnate, John Talbot, earl of Shrewsbury, were killed fighting at Northampton, the Derbyshire gentry were no longer die-hard Lancastrians. The previous year they had avoided fighting at Blore Heath and Ludford Bridge. Indeed, with the lack of strong royal or magnate authority, they had resorted to self-regulation, attempting to reconcile their recent differences.[26] Although trouble would still arise into the 1460s, the gentry network continued to work together. Both before and after the Yorkist accession in 1461, families such as the Blounts, Cockaynes, Fitzherberts, Frauncheyses, Bradbournes, Montgomerys and Vernons can be seen co-witnessing charters.[27]

Perhaps surprisingly, many of the families involved in the attack on Blount's property in 1454 feature among those individuals who, from 1465, were to be depicted wearing Yorkist livery collars on their monuments: Nicholas Montgomery and Nicholas and Ralph Fitzherbert were included on the list of those

---

[22] J.C. Cox, 'Political History', in *VCH Derbys.*, ii, pp. 106–7.
[23] Castor, *The King, the Crown, and the Duchy*, pp. 200–6.
[24] C. Rawcliffe, *The Staffords, Earls of Stafford and Dukes of Buckingham, 1394–1521* (Cambridge, 1978), pp. 19–20.
[25] A. Carrington and W.J. Andrew, 'A Lancastrian Raid in the Wars of the Roses', *DAJ*, 34 (1912), 33–49.
[26] Castor, *The King, the Crown, and the Duchy*, pp. 302–5.
[27] DRO, 231 M/T150; Jeayes, 1395, 1596, 1597, 2678.

indicted, although the names of the latter two were subsequently crossed out.[28] The families had not, however, forgotten their duchy links. With the accession of Edward IV in 1461, the duchy had been detached from the Lancastrians and was now in the hands of the Yorkist king. The depiction of the Yorkist suns and roses livery collar on their memorials, however, could still be a statement of their strong ties with the Tutbury honour. In some respects their loyalty was still directed towards the duke of Lancaster, who now happened to be the Yorkist king.

Ties of locality: kinship, tenure and office

Many of the individuals commemorated had strong kinship ties, some with more than one family (see Appendix 1). It is also possible to illuminate local connections through deeds, especially enfeoffments and wills.[29] Although there are problems with definition, it may be possible to describe the links between some of these individuals as friendships. There is evidence of close ties between several generations of families and there was clearly an element of mutual trust and responsibility involved in their relationships.[30]

By the fifteenth century, the Fitzherbert family had resided at Norbury for several hundred years, having been granted the manor by Tutbury Priory in 1125 for an annual rent of 100s.[31] In 1451 a settlement was reached with the priory whereby the yearly rent was released in exchange for family estates in Osmaston, Foston and Church Broughton.[32] One of the arbitrators in the 1451 settlement was a member of the Bothe family, with whom the Fitzherberts had enjoyed close ties for several decades, after Nicholas (d. 1473) had married Alice, daughter of Henry Bothe of Arleston (Derbyshire), in 1416. Her father presented to the living at Norbury in 1424, and remained patron until 1461.[33] In addition to their manor at Norbury, the Fitzherberts also held land at Birchwood, Snelston and Cubley, where they were neighbours to the Montgomery family.[34] In his will of 1483, Ralph Fitzherbert left 6s. to the churches at Snelston and Cubley, where the mausoleum of the Montgomery family was situated. Ralph's son and

---

[28] TNA, KB 9/12/1, mems. 13a, 15, 24; *Derbyshire Gentry*, p. 135.
[29] N. Saul, *Scenes from Provincial Life: Knightly Families in Sussex, 1280–1400* (Oxford, 1986), p. 62.
[30] P. Maddern, '"Best Trusted Friends": Concepts and Practices of Friendship among Fifteenth-Century Norfolk Gentry', in N. Rogers (ed.), *England in the Fifteenth Century: Proceedings of the 1992 Harlaxton Symposium*, Harlaxton Medieval Studies, IV (Stamford, 1994), pp. 100–17; C.E. Moreton, 'A Social Gulf? The Upper and Lesser Gentry of Later Medieval England', *Journal of Medieval History*, 17 (1991), 255–62, at 257–8.
[31] SRO, D641/5/T20/2. A copy of the original grant is also kept in Swynnerton MSS.
[32] Historical Manuscripts Commission, *The Cartulary of Tutbury Priory*, ed. A. Saltman (London, 1962), no. 89.
[33] L.J. Bowyer, *The Ancient Parish of Norbury* (Ashbourne, 1953), p. 71; Jeayes, 1769.
[34] A.D. Smith, *Derbyshire Landholdings in the Fifteenth Century, The Lay Subsidy of 1431* (privately published, 1999), appendix, table II.

heir John (d. 1531) left bequests to Repton church, where Thomas Fraunceys (d. 1482) lay buried.[35]

Although Nicholas Fitzherbert served as sheriff for Derbyshire and Nottinghamshire, and as an MP under the Lancastrians, it is clear that by the 1460s he had reconciled himself to the Yorkists, serving as JP and sitting on various commissions until his death, and being selected as sheriff in 1465. He was regularly named as a tax collector in the county, a task he would often carry out with John Curzon, Thomas Fraunceys and Robert Barley.[36] In the early 1460s, Nicholas and other local gentry, including members of the Blount and Curzon families, were ordered to arrest the troublesome John and Roger Vernon, and their close associate, John Cockayne. In 1471 and again the following year, alongside the duke of Clarence, William, Lord Hastings, Walter Blount (by then Lord Mountjoy) and John Bothe, Nicholas sat on commissions of array in Derbyshire.[37] Together with members of the Bothe and Fraunceys families, he was a regular presence on the quorum during the 1460s. His training as a lawyer brought him into contact with other local gentry, and with other members of his family he carried out various legal duties for families, including the Cockaynes.[38] The apparent Yorkist leanings of Nicholas and his son Ralph are compounded by their association with Thomas Powtrell from the 1470s. Powtrell provided a strong Yorkist administrative presence in Derbyshire. He worked in local government, employed by Walter Blount, the only member of the county gentry who could be described as a staunch Yorkist, and was created deputy steward of Tutbury in 1480.[39] He was named as a feoffee by Elizabeth Fitzherbert, Ralph's widow, in 1484.[40] Although Nicholas's son Ralph was not such a ubiquitous figure, he did join several commissions of the peace during the 1470s and early 1480s, frequently alongside representatives of the Fraunceys and Curzon families.[41]

Ralph's son and heir, John Fitzherbert (d. 1531), ran into difficulties with various individuals, not least his wife. John had married Benedicta, the daughter of John Bradbourne, in the late fifteenth century. By the time he made his will in 1517, however, they had parted. Benedicta had, according to John, been unfaithful,

---

[35] SRO, D641/5/T(S)/4/1; LRO, B/A/1/14, fol. 106v.
[36] J.C. Wedgwood (ed.), *History of Parliament 1439–1509*, 2 vols (London, 1936–38), ii, *Biographies of Members of the Commons House*, p. 42; E.A. Ayres, 'Parliamentary Representation in Derbyshire and Nottinghamshire in the Fifteenth Century', University of Nottingham, unpublished MA thesis (1956), pp. 229–37.
[37] *CPR 1461–67*, pp. 31, 102, 135, 304; *CPR 1467–77*, pp. 284, 350.
[38] *Derbyshire Gentry*, pp. 60, 102; TNA, E 159/234 mems. 112, 121, 181, 182.
[39] G. Wrottesley, 'Extracts from the Plea Rolls, Temp. Edward IV, Edward V and Richard III', *Staffordshire Historical Collections*, New Series, 6, Part I (1903), 135; *Derbyshire Gentry*, pp. 88, 91, 102.
[40] SRO, D641/5/T(S)/4/2.
[41] *CPR 1467–77*, p. 408; *CPR 1476–85*, pp. 395, 557.

displaying a 'lewde and vile disposicion' to her husband.⁴² He ensured that she received no property or dower, meticulously passing on his goods and chattels to his relatives and friends in order that she would receive nothing. Furthermore, John declared his eldest daughter Anne, who had married John Welles, illegitimate and disinherited her. This led to problems at John's funeral on 25 July 1531, when members of the Welles family arrived uninvited to demand their part of the inheritance. A riot promptly ensued, with John's younger brother and heir, Anthony, being ushered away by relatives fearing for his life.⁴³ By the time he made his will, John had settled his past grievances with Anthony in order to perpetuate the Fitzherbert name. When added to several pardons he received at the turn of the fifteenth century, this history suggests John had a rather troubled life.⁴⁴ With no male heir to contribute to the family's succession, perhaps John commissioned the lavish tombs for his father and grandfather to mask his personal failures and stress family continuity. His own memorial, in stark contrast to those of his relatives, is a simple table tomb with brass inscription on top. It lies under the arch in his chapel at Norbury.

John of Etwall, a younger son of Nicholas and uncle to John, was another prominent local individual. Having connections with the Yorkist court, he may have had an influence in commissioning the tombs of his father and brother. The two livery collars on the effigies of Nicholas and Ralph are not in fact the only depictions of suns and roses collars in the church. On the north tomb chest panel of Nicholas's tomb are depictions of eight sons from his first marriage. The seventh and eighth both wear the Yorkist livery collar, and perhaps one of these represents John of Etwall. John owned land at Etwall and Ash in Derbyshire, where he was neighbour to the Bothe family, and his work brought him more often than not to London, where he held property in Hackney, and where he requested to be buried in St Bartholomew's, Smithfield.⁴⁵ His career centred on the exchequer; he worked as a teller in the 1470s and was granted the office of king's remembrancer on 31 May 1480.⁴⁶ His position brought him benefits. In 1461 he was granted a piece of land called 'Prince Fee' in Derbyshire, for twelve years. In December 1470 he and William Knyvet were granted the same land for seven years, to be farmed at 22s. 4d. a year. The grant was reissued the following year to Fitzherbert and Thomas Thwaytes, chancellor of the exchequer.⁴⁷ John's

---

⁴² LRO, B/A/1/14, fol. 109v.
⁴³ TNA, STAC 2/22/159; 2/25/19.
⁴⁴ SRO, D641/5/T20/14; Swynnerton MSS, i, no. 14; ii, p. 15.
⁴⁵ TNA, PROB 11/13, fol. 158v; Derby Local Studies Library, Derbyshire Deeds, 716, 721, 1863; Jeayes, 1203, 1204; *CIPM* Henry VII, ii, no. 631.
⁴⁶ *CPR 1476–85*, p. 202.
⁴⁷ *CFR 1461–71*, pp. 35, 288; *CFR 1471–85*, p. 59; D. Grummitt, 'Public Service, Private Interest and Patronage in the Fifteenth-Century Exchequer', in L. Clark (ed.), *The Fifteenth Century*, III: *Authority and Subversion* (Woodbridge, 2003), p. 152.

work took him around the country, and in 1475 he and John Sorell, another teller, travelled on Edward IV's French expedition.[48] His connections with the Yorkist court are confirmed by a medical prescription for his weeping eyes in British Library Harleian MS 1628, a collection of medical recipes for individuals associated with Edward IV's court.[49] Perhaps the Fitzherberts' attachment to the house of York was therefore a little stronger than we may at first expect. It should, however, be stipulated that there is no evidence to suggest that the family were politically active supporters of the regime; they are not recorded as having participated in any military encounters, although they clearly served as trusted administrators in the area under the Yorkists.

Partly because of the scant records of the Bothe family, there is confusion over the exact relationship between Roger Bothe II and Nicholas Fitzherbert. They have been described as brothers-in-law, although this could not have been possible, as Alice Bothe's father was Henry of Arleston (as the inscription on her memorial at Norbury testifies), and Roger's father was Roger I (d. 1467). It is possible that Alice was sister to Roger I. Either way, the Arleston and Sawley branches of the family were closely related, stemming from the Dunham Massey Bothes in Cheshire.[50] The Bothes and Fitzherberts shared close family ties, and their links were certainly durable. Alice's father, Henry, acted as guardian to Nicholas Fitzherbert, and their close affinity is still observable in 1451, when Henry's son John awarded in favour of his in-laws in their dispute with Tutbury Priory.[51] Nicholas and Ralph Fitzherbert acted as feoffees for the Bothes in the 1430s.[52] In 1470 William Bothe was acting as a feoffee for Ralph Fitzherbert, and in 1517 another William Bothe, chantry priest at Norbury, witnessed John Fitzherbert's will.[53] In addition, the two families held land in the same areas, for example at Hilton.[54] John and William Bothe sat on several commissions in the county from the 1460s, accompanying the Fitzherberts and Thomas Frounceys,

---

[48] *Harleian 433*, iii, pp. 128, 130, 155; *CPR 1467–77*, pp. 408, 428, 491; *CPR 1476–85*, p. 563; *CFR 1471–85*, pp. 159, 263, 283; F.P. Barnard (ed.), *Edward IV's French Expedition of 1475: The Leaders and Their Badges* (Oxford, 1925), pp. 1–2.

[49] T. Lang, 'Medical Recipes from the Yorkist Court', *The Ricardian*, 20 (2010), 100.

[50] J.C. Cox, *Notes on the Churches of Derbyshire*, 4 vols (Chesterfield and London, 1875), iii, p. 235; L.M. Angus-Butterworth, *Old Cheshire Families and Their Seats* (Manchester, 1932), pp. 159–74; L. Jewitt, 'The Booths or Bothes, Archbishops and Bishops, and the Derbyshire Family to which They Belonged', *The Reliquary*, 25 (1884–85), 33.

[51] DRO, D31M/E451; Jeayes, 1769.

[52] Every MSS, 3184, 3196, 3538.

[53] Swynnerton MSS, i, no. 15; SRO, D641/S/T20/15; LRO, B/A/1/14, fol. 110v.

[54] C. Glover and P. Riden (eds), *William Woolley's History of Derbyshire*, Derbyshire Record Society, 4 (Chesterfield, 1981), p. 108. The Wynter family granted land to Ralph Fitzherbert in 1462, and William Bothe of Arleston in 1494: SRO, D(W)1734/J/986 and 987.

among others. The Bothes also regularly sat on the county bench during the second half of the fifteenth century.[55]

Roger Bothe's interests also took him further afield, and it is perhaps in this context that we can interpret the Yorkist collar on his brass. In c. 1473 his sister Isabel married Ralph Neville, the future third earl of Westmorland. Although the Westmorland Nevilles had avoided committing themselves politically during the early years of Edward IV's reign, by the 1470s Ralph was currying favour. Created knight of the Bath in 1475, he was serving the duke of Gloucester by 1477, and in the following year the duke stayed at the Nevilles' home, Raby Castle.[56] The tomb effigy of Ralph's uncle, the second earl (d. 1484), at Brancepeth bore a Yorkist livery collar with Richard III's boar pendant, possibly another aspect of his nephew's strategy to win Yorkist favour.

Roger Bothe's links with the Westmorland Nevilles undoubtedly stemmed from his uncle Laurence, bishop of Durham from 1457 to 1476, when he was translated to the archbishopric of York. Though at first a Lancastrian (he had been chancellor to Margaret of Anjou in the 1450s), he eventually reconciled himself with the house of York. Becoming guardian to the young prince of Wales in 1471, he was created lord chancellor two years later and enjoyed the king's favour until his death in 1480.[57] Despite earlier tensions, relations between Bishop Bothe and the Westmorland Nevilles had improved by the time his niece married Ralph, and in 1482 several of the Bothes were named as feoffees by Ralph and Isabel.[58] Laurence's nephew John, bishop of Exeter, had closer links with the Yorkists, serving as secretary to Edward IV. In 1463 the king wrote of his 'entyerely belovette clerc', for whom he held 'very trew hert zele and affeccion'.[59] Roger's illustrious clerical relatives clearly had close links to the Yorkist government. It could well have been his uncle Laurence who commissioned his and his father's brasses at Sawley, complete with the Yorkist collar on his nephew's memorial.

To the west of Sawley and some ten miles north-east of Norbury lies Bradbourne, home of the Bradbourne family. By the early fourteenth century the family had also acquired the manor of Heage, north of Derby.[60] The location of their estates, not surprisingly, brought them into contact with their fellow gentry families in south-west Derbyshire: the Vernons, Cockaynes, Frauncesyes, Mont-

---

[55] *CPR 1461–67*, p. 102; *CPR 1467–77*, p. 350; *CPR 1476–85*, p. 557; *Derbyshire Gentry*, appendix 9a.
[56] J. Petre, 'The Nevills of Brancepeth and Raby 1425–1499, Part II 1470–1499: Recovery and Collapse', *The Ricardian*, 6 (1982), 2–13; R. Davies (ed.), *Extracts from the Municipal Records of the City of York, during the Reigns of Edward IV, Edward V and Richard III* (London, 1843), pp. 98–9.
[57] E. Axon, 'The Family of Bothe (Booth) and the Church in the 15th and 16th Centuries', *Transactions of the Lancashire and Cheshire Antiquarian Society*, 53 (1938), 49–56.
[58] Historical Manuscripts Commission, *Rutland*, iv, p. 87.
[59] C.H. Cooper, *Annals of Cambridge*, 5 vols (1842–1908), i, p. 210.
[60] M. Wiltshire and S. Woore, *Medieval Parks of Derbyshire: A Gazetteer with Maps, Illustrations and Historical Notes* (Ashbourne, 2009), p. 96.

gomerys and Fitzherberts were closely associated throughout the century.[61] In addition, alongside Henry Bothe, the Poles of Radbourne and the Curzons of Kedleston, John Bradbourne's father, Henry, had been a member of Henry, Lord Grey's retinue in the 1430s. The majority of the retinue was absorbed into Humphrey Stafford's affinity after Grey's death in 1444. Sir Richard Vernon, another Stafford annuitant, was John Bradbourne's father-in-law. Bradbourne was thus also related to John Cockayne (d. 1505), who married another of Vernon's daughters.[62]

John Bradbourne's daughter, Benedicta, had married John Fitzherbert some time before her father's tomb was built. Despite the subsequent difficulties between Benedicta and her estranged husband, their families appear to have remained close. Isabel, the widow of John Bradbourne's grandson (another John), left estates in Netherton and Hampstall Ridware to the Fitzherbert family for the kindness and friendship they had shown towards her and her late husband, and in 1510 John and Anthony Fitzherbert, and Humphrey and John Bradbourne were named feoffees by Sir Ralph Longford.[63] In 1500 Anne, the widow of John (d. 1488), bequeathed to Anne Fitzherbert a 'coler of the kynge lyverey wt a flor of golde at hyt'.[64] Although it is tempting to postulate that this is the same collar depicted on John Bradbourne's monument, it is unlikely. The description of the flower of gold may refer to the Tudor rose, which can be seen on the pendants to the SS livery collars depicted on the effigies of Ralph Pole at Radbourne and John Curzon at Kedleston (see Figure 6).

Bradbourne played little part in local government, although he did undertake some minor administrative duties for the Yorkists. In 1468 he was a tax collector in Derbyshire, but perhaps more significant is a grant of several manors in Essex by Thomas Ferrers in March 1459. The other grantees included the duke of York, the earl of Warwick and Henry, Viscount Bourchier.[65] Although this is evidence of an early association with the Yorkist hierarchy, it appears to be the extent of Bradbourne's relations with York. His absence from the records is explained by the fact that he spent a period of time fighting for Ferdinand and Isabella in Spain, where it is probable he was awarded the Order of Granada. The badge of the order can be seen on the effigy of Humphrey Bradbourne, John's great-grandson, which lies next to John's tomb. On his wife's effigy is displayed a necklace of cockleshells, evidence that she too travelled with her husband, evidently undertaking a pilgrimage to the shrine of St James at Santiago de Compostela.

---

[61] SRO, D641/5/T; *CCR 1441–47*, p. 289; Jeayes, 2678, 2394; Every MSS, 3167, 3244.
[62] *Derbyshire Gentry*, pp. 66–8; A. Compton Reeves, 'Some of Humphrey Stafford's Military Indentures', *Nottingham Medieval Studies*, 16 (1972), 80–91.
[63] Swynnerton MSS, ii, p. 17; Jeayes, 1359.
[64] LRO, B/A/1/13, fols. 245v–248v. Anne had since married John Kniveton.
[65] *CFR 1461–71*, p. 230; *CCR 1454–61*, p. 324.

Robert Barley (d. 1467), whose main residence at Barlow lay in the north of the county, has perhaps rightly been labelled a trimmer.[66] He served as a JP during the 1450s, sat on the Lancastrian commission of array in December 1459, and was returned to the Lancastrian parliament at Coventry in November the same year. He was also named as a knight of the shire in the predominantly Yorkist parliament of July 1455. After December 1460 it appears that he retired from the bench, although he was a tax collector, alongside representatives from the Fitzherbert and Fraunceys families, in July 1463.[67] It is unlikely that he was ever a staunch Lancastrian, however, as he had served as an esquire to Humphrey, duke of Gloucester, during the 1430s.[68] Perhaps it was his son (another Robert) who bore a stronger allegiance to the house of York. In 1469 he enfeoffed his estate to, among other individuals who owned land in the north of the county, the duke of Clarence and the earl of Warwick. It is possible that he was a retainer of Clarence.[69] In 1473 Henry, Lord Grey, by then a supporter of the house of York, quitclaimed the manor of Stoke in Derbyshire to Robert for 200 marks, perhaps having been persuaded by the king.[70] Perhaps the suns and roses collar on Robert senior's tomb is therefore more an assertion of his son's Yorkist connections than his own.

Locally, the Barleys were associated with the Fitzherbert family. Both acted as feoffees for Alfred Longford in 1434, and the two families were plaintiffs in an action against Richard Paynell over land in Derby in 1528.[71] A strong, durable association with the Cockaynes was forged after Robert's daughter, Agnes, married Thomas, son of John Cockayne in *c*. 1458. Not surprisingly, the Cockayne arms featured prominently in the glass of Barlow Hall and in the church; Chaloner's 1611 visitation noted that several of the shields on Robert's memorial celebrated the union between the two families.[72] Another compelling link, this time from further afield, attracts attention: in 1479 Robert Barley of Barlow was named executor of Nicholas Stafford, 'late of Shrewsbury'.[73] In addition, Tilley cites an enfeoffment between a John and Johanna Stafford and Robert Barley the elder and the younger, of land in Youlgreave and Little Longstone in

---

[66] *Derbyshire Gentry*, p. 115.
[67] *CPR 1452–61*, pp. 663–4, 558; *CFR 1476–85*, pp. 100, 105; Ayres, 'Parliamentary Representation', pp. 243–4.
[68] W.C. Metcalfe, 'Pedigrees Contained in the Visitations of Derbyshire, 1569 and 1611', *The Genealogist*, New Series, 7 (1891), 5; Wedgwood (ed.), *History of Parliament*, ii, p. 42.
[69] Nottingham, Nottinghamshire Archives, Portland Collection, DDP/CD/111.
[70] TNA, CP 25/1/39/46.
[71] Jeayes, 1395; TNA, CP 25/2/6/29.
[72] M. Barlow, *Barlow Family Records* (London and Derby, 1932), plate 7.
[73] J.P. Yeatman, *The Feudal History of the County of Derby*, 6 vols (London and Birmingham, 1886–1907), iv, section viii, p. 422.

Derbyshire.[74] Appropriately, a Nicholas Stafford of Shrewsbury (d. 1471) has a memorial brass featuring a suns and roses collar in St Mary's Church, Shrewsbury (Shropshire). Could this be another example of close associates wearing the Yorkist livery collar on their monuments?

The family of Robert Barley's son-in-law, Thomas Cockayne, owned several estates in the county, including Middleton by Youlgreave and Clifton, and came into possession of their chief seat at Ashbourne in the fourteenth century, which they held under the duchy of Lancaster until the seventeenth. They were a prominent Derbyshire family. Sir John Cockayne (d. 1438) served as sheriff and MP during the first half of the century, and regularly sat on the county bench. His tomb lies in the Cockayne mausoleum at Ashbourne, where he is depicted wearing the Lancastrian SS livery collar. His uncle, Sir John Cockayne of Bury Hatley (Bedfordshire), was created chief baron of the exchequer in 1400.[75] Sir John's son and heir, John (d. 1505), did not, however, enjoy his ancestors' success. No doubt irritated by his mother's longevity (she outlived her husband by some thirty years, retaining the majority of the family's inheritance), John was frequently in trouble, with violence erupting with his stepfather Thomas Bate, the Shirleys, the Okeovers and the Bassetts at various times.[76] With the death of his son Thomas, in 1488, John was forced into a one-sided marriage arrangement between his grandson, Sir Thomas (d. 1537), and a daughter of John Fitzherbert of Etwall.[77] This Thomas, knighted at the siege of Tournai in 1513, revived his family's fortunes, referred to on his epitaph in Ashbourne church.[78]

The family's close association with the Barleys strengthened after Thomas Cockayne married Agnes Barley in the late 1450s, an association proclaimed through the depiction of the Barley arms on the tomb of Thomas at Youlgreave, and on the tomb of his son, Sir Thomas, at Ashbourne. The arms of Fitzherbert also appear on the Ashbourne tomb: Sir Thomas married Barbara Fitzherbert in the 1490s. It appears that, by this time, any old wounds between these two families had begun to heal. The Fitzherberts and Cockaynes had earlier connections: Sir John Cockayne had been a feoffee of Nicholas Fitzherbert's estates during his minority.[79] But trouble flared up during the second half of the century over the possession of 500 acres of land at Clifton, only to be rectified through

---

[74] J. Tilley, *The Old Halls, Manors and Families of Derbyshire*, 4 vols (London, 1892–1902), iii, p. 135.

[75] Smith, *Derbyshire Landholdings*, p. 8; table 5; *List of Sheriffs for England and Wales*, PRO Lists and Indexes, 9 (London, 1898), pp. 102–6; Ayres, 'Parliamentary Representation', pp. 44–54.

[76] *Derbyshire Gentry*, p. 134. See TNA, KB 9/250, mem. 45; KB 9/12/1, mem. 10; G. Wrottesley, 'Extracts from the Plea Rolls, 34 Henry VI to 14 Edward IV', *Staffordshire Historical Collections*, New Series, 4 (1901), 110–11.

[77] *CIPM* Henry VII, ii, no. 832.

[78] Wilson-Lee, 'Dynasty and Strategies, Part 1', 97.

[79] DRO, D231M/E451; D231M/T308; Jeayes, 1769, 2678; Saltman (ed.), *Cartulary of Tutbury Priory*, no. 317.

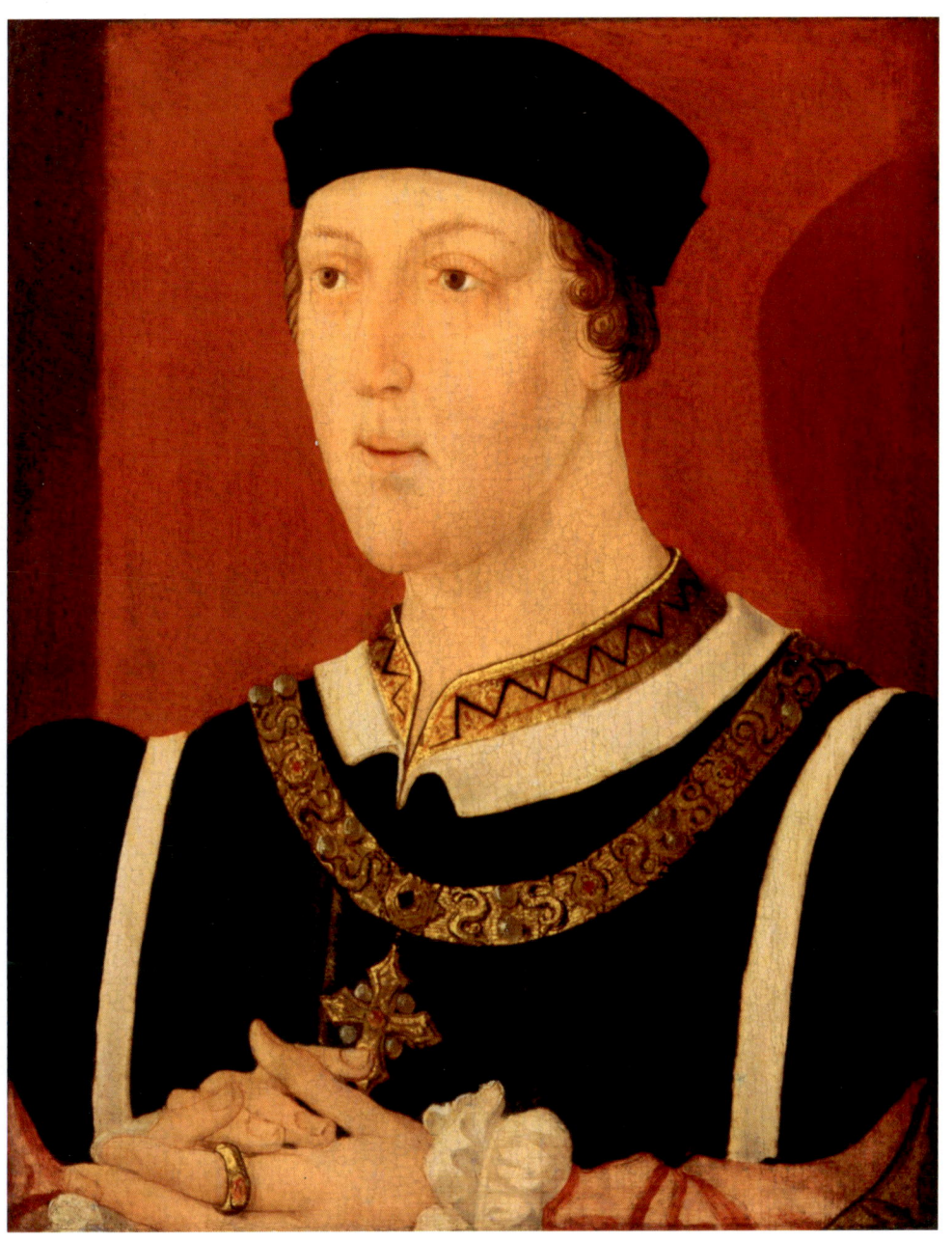
Plate 1. Henry VI portrait, unknown artist (*c.* 1540).

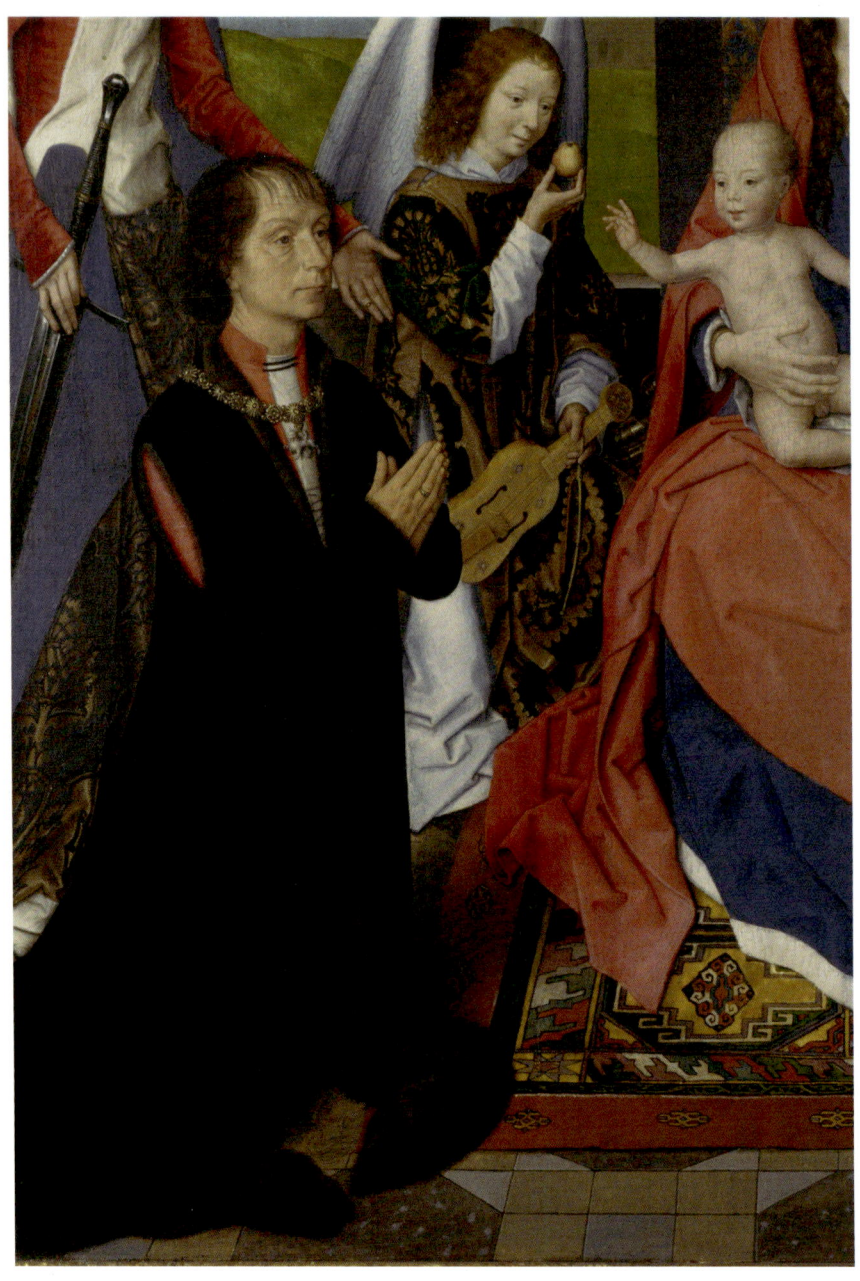

Plate 2. Sir John Donne portrait, Donne Triptych, Hans Memling (*c.* 1475).

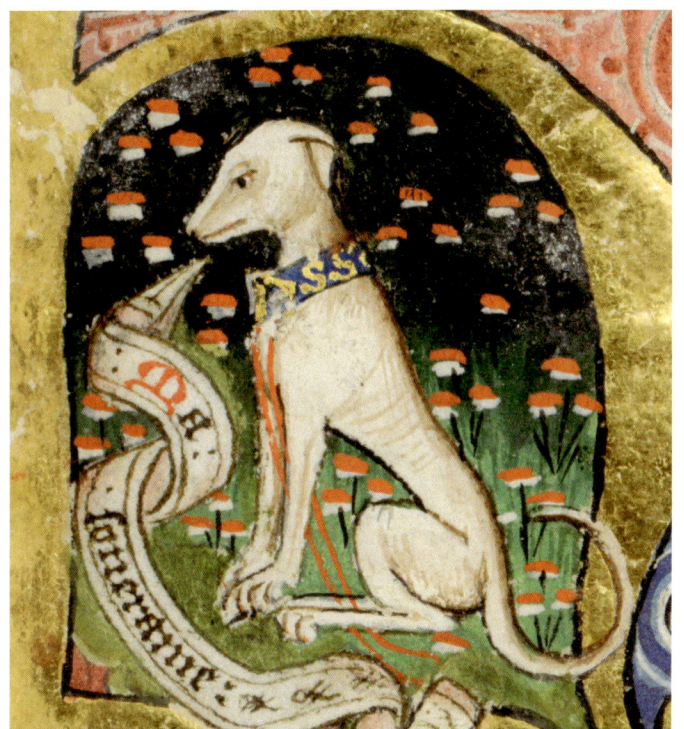

Plate 3.
SS dog collar worn by a white greyhound, Henry IV's beast, accompanied by the king's motto *Ma soueraine*; *Statutes of England* (1420s).

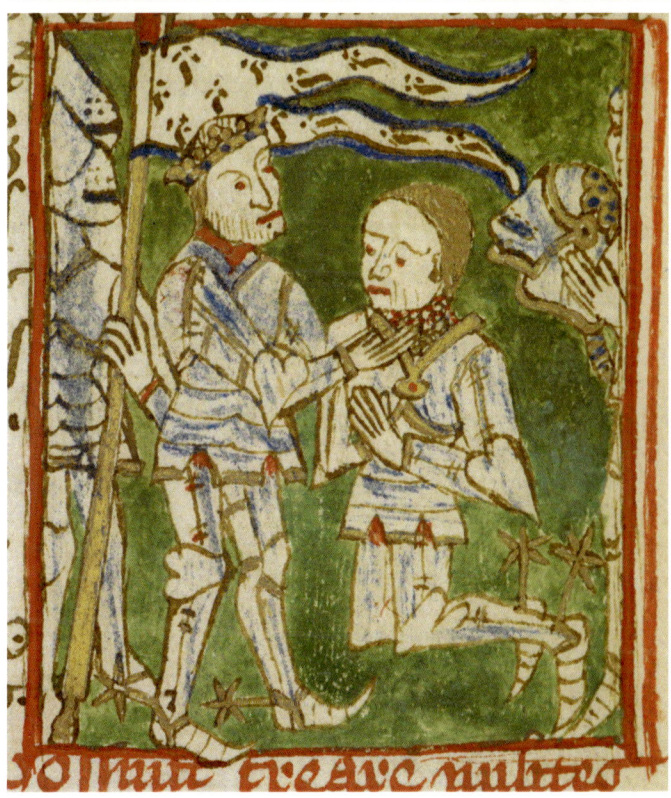

Plate 4.
A knight is awarded a collar by the king (*c.* 1458).

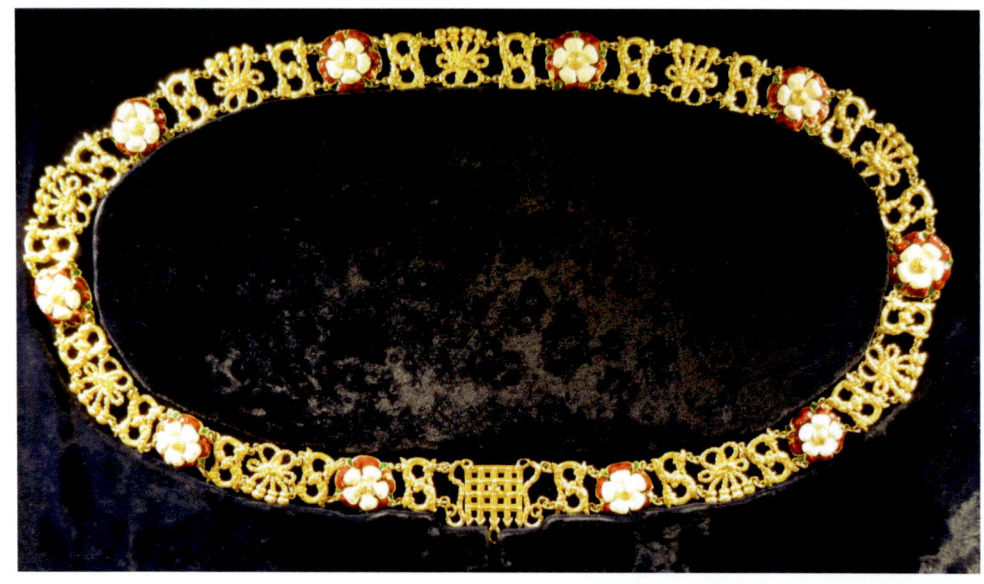

Plate 5.
The Lord Mayor's collar.

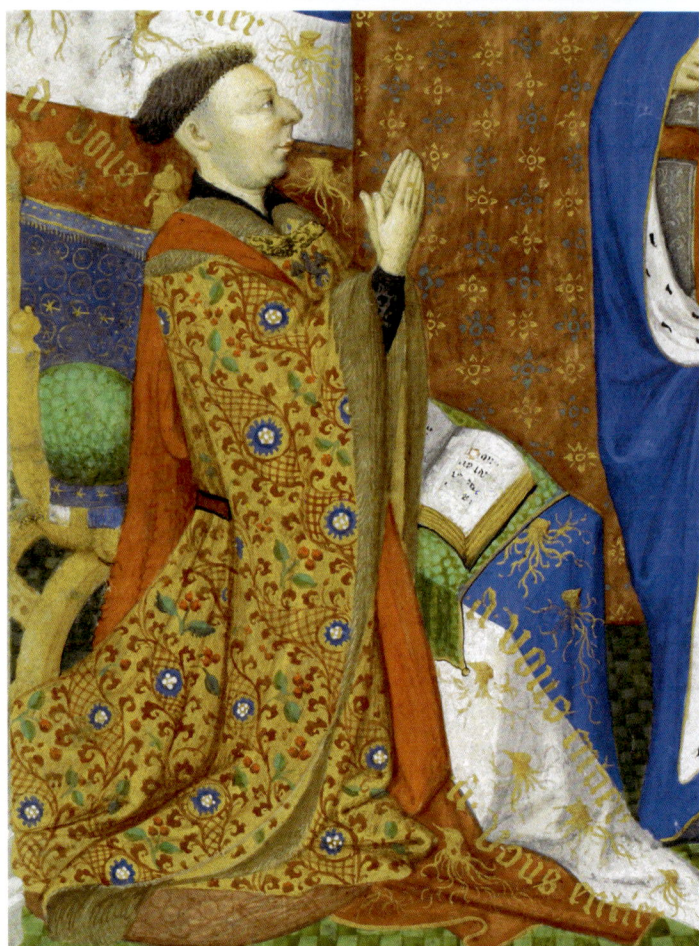

Plate 6.
John, duke of Bedford portrait, from the *Bedford Hours* (c. 1423).

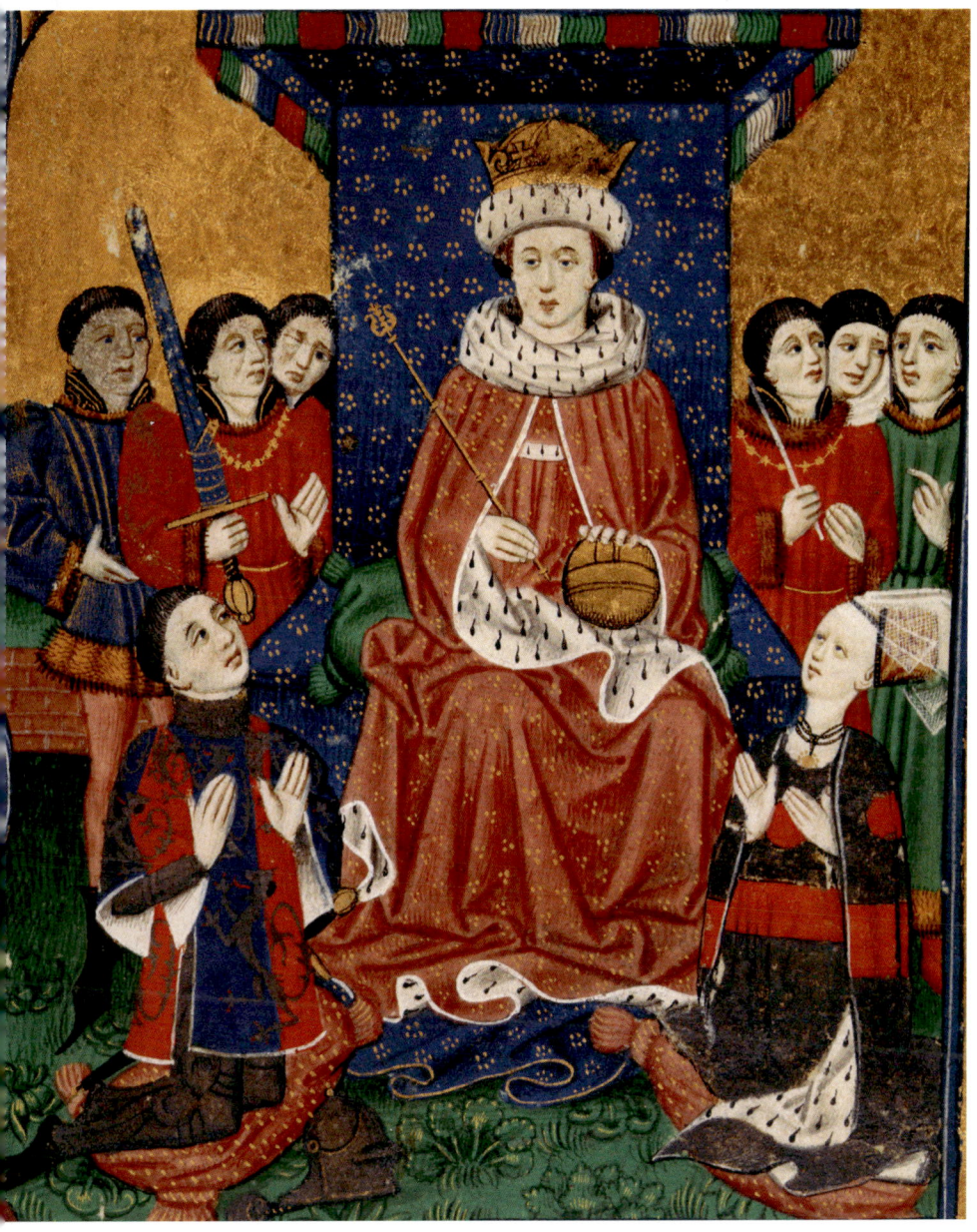

Plate 7. William Herbert and his wife kneel before Edward IV, in John Lydgate's *Troy Book* (c. 1461–62).

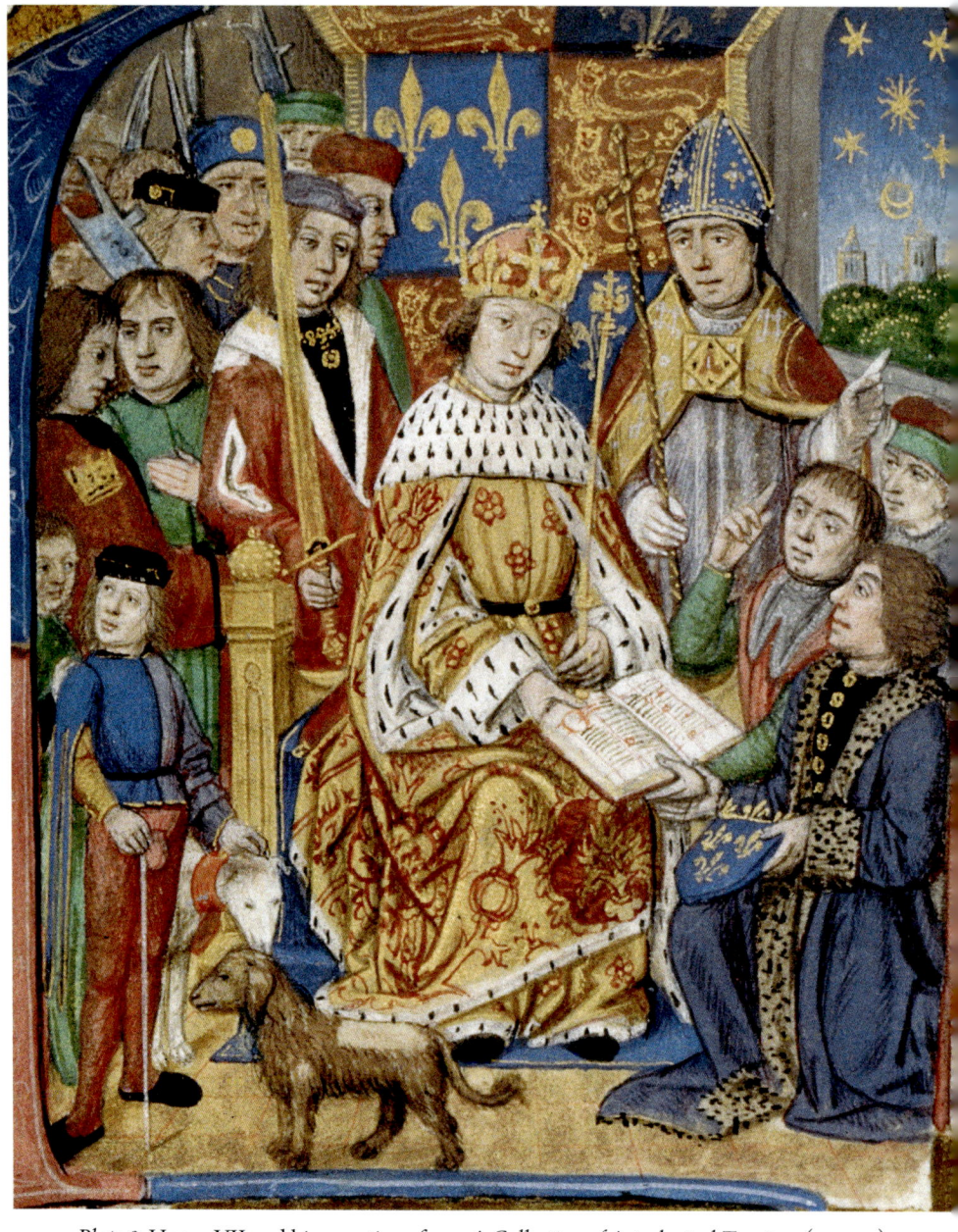

Plate 8. Henry VII and his courtiers, from *A Collection of Astrological Treatises* (c. 1490).

Plate 9 [facing above]. Tomb of William Herbert and his wife, Tintern Abbey; the *Herbertorum Prosapia*.

Plate 10 [facing below]. Military ordinance of Charles the Bold; Master of Fitzwilliam 268 (1475).

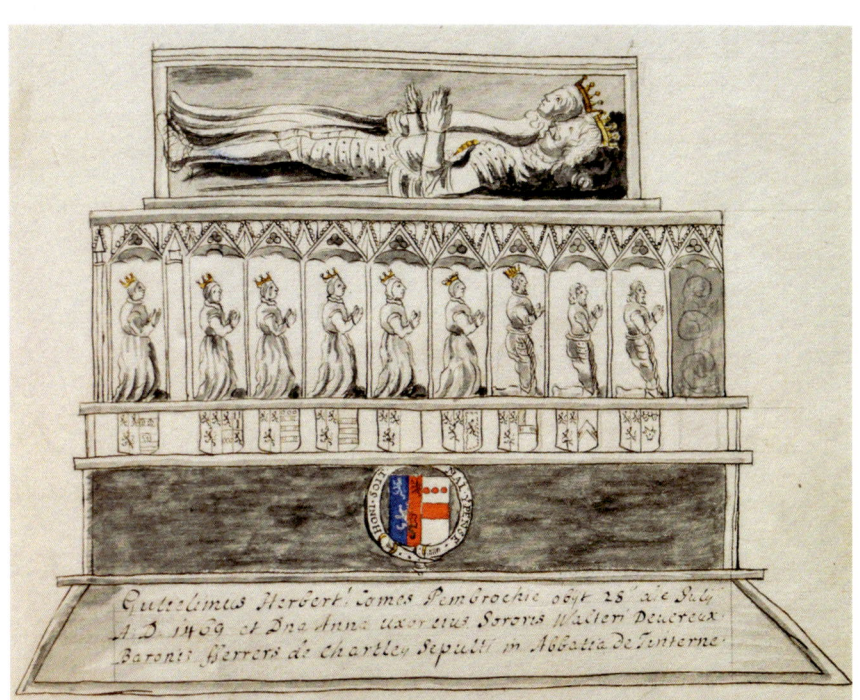

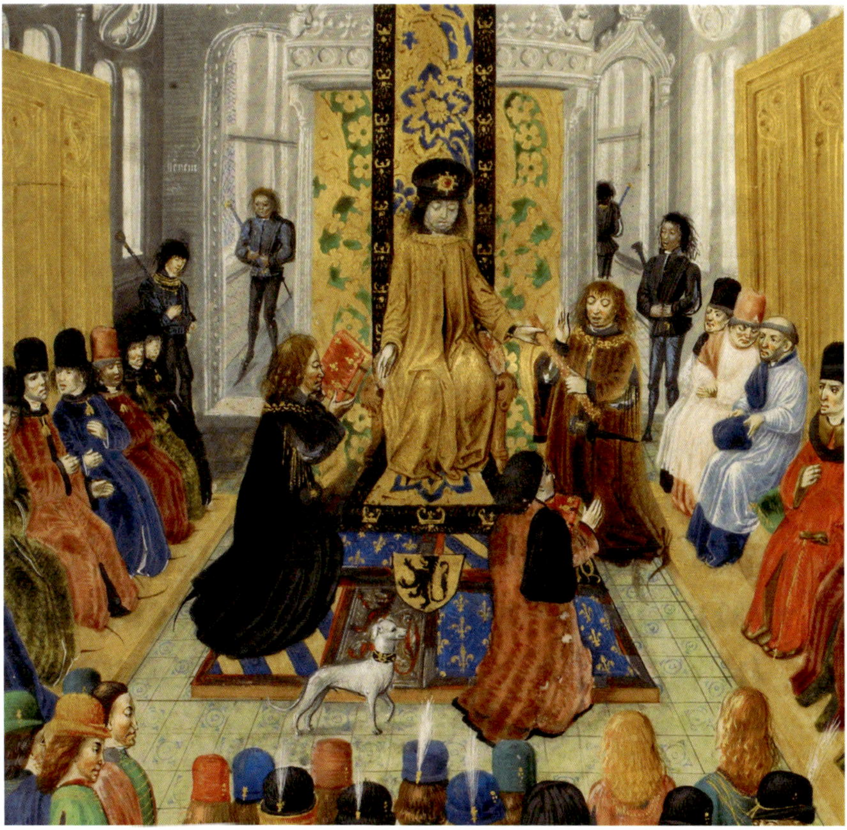

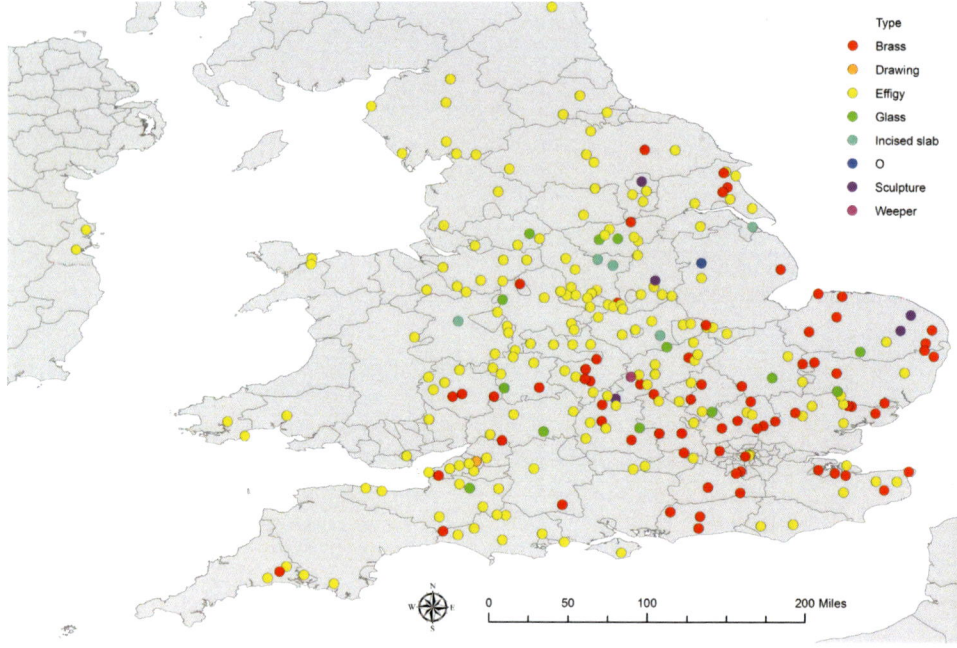

Map 1. Geographical distribution of livery collars in England, Wales and Ireland.

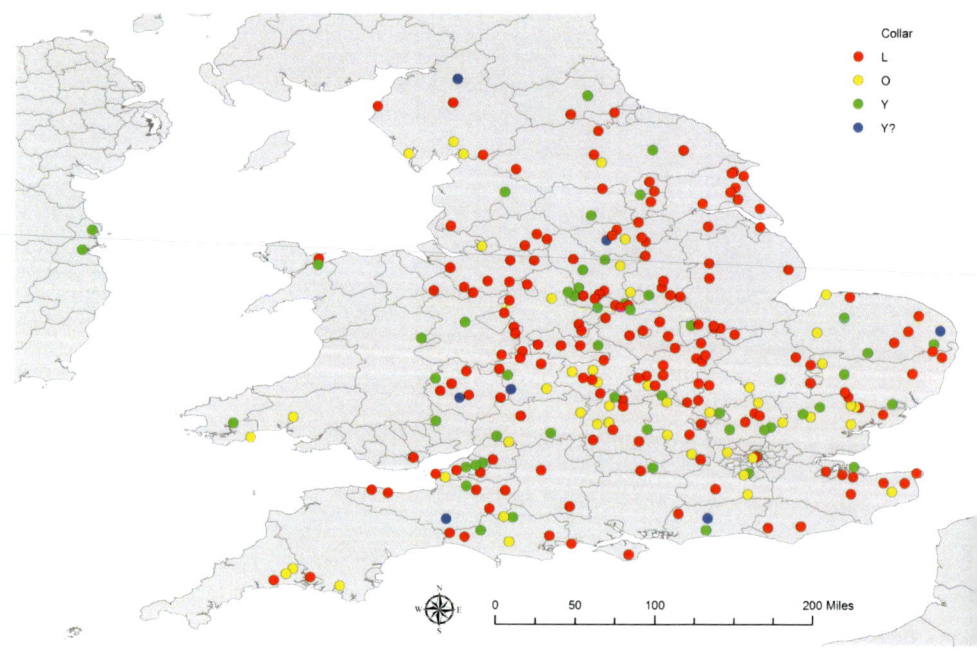

Map 2. Distribution of livery collars according to type.

the arbitration of William, Lord Hastings, in 1481.[80] Subsequently it seems the relationship became more amicable. Four members of the Fitzherbert family were mentioned as feoffees by John Cockayne in c. 1500,[81] and in the 1531 riot at Norbury Sir Thomas Cockayne was on hand to protect Sir Anthony Fitzherbert from the Welles aggressors.

The Cockaynes also had a long-standing association with the Vernon family throughout the fifteenth century, particularly after John (d. 1505) had married Agnes, daughter of Sir Richard Vernon.[82] John Cockayne was frequently on hand to witness Vernon land grants, and the families regularly witnessed deeds together.[83] As will be seen, the Vernons joined the Cockaynes in developing a reputation for being a rather volatile family during the century, yet the two families also nurtured a spiritual bond. In the last decade of the century, Thomas and John Vernon, younger sons of Sir Henry (d. 1515), founded a chantry dedicated to St Mary in the south aisle of Youlgreave church. It was either in or near this chapel that Thomas Cockayne had been buried several years before.[84]

Was Thomas Cockayne a Yorkist? There are some connections. He was one of many local gentry to be retained by William, Lord Hastings, and in 1469 Isabel, the widow of Sir John Cockayne, enfeoffed the duke of Clarence and the earl of Warwick. The family therefore had some connection with the Yorkist hierarchy.[85] As far as the depiction of the Yorkist livery collar on Thomas's effigy is concerned, perhaps the link with his father-in-law, Robert Barley, is more pertinent. As was the case with all the individuals examined here, it is possible that the Cockayne family was emulating a close relative by depicting the same livery collar on Thomas's effigy.

The Frauncys family had several landholdings in the county. In 1431 Isabell Frauncys was assessed at £22 33s., with the manor of Foremark, purchased from the Vernons in 1387, being the family's principal residence.[86] Another branch of the family had resided at Ticknall in Derbyshire since at least the thirteenth century. An alabaster slab commemorating Thomas, Richard and William Fraunceys of Ticknall, who died in the early sixteenth century, was noted in the old chapel at Ticknall in 1710, although the chapel was destroyed in the 1840s to make way for a new church.[87] Another manor, Stanton, was held in moieties by both

---

[80] CCR 1476–85, p. 223.
[81] CIPM Henry VII, ii, no. 832. Also see no. 631, and Jeayes, 90.
[82] Derbyshire Gentry, pp. 67, 132.
[83] Jeayes, 2394, 1394; Derbyshire Gentry, appendix 6; TNA, CP 25/39/47; Stafford, William Salt Library, S. Ms. 459/3.
[84] Cox, Churches of Derbyshire, ii, p. 317.
[85] BL, Harleian MS 1096, fols. 24b–28.
[86] Smith, Derbyshire Landholdings, table 5; appendix, table 2; Tilley, Halls, Manors and Families, iv, p. 65.
[87] Cox, Churches of Derbyshire, iii, pp. 461–2.

branches of the family during the fifteenth century.[88] With their main interests lying in the south-west of the county, the Frauceyses were in close contact with the Fitzherberts, Montgomerys, Bradbournes and Cockaynes, and with Robert Barley in the 1440s.[89] They undertook important administrative duties within Derbyshire and, alongside the Montgomerys, in Staffordshire, particularly in the first half of the century. Though perhaps not as prominent in the county as his father, who was elected to parliament in 1437, Thomas (d. 1482) regularly sat on the quorum from 1458 until his death, and in July 1463 he was chosen as a tax assessor alongside Nicholas Fitzherbert and Robert Barley.[90]

The Frauceys family shared strong kinship ties with the Somersal branch of the Fitzherberts. Robert Frauceys, father of Thomas, married, as his second wife Elizabeth, the widow of John Fitzherbert, shortly before 1460, and in July that year he granted to his Fitzherbert stepson all his land entitlements in Somersal Herbert. In addition, Margaret and Cicely, Robert's daughters from his first marriage to Anne Clinton, married Nicholas and William Fitzherbert (the sons of John of Somersal) respectively. It was through his marriage to Margaret that Nicholas Fitzherbert inherited Tissington.[91] Thomas Frauceys took as his wife Isabel, daughter of Nicholas Montgomery of Cubley. As there was a succession of Montgomery heirs named Nicholas, it is difficult to ascertain who the father of Isabel was. The two most likely candidates are Sir Nicholas (d. 1435), or his son Nicholas (d. 1465).[92]

The Montgomerys were a senior and well-established Derbyshire family. Their ancestor, Roger Montgomery, was a kinsman of William the Conqueror. They held their principal manor of Cubley under the Ferrers from as early as the twelfth century, with additional estates at Snelston, Sudbury, Rodsley and Marston Montgomery.[93] They had close ties with the Fitzherberts, in addition to being their overlords at several of their estates, such as Sudbury.[94] The families also shared a mutual associate in Thomas Powtrell, the prominent Yorkist administrator in the area. Their interests expanded into Staffordshire, where they received extensive lands after 1066.[95] The heads of the family regularly held

---

[88] D. Hillyard, 'Stanton by Bridge: Some Early Incumbents', *DAJ*, 66 (1946), 40–7; DRO, D2375M/53/6.

[89] Every MSS, 3163, 3167, 3271, 3454, 3544; *CCR 1441–47*, pp. 30, 34.

[90] Ayres, 'Parliamentary Representation', pp. 197–201; *CPR 1452–61*, pp. 663–4; *CPR 1467–77*, pp. 248, 408; *CPR 1476–85*, p. 557; *CFR 1461–71*, p. 100.

[91] Swynnerton MSS, ii, p. 226; Jeayes, 2166; Tilley, *Halls, Manors and Families*, iv, p. 65.

[92] *Derbyshire Gentry*, appendix 5b; Mundy MS, pp. 94–94B.

[93] D. and S. Lysons, *Derbyshire*, p. 94; Wiltshire and Woore, *Medieval Parks*, pp. 58, 116, 146, 162, 170.

[94] TNA, C 140/17/20; Jeayes, 2288; *CIPM Henry VII*, ii, no. 628. For links with other local families, see Jeayes, 1874, 2081, 2394, 2398; Yeatman, *Feudal History*, iv, section vii, p. 145.

[95] T. Harwood, *A Survey of Staffordshire: Containing the Antiquities of that County by Sampson Erdeswick, Esq.* (Westminster, 1820), p. 1.

the shrievalty in both Derbyshire and Staffordshire, and served as knights of the shire during the first two decades of the century.[96] Sir Nicholas and his son John sat on the county bench and various other commissions in Staffordshire and Derbyshire from the 1480s to 1510.[97] Sir Nicholas (d. 1494) continued a family tradition of royal service by being named an esquire of the body to the Yorkist kings. It is possible that he was one of the very few Derbyshire gentry who fought for Richard III at Bosworth, although if this was the case he quickly found favour with Henry Tudor, confirmed by his knighthood at the inauguration of the prince of Wales in 1489.[98]

The Montgomerys end the examination of those whose monuments feature Yorkist livery collars. It is now time to investigate those depicted wearing the Lancastrian or, to be more precise, Tudor livery collar of SS. Here we have a smaller group, again with discernible links, although this is not to say they were not associated with the families considered above. Were they 'Lancastrians'? Some certainly became trusted servants of Henry Tudor, while others were perhaps reflecting on their family's past service to the house of Lancaster when they contemplated the design of their tombs.

The Poles inherited Radbourne manor through the marriage of Peter, Ralph's (d. 1492) grandfather, to Elizabeth, niece and heiress of Sir John Chandos (d. 1370). The family also gained a moiety of the manor and advowson of the church at Mugginton through the Chandos inheritance, thus connecting them with the Knivetons.[99] With several generations of the family providing lawyers during the fifteenth century, it was natural that their skills were utilised in the county and also by the duchy of Lancaster. Peter (d. c. 1444) followed his father into the legal profession and entered the duchy council in 1402. He was also closely involved in the administration of the county, and performed duties as an attorney. His son Ralph (d. c. 1460) continued the tradition; named chief justice at Lancaster in 1456, he later became a justice of the King's Bench.[100] Alongside John Curzon, Ralph carried out the majority of the work on the county bench until 1460, and made regular appearances on commissions.[101] Despite being appointed sheriff in 1476, his son Ralph (d. 1492) is conspicuously absent from the records. He failed to sit on the county bench (he may not have been a trained lawyer) and

---

[96] *List of Sheriffs*, pp. 102–6; J.C. Wedgwood, *Collections for a History of Staffordshire* (1912), pp. 272–94; Ayres, 'Parliamentary Representation', pp. 91–100; 114–22.
[97] *Derbyshire Gentry*, appendix 9a; CPR 1476–85, pp. 393, 396, 401, 491, 573; CPR 1485–94, pp. 178, 318, 354.
[98] W.A. Shaw, *The Knights of England*, 2 vols (London, 1916), i, pp. 16, 140, 143.
[99] I.H. Jeayes, *Descriptive Catalogue of the Charters and Muniments in the Possession of Reginald Walkelyne Chandos-Pole Esq.*, at Radbourne Hall (London, 1896), p. xv; Mundy MS, v, pp. 215–232A; Jeayes, *Radbourne Hall*, 470.
[100] Somerville, *History of the Duchy*, i, pp. 453, 451, 469.
[101] CPR 1452–61, pp. 107, 153, 300–6, 557, 564, 663.

was not named on any of the Derbyshire commissions. Ralph's kinsman, John Pole of Hartington, enjoyed the favour of Edward IV for a brief period, and was knighted in the late 1460s. His privileged position did not last, however. In 1478 he was forced to sell his manors of Hartington and Sheen, perhaps because of his involvement in the Readeption of Henry VI in 1470. His reputation was hardly helped when he was accused of acting as an accessory to the murder of John Meycok in the early 1470s. In addition, Ralph of Radbourne was sued by Sir John Gresley and Sir William Trussell (both in Yorkist favour at the time) for forcible entry into land at Rugeley (Staffordshire).[102]

The Poles were close companions of the Curzons of Kedleston throughout much of the century. In the 1430s Ralph Pole and John Curzon formed part of Henry, Lord Grey's retinue in the region, and both entered Humphrey Stafford's affinity on Grey's death.[103] Both individuals can regularly be found co-witnessing charters, and their heirs were still working together, alongside Nicholas Kniveton, into the 1490s.[104] In June 1453 Pole and Curzon were granted the manor of King's Newton in Derbyshire by the king, and before his death in 1492 Ralph had enfeoffed John Curzon in the manor of Radbourne to the use of his will. In return, Richard Curzon enfeoffed Kedleston manor to the Poles and the Knivetons before he died in 1496.[105] The relationship between the two families continued into the sixteenth century, when German Pole was granted the wardship and marriage of Richard Curzon in 1517.[106] It is to the Curzon family that we now turn our attention.

By the fifteenth century the Curzons' connection with Derbyshire spanned several hundred years. Their main residence, Kedleston, came into their hands during the reign of Henry I, and had been part of the Ferrers' vast estates in the region. Their other manors included Weston Underwood and Wingerworth, and another branch of the family made their residence at Croxall.[107] They were a prestigious family with a proud history of service to the house of Lancaster. John's grandfather (another John, d. 1405) was one of Henry IV's esquires of the body, and a member of his privy council. The family's importance in the county continued under his son, who served as sheriff, was knight of the shire on several occasions, and frequently sat on the county bench.[108] His son John (d. c. 1492) also served as sheriff on two occasions, in 1472 and 1486, and sat on various

---

[102] *Derbyshire Gentry*, pp. 10, 24; CCR 1468–76, p. 144; 1476–85, p. 139; Wrottesley, 'Plea Rolls, 34 Henry VI to 14 Edward IV', 174, 190.
[103] Compton Reeves, 'Military Indentures', 83–4.
[104] Every MSS, 3163, 3235, 3244, 3519; Jeayes, *Radbourne Hall*, 572, 575, 615, 660, 666, 667; Derbyshire Deeds, 2082.
[105] CPR 1452–61, p. 82; CIPM Henry VII, i, no. 776; CIPM Henry VII, iii, no. 1040.
[106] Jeayes, *Radbourne Hall*, 714.
[107] Smith, *Derbyshire Landholdings*, p. 11.
[108] Ayres, 'Parliamentary Representation', pp. 12, 170–8; *Derbyshire Gentry*, appendix 9a.

commissions within the county, and either he or his father was appointed to the Lancastrian commission of array against the Yorkists in December 1459. He sat on the county bench from 1475 until his death in c. 1492.[109]

The Curzons were also associated with the Knivetons. Margaret, the sister of John (d. c. 1459), married, as her second husband, Thomas, head of the Kniveton family, before 1443. Though the evidence for the association between these two families is not as copious as that with the Poles, they co-witnessed several land transactions and acted as feoffees together from the date of the marriage.[110]

The Mercaston branch of the Kniveton family to which Nicholas (d. 1500) belonged made the manor their main residence during the mid-fourteenth century, with the senior branch continuing to live at Bradley. The family also held land at Kniveton, where they were neighbours of the Cockaynes.[111] It was either Nicholas or his father, also Nicholas (d. c. 1494), who made extensive additions to the church at Mugginton, including the upper portion of the tower and the south aisle chapel, in which they were buried. In addition, Nicholas installed the east window in the chapel which once contained the figures of him and his wife, and an inscription asking the onlooker to pray for their souls.[112] The shields on Nicholas's tomb reflected their family alliances. On the south side of the tomb chest was a shield depicting the arms of Kniveton impaling Curzon: it will be recalled that Thomas Kniveton (Nicholas's grandfather) had married Margaret Curzon in the 1440s. On the tomb slab is a shield featuring the arms of Kniveton impaling those of Montgomery: John, son and heir of Nicholas, married Joan, daughter of Sir Nicholas Montgomery of Cubley. The family shared in the patronage of the church at Mugginton with the Poles of Radbourne, after the latter inherited a moiety of the advowson early in the fifteenth century.[113]

It is difficult to distinguish between Nicholas (d. 1500) and his father, also Nicholas (d. c. 1494). This is compounded by the fact that their dates of death were so close. Occasionally, we are helped by the records identifying the son as Nicholas 'the younger'. We can therefore be certain that it was he who served as sheriff of Nottinghamshire and Derbyshire in 1493. Equally, it was his father who served in the same capacity in 1489, and this was probably his final role in local government. It was probably also the father who served as sheriff in 1466. It is therefore safe to assume that it was his son who sat on the county bench from the mid – to late 1490s.[114] It is clear that the Knivetons were held in reasonably high esteem by the Yorkists: in May 1483 it was probably the son who was appointed

---

[109] *List of Sheriffs*, pp. 102–6; *CPR 1452–61*, pp. 408, 588; I. Rowney, 'The Curzons of Fifteenth-Century Derbyshire', *DAJ*, 103 (1983), 111.
[110] Rowney, 'The Curzons', 108; Jeayes, *Radbourne Hall*, 568, 587, 589, 663.
[111] Glover and Riden (eds), *Woolley's History of Derbyshire*, p. 210.
[112] Mundy MS, v, p. 216.
[113] Cox, *Churches of Derbyshire*, iii, pp. 219–20, 215.
[114] *List of Sheriffs*, pp. 102–6; *Derbyshire Gentry*, appendix 9a.

bailiff of Chesterfield and Scarsdale.[115] It was, however, in the service of Henry Tudor that he thrived. Now an esquire for the body, he was created steward of Tickhill in 1488 for life and was named parker of Shottle in 1492; he and his father had been parkers of Ravensdale since 1485. He was also awarded the stewardship of Scarborough in September of the same year.[116] The representation of the portcullis as a pendant to his SS collar suggests that he owed his rewards to the patronage of Margaret Beaufort, mother of Henry VII.

Three other individuals merit discussion: Sir Henry Vernon (d. 1515), Sir Henry Pierrepont (d. 1499), and Sir John Savage IV (d. 1495). Although they were not buried in Derbyshire, they had strong associations with the county gentry and their effigies also feature a livery collar. As may have been the case with the individuals examined above, the decision to depict a collar on their memorial was motivated by their connections with other collared individuals with whom they were closely related or affiliated.

The Vernons were the only Derbyshire family who could be labelled Lancastrians in our period. Sir Henry's father, Sir William (d. 1467), who was at one time treasurer of Calais and constable of England, saw his role in Derbyshire politics lessen with the accession of the Yorkists in 1461,[117] and proceeded to involve himself in various troubles in the county, either directly or indirectly, until his death.[118] Interestingly, Sir William's memorial brass at Tong, perhaps prudently, does not feature a livery collar. The Vernons' fortunes improved somewhat during the 1470s, with Sir William's son Henry sitting on the Derbyshire peace commissions, and serving as MP in 1478.[119] Henry was also made an esquire of the body for Edward IV, and regranted some of the High Peak offices which had been taken away from his family. He refused, however, to answer the calls for support from the duke of Clarence, Edward IV and Richard III when requested.[120] Before Bosworth in 1485, Richard sternly wrote to him asking for men, 'uppon payne of forfaicture unto us of all that ye may forfaict and loose'. In fact, Vernon probably joined his brother-in-law, Sir Gilbert Talbot, and fought against Richard at Bosworth. It was in the service of Arthur, prince of Wales, that he excelled from the 1490s. He was named comptroller of his household in April 1492, and from 1494 acted as governor to the prince. He was also dubbed a knight of the Bath at the creation of Arthur as prince of Wales in 1489, and created steward of the High Peak in 1507.[121] With their main residence being Haddon

---

[115] *CPR 1476–85*, p. 351; *Harleian 433*, i, p. 36.
[116] TNA, DL 42/21, fols. 67v, 98, 99v; *CPR 1485–94*, pp. 6, 252.
[117] *Derbyshire Gentry*, p. 139.
[118] *CPR 1461–67*, pp. 31, 135, 304; Wrottesley, 'Plea Rolls, 34 Henry VI to 14 Edward IV', 110–11; Wrottesley, 'Plea Rolls, Edward IV, Edward V and Richard III', 150–1.
[119] *Derbyshire Gentry*, p. 116; appendix 10; *CPR 1476–85*, pp. 395, 400.
[120] Historical Manuscripts Commission, *Rutland*, iv, p. 188.
[121] H. Kirke, 'Sir Henry Vernon of Haddon', *DAJ*, 42 (1920), 9–11, 13–15.

Hall, Henry's family was closely involved with the Derbyshire gentry; indeed they were related to several of the families including the Bradbournes and the Cockaynes, a family with whom they shared a close affinity.[122] However, the Vernons' interests increasingly lay beyond the county boundaries and were focused on a higher social milieu, particularly after Henry entered the Tudor court. This is confirmed by his marriage into the Talbot family, and his decision to be buried alongside his ancestors at the family mausoleum at Tong, where both his grandfather, Sir Richard (d. 1451), and his son Richard (d. 1517) wear a collar of SS on their effigies. There are stylistic similarities between the effigies of Vernon and his grandfather-in-law John Talbot, first earl of Shrewsbury (d. 1453), whose freestone tomb was erected at St Alkmund's in Whitchurch (Shropshire).[123]

Sir Henry's will provides us with another mention of a collar. Although he does not state whether it was a livery collar, this was probably the case, as many testators refer to 'chains' in their wills, possibly to distinguish them from livery collars.[124] Among his bequests Henry states, 'I wyll my eldest son have my Coler of gold'.[125] As was the case with Anne Kniveton, here a livery collar was deemed worthy of being bequeathed to a loved one. It was clearly an expensive item. Made of gold, this was a prestigious example, awarded to the king's most trustworthy associates. Perhaps this was the SS collar worn by Henry on his effigy, no doubt awarded in connection to his service to Prince Arthur.

Sir Henry Pierrepont was a Yorkist supporter, fighting for Edward IV at Tewskesbury and being knighted after the battle. Though his principal estates lay in Nottinghamshire, Pierrepont had significant interests in the north of Derbyshire, particularly around Chesterfield. He regularly witnessed charters with a group of gentry from the area, including the Frechevilles, Bullocks, Foljambes and Barleys. It was with the Barleys that Henry was most involved, as for several decades in the middle of the century their names appear together in land transactions. Robert Barley (d. 1467) and Pierrepont were also both members of the guild of the Holy Cross in All Saints' Church, Chesterfield.[126]

It was for the Yorkist regime that Sir Henry was most active, serving in various local offices in Nottinghamshire, although he evidently reconciled himself to Henry Tudor as he sat on the county bench until 1493. For much of his life he

---

[122] Jeayes, 2394, 2398; William Salt Library, S. Ms. 459/3.

[123] H. Gilderdale Scott, '"This Little Westminster": The Chantry-Chapel of Sir Henry Vernon at Tong, Shropshire', *Journal of the British Archaeological Association*, 158 (2005), 46–81.

[124] See, for example, the 1489 will of Sir Henry Pierrepont, who left his 'old cheyne' to his nephew and heir: University of York, Borthwick Institute for Archives, Archbishops Register, 23, fol. 370v.

[125] D.G. Edwards (ed.), *Derbyshire Wills Proved in the Prerogative Court of Canterbury 1393–1574*, Derbyshire Record Society, 26 (Chesterfield, 1998), pp. 44–50.

[126] Jeayes, 2475, 2521, 2564; P. Riden and J. Blair (eds), *Records of the Borough of Chesterfield and Related Documents 1204–1835* (Chesterfield, 1980), pp. 176–7; Jeayes, 2317.

sought to revive his family's fortunes, fighting to win back several manors which Ralph, Lord Cromwell, had claimed during the 1440s. It appears that towards the end of his life Sir Henry was a rather isolated figure. He died childless; it appears that his wife had predeceased him and his will makes no mention of other local gentry. The Yorkist collar on Henry's effigy is a rarity in the county. It seems that he could not entirely distance himself from his past Yorkist sympathies. This is one example of a handful of tombs erected after the Tudor accession to the throne in 1485 which depict a livery collar expressing allegiance to the previous regime. His will, dated 23 October 1489, states that his executors were to erect a suitable monument at Holme Pierrepont, 'if I make it not in my life days'.[127] It is clear from the wording that the tomb had not yet been constructed.

Despite the family settling in Cheshire, the Savages had land interests in Derbyshire, including the manor of Stainsby with which they were associated since the thirteenth century. During the late fifteenth century they were steadily building up their interests in the county, for example at Pinxton. The family were Derbyshire gentry, with close links with the Fitzherbert family in particular. Both Ralph and Elizabeth Fitzherbert bequeathed items of clothing to John Savage (probably the father) in their wills.[128]

A homogenous group

Not surprisingly, there were links between those individuals who are depicted wearing a Yorkist collar, and those wearing the Lancastrian collar on their monuments. This can be seen in several marriages between 'Yorkist' and 'Lancastrian' families, such as those between John Pole of Radbourne (Ralph's son and heir) and Jane, daughter of John Fitzherbert of Etwall, in 1473, and John Kniveton (son and heir of Nicholas, d. 1500) and Margery, daughter of Sir Nicholas Montgomery, early in the sixteenth century. Further links can be identified through land transactions, with members of the Curzon and Vernon families witnessing deeds with the Fitzherberts, among others.[129] The Bradbourne chantry foundation at Ashbourne is a further example of families from the south-west of the county acting together, some of whom put aside past differences. Anne Kniveton (John Bradbourne's widow), Henry Vernon, Nicholas Montgomery, John Cockayne, John Fitzherbert, and several members of the Kniveton family (chiefly from the Bradley branch into which Anne had married) obtained a licence in May 1485 to found a perpetual chantry for two priests at St Oswald's altar in Ashbourne church, to pray for the souls of the king, the Bradbournes and their close

---

[127] See below, p. 143.
[128] D. and S. Lysons, *Derbyshire*, p. cxlv; Derby Local Studies Library, Brookhill Hall Collection, Calendar of Deeds, 16962, 16963, 16964; SRO, D641/5/T(S)/4/1; D641/5/T(S)/4/2.
[129] Jeayes, *Radbourne Hall*, 638; Mundy MS, v, p. 216B; Jeayes, 1596, 1597, 1600.

associates. A similar chantry was established in the chapel of St Mary at Heage, which had recently been erected by the Bradbournes. In 1500 the same individuals were mentioned in Anne's will, in which lands were enfeoffed for the chantry. Anne left bequests to the Fitzherberts and John Cockayne, and named her son Humphrey Bradbourne, Roger Vernon, and John Fitzherbert of Norbury among her executors.[130]

With these examples in mind, and whilst still acknowledging the influence of the closer family ties between the individuals investigated above, it is also appropriate to take a broader perspective and see the two groups of Yorkist and Lancastrian collar wearers as a whole, linked through a mutual pride in royal service, whether it was under the Lancastrians or the Yorkists. The appearance of a livery collar on a monument was a distinguishing mark of honour which created a distinct gentry group within the county, a livery collar 'club', as it were. When looking for wider ties which brought all the individuals together, the duchy of Lancaster's honour of Tutbury is an appropriate place to begin.

The Tutbury honour

In the great east window of Ashbourne church are featured coats of arms of families who held land within the honour of Tutbury during the fourteenth and fifteenth centuries. In 1611 a total of sixty-one coats of arms were recorded. Of the remaining arms, the majority are still in the east window, with the rest now in the clerestory windows of the north transept. The glass, most of which dates from the 1390s, included the arms of the duchy of Lancaster, John of Gaunt as duke of Lancaster, and other familiar families including Montgomery, Bradbourne, Curzon, Pole, Fraunceys, Cockayne and Fitzherbert of Norbury.[131] The heraldic arms in the stained glass remain a vivid testament to the pride of these local families in their long-standing association with the duchy.

The Tutbury honour formed part of the vast earldom of Lancaster and became the largest receipt in the duchy. It was formed from the Ferrers estates in the region, which were confiscated by the crown in 1269, and the castle at Tutbury was at the heart of an estate which covered much of east Staffordshire and south-west Derbyshire, although the majority of its lands lay in the latter county. Including the chases of Needwood and Duffield Frith, Tutbury honour dominated south-west Derbyshire, with High Peak being another duchy influence further north. The duchy was the largest landholder in the county.[132] John

---

[130] *CPR 1476–85*, pp. 524–5; *Harleian 433*, i, p. 277; LRO, B/A/1/13, fols. 245v–248v.
[131] F. Jourdain, 'The Heraldic Stained Glass in Ashbourne Church, Derbyshire', *DAJ*, 3 (1881), 90–4.
[132] J.R. Birrell, 'The Honour of Tutbury in the Fourteenth and Fifteenth Centuries', University of Birmingham, unpublished MA thesis (1962), pp. 1–2; N.J. Tringham, 'Honour of Tutbury', in *The Victoria County History of the County of Stafford*, 14 vols (1908–2013), x, pp. 9–20.

of Gaunt, duke of Lancaster, and his wife Blanche held Tutbury close to their hearts; they made extensive alterations to the castle, and Gaunt regularly used its hunting chases. With the coronation of Henry IV in 1399 the Lancastrian estates, including Tutbury honour, merged with the crown. Henry would nurture a close association with the Derbyshire gentry. In 1399 his retinue included members of the Cockayne, Montgomery, Bothe, Curzon, Bradbourne and Fraunceys families.[133]

Given the significant presence of the honour in the county, it is not surprising that the Derbyshire gentry were heavily involved with the duchy. Many of the families we have been considering were duchy tenants;[134] they also held duchy offices. From the steward, constable and receiver of the honour, to the local bailiffs, reeves, forest officials and keepers of fees and franchises, there was an abundance of offices to be filled by the local gentry, and many of the families served the honour:[135] the Poles, Curzons and Montgomerys held the major offices of steward and constable of Tutbury Castle; the Cockaynes were granted the stewardship of Ashbourne; and the Barleys, Bradbournes and Knivetons enjoyed a hereditary right to the office of foresters of fee in Peak forest and Duffield Frith. Several families were also employed as keepers of the duchy parks. Deer caught in the forests were often given to favourites such as the Poles, and pasture would be leased off to trustworthy duchy servants.[136] Many had been associated with duchy service since the fourteenth century; the gentry connection with the duchy was intimate and long-standing.

Under Henry V, Lancastrian allegiance within the duchy became subservient to crown allegiance as the king sought to bring the affinity under his authority as king, rather than as duke of Lancaster. After the weak royal leadership of Henry VI, Edward IV continued the trend, and under the control of royal favourites such as William, Lord Hastings, a direct link to the Yorkist crown was forged. Under Edward, the duchy lands were no longer treated as the private possession they had been by Henry IV, but were held under the crown. Particularly from the 1470s, a stronger royal presence in the area developed, with the king showing a particular interest in the duchy affinity. He gathered the local gentry together at Burton Abbey in March 1474, appointed Hastings as steward, and made Nicholas Montgomery his deputy.[137] Edward reorganised the duchy administration, with Thomas Tremayl, the attorney general, spending over a month in the area

---

[133] Castor, *The King, The Crown, and the Duchy*, p. 202.
[134] Yeatman, *Feudal History*, ii, section ii, pp. 489–90; S. Shaw, *The History and Antiquities of Staffordshire*, 2 vols (London, 1798–1801), i, p. 43.
[135] I.S.W. Blanchard, *The Duchy of Lancaster's Estates in Derbyshire 1485–1540*, Derbyshire Archaeological Society Record Series, 3 (1971, for 1967), pp. 16–19.
[136] Somerville, *History of the Duchy*, i, pp. 381–3, 539–57; Birrell, 'Honour of Tutbury', pp. 110–22; J.C. Cox, 'Forestry', in *VCH Derbys.*, i, pp. 397–426.
[137] *Derbyshire Gentry*, p. 88.

identifying improvements and drawing up a new rental in the High Peak.[138] Edward also ordered extensive repairs to property. In the late 1470s £75 was spent on restocking the deer and rebuilding the hunting lodges in Needwood Forest and Duffield Frith.[139] Though the larger duchy affinity in the area was beginning to break down from the 1430s, the gentry of south-west Derbyshire, regardless of their inevitable disagreements, would continue to serve the duchy. Their loyalty was directed towards the honour rather than any particular steward, and through the honour to the crown.[140] Perhaps some of the Yorkist collars shown on the monuments of the local gentry from 1465 onwards can be regarded as an assertion of their continuing duchy connections. The honour of Tutbury was effectively brought under crown control, with the crown being in the hands of the Yorkists, with a brief interlude, from 1461 to 1485. The livery collar thus represented the enhanced importance of those gentry associated with the duchy.

Although the principal local duchy appointments increasingly went to court favourites such as Hastings and Walter Blount, Lord Mountjoy, the gentry of south-west Derbyshire continued to work for the duchy, with some families developing a more prominent connection than previously. When Nicholas Montgomery was created deputy steward of Tutbury in 1474, the family's traditional association with the duchy was renewed.[141] The Bradbournes continued their involvement with Duffield Frith: John was a forester of Hulland Ward in 1472, and his family were parkers of Mansell into the 1490s.[142] Sir John Savage (d. 1495) was created steward at Halton in 1465, and another family to benefit from the Yorkist accession was the Fitzherberts, with Nicholas, Ralph and John working for the duchy as bailiffs and feodaries from the 1460s. Their kinsman, William Bothe, also worked his way up the duchy hierarchy, being named deputy constable of Melbourne in 1495.[143] In a 1482 list of the offices and fees of the Tutbury honour, John Fitzherbert was named as parker of Mansell, John Fraunceys and John Curzon as parkers of Postern, and Nicholas and Walter Fitzherbert of Somersal as parkers of Colebrook Ward in Duffield Frith.[144] With the Tudors securely on the throne, the Vernon family were finally regranted their major duchy offices in the county, with Sir Henry appointed as High Peak steward for life in 1507. Other individuals to benefit from Henry VII's favour included Sir John Savage

---

[138] Somerville, *History of the Duchy*, i, pp. 250–1.
[139] I.S.W. Blanchard, 'Economic Change in Derbyshire in the late Middle Ages, 1272–1540', University of London, unpublished PhD thesis (1967), p. 78; Birrell, 'Honour of Tutbury', pp. 119, 237.
[140] Horrox, *Richard III*, pp. 46, 212; I. Rowney, 'The Hastings Affinity in Staffordshire and the Honour of Tutbury', *Historical Research*, 57 (1984), 42, 45; *Derbyshire Gentry*, p. 92.
[141] Somerville, *History of the Duchy*, i, pp. 540–1.
[142] Cox, 'Forestry', p. 418. The family held land in severalty in Duffield: TNA, DL 29/375/6229; Blanchard, *Estates in Derbyshire*, p. 96.
[143] Somerville, *History of the Duchy*, i, pp. 511, 547–9, 557; *Harleian 433*, i, p. 110.
[144] *Harleian 433*, iii, pp. 199–203.

(d. 1492), awarded many offices including High Peak steward for his loyalty at Bosworth, and Nicholas Kniveton (d. 1500), made Tickhill steward in 1488.[145]

Another aspect of duchy patronage favoured by Edward IV was leasing duchy lands and rights. Used as a form of reward for trusted servants, leasing 'implicitly carried with it a delegation of royal power',[146] and a degree of honour was bestowed on the lessee. Alongside leases, another area from which the gentry benefited was the lead trade. Derbyshire was a major exporter of lead to Europe in the later Middle Ages, with the mines at Wirksworth and High Peak forming part of the estates of the duchy, which claimed the mineral duties of lot and cope. The duties were farmed out to favoured individuals from the middle of the fifteenth century, and families including the Foljambes, Vernons and the Fitzherberts competed to obtain the leases.[147] A lease of the Wirksworth mines was made to John and Robert Fitzherbert in 1461 for ten years, followed by John and Ralph Fitzherbert, with John Fitzherbert and John Savage the lessees from 1486 to 1491.[148] The relatively small number of families who were involved in duchy service constituted a close-knit group, and included the Fitzherberts, the Montgomerys and the Agards of Foston, who filled many duchy offices throughout the century. In his will of 1516, John Agard remembered his past duchy lords and colleagues, asking for prayers for the duke of Clarence, William, Lord Hastings, and Walter Blount, Lord Mountjoy. John and Anthony Fitzherbert also got a mention, and were named as witnesses.[149]

It is not implausible to suggest that King Edward, on his visit to Burton Abbey in 1474, distributed some of the livery collars which were then depicted on local monuments. Equally, after 1485 the SS collars seen on the Curzon, Pole, Kniveton and Vernon monuments may also be partly explained as an assertion of their duchy service, the duchy now being under the control of the new Tudor regime. The dynastic, or political, significance of the livery collars to the Derbyshire group should therefore not be over emphasised. Other, more localised, considerations were apparently more applicable to some of these individuals and their families.

William, Lord Hastings

King Edward's leading magnate was a prominent figure in Tutbury. When Hastings began to build up his retinue in the early 1470s, it was to the pre-existing duchy affinity that he turned. The affinity of the duke of Clarence, lord of Tutbury

---

[145] Somerville, *History of the Duchy*, i, pp. 551–2; TNA, DL 29/22/389; Somerville, *History of the Duchy*, i, pp. 528–9, 550–1.
[146] *Derbyshire Gentry*, p. 89.
[147] J.H. Lander, 'Lead Mining', in *VCH Derbys.*, ii, pp. 323–48.
[148] TNA, DL 42/20, fol. 85v; DL 37/54, mem. 2r. See DL 29/403/6468–76, DL 29/184/2932–39.
[149] *Derbyshire Gentry*, pp. 89–92; Somerville, *History of the Duchy*, i, pp. 543, 547; LRO, B/C/10ii/1.

between 1464 and 1473, also comprised members of the duchy affinity. Although less is known about specific individuals retained in Derbyshire, we can be fairly certain that John Curzon and Henry Vernon were his men.[150] Hastings retained at least ninety individuals during the period 1461–83, with thirty-two coming from Derbyshire, making it the county from which the largest percentage was drawn. Of the individuals and families discussed above, the following were retained by Hastings (in chronological order): Nicholas Kniveton, Ralph Fitzherbert, Ralph Pole, Thomas Cockayne, Humphrey Bradbourne, son and heir of John (d. 1488), Henry Vernon and Nicholas Montgomery. In addition, Hastings retained Thomas and John Curzon of Croxall, eschewing the Kedleston branch of the family. Although the families of Bothe and Fraunceys appear not to have been retained, they were probably in favour with Hastings, as evidenced by their regular appearance on the county bench.[151]

Much has been written on the Hastings affinity.[152] What is important here is the fact that a significant proportion of our collared individuals joined his affinity. He may have acted as a focus for the duchy affinity, which had begun to lose its connection to the crown under Henry VI. King Edward had a significant influence in the creation of the Hastings affinity and the restructuring of the honour's administration.[153] The crown link can hardly have been lost on the Derbyshire gentry. The loyalty of the affinity towards Hastings himself has been questioned, although it has been argued more recently that he successfully re-established stability in the Tutbury honour after a period in which the old affinity had begun to break down.[154] But the emphasis should perhaps be placed on Hastings's link with the Tutbury honour. The core of his affinity lay in the honour; indeed, the majority of his retainers were from those Derbyshire and Staffordshire families connected with the duchy. On Hastings's death in 1483, it is perhaps not surprising that Simon Stallworth, when writing to Sir William Stonor, stated: 'All the lord Chamberleyne mene be come my lordys of Bokynghame menne.'[155] Henry Stafford, duke of Buckingham, was created Tutbury steward soon after Hastings's demise.

When considering the abundance of extant Yorkist collars on Derbyshire monuments, it is tempting to speculate that this may be due to the prevalence of

---

[150] Hicks, *Clarence*, pp. 166–73.
[151] Dunham, appendix A; appendix B; *Derbyshire Gentry*, p. 107.
[152] Dunham; Rowney, 'The Hastings Affinity', 35–45; T. Westervelt, 'The Changing Nature of Politics in the Localities in the Later Fifteenth Century: William Lord Hastings and His Indentured Retainers', *Midland History*, 26 (2001), 96–106.
[153] Rowney, 'The Hastings Affinity', 35–45; Walker, *Lancastrian Affinity*, p. 254; *Derbyshire Gentry*, p. 88.
[154] Westervelt, 'Changing Nature of Politics', 99–102.
[155] C. Carpenter (ed.), *Kingsford's Stonor Letters and Papers 1290–1483* (Cambridge, 1996), pp. 160–1.

Hastings's retainers in the area. However, they are collars which predominantly depict the lion (or, in one case, boar) pendant, not a Hastings badge. Nor indeed do they depict the bull badge of the duke of Clarence. Although a proportion of those retained by Hastings do feature a Yorkist collar on their effigies, the emphasis appears to be on their association with the crown, in this case Edward IV and Richard III, rather than a magnate.

Evidence of absence: monuments which have no collar

Not unexpectedly, there are examples of monuments in the county from this period which do not have a collar. Did these individuals share the same close ties as those whose memorials do feature a collar? The first thing to note is that the majority of the families came from the north of the county. Though this does not preclude them from having a collar on their monuments (see Robert Barley), it places them further away geographically from the main cluster of collared individuals, whose land interests lay in the south of the county.

One family who eschewed livery collars on their monuments were the Stathums, whose mausoleum is at Morley. In the church can be found memorial brasses commemorating John Stathum (d. 1454) and his wife Cecily Cornwall, Sir Thomas Stathum (d. 1469) and his wives Elizabeth, daughter of Robert Langley, and Thomasine, daughter of John Curzon. Henry (d. 1480), brother and heir to Sir Thomas, is also represented in a brass, alongside his three wives: Anne, daughter of Thomas Bothe of Dunham Massey (Cheshire), Elizabeth, daughter of Giles St Lowe and Margaret, daughter of John Stanhope.[156] The Stathums quickly built up their prominence in the county after inheriting Morley in the fourteenth century. Henry served as sheriff in 1474, and in 1466 Sir Thomas became another of the Derbyshire gentry retained by Hastings.[157] Both brothers served infrequently on the county bench during the 1460s. The male line ended with the death of Henry in 1485, when the Sacheverell family acquired the manor of Morley through the marriage of John Sacheverell (d. 1485) to Henry's daughter and heir, Joan Stathum.

The only link with collared individuals is the marriage between Sir Thomas Stathum and Thomasine, a daughter of John Curzon (d. c. 1459). In addition, Henry married as his first wife Anne Bothe, who was a member of the Dunham Massey branch of the family. The Bothes of Sawley originated from this line, although Anne was not from the Derbyshire branch. A limited involvement with other Derbyshire gentry referred to in this chapter may be the reason why none of the families are mentioned in Sir Thomas Stathum's detailed will of 1469. His

---

[156] W. Lack, H.M. Stuchfield, and P. Whittemore, *The Monumental Brasses of Derbyshire* (London, 1999), pp. 146–51.
[157] *Derbyshire Gentry*, appendix 9a; appendix 10; Dunham, appendix A; appendix B.

executors are his wife and two brothers, Henry and Nicholas, and Henry Killingworth, abbot of Darley, is named supervisor.[158] There may be an explanation as to why three generations of the Stathum family are depicted without livery collars on their church monuments. The memorials have been interpreted as a coherent group. All are figure brasses, and all share a similar composition. It appears those members of the family who commissioned the memorials were following the pattern set by John (d. 1454), with the repetition of the Morley family arms (*argent, a lion rampant double queued sable crowned or*) stressing the continuity of lordship.[159] In his will, Sir Thomas was explicit in his instructions for the composition of his brass, adopting a pattern that followed his father's memorial, which was subsequently copied by his brother Henry. Perhaps the absence of collars on any of these memorials is not entirely a coincidence. It is possible that the family made a choice not to include depictions of them on their monuments. The will of Sir Thomas is evidence that the family closely involved themselves in the composition of their memorials. In addition, it should be noted that in 1466 Sir Thomas was indicted for illegally distributing his own livery to several Derbyshire individuals.[160] Perhaps the whole issue of depicting livery of any kind on his brass was therefore thought best avoided. Other individuals from the county whose monuments do not depict a livery collar include:

> Richard Barley (d. c. 1491), St John the Baptist's, Dronfield
> Richard Curzon (d. 1496), All Saints', Kedleston
> Eyre family brasses (Robert I, d. 1459; Robert II, d. c. 1500 and Ralph, son of Robert I), St Michael's and All Angels', Hathersage
> John Foljambe (d. 1499), St Mary's, Sutton Scarsdale
> Peter Frecheville (d. c. 1504), St John the Baptist's, Staveley (head and shoulders missing)
> Robert Lytton (d. 1483), St John the Baptist's, Tideswell
> Sir Sampson Meverell (d. 1462), St John the Baptist's, Tideswell
> John Rolleston (d. 1482), St James's, Swarkestone

The salient observation to make is that, although some may have held the local offices one would expect of families of gentry status, the majority of the individuals with no collar on their monuments do not appear to have shared the close kinship ties which have been identified among the collared individuals. Indeed, with reference to the Stathum family, it may be possible that they chose to avoid depicting the livery collar on a succession of their memorials. In addition, the

---

[158] TNA, PROB 11/6, fol. 1.
[159] J. Denton, 'Genealogy and Gentility: Social Status in Provincial England', in R. Radulescu and E.D. Kennedy (eds), *Broken Lines: Genealogical Literature in Late-Medieval Britain and France* (Turnhout, 2009), pp. 143–58.
[160] TNA, KB 29/77, fol. 29r.

individuals did not appear to have had close ties with the Tutbury honour: none of the families had their arms depicted in the east window at Ashbourne church.

The monuments

Derbyshire has an abundance of alabaster tombs and effigies. The principal alabaster quarries during the medieval period were located in Staffordshire and Derbyshire. In Derbyshire the gypsum ridge can be found along the whole of the Trent valley, but is most easily worked at Chellaston, where it lies near the surface. Chellaston lies approximately ten miles east of Tutbury, and lay within the honour. Records show that alabaster was being quarried there from at least 1374.[161] Indeed, the Chellaston workshop of Thomas Prentys and Robert Sutton was one of the most important and well documented in the first half of the fifteenth century, when they were contracted to produce effigies for such prestigious families as the Montagu earls of Salisbury.[162] It appears that Nottingham was also home to a number of alabastermen, particularly after the 1470s. In 1496 it was a Nottingham craftsman, Walter Hylton, who was contracted to make the tomb for Richard III.[163] Jane Crease has recently identified at least one Yorkshire workshop contemporary to the Prentys and Sutton enterprise at Chellaston.[164] Although it is not certain that these workshops were based in York itself, there is evidence to suggest that alabaster was being worked in the city by the second half of the fifteenth century, as several alabasterers are mentioned in the Freemens' rolls from 1456.[165] Later in the century the alabaster trade moved to Burton-upon-Trent; a 1508 contract with Burton alabastermen Henry Harpur and William Moorecock can be linked to the Montgomery tomb at Cubley.[166] The monuments at Norbury, Radbourne, Kedleston, Repton, Youlgreave and Ashbourne are fine examples of alabaster workmanship.[167]

---

[161] R. Lethbridge Farmer, 'Chellaston Alabaster', *DAJ*, 38 (1916), 135; F. Cheetham, *Alabaster Images of Medieval England* (Woodbridge, 2003), pp. 12–13; N. Ramsay, 'Alabaster', in J. Blair and N. Ramsay (eds), *English Medieval Industries* (London and Rio Grande, 1991), p. 31; W.H. St John Hope, 'On the Early Working of Alabaster in England', *Archaeological Journal*, 61 (1904), 221–40.

[162] Bayliss, 'Indenture', 22–9.

[163] R. Edwards, 'King Richard's Tomb at Leicester', *The Ricardian*, 3 (1975), 8–9.

[164] J. Crease, '"Not Commonly Reputed or Taken for a Saincte": The Output of a Northern Workshop in the Late Fourteenth and Early Fifteenth Centuries', in *Monumental Industry*, pp. 136–60.

[165] Ramsay, 'Alabaster', p. 34; Crease, '"Not Commonly Reputed or Taken for a Saincte"', p. 156.

[166] See below, p. 140.

[167] H. Lawrance and T.E. Routh, 'Derbyshire Military Effigies, III', *DAJ*, 48 (1926), 38–9.

Yorkist collars

Nicholas Fitzherbert (d. 1473) and his son and heir Ralph Fitzherbert (d. 1484), St Mary's and St Barlok's, Norbury

Nicholas: single tomb in the south side of the chancel with a recumbent effigy lying on top, the feet resting on a lion with an angel holding a shield on its back. He wears a Yorkist collar of three-dimensional suns and roses, with a lion pendant (Figure 3).

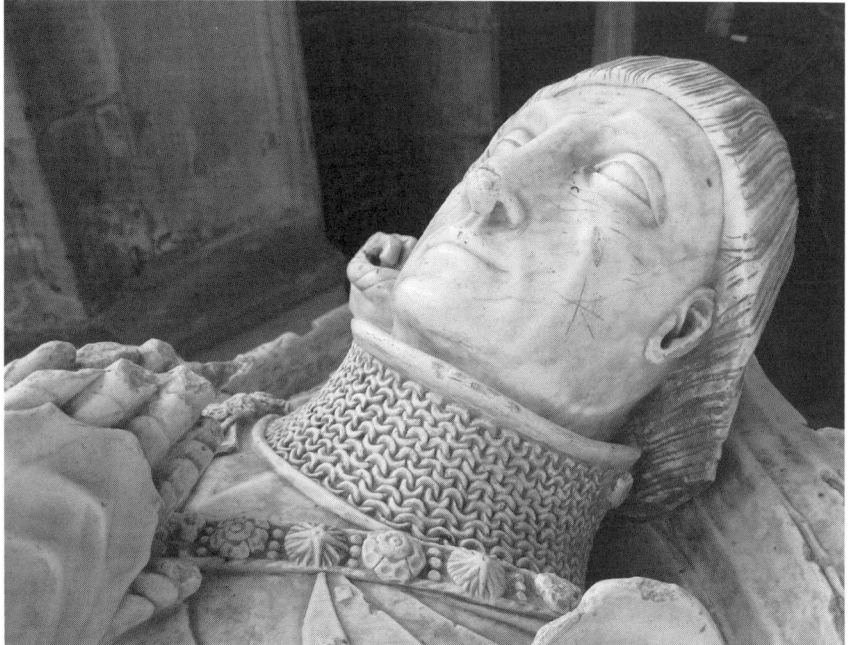

Figure 3. St Mary's and St Barlok's, Norbury (Derbyshire). Nicholas Fitzherbert (d. 1473).

Ralph: tomb in the north side of the chancel with the effigies of him and his wife Elisabeth, heiress of John Marshall of Upton (Leicestershire), lying on top. He wears a similar collar to his father, but has a boar pendant.

Nicholas carried out extensive building in the church and hall at Norbury.[168] This was acknowledged by the now lost inscription which once adorned the east end of his tomb, recorded by Peter Le Neve:

---

[168] J.C. Cox, 'Norbury Manor House and the Troubles of the Fitzherberts', *DAJ*, 7 (1885), 221–59.

> An MCCCC seventy and three
> Yeres of our Lord passed in degree
> The body that beried is under this stone
> Of Nicol Fitzherbert Lord & Patrone
> Of Norbury with Alis the daughter of Henry Bothe
> Eight sonnes & five daughters he had in sothe
> Two sonnes & two daughters by Isabel hys wyfe
> So seventeen children he had in hys lyfe.
> This church he made of his own expense
> In the joy of Heaven be his recompense
> And in the mooneth of November the nineteenth day
> He bequeathed his soule to everlasting joy.[169]

In fact, Nicholas built the north aisle and the south-east chapel of the church. It is also possible that he began work on the tower and the south-west chapel, the building being completed by his grandson John (d. 1531) towards the close of the century. John also raised the nave walls and added a clerestory.[170] As requested in his will, John's tomb is situated in the south-west chapel, 'leyde undre the newe arche beneathe the stepull or ells wher God shall otherwyse dispose it'.[171] The monuments of Nicholas and Ralph are not in their original positions. That of Nicholas once stood under the arch in the south-east chapel, and the tomb of his son sat opposite, inside a carved oak screen at the east end of the north aisle. They were moved to their present positions in c. 1842.[172]

In addition to the splendid tombs there are remnants of fifteenth-century glass in the church windows. The large east window houses fragments once contained in the nave and includes heraldic arms celebrating links with various local families such as the Montgomerys of Cubley and the Poles of Radbourne. In addition, the initials F, N, A, I and J (representing Fitzherbert, Nicholas, his first wife Alice, and John) appear alongside several golden suns. These could be interpreted as Yorkist symbols, the sun in splendour motif being adopted by Edward IV early in his reign. It is perhaps more prudent to suggest that they were intended to convey a dual meaning: the religious significance of the sun should not be disregarded. If it is the case that they were to be viewed as Yorkist emblems, through explicitly linking the initials of family members with the motif, the Fitzherberts were symbolically associating themselves with the royal house, serving to emphasise their honour and status. Another subtle reference to

---

[169] BL, Harley MS 3606, fol. 21. For Ralph's inscription see BL, Harley MS 3607, fol. 8.
[170] Cox, *Churches of Derbyshire*, iii, p. 233.
[171] LRO, B/A/1/14, fol. 106v.
[172] For the original tomb positions see T. Bateman, *Vestiges of the Antiquities of Derbyshire, and the Sepulchral Usages of Its Inhabitants, from the Most Remote Ages to the Reformation* (London, 1848), pp. 231–2.

the Yorkist associations of the family can be found in the depiction of St Antony in the south window of the south-east chapel. Antony is represented in traditional style, with a hog (sometimes referred to as a pig) standing at his feet with a bell around its neck. The saint had a particular significance to the house of York. In the north transept window at Canterbury, Antony was included among the various attendant saints. The same saint features on the tomb of the Yorkist supporter Sir Richard Croft (d. 1509) at Croft Castle in Herefordshire. It should also be recalled that Richard III's badge was the white boar, although a direct link with St Antony's boar cannot be proven.[173]

It has been suggested that the tombs of Nicholas and Ralph and his wife were commissioned by John Fitzherbert after the death of his mother in 1491.[174] It is striking that the tombs feature such a prominent expression of Yorkist allegiance, considering the possibility that they were commissioned some time after the accession of Henry Tudor in 1485. They are not, however, the only local examples. The tomb effigies of Sir Henry Pierrepont at Holme Pierrepont, in neighbouring Nottinghamshire, and Sir John Savage (d. 1495) at Macclesfield also feature the livery collar of suns and roses. As noted above, it is clear from Pierrepont's will that his monument was not begun until after 1489.[175] Perhaps in choosing to depict the Yorkist symbol these individuals were hedging their bets. After all, Henry Tudor had been in power for only a short period, and the political situation had hardly been stable over the previous decade. Who was to say that the Yorkist faction would not soon return to power? Perhaps such a depiction was deemed acceptable because those commemorated were dead after all. It should also not be forgotten that Henry had married Elizabeth of York, and that something of a spirit of reconciliation was in the air. However, the unwillingness of the new king to show leniency to those with an affinity to the previous regime suggests that Henry was not prepared to tolerate expressions of

---

[173] I am grateful to Geoffrey Wheeler for his comments on this subject.
[174] Bowyer, *Norbury*, p. 85; K. Wilson-Lee, 'Representations of Piety and Dynasty: Late-Medieval Stained Glass and Sepulchral Monuments at Norbury, Derbyshire', *DAJ*, 131 (2011), 226–44, at 229–34. For an earlier date of *c.* 1480–85 see M. Downing, *Military Effigies of England and Wales*, 8 vols (Shrewsbury, 2010–13), i, p. 127. For the purpose of this study a date of the mid-1490s, after the death of Ralph's wife Elizabeth, is accepted. If the tomb was made between Ralph's death and Elizabeth's (1484–91), and was commissioned by her, then it is likely that she would have depicted herself as a widow.
[175] Borthwick Institute for Archives, Archbishop's Register, 23, fol. 370r.

Yorkist allegiance on his subjects' memorials. Such depictions of Yorkist collars are significant, and warrant further research.[176]

Roger Bothe II (d. 1478), All Saints', Sawley

The London style 'D' brass of Roger and his wife Margaret (Stanley) above three sons (now lost) and six daughters, which lies on a Purbeck slab, is located in the north-east side of the nave. The marginal inscription is now partly erased although a fuller inscription was recorded in 1705.[177] Roger has a suns and roses collar around his neck. On the tomb panels are several roses and what appear to be the remnants of a *rose-en-soleil* badge, which have hitherto not been commented on by scholars. A similar altar tomb to his father, Roger I (d. 1467)

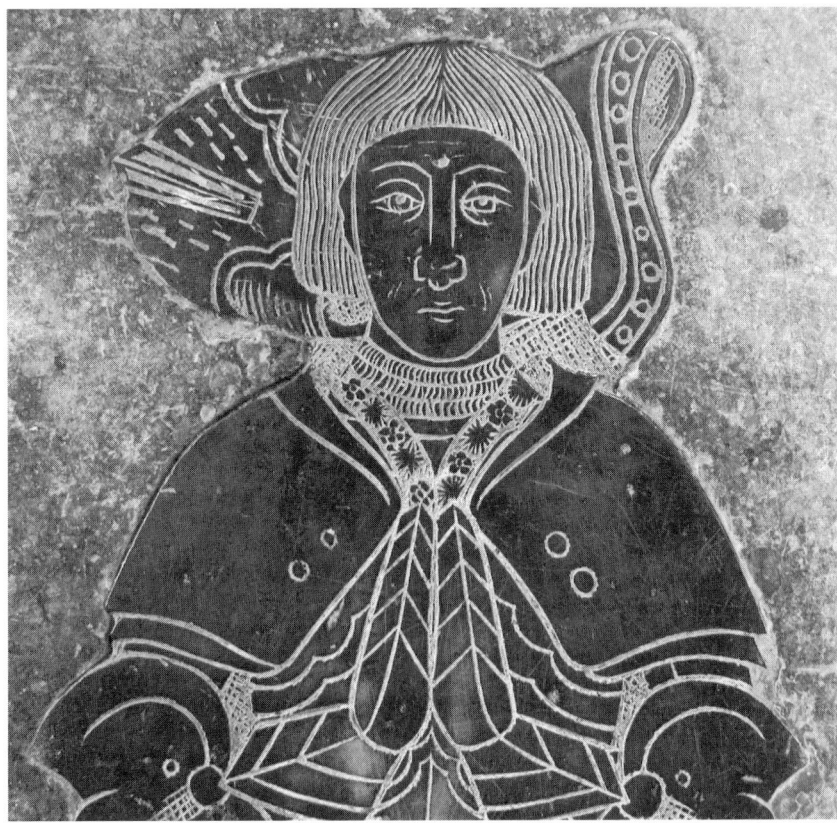

Figure 4. All Saints', Sawley (Derbyshire). Roger Bothe (d. 1478).

---

[176] I am currently researching this topic, with the intention of publishing the outcomes.
[177] See Cox, *Churches of Derbyshire*, iv, p. 390.

lies in the chancel. The tombs were probably commissioned at the same time (Figure 4).[178]

John Bradbourne (d. 1488) St Oswald's, Ashbourne

The tomb chest with recumbent effigies in prayer of John and his wife Anne, daughter of Sir Richard Vernon, lies in the Lady Chapel – today called the Boothby Chapel – among many other monuments to the Cockayne and Boothby families. Of the tombs panels, only the north is original; it features angels holding frontal shields. Until c. 1840 the tomb stood in the family's chantry chapel in the south transept, founded by John and Anne in 1484. Around John's neck is an almost completely worn collar, once of suns and roses; one rose can still be discerned.[179] The slender collar shares similarities with those depicted on the effigies at Melbury Sampford (Dorset), thought to represent members of the Browning family.

Robert Barley (d. 1467), St Lawrence's, Barlow

The full-length incised effigies of Robert and his wife Margaret, daughter of Sir Henry Delves of Doddington (Cheshire), are depicted on an alabaster slab in the Lady Chapel. Now a mural, the slab was once set into the floor. Robert wears a much worn collar of suns and roses around his neck. A visitation of the church in 1611 recorded the inscription and details of the original five shields which once adorned the memorial.[180]

Thomas Cockayne (d. 1488), All Saints', Youlgreave

Thomas's small effigy (3' 6" in length) lies on a modern tomb chest and is situated in the centre of the chancel. Until c. 1835 it was positioned in the Lady Chapel in the south aisle. Thomas wears a suns and roses collar around his neck with a lion pendant. The tomb was restored in c. 1870, when the anachronistic moustache was added to the effigy (Figure 5).[181]

In 1488 Thomas was killed in a fight with Thomas Burdett on his way from his family's residence at Pooley (Warwickshire), to Polesworth church.[182] Many have speculated on why the tomb is so small. The usual explanation of this being

---

[178] Lack, Stuchfield and Whittemore, *Monumental Brasses*, pp. 179–83; R.R. Rawlins, *Churches and Chapels in the County of Derby*, 3 vols (1819–23), iii, p. 374; Jewitt, 'The Booths', 36.

[179] E.A. Sadler, 'The Family of Bradbourne and Their Monuments in Ashbourne Church', *DAJ*, 57 (1936). For a description of the tomb in its original location see *The History and Topography of Ashbourn, the Valley of the Dove, and the Adjacent Villages* (no author, Ashbourne, 1839), pp. 67–9.

[180] Derby Local Studies Library, MS 6341, fol. 33v.

[181] Lawrance and Routh, 'Derbyshire Military Effigies', 47–8; Cox, *Churches of Derbyshire*, ii, pp. 322–8; A.E. Cockayne, *Cockayne Memoranda: Collections towards a Historical Record of the Family of Cockayne* (Congleton, 1869), p. 22.

[182] Dugdale, *Warwickshire*, p. 809.

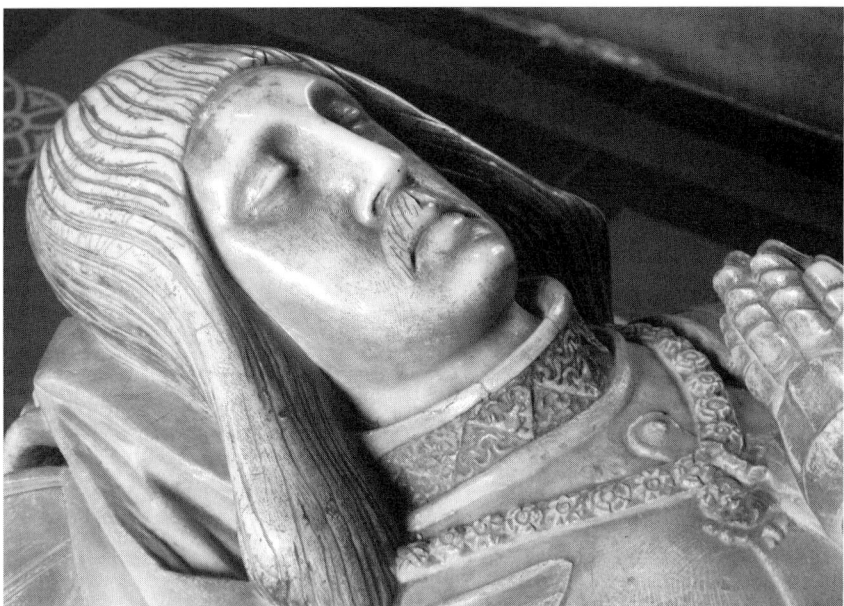

Figure 5. All Saints', Youlgreave (Derbyshire). Thomas Cockayne (d. 1488).

a child's tomb can be discounted as Thomas was of age and had children when he died. One explanation may have been a lack of disposable income. The family were in a precarious financial position during the late fifteenth century, so this may have dictated the size of the tomb. It is possible that his father also intended to be buried at Youlgreave, and commissioned a smaller tomb for his son in order to distinguish between the two memorials. It should also be noted that Thomas was not buried in the family mausoleum at Ashbourne. This is perhaps evidence that his family did not think him worthy enough to be interred among his more illustrious relatives. It should also be remembered that, unlike his relatives interred at Ashbourne, Thomas was evidently not a Lancastrian supporter. Burial next to his ancestors would perhaps have been considered impolitic, and may explain his burial elsewhere.

Thomas Fraunceys (d. 1482), St Wystan's, Repton

The full-length effigy of Fraunceys lies on a tomb chest with some original panels featuring large shields. Now next to the stairway to the crypt, the tomb was originally in the east end of the north aisle, subsequently placed outside the church, then moved into the crypt.[183] Thomas wears a suns and roses collar with a lion pendant. It has traditionally been thought that the effigy represents Sir Robert

---

[183] R. Bigsby, *Historical and Topographical Description of Repton, in the County of Derby* (London, 1854), pp. 129–30.

Fraunceys, who settled in Foremark in the late fourteenth century.[184] This is not possible, as he died in 1420, decades before the Yorkist accession to the throne and the introduction of the suns and roses collar. Another candidate is his son Robert (d. c. 1463). This is more plausible, but the lion of March pendant on his collar would make this an extremely early example. It is likely, therefore, that the tomb is that of his son Thomas (d. 1482). If this is the case, it is probable that the tomb was made earlier, during the lifetime of the deceased.[185]

Nicholas Montgomery (d. 1465), St Andrew's, Cubley

The tomb chest decorated with angels holding frontal shields lies in the north side of chancel. Montgomery's head, which rests on a helm, wears a bascinet with orle, featuring the sacred monogram 'Ihc'. A collar of suns and roses is around his neck. Traditionally, this tomb has been attributed to Sir Nicholas Montgomery (d. 1435).[186] This poses problems, as the Yorkist collar is from a later period. The figure is therefore more likely to represent his son Nicholas (d. 1465). Although the armour appears to date from an earlier period, the effigy could well represent this individual.[187] If this is the case, the appearance of a Yorkist livery collar is still rather baffling as there appears to be no evidence of Nicholas supporting the house of York. Perhaps the collar is more an expression of the Yorkist loyalties of his family, rather than the individual it was erected to commemorate. As has been demonstrated, Sir Nicholas (d. 1494) had Yorkist connections.

Opposite, on the south side of the chancel, is a panel from the tomb of Sir Nicholas. This is all that remains of his sepulchre, which once featured a memorial brass, recorded by Ashmole.[188] In seven niches on the panel are featured several individuals, in the second niche is the figure of a man in armour wearing a chain with the remnants of what appears to be an animal pendant. In the third is a figure of a man in civilian costume wearing a chain with a rose pendant. It is not possible to identify these individuals, although one may depict John Montgomery (d. 1513), son and heir of Sir Nicholas, who was the last male head of the family. It is likely that Henry Harpur and William Moorecock from

---

[184] Cox, *Churches of Derbyshire*, iii, p. 438.
[185] Lawrance and Routh, 'Derbyshire Military Effigies', 43. A date of c. 1465 has been suggested by Mark Downing: *Military Effigies*, i, p. 132.
[186] H. Lawrance and T.E. Routh, 'Medieval Military Effigies in Derbyshire, II', *DAJ*, 47 (1925), 150.
[187] Personal correspondence with Mark Downing. Part of a now-lost inscription from a tomb in the chancel was recorded by Elias Ashmole in c. 1660: 'Hic jacet Dns Nicholas Montgomerie miles qui obit 27 Martii 1435': Cox, *Churches of Derbyshire*, iii, p. 98. It is possible that this refers to the tomb in question, in which case it does indeed represent the Sir Nicholas who died in 1435. Equally, it could have been on a now-lost tomb, as the chancel was once filled with Montgomery monuments: Bateman, *Antiquities of Derbyshire*, p. 201.
[188] Derby Local Studies Library, DL84.

Burton-upon-Trent built this tomb.[189] It was these alabastermen who were contracted to make the tomb of Henry Foljambe (d. 1504) and his wife Benedicta in All Saints', Chesterfield. Indeed, Foljambe's executors had Montgomery's memorial in mind when they asked Harpur and Moorecock:

> to make a tomb for Henry Foljambe, husband of Bennett, in St Mary's quire, in the church of All Hallows, in Chesterfield, and to make it as good as is the tomb of Sir Nicholas Montgomery at Colley, with eighteen images under the table, and the arms upon them, and the said Henry in copper and gilt upon the table of marble, with two arms at the head and two arms at the feet of the same, and the table of marble to be of a whole stone and all fair marble.[190]

The contract gives us a clear idea of the appearance of Montgomery's tomb and brass, which cost £10. It also serves to remind us that the local gentry were more than aware of the design and appearance of their associates' monuments, and often sought to emulate them.

Lancastrian/Tudor collars

Ralph Pole (d. 1492), St Andrew's, Radbourne

The recumbent effigies of Ralph and his wife Elizabeth, daughter and heir of Reginald Moton of Peckleton (Leicestershire), lie on a modern plinth in the Pole chapel at the east end of the north aisle. Ralph wears a collar of SS with a rose pendant around his neck. The effigies and collar details are similar to those of John Curzon III and his wife at Kedleston. Some have attributed this tomb to Ralph's son John and his wife Jane. This is unlikely, as John predeceased his father, leaving his son German as heir. Ralph also founded the chantry chapel, dedicated to St Nicholas, in which he is buried.[191]

St Andrew's Church once had several altars, one of which was dedicated to St Zitha/Sitha.[192] Although it cannot be proven that this particular dedication was connected to the Pole family, there may be a link with the Fitzherberts, as it is possible that it is the figure of this saint which is depicted in the east window of

---

[189] S.A. Jeavons, 'The Church Monuments of Derbyshire, the Sixteenth and Seventeenth Centuries, Part 1', *DAJ*, 84 (1964), 53–7.
[190] J.C. Cox, 'Derbyshire Monuments to the Family of Foljambe', in his *Memorials of Old Derbyshire* (London, 1907), p. 108.
[191] Jeayes, *Radbourne Hall*, 674; *CPR 1485–94*, p. 431; Jeayes, *Radbourne Hall*, p. xxvi.
[192] Cox, *Churches of Derbyshire*, iii, p. 260.

the south-east chapel at Norbury.¹⁹³ Incidentally, the same saint also features on the tomb of Sir Richard Croft at Croft Castle, alongside St Antony (page 135).

John Curzon III (d. c. 1492), All Saints', Kedleston

The recumbent effigies of John and his wife Joan (Bagot) lie on a tomb chest decorated with angels holding frontal shields, saints and kneeling figures, in the south transept. His head rests on a helm and he wears a skull cap.¹⁹⁴ John wears a collar of SS with a rose pendant. The tomb of John's father, John II (d. c. 1459), once stood near his son's monument, but is now situated in the south wall of the chancel. He also wears a collar of SS. Perhaps this influenced his son's decision to depict the same collar on his own memorial (Figure 6).

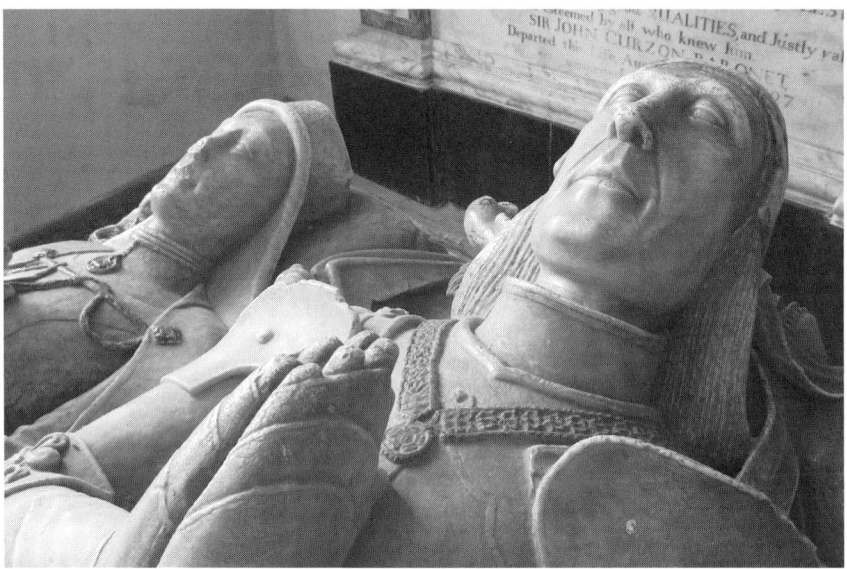

Figure 6. All Saints', Kedleston (Derbyshire). John Curzon (d. c. 1492) and his wife, Joan.

Nicholas Kniveton (d. 1500), All Saints', Mugginton

The London style 'D' brass of Nicholas, in armour, and his wife Joan (Mauleverer) lies on an altar tomb in the south chapel, erected by the Kniveton family during the late fifteenth century. The tomb originally stood under an archway which once separated the south chapel from the chancel. Nicholas wears a collar of SS with a Beaufort portcullis pendant. The full marginal inscription was recorded in 1569. The brass was once thought to date from c. 1475, but the

---

¹⁹³ St Edith has been suggested as an alternative attribution: Bowyer, *Norbury*, p. 71.
¹⁹⁴ Similar headgear is worn by Sir Roger Tocotes (d. 1492) at St Owen's, Bromham (Wiltshire).

portcullis pendant makes it datable to after 1485, as the Beaufort portcullis was adopted by Henry Tudor after his accession to the throne (Figure 7).[195]

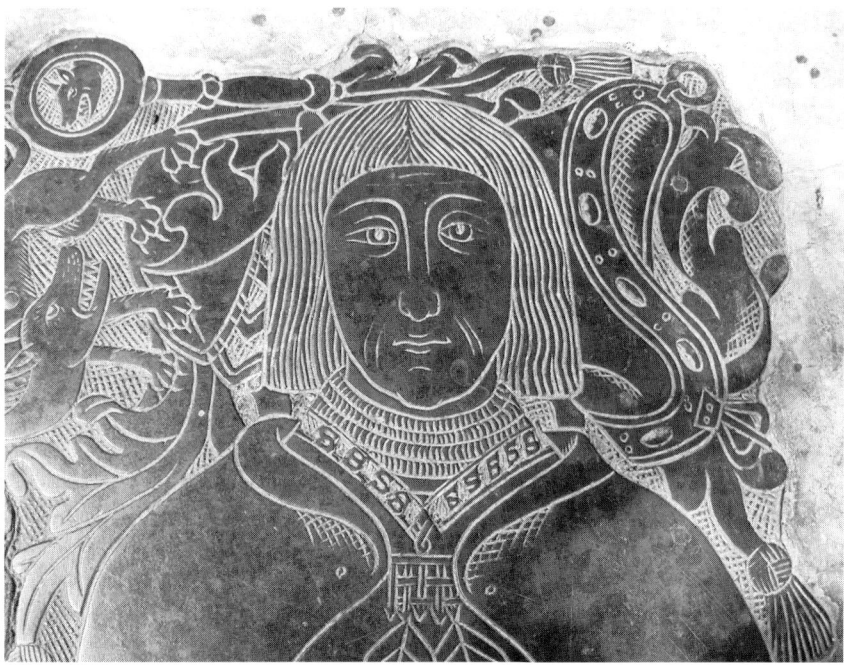

Figure 7. All Saints', Mugginton (Derbyshire). Nicholas Kniveton (d. 1500).

Additional individuals

Sir Henry Vernon (d. 1515), St Bartholomew's, Tong (Shropshire)

Although this monument lies outside the period under investigation, the Vernon family were Derbyshire gentry, and their mausoleum at Tong contains several examples of the SS collar. Sir Henry was buried at Tong alongside his wife Anne Talbot, daughter of the earl of Shrewsbury, whom he married in 1467.

---

[195] Lack, Stuchfield and Whittemore, *Monumental Brasses*, pp. 156–8; Stephenson, *List of Monumental Brasses*, p. 85; Derby Local Studies Library, MS 6341, fol. 15r; Mundy MS, v, pp. 215–16B; M. Norris, *Monumental Brasses: The Memorials*, 2 vols (London, 1977), i, p. 137. For the tomb in its original position see Rawlins, *Churches and Chapels*, iii, pp. 333–4.

His sandstone tomb is situated beneath a broad arch in the wall between the nave and his chapel. He is depicted wearing a large collar of SS.[196]

Sir Henry Pierrepont (d. 1499), St Edmund's, Holme Pierrepont (Nottinghamshire)

Sir Henry's superb effigy lies on a tomb chest decorated with cusped lozenge panels containing small shields, next to the south wall of the church. The monument, along with the tomb at nearby Strelley, commemorating John Strelley (d. 1501), was probably the product of a local Nottingham workshop.[197]

Sir John Savage IV (d. 1495), St Michael's, Macclesfield (Cheshire)

The alabaster effigies of Sir John and his wife Catherine, daughter of Thomas, Lord Stanley, lie next to the south wall of the chancel. Sir John wears a collar of suns and roses, and his wife has a collar of roses about her neck. He was created knight of the Bath in 1465. Several other monuments to his family can be found in the church. Although attributing the various effigies to specific family members is open to conjecture, it is possible that this effigy is that of his son Sir John Savage V, who predeceased his father, dying at the siege of Boulogne in 1492. He joined Henry Tudor at Bosworth, where he commanded the left wing. For his services to Henry, John was granted the majority of the lands of Francis, Viscount Lovell. He was created knight of the Garter in 1489.[198] It is therefore unlikely that he would have been depicted wearing a Yorkist collar. Another effigy in the church features a collar of plain chain links, ending in a damaged pendant. It is this figure which is thought to represent Sir John Savage V.

Two earlier tombs

Earlier generations of the Cockayne and Vernon families were also depicted wearing livery collars – in both cases Lancastrian – on their tomb effigies. Among the series of six Cockayne family monuments in the Boothby Chapel at Ashbourne are the alabaster tomb and double effigies of Sir John Cockayne (d. 1438) and his first wife Margaret (d. c. 1420). The tomb may have been erected during the early 1440s; the horned headdress worn by Margaret dates from this period. The tomb commemorates a successful and powerful local landowner, whose reputation certainly supersedes that of his second son and heir John (d. 1505), whose mother was Sir John's second wife Isabel Shirley.[199] The tomb of Sir

---

[196] Gilderdale Scott, '"This Little Westminster"', 46–81.
[197] Gardner, *Alabaster Tombs*, p. 73.
[198] G. Ormerod, *The History of the County Palatine and City of Chester*, 3 vols (London, 1819), i, pp. 525–8; *Harleian 433*, i, pp. 207, 209; iii, p. 200; Mundy MS, v, p. 270E.
[199] Wilson-Lee, 'Dynasty and Strategies, Part 1', 92–3; E.A. Sadler, 'The Ancient Family of Cockayne and Their Monuments in Ashbourne Church', *DAJ*, 55 (1935), 14–39; Gilderdale Scott, '"This Little Westminster"', 46–81.

Richard Vernon (d. 1451), grandfather of Sir Henry (d. 1515), and his wife Benedicta Ludlow, can be found among the family tombs at Tong. In this instance both husband and wife wear SS collars. As with Sir John Cockayne, Vernon had an illustrious career, his achievements culminating in his appointment as treasurer of Calais in 1444. Vernon was the first of several generations of his family to include an SS collar on their tombs at Tong, and we have seen that Sir John Cockayne's grandson's effigy at Youlgreave – the next family monument to be erected – also features a livery collar, this time a Yorkist example. Although the two Cockayne collars would appear to signify allegiance to opposing factions, it should be kept in mind that both represent continuity of service to the crown in some form. It should also be remembered that, during Sir John's time, there was no Yorkist collar, nor indeed an opposing Yorkist faction. Perhaps the tombs of Cockayne and Vernon can be seen as the inspiration, as it were, for the appearance of subsequent tombs in Derbyshire whose monuments went on to depict collars. Although neither married into the other families considered here, the form of their effigies would have been well known, and no doubt these earlier monuments influenced the decision by other local families to continue the trend of including collars on their own monuments.

Conclusions

It is important to draw out the distinction between why individuals were awarded a collar, and why they or their family chose to depict the artefact on their monument. It may well have been the case that the individuals discussed here received a collar due to their membership of Hastings's, or indeed the duke of Clarence's, retinues, the link to the crown being made through their lords. But other, more personal ties of kinship and tenure may help to explain why the group chose to depict them on their memorials. It is important to remember that we are considering conscious choices, choices by the individual or family to request a livery collar to be included on a tomb.

If one sees a Yorkist or Lancastrian livery collar on a memorial, it is obvious that the individual, or the individual's family, is asserting their political allegiance to the respective regime. However, I have attempted to demonstrate that few of the individuals were staunchly Lancastrian or Yorkist. Some, such as the Vernons, may have been, but can we say the same of Robert Barley? Most chose to eschew fighting for either side in the civil wars; indeed many opted for the gentry's typical pragmatic approach and made themselves amenable to whichever faction held power.[200] There is no evidence that Nicholas or Ralph Fitzherbert,

---

[200] Although some families such as the Barleys and Cockaynes saw military service prior to 1453, this did not continue during the Wars of the Roses: J. Denton, 'The East-Midland Gentleman, 1400–1530', Keele University, unpublished PhD thesis (2006), pp. 187–99.

for example, were members of the Yorkist royal household. Although the land grants and lead leases given to the Fitzherberts and other families were the types of reward given to members of the household, they were not exclusive to royal servants.

The appearance of the livery collar on memorials in the area is indicative of the collective identity of the local gentry and the nature of political feeling among them. What, for example, happened after the end of Lancastrian rule in 1461? If the appearance of livery collars on monuments is a barometer, then the answer is apparently very little. The practice of placing livery collars on memorials in the county was continued, albeit with Yorkist equivalents, until c. 1485 when they were again superseded by Tudor SS collars. Of those families who attacked the residence of Walter Blount in 1454, many of the next generation were keen to impress their loyalty to the crown after 1461 through their collars. Yet they had not necessarily switched their allegiances. The majority of those individuals who included a Yorkist collar were neither politically active for the Yorkists, nor closet Lancastrians. They were, therefore, continuing to express their service and allegiance to the crown through the livery collar. This may, of course, have been due to a desire to rectify their rather partisan behaviour at Elvaston in 1454, although it should be stressed that they were then targeting an individual who, in their eyes, had withdrawn his support for the king: they were again stressing their loyalty to the crown. Any local disturbances involving collared families such as the Cockaynes cannot be discerned as politically motivated, although the actions of members of the Vernon family in the mid-1460s may have been due to a perceived lack of recognition from Edward IV, particularly for Sir William (d. 1467), whose brass at Tong does not feature a livery collar. The explanation for this group solidarity may be due partly to the geographical and tenurial context in which the local gentry resided: the influence of Tutbury honour. A geographically compact honour, with several generations of families holding the principal offices, produced a feeling of duty and pride associated with one of the duchy's more prestigious honours. With the accession of the Yorkists came a new duke of Lancaster: Edward IV.

Susan Wright stressed that it is difficult to identify relationships between Derbyshire families.[201] It is true that many alliances between families, indeed between a lord and his affinity, were transient and liable to change at a whim, but it is clear that a marriage constituted an effective relationship. Despite the rather business-like considerations involved in marriage settlements, such an alliance must reflect a degree of trust and mutual understanding between families, as both parties had to work together. With many of the individuals featured here, a connection can be made with another individual, closely related through marriage, who also chose (or at least their family chose) to depict the same livery

[201] *Derbyshire Gentry*, p. 63.

collar on their monuments. Perhaps here we have a recognition, or statement, of their kinship bonds through a shared symbol. In this respect, the collar represents a moment in time, the relationship between the families at the time the monument was commissioned. For some, such as the Fitzherberts and Bothes, it also represented more durable ties. It may have been from the closest family associates (in most cases in-laws, see Appendix 1) that the strongest motivation to depict a collar was derived. If this was the case, then it is worth noting the dates between the various pairs of influence. The tombs of Montgomery and Frauncys were constructed at approximately the same time, probably during the mid-1460s. The gap between the construction of the Bothe brass and the Fitzherbert monuments could have been as little as a couple of years. Equally, the Bradbourne tomb was probably erected at about the same time as the Fitzherberts' monuments. The tombs of Pole and Curzon, which are very similar in appearance, were likely to have been built during the same period (1490–1500), with Kniveton's brass erected at approximately the same time. The only discernible long gap is that between the construction of the Barley incised slab and his son-in-law Thomas Cockayne's tomb: between ten and fifteen years. When pairing the monuments to their closest family associates, there does not, therefore, appear to have been a substantial lapse of time between their construction.

It is also appropriate to consider the group as a whole. Through their close geographical and professional ties, and particularly their long-standing collective affinity with the Tutbury honour, and despite their disputes during the 1440s and early 1470s, all the families were associated through service to the honour. The depiction of the livery collar put into stone their bonds and their collective responsibility derived through duchy service. With a stronger crown presence in the area after 1470, albeit in the form of Hastings, a particular pride would have been derived from duchy service, a pride that was to continue into the sixteenth century. Apart from Hastings, who was very much the king's lieutenant in the region, and to a lesser extent the duke of Clarence, a lack of meaningful magnate power during the period would have encouraged the families concerned to feel a closer association to the crown through their duchy service.

This chapter has demonstrated that, when considering the motivations behind the appearance of a livery collar on a monument, one must consider a variety of overlapping influences, and several levels of relationships between families. Although it would be wrong to entirely dismiss the political significance of the livery collar (which, we should remember, essentially represented allegiance to one's lord), when examining the Derbyshire gentry a consideration of other ties is required to help to explain the appearance of the collar. It serves to remind us that the political or dynastic significance associated with a livery collar on a church monument is in some cases too simple an interpretation.

5

Livery Collars in Wales and the Edgecote Connection

We now travel west to examine the depiction of livery collars on church monuments in Wales, to provide both a comparison and a contrast to the study of Derbyshire. The aims are the same: to identify the motivations behind a group of individuals and their families choosing to depict livery collars on their church monuments, and to elucidate the links between them. Were the same motivations identified in Derbyshire, in particular ties of kinship and geography, present among other clusters of individuals who were depicted with livery collars on their memorials? Were there additional factors specific to the Wales network? The context is again a geographical area, principally the south of Wales, a region which provided the core of the affinity of William Herbert, earl of Pembroke (d. 1469), during the 1460s. However, a supplementary theme is addressed in the form of an event – the battle of Edgecote in 1469, at which a significant proportion of Herbert's affinity were killed fighting for Edward IV. Did this catastrophic event for the house of York provide an additional stimulus for choosing to depict a livery collar on a memorial? The focus here is on the collar both as a political statement and as an affirmation of kinship and geographical ties. With this group political conviction, hitherto the conventional meaning attributed to the livery collar by historians, was indeed a salient motivation when it came to making the decision whether to depict the artefact on one's tomb.

Though the English gentry may have amused themselves at Welsh patronymics and their obsession with 'old pedegris',[1] the Welsh played an integral part in the Wars of the Roses. The contributions of Jasper Tudor, uncle to Henry VII and a constant thorn in the Yorkists' side, and Sir Rhys ap Thomas, whose contingent proved vital to Henry in 1485, have been acknowledged by historians.[2] Up to the accession of Edward IV in 1461, Yorkist military strength was drawn primarily from the Welsh Marches, the duke of York's Mortimer estates providing fertile recruiting territory. It was their Mortimer lineage which drew the people of the

---

[1] *PL*, iii, pp. 118–19.
[2] R.A. Griffiths, *Sir Rhys ap Thomas and His Family: A Study in the Wars of the Roses and Early Tudor Politics*, 2nd edn (Cardiff, 2014).

Marches to York and his son, the earl of March, and it was Marcher men who triumphed at the battle of Mortimer's Cross in February 1461, paving the way for the earl's proclamation as king in London.[3] Edward's Mortimer lineage and descent from Gwladus Ddu, daughter of Llywellyn the Great, was celebrated by Welsh poets Lewis Glyn Cothi and Guto'r Glyn, who saw him as a Welsh (or British) king and potential unifier of their nation. Indeed, according to Gutyn Owain, Guto'r Glyn was awarded a livery collar by Edward for his panegyric.[4]

It was William Herbert, earl of Pembroke, executed after fighting for Edward at the battle of Edgecote in 1469, who provided the leadership for the Welsh Yorkists during the 1460s.[5] His affinity, which included families such as the Vaughans of Bredwardine (Herefordshire) and the Wogans of Wiston (Pembrokeshire) provides the focus here. The families were closely connected through ties of blood and tenure, considered so important to the Welsh gentry and celebrated by their poets. Many were politically active, serving the house of York in various capacities, some at a national level, and many were to die at Edgecote. Of the church monuments in Wales which feature the Yorkist livery collar, all individuals commemorated either died, or were closely connected to those who died, at the battle. As they were slain fighting for their king, the appearance of the livery collar on their monuments may well have been a demonstration of their comradeship on the battlefield. Although kinship ties and geographical associations were meaningful stimuli for the inclusion of a livery collar on their tomb effigies, the Yorkist collars were also an assertion of political loyalty among the group. The following individuals and their tombs are the focus of analysis:

William Herbert, earl of Pembroke (d. 1469), Tintern Abbey (Monmouthshire), no extant tomb
Sir Richard Herbert (d. 1469), Priory Church of St Mary, Abergavenny (Monmouthshire)
?Sir Richard Herbert (c. 1470–80), St Nicholas's, Montgomery (Montgomeryshire)

[3] H.T. Evans, *Wales and the Wars of the Roses* (Cambridge, 1915), pp. v–vi; Edward Hall, *Chronicle*, ed. H. Ellis (London, 1809), p. 251; J.H. Harvey (ed.), *William Worcestre Itineraries* (Oxford, 1969), pp. 203–5.
[4] I. Williams and J.L. Williams (eds), *Gwaith Guto'r Glyn* (Cardiff, 1939), pp. 157–9; G. Williams, *Renewal and Reformation, Wales c. 1415–1642* (Oxford and New York, 1993), p. 211; I. Williams, 'Guto'r Glyn', *Welsh Biography Online*, 2009 (http://wbo.llgc.org.uk/en/s-GUTO-GLY-1440.html, accessed 18 May 2013).
[5] For Herbert, see the *Herbertorum Prosapia* (*HP*), a late seventeenth-century copy of a family history written earlier that century. D.H. Thomas's 1967 unpublished University of Wales MA thesis, 'The Herberts of Raglan as Supporters of the House of York in the Second Half of the Fifteenth Century' was published as a book, *The Herberts of Raglan and the Battle of Edgecote 1469* (Enfield, 1994). Also see R.A. Griffiths, 'Herbert, William, First Earl of Pembroke (c. 1423–1469)', *Oxford Dictionary of National Biography*, Oxford University Press, 2004; online edn, 2008 (www.oxforddnb.com/view/article/13053, accessed 12 May 2012).

Thomas Vaughan (d. 1469), St Mary's, Kington (Herefordshire)
Sir Henry Wogan (d. 1475), Scolton Manor Museum (Pembrokeshire)
William Griffith (d. c. 1483), St Tegai's, Llandegai (Gwynedd)

Brothers in arms: the battle of Edgecote, 26 July 1469

The battle of Edgecote should be seen in the context of growing animosity between Richard Neville, earl of Warwick, and the king and his most intimate advisers, including William Herbert, during the late 1460s. Despite having worked for Warwick earlier in his career, Herbert's favours from the king had steadily angered Neville, most notably the marriage of the queen's sister Mary Woodville to his eldest son William in 1466.[6] The following year, Herbert's involvement in the capture of a messenger, whose letters implicated Warwick in a Lancastrian plot with Margaret of Anjou, further antagonised the earl's relationship with Herbert and the king. In the resulting interrogation, the messenger suggested that Warwick had colluded with the Lancastrians, leading the earl to angrily rebuke those responsible for the arrest as traitors. Herbert was now one of Warwick's primary opponents, alongside his Woodville kinsmen Earl Rivers and Lord Scales. Once a mere 'meane gentleman', Herbert was given an earldom as a result of his close friendship with the king. He was one of the obstacles to power Warwick felt necessary to remove.[7]

A series of insurrections in Yorkshire during the spring of 1469 culminated in the Robin of Redesdale rebellion, probably captained by Sir John Conyers, a cousin of the earl of Warwick. On 12 July Warwick and the king's brother, the duke of Clarence, issued an open letter from Calais, naming 'certeyne ceducious persones', including William Herbert, Humphrey Stafford, recently created earl of Devon, Lord Scales and other Woodvilles. Warwick had married his eldest daughter Isabel to Clarence the previous day, in defiance of the king's wishes. With the king in Nottingham, Herbert and the earl of Devon were ordered to raise reinforcements in Wales and the West Country. Meanwhile the northern rebels travelled south, past Nottingham, in order to meet the earl of Warwick.[8]

---

[6] *CPR 1452–61*, p. 549; J. Beverley Smith and T.B. Pugh, 'The Lordship of Gower and Kilvey in the Middle Ages', in T.B. Pugh (ed.), *Glamorgan County History, III, The Middle Ages* (Cardiff, 1971), pp. 260–1. The marriage contract is printed in *HP*, pp. 52–4.

[7] J. Stevenson (ed.), 'Wilhelmi Wyrcester Annales Rerum Anglicarum', in Stevenson (ed.), *Letters and Papers Illustrative of the Wars of the English in France during the Reign of Henry VI*, Rolls Series, 2 vols in 3 (London, 1861–64), ii, part 2, p. 788; M. Hicks, *Warwick the Kingmaker* (Oxford, 1998), pp. 259, 264–71; Jean de Waurin, *Recueil des chroniques et anchiennes istoires de la Grant Bretaigne*, ed. W. Hardy, Rolls Series (1891), p. 545; Hall, *Chronicle*, p. 273; Stow, *Annales*, p. 421.

[8] Halliwell (ed.), *Chronicle*, pp. 6, 46; Riley (ed.), *Croyland*, p. 446.

Though contemporary and near-contemporary accounts of the battle are occasionally confused and contradictory, it is possible to outline the principal events.[9] The armies met, possibly by chance, near Banbury. There appears to have been an initial skirmish on 24 July, in which a contingent of 2,000 royalist troops, led by Sir Richard Herbert and the earl of Devon, 'wer clene discomfited and scatered' and returned to the main army.[10] After a second skirmish the following day, in which Warwick's cousin Sir Henry Neville was captured and executed,[11] an altercation occurred between Pembroke and Devon regarding lodging at Banbury, resulting in the latter withdrawing his troops, the majority of which were archers.[12] The main battle was fought the following day, at Danes Moor near Edgecote, approximately three miles from Banbury. Herbert's troops, the best in Wales according to Warkworth, without the aid of Stafford's men, acquitted themselves well and at one point were close to victory. However, the arrival of John Clapham with the vanguard of Warwick's army, 'hauyng borne before them the standard of the Erle with the white Bere, Cryenge a Warwycke a Warwycke', changed the course of the battle. Thinking Warwick's main army had arrived, the royalists were routed. Approximately 5,000 Welshmen were slain. The earl of Pembroke and his brother, Sir Richard Herbert, were captured along with ten of their captains and beheaded at Northampton in the presence of Warwick on 28 July. The earl had made a codicil to his will shortly before his death, instructing his brother Thomas to take care of his affairs. This wish was not fulfilled, as Thomas was later killed in Bristol, apparently tracked down and murdered, no doubt on Warwick's orders. The Woodvilles were executed at Coventry on 12 August, and the earl of Devon was captured and beheaded at Bridgwater on 17 August. He was buried in the Lady Chapel at Glastonbury, as requested in his will.[13] Warwick's personal feud with Herbert was now over, his bloody revenge had been taken and his objectives met. With the senior Herberts dead, their place at the centre of the English polity, and their dominance in Wales, had been curtailed.

Herbert's affinity at Edgecote included many members of his own family, including his brother Sir Richard, another Richard 'bastard', William, his half-brother, and John, another of his brothers or cousins. Thomas Vaughan of

---

[9] Ross, *Edward IV*, pp. 129–32; W.G. Lewis, 'The Exact Date of the Battle of Banbury, 1469', *Bulletin of the Institute of Historical Research*, 55 (1982), 194–6.

[10] Riley (ed.), *Croyland*, p. 446; Hall, *Chronicle*, p. 273; P.A. Haigh, '… *Where Both the Hosts Fought …' The Rebellions of 1469–1470 and the Battles of Edgecote and Lose-Cote-field* (Heckmondwicke, 1997), pp. 32–4.

[11] It may have been Neville's father Lord Latimer who was executed: 'Hearne's Fragment', in J.A. Giles, *The Chronicles of the White Rose of York*, 2nd edn (London, 1845), pp. 5–30, at p. 24.

[12] Halliwell (ed.), *Chronicle*, p. 6; Thomas and Thornley (eds), *Great Chronicle*, p. 209.

[13] Halliwell (ed.), *Chronicle*, pp. 6–7; 'Hearne's Fragment', p. 24; Riley (ed.), *Croyland*, p. 446; TNA, PROB 11/5, fol. 216r; TNA, PROB 11/5, fols. 227v–229r.

Hergest, Pembroke's half-brother, was the leading representative of his family. The Donnes of Kidwelly were also present, as were members of the Morgan and Havard families of Brecon. Sir Richard Herbert and Thomas Vaughan, both depicted wearing the Yorkist livery collar on their monuments, were killed. The effigy of Sir Henry Wogan (d. 1475) features the same collar; his son Sir John was also killed. A total of 168 'worthier persons' died fighting for the royalist cause at the battle.[14]

It is likely that those who fought at Edgecote, or their surviving kin, saw themselves as brothers in arms. The culture of ritual brotherhood was popular among the gentry and aristocracy of western Europe between the eleventh and seventeenth centuries. The bond was instigated through a reciprocal oath or letter which promised service, counsel and succour. The ritual was frequently accompanied by the exchange of a token such as a necklace, this exchange of a material item confirming the bond. There were often kinship links between sworn brethren, and, for those not related, the powerful familial nature of the relationship was explicitly expressed through referring to each other as brother in wills.[15] Exceptionally, the link was literally put into stone. An inscribed marble slab in Constantinople commemorating Sir William Neville and Sir John Clanvowe, who both died in 1391, depicts their two helmets facing one another in an attempt to visualise their friendship.[16] Unusually, their two shields impale the Neville arms with those of Clanvowe. Heraldry was therefore being utilised to advertise their comradeship. Although there is no evidence to support the suggestion that any of the principal players among the Yorkist ranks at Edgecote were sworn brethren, it is helpful to interpret their relationship within this context. Perhaps the inclusion of livery collars on the tombs of those who fought and died at the battle was to some degree inspired by their links through combat, a visual manifestation of their ties in death.

In Chapter 3 I introduced the concept of fictive kinship, and its applicability when viewing groups of collar wearers. In the case of those individuals in Wales and Derbyshire who have been the focus of investigation, all were related: they *were* kin. In these instances it is more appropriate to interpret the collective inclusion of collars on their memorials as an attempt to affirm, or more appropriately to reaffirm, their ties. For the Herbert affinity, perhaps the collars acted to reinforce long-standing bonds of kin and tenure which had been severely traumatised by what was, in effect, mass death; the core of the affinity had after all been wiped out. In this respect, the memorials were just as much a solace for

---

[14] Harvey (ed.), *Itineraries*, pp. 340–1; Halliwell (ed.), *Chronicle*, p. 7.
[15] Keen, 'Brotherhood in Arms', 1–17; E.A.R. Brown, 'Ritual Brotherhood in Western Medieval Europe', *Traditio*, 52 (1997), 357–81.
[16] S. Düll, A. Luttrell and M. Keen, 'Faithful into Death: The Tomb Slab of Sir William Neville and Sir John Clanvowe, Constantinople 1391', *Antiquaries Journal*, 71 (1991), 174–90, esp. 183–5.

the living as a commemoration of the dead. We are therefore brought back to a significant theme: the use of livery collars on memorials as a manifestation, and indeed perpetuation, of the collective identity of the deceased and their kin.

William Herbert, earl of Pembroke (d. 1469)

Herbert's links with the house of York were fostered by his father Sir William ap Thomas, who served as Richard, duke of York's chief steward of Usk and Caerleon from the 1430s. He was a member of York's ducal council as early as 1441, and was still working for the duke a year before his death in 1445.[17] The effigies of William and his wife Gwladys Ddu lie in the centre of the Herbert chapel at Abergavenny. The tomb was probably commissioned after the death of Gwladys in 1454. William is depicted wearing a collar of SS, the first of a succession of Herbert monuments to feature a livery collar on their memorials (Figure 8). As instigator of the family's rise to national prominence it is perhaps fitting that he was the first to feature a royal collar on his tomb effigy, a practice that was repeated by subsequent generations of his family. Herbert took over his father's responsibilities at Usk and Caerleon in 1450, and his support for York continued throughout the mid-1450s. In May 1454 Sir Walter Devereux, Herbert's father-in-law, wrote to the duke to report that Herbert 'saith he is noo monis mon but only youres'.[18] It can be safely assumed that the subsequent violent activities of Herbert had the tacit backing of York.

In 1456 Herbert's affinity, which included Devereux and members of the Vaughan family, were involved in disturbances in Hereford which were instigated by the murder of Watkin Vaughan, eldest son of Sir Roger Vaughan of Bredwardine. Herbert took control of the city and forced the justices of the peace to condemn several burgesses for their supposed murder of Vaughan. They were immediately hanged by Herbert. Subsequently the Devereux/Herbert/Vaughan affinity carried out several raids in Herefordshire, with Herbert's brothers Richard and Thomas being heavily implicated.[19] In August their 2,000 strong affinity captured and imprisoned Edmund Tudor, earl of Richmond, at Carmarthen Castle, then under the jurisdiction of the duke of York. They then moved on to Aberystwyth Castle, where York was constable, where they proceeded to hold illegal sessions and release several prisoners.[20] In September Herbert and

---

[17] NLW, Badminton Deeds, 1044; Nicolas (ed.), *Privy Council*, v, pp. 136–8; Johnson, *Richard of York*, pp. 17, 240; BL, Egerton Charters, 7358.

[18] NLW, Llangibby MSS, C899; Badminton Deeds, 976, 977; BL, Cotton MS Vespasian F VIII, fol. 99r, in Pugh, 'Magnates, Knights and Gentry', p. 92. Herbert married Devereux's daughter Anne in 1449.

[19] A. Herbert, 'Herefordshire, 1413–61: Some Aspects of Society and Public Order', in Griffiths (ed.), *Patronage, The Crown and The Provinces*, pp. 103–22; TNA, KB 9/35.

[20] Storey, *End of the House of Lancaster*, pp. 179–81.

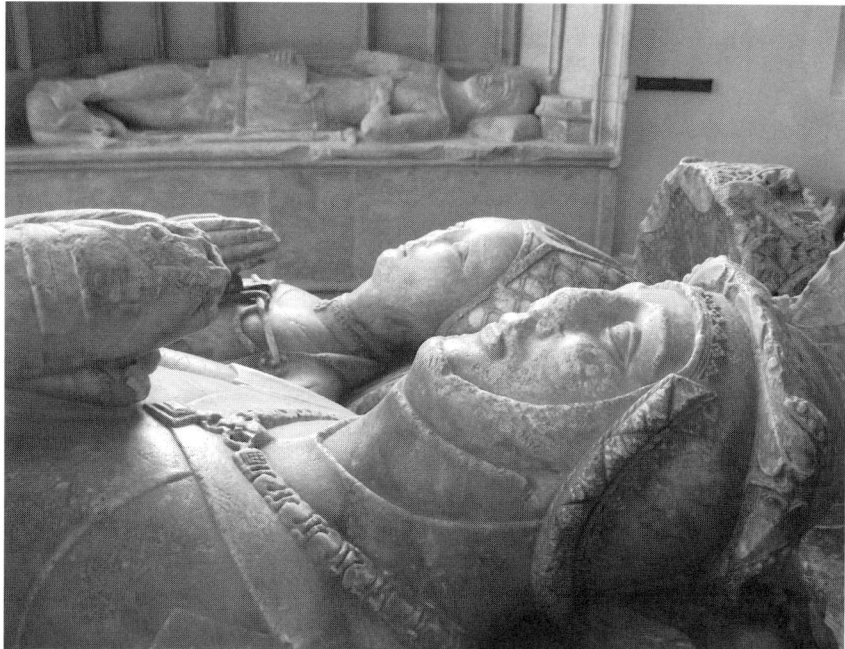

Figure 8. Priory Church of St Mary, Abergavenny (Monmouthshire). Sir William ap Thomas (d. 1445) and his wife, Gwladys.

Devereux were summoned before the great council at Coventry. Devereux was sent to Windsor Castle and the council advised that Herbert be imprisoned in the Tower, but he soon escaped, and in October he was coordinating raids in Glamorgan and Llandaff from his base at Abergavenny. He was subsequently declared a rebel with 500 marks offered for his detainment.[21] In May of the following year, as the indictments against him and his affinity proliferated, Herbert was reconciled with the king at Leicester. He was pardoned alongside his brothers-in-law Thomas and Roger Vaughan at Coventry in June, perhaps in an effort by the court to wrestle his support away from the duke of York.[22]

This was not the first time that Herbert and his brothers-in-law had been involved in riotous behaviour. In July 1453 they appeared before the king's council after involving themselves in the Glamorgan dispute between the earl of Warwick and the duke of Somerset.[23] It appears the families of Herbert and Vaughan

---

[21] *CCR 1454–61*, pp. 158, 174; TNA, KB 9/35.
[22] *PL*, iii, p. 118; *CPR 1452–61*, pp. 353, 360, 367; Evans, *Wars of the Roses*, pp. 98–100.
[23] Herbert was Warwick's sheriff of Glamorgan: T.B. Pugh, 'The Marcher Lords of Glamorgan, 1317–1485', in Pugh (ed.), *Glamorgan County History*, p. 196; G.T. Clark, *Cartae et Alia Munimenta quae ad Dominium de Glamorgancia pertinent*, 6 vols (Cardiff, 1910), v, 1634.

shared a penchant for violent action to attain their goals. The amalgamation of the two families into a formidable affinity, each providing a significant show of manpower, meant that their goals were frequently attained. Well before the fateful battle of Edgecote, the two families evidently shared a close solidarity and sense of loyalty to one another.

If the Lancastrian court had wished to win the support of Herbert they were to be disappointed. After the battle of Northampton on 10 July 1460, and with York and the Nevilles now firmly in control of the government, Herbert, Devereux and Sir Roger Vaughan were ordered to restore order in Wales. After the death of York at Wakefield in December, Herbert and his brother Sir Richard, alongside Devereux and Sir Roger Vaughan, were considered the chief supporters of York's son Edward, earl of March.[24] It was Herbert's affinity which formed the core of Edward's victorious army at the battle of Mortimer's Cross in February 1461: William Worcester lists Sir Richard Herbert, Sir Roger Vaughan and Philip Vaughan (singled out as 'the most noble esquire of lances among all the rest') among Edward's leading captains. It is likely that Roger's brother Thomas was also present.[25] At a meeting at Baynard's Castle on 3 March, in which the decision was taken that Edward should be made king, William Herbert was present among the Yorkist inner circle. The following day he was at Westminster to witness Edward's proclamation as king. It is clear that Herbert was by now a trusted and intimate servant of Edward, one of his few 'chosen and faithful'. His military support had given Edward victory over Jasper Tudor's Lancastrian army at Mortimer's Cross. Indeed, Tudor acknowledged the importance of the 'traitors Marche, Herbert, and Dunns with their affinityes' in a letter to Roger Puleston on 25 February.[26] A few months later Lewis Glyn Cothi described how Herbert had 'triumphed with [the] white roses' of Edward in the north of England.[27] Not for the first time, Herbert was being explicitly linked with one of the badges of the Yorkists, thus symbolising his close affinity and loyalty to the royal house.

Herbert's influence at the centre of Edward's polity would increase until his death in 1469. There is no more graphic illustration of his close relationship with the king than an illustration in John Lydgate's *Troy Book*, c. 1461–62 (Plate 7).[28]

[24] CPR 1452–61, pp. 549, 602; Nicolas (ed.), *Privy Council*, vi, pp. 304–5; J. Nasmith (ed.), *Itineraria Symonis Simeonis et Willelmi de Worcestre* (Cambridge, 1778), p. 328.
[25] Harvey (ed.), *Itineraries*, pp. 203–7.
[26] Stevenson (ed.), 'Wilhelmi Wyrcester Annales', p. 777; Gairdner (ed.), *Historical Collections*, pp. 214–15; C.L. Kingsford, *Chronicles of London* (Oxford, 1905), pp. 173–4; Rymer, *Foedera*, xi, p. 473. 'Dunn' was Sir John Donne of Kidwelly (d. 1503) (Plate 2). He was an esquire of the body to the king, and shared close connections with the Herberts and Vaughans. He was buried near to Edward in St George's Chapel, Windsor, as requested in his will: TNA, PROB 11/13, fol. 94v.
[27] NLW, 6512, 1C, fol. 4: translation of 'Syr Wiliam Herbart'; W. Davies and J. Jones (eds), *Gwaith Lewis Glyn Cothi* (Oxford, 1837), pp. 58–64.
[28] BL, Royal MS 18 D II, fol. 6.

Herbert and his wife are depicted kneeling before Edward IV. Their arms and mottos, *e las sy longuement*, and *De toute* are included in the composition. There appears to have been an attempt to show direct eye contact between Herbert and his sovereign, accentuating their personal relationship. Although neither Herbert nor his wife is wearing a livery collar, the two household servants either side of Edward, clad in red royal livery, are wearing Yorkist suns and roses collars, the first extant depiction of the Yorkist livery collar in manuscript form. Their positions, directly above Herbert and his wife, symbolise their service to the king: they literally sit under the representation of his power and dignity. The positioning of the two servants wearing livery collars, immediately to the left and right of Edward, is also perhaps a statement of the nature of royal power, a reflection of the propagation, as it were, of the royal power and majesty outwards from the person of the king. The image is directly comparable to another dating from c. 1490, depicting Henry VII and his courtiers reviewing a book of astrology. In a very similar depiction to the miniature in the *Troy Book*, the figure directly to the left of the king bears the sword of estate, and he too wears a livery collar, this time that of SS (Plate 8).

Inevitably Herbert's support for Edward after his coronation resulted in a plethora of commissions and grants in Wales and the Marches. He and Walter Devereux were ordered to rid south Wales of the Lancastrian threat during the spring of 1461, and Herbert was created chief justice and chamberlain of south Wales – an office in which he wielded full authority as principal representative of the king – and steward of the royal counties of Carmarthenshire and Cardiganshire. He and his brothers Thomas and John were commissioned to recover the lands of Jasper Tudor, earl of Pembroke, and were involved in various other commissions in south Wales during the summer.[29] In September the Herbert brothers and Devereux were granted custody of the lands of the duke of Buckingham during his minority, and Herbert was made steward of Brecon, Huntington and Hay, and effectively given control of the lordship of Newport.[30] In a characteristic act of nepotism on the part of Herbert, his brother Sir Richard was made sheriff of Wentloog and seneschal of Machen shortly after.[31] Indeed, the Herberts and Vaughans had been working together to acquire land in Wentloog and Machen since the early 1450s, and this association would continue into the sixteenth century.[32] By September Herbert and Devereux, now Lords

---

[29] CPR 1461–67, pp. 7, 30, 38; R.A. Griffiths, *The Principality of Wales in the Later Middle Ages: The Structure of Personnel and Government, I. South Wales, 1277–1536* (Cardiff, 1972), pp. 22–30, 155–6.

[30] CPR 1461–67, pp. 43, 100; T.B. Pugh (ed.), *The Marcher Lordships of South Wales 1415–1536, Select Documents* (Cardiff, 1963), p. 21.

[31] NLW, Tredegar MSS, 12/4; Alice M. Dixon Collection, II, 7, 8.

[32] NLW, Tredegar MSS, 110/74; Alice M. Dixon Collection, II, 6; Tredegar MSS, 27/23, 27/24, 27/17, 27/28, 90/65, 98/53, 90/96, 90/87.

Herbert and Ferrers, were hard at work rooting out Lancastrian resistance in Wales. The king's judgement of their abilities was made clear in a letter written in September: 'As for any grete doing in Wales I trust God we shal not doubte. The Lord Herbert and the Lord Ferrers ... ben gone afore to clense the countreye afore us.'[33] Trust and a supreme confidence now underpinned the relationship between Herbert and the king. They shared a close affinity, and it would not be an exaggeration to suggest that they had become close friends.

The next task was to take the remaining Lancastrian castles in Wales. The captain of Pembroke Castle, Sir John Skydmore, surrendered on 30 September 1461, and received a pardon from Herbert. Skydmore was, however, soon relieved of his lands, those in Herefordshire being given to Sir Richard Herbert, thus extending his territorial interests into an area dominated by the Vaughans. It was suggested that the Herberts had persuaded the king, 'by mervelous pryvat labour', to forfeit the lands, in a gesture suggestive of personal favour.[34] At Pembroke was found the infant Henry Tudor, who was taken to Raglan, where he was brought up by Lady Herbert. For a fee of £1,000 her husband was granted Tudor's custody and marriage. Herbert was granted the extensive lands of Jasper Tudor in February of the following year, by which time all the Welsh castles in Lancastrian hands, save Harlech, had surrendered to the king. Herbert had ensured that 'the moost part of gentilmen and men of worship are comen yn to the king and have grace, of all Wales'.[35] The grants continued apace, including that of the lordship of Haverfordwest, thus connecting Herbert to an area in which his kin the Wogans and the Vaughans were closely associated.[36] He also acquired the manors of Crickhowell from Thomas Pauncefote, and Tretower. Both were amalgamated to form a separate lordship in 1463. Herbert later entrusted Tretower Court to Sir Roger Vaughan, who made it his chief residence.[37] Raglan, the Herbert *caput honoris*, was elevated into a royal lordship in 1465, in the process becoming the final Welsh Marcher lordship to be created. The estate was augmented with land from the royal lordship of Usk.[38] Herbert, already one of Edward's intimates as a king's knight, was created a knight of the Garter in March 1462. His place at the heart of the king's inner circle was secured, and there he would remain until his death at Edgecote seven years later.

---

[33] H. Ellis (ed.), *Original Letters Illustrative of English History*, 1st Series, 3 vols (London, 1824), i, pp. 15–16.

[34] *PROME*, Edward IV, Parliament of October 1472 to March 1475, First Roll, mems. 21–22; Thomas, 'The Herberts', pp. 67–8.

[35] Hall, *Chronicle*, pp. 285–7; Evans, *Wars of the Roses*, p. 192; *CPR 1461–67*, p. 114; *PL*, iii, p. 312.

[36] *CPR 1461–67*, p. 119; NLW, Picton Castle MSS, 12.

[37] *CCR 1461–68*, p. 149; *CPR 1461–67*, p. 268; G. Owen, *The Description of Penbrokshire*, 3 vols (1892–1906), i–ii, p. 29.

[38] *CPR 1461–67*, p. 425; Griffiths, 'Herbert, William, First Earl of Pembroke (c. 1423–1469)'.

Grants, offices and commissions continued to be showered on Herbert into the mid-1460s. Given the stewardships of the duchy of York lordships of Usk, Caerleon and Clifford, and of the lordships of Builth, Dinas and Ewyas, and made chief forester of the royal forest in south Wales, he had secured hegemony in the region. His powers in the north were extended in 1467 when he was made chief justice of north Wales, steward of the lordships of Denbigh and Montgomery, and constable of Harlech Castle, the final Lancastrian stronghold in the country.[39] In July 1468 a commission was given to the Herbert brothers, Sir Roger Vaughan and others to quash the Lancastrian threat in the north. After Sir Richard Herbert defeated a force led by Jasper Tudor at Denbigh, the town was devastated, 'clere defacid with fier by hostilite'. The Herberts then proceeded to savage Gwynedd. Punitive measures were harsh: seven brothers were executed on Anglesey, despite the protestations of their mother.[40] Harlech Castle, despite it being 'so stronge that men sayde that hyt was impossybylle unto any man to gete hyt', finally capitulated on 14 August.[41] Although a pardon was issued by Herbert, several of the garrison were taken to London, where Thomas Elwyk and John Trueblode were executed.[42] Victory had finally been achieved, leaving Herbert 'the onlye and entire comaunder of Wales'.[43] His reward: the earldom of Pembroke, bestowed on him on 8 September 1468. His influence was without comparison; his close affinity with the king had been rewarded with unprecedented power in the region and beyond. Of course the relationship was mutually beneficial: the king safeguarded an area in which Lancastrian resistance had lingered, and Herbert's ambitions had been fulfilled.

The Herbert hegemony in Wales declined under William's heir, William (d.1490), although the family's connections with the house of York were not entirely extinguished. William accompanied the king on his procession through London after the battle of Tewkesbury in May 1471, was present at the Garter feast in 1472, and travelled with the king's expedition to France in 1475.[44] However, in 1479 Herbert was forced to surrender the earldom of Pembroke in exchange for the earldom of Huntingdon.[45] With the accession of Richard III in 1483, Herbert's fortunes took an upward turn, culminating in his marriage to the king's illegitimate daughter Katherine in 1484. This was followed by several grants, offices and annuities, including the issues of the lordship of Haverfordwest where the

---

[39] *CPR 1461–67*, pp. 526–7; *CPR 1467–77*, pp. 41, 22, 79, 154.
[40] *CPR 1467–77*, pp. 102–3; Stevenson (ed.), 'Wilhelmi Wyrcester Annales', p. 791.
[41] Gairdner (ed.), *Historical Collections*, p. 237; Owen, *Description of Penbrokshire*, pp. 27–8.
[42] NLW, Peniarth Estate MSS, CA1; 'Pardon to Rhys ap Griffith ap Aron, of Peniarth, and Others', *Archaeologia Cambrensis*, 15 (1860), 309–12.
[43] Owen, *Description of Penbrokshire*, p. 28.
[44] C.L. Kingsford, *English Historical Literature in the Fifteenth Century* (Oxford, 1913), p. 381; HP, p. 68.
[45] *CChR 1427–1516*, p. 250; *PROME*, Edward IV, Parliament of January to February 1483, mem. 14.

Herberts and Wogans had tenurial interests, and the stewardship of Usk, thus continuing the family's close association with the duchy of York estate.[46] He did not, however, resist Henry Tudor in 1485, and was pardoned in 1486.

Kinship and tenurial ties

As was the case with Derbyshire, the individuals and their families which form the focus here shared close bonds of kinship and tenure. The Herberts and Vaughans had been associated through kinship for several decades before Edgecote. Sir Roger Vaughan of Bredwardine fought at Agincourt in the retinue of David Gam, whose daughter Gwladys Ddu he had married some years before. Both he and his father-in-law died on the battlefield, tradition has it after having been knighted by Henry V.[47] William Herbert's father Sir William ap Thomas later married Gwladys Ddu, Vaughan's widow. She and Vaughan had three sons: Watkin, Thomas of Hergest and Sir Roger of Tretower, who were brought up with their half-brothers William Herbert and Sir Richard Herbert at Raglan Castle, in the duke of York's lordship of Usk.[48] Not surprisingly, these individuals became close allies. In his will of 16 July 1469, William Herbert referred to Sir Roger Vaughan of Tretower as his 'brother' alongside Sir Richard Herbert. They were both to be prayed for, second only to his immediate kin.[49] As their predecessors had done before them, many members of these two families were to die fighting for their king at the battle of Edgecote.

Despite trouble during the mid-1470s involving the bastard sons of Pembroke and two sons of Sir Roger Vaughan, the close relationship between the families continued. Any lingering tensions had apparently healed by 1484, when William Herbert, earl of Huntingdon, enfeoffed his estates to his mother, John Herbert, Sir Thomas Vaughan, Thomas Vaughan of Bredwardine, Walter Vaughan of Kington and William Vaughan of Clifford. In 1478 Sir Thomas and John Vaughan were also included in an enfeoffment of Dunster and Minehead.[50]

Thomas and Sir Roger Vaughan, step-brothers to William Herbert, were crucial members of the earl's affinity. Their support extended Herbert's influence eastwards into England, with their wider kinship network providing additional manpower for his affinity. From their early mutual links with the duke of York, dating back to the 1430s,[51] to their support at Edgecote, the two families were closely allied. From the 1430s, members of the various branches of the Vaughan

---

[46] *CPR 1476–85*, pp. 431, 538; *Harleian 433*, i, pp. 94, 139, 269; iii, pp. 105, 193.
[47] Thomas and Thornley (eds), *Great Chronicle*, p. 93; *HP*, pp. 36–7; Thomas, 'The Herberts', p. 2; R.W. Banks, 'On the Family of Vaughan of Hergest', *Archaeologia Cambrensis*, 26 (1871), 23–4.
[48] For Raglan, see J.R. Kenyon, *Raglan Castle* (Cardiff, 2003).
[49] *HP*, p. 56; Thomas, 'The Herberts', pp. 288–9.
[50] *CPR 1467–77*, p. 429; *HP*, pp. 68, 72–3, 77.
[51] NLW, Badminton Deeds, 1044, 1103, 1742.

family were involved in land transactions with the Herberts, and the two families regularly co-witnessed deeds. The Vaughans were also employed by the Herberts as stewards, bailiffs and reeves on their estates, and the bonds continued into the sixteenth century.[52] The relationship was not, of course, one sided. Through Herbert's influence, the Vaughan brothers and their kin were able to secure favour with the king in the form of offices and grants. From his main residence at Hergest, Thomas Vaughan's influence stretched into Wales, where he served as receiver of the Stafford lordships of Brecon and Hay, in addition to Huntington (where he was also constable), in the 1450s.[53] An early indication of his loyalty to Edward IV came in the autumn of 1461 when he was reappointed receiver of these lordships during the minority of the duke of Buckingham. He was also made mayor of Newport by 1459, and named as receiver by Herbert after he took custody of the lordship in 1461.[54] Along with his Herbert kin, he remained a staunch Yorkist throughout the 1460s. The two families were regularly entrusted to work together for the crown, emphasising an effective working relationship not only with one another, but also with their king.

In addition to being William Herbert's brother-in-law through his marriage to Herbert's sister Margaret, Sir Henry Wogan (d. 1475) was also closely related to the Vaughans through the marriage of his daughter Elizabeth to Watkin Vaughan (d. 1456).[55] When compared to his in-laws, Sir Henry has left little impression in the records. Alongside Sir William ap Thomas, he was a prominent member of Humphrey, duke of Gloucester's retinue and, with Thomas Herbert, was arrested with the duke in 1447. It may have been that Sir Henry and William developed a close bond through their service on Gloucester's council, a relationship which resulted in the marriages between the two families.[56] It was probably as a result of Gloucester's favour that Wogan served as deputy justiciar of south Wales between 1442 and 1446, and again in 1455. He also served as seneschal of Pembroke and Haverford during the 1440s and 1450s. It is probable that he fought alongside Herbert at Mortimer's Cross in 1461, and his son John fought and died at Edgecote.[57]

---

[52] NLW, Badminton Deeds, 10, 11, 12, 1103, 1105–6, 1519; Tredegar MSS, 27/24, 12/5, 90/87, 110/74; Badminton Manorial, I, 6, 23/24; I, 1577, 1578, 1582, 1584, 1587; I, 1501–3, 1509–10, 1560a, 1561–2, 1564, 1568, 2610; Tredegar MSS, 27/28.
[53] C.J. Robinson, *Herefordshire Mansions and Manors* (London, 1872), pp. 184–5; Pugh, *Marcher Lordships*, p. 246.
[54] NLW, Tredegar MSS, 62/34; NLW, Badminton Manorial, 1503.
[55] P.C. Bartrum, *Welsh Genealogies AD 1400–1500*, 18 vols (Aberystwyth, 1983), iii, p. 451; G.T. Clark, *Limbus Patrum Morganiae et Glamorganiae* (London, 1886), pp. 280–1; F. Green, 'The Wogans of Pembrokeshire', *West Wales Historical Records*, 6 (1916), 169–232, at 194–5.
[56] Kingsford, *Historical Literature*, p. 363; Thomas, 'The Herberts', p. 15.
[57] Griffiths, *Principality of Wales*, pp. 150–1; BL, Sloane Charters, xxxii, 5, 20; Harvey (ed.), *Itineraries*, pp. 340–1.

The Herberts shared land interests with the Wogan family in Haverfordwest and, particularly after William Herbert's grant of the lordship in 1462, his family were brought into close contact with the Wogans of Boulston and the Vaughans.[58] In 1422 Henry, Margaret and a John Vaughan, chaplain, granted a burgage in 'le Marketstreet' in Haverfordwest, and Henry was renting out lands in Corby (near Wiston) during the 1450s. The link with the Herbert family was long-standing. During the 1470s Henry Wogan of Boulston served as steward of Haverfordwest for the earl of Huntingdon.[59]

As with Wogan, there is a paucity of source material regarding William Griffith. Although there is no evidence that William fought at Edgecote, Henry Griffith, probably a relative, was regularly associated with the Herbert affinity from the 1450s.[60] Despite the apparent lack of military activity there is, however, once again a kinship link with the Herberts. William's granddaughter Jane married Sir William Herbert (d. c. 1518), son and heir of Sir Richard of Coldbrook (d. 1469), thus expanding the Griffiths' interests into the south of Wales. During the 1480s Sir Walter and William Herbert served as witnesses to deeds concerning their new Griffith kin. Sir Walter Herbert was also involved in the recovery of lands by Joan Griffith, Jane's mother, in 1506.[61]

Another family warrants consideration: the Berkeleys of Berkeley Castle. Although their links with the Herberts were not as strong as those between the families discussed above, and the family did not fight at Edgecote, they at least allow us to introduce another example of the livery collar being utilised on church monuments as a symbol of family identity. Sir William ap Thomas's first wife was Elizabeth Bluet, heiress of Sir John Bluet of Raglan and widow of Sir James Berkeley. It was through Elizabeth that the Herberts' long association with Raglan came into fruition. When Elizabeth died in 1420, William married Gwladus Ddu, although his stepson James, Lord Berkeley (d. 1463), who had been born and raised in Raglan Castle, allowed him to continue residing at Raglan for the term of his life. In 1432 a deal was struck with Berkeley whereby William bought the manor and castle at Raglan for 1,000 marks. The sale of Raglan was probably precipitated by the protracted difficulties Berkeley faced over the inheritance of the Berkeley estates with his cousin Elizabeth Berkeley, sole child of Thomas, Lord Berkeley (d. 1417), and her husband Richard Beauchamp, earl of Warwick. The struggle was ultimately resolved in a skirmish at Nibley Green

---

[58] *CPR 1446–52*, p. 272; *CPR 1452–61*, p. 561; *HP*, pp. 39–40.
[59] NLW, Picton Castle MSS, 19; Eaton Evans and Williams Collection, 22; Prendergast, Haverfordwest, Pembrokeshire Record Office, HDX/337/42; H. Owen (ed.), *A Calendar of the Public Records relating to Pembrokeshire*, Cymmrodorion Record Series, 3 vols (London, 1911–18), i, pp. 53–4, 134.
[60] BL, Additional Charters, 1816; *CFR 1452–61*, pp. 36–7; *CPR 1467–77*, p. 54.
[61] *HP*, p. 102; Bartrum, *Welsh Genealogies*, viii, pp. 1265–7; NLW, Badminton Deeds, 978; Powis Castle Deeds, 11137.

in March 1470, where Thomas Talbot, Viscount Lisle, was killed. It was during the 1430s that William ap Thomas began to build the castle at Raglan into the impressive fortress we see today.[62]

James, Lord Berkeley, was buried in the family chapel which he had erected at Berkeley, where his alabaster tomb survives. The effigy, the style of which suggests a later date than that of his death in 1463, lies on a high tomb chest. He is represented with long hair and wearing a tabard depicting the family arms, *(gules), a chevron between ten crosses pattée (gules)*. He wears a Yorkist suns and roses livery collar. A smaller effigy, measuring 4' 10", lies next to him on the same tomb chest and is almost identical. It also features a Yorkist collar. It has been suggested that this represents Berkeley's second son James, who died fighting in France in 1452.[63] The inclusion of a Yorkist livery collar makes it more likely that the effigy in fact represents another of Berkeley's sons. Just under twenty miles south of Berkeley is the Lord Mayor's Chapel, formerly the chapel of St Mark's Hospital, Billeswick, Bristol. On a high tomb chest, under a Berkeley arched canopy, lie the effigies of Sir Maurice Berkeley (d. 1464) and his wife Ellen (d. c. 1475). Sir Maurice wears a Yorkist collar of suns and roses with an oblong shaped pendant. The effigy was reworked during the 1501 refurbishment of the Berkeley monuments in the church. In addition, the effigies of Thomas and Alice Bridges in Gloucester Cathedral, dating from *c.* 1410, are featured wearing SS collars. Alice was daughter and co-heir of Sir Thomas Berkeley of Coberley.[64]

Here we may have another example of the family of the deceased influencing the decision to place a collar on an effigy.[65] As James, Lord Berkeley, apparently died some years before the construction of his tomb, perhaps his son William (d. 1492) may have been responsible for its composition. He was more closely associated with the Yorkist court than his father had been. Made a viscount by Edward IV in 1481, he was given the title of the earl of Nottingham by Richard III in 1483, although he also found favour with Henry Tudor who created him marquis of Berkeley in 1489. It may be the case that he ordered the construction of his father's tomb at some point before Bosworth in 1485. The inclusion of livery collars on the tombs at Berkeley not only reflects the family's connections with the house of York, but also places them with a family tradition, begun with the erection of the Bridges tomb at Gloucester Cathedral.

---

[62] R.A. Griffiths, 'Lordship and Society in the Fifteenth Century', in R.A. Griffiths (ed.), *The Gwent County History*, 5 vols (Cardiff, 2004–13), ii, pp. 262–3.
[63] M.E. Bagnall-Oakeley, 'On the Monumental Effigies of the Family of Berkeley', *Transactions of the Bristol and Gloucestershire Archaeological Society*, 15 (1892), 99–100.
[64] I.M. Roper, *The Monumental Effigies of Gloucestershire and Bristol* (Gloucester, 1931), pp. 52–7; Friar, p. 76.
[65] As we have seen with the Yorkist collar on the effigy of Ralph Neville, earl of Westmorland, at Brancepeth.

In some cases the kinship associations between the families of the Herbert affinity were continued over several generations, this was particularly the case with the Herberts and the Vaughans. Each family was to some extent related to every other family (see Appendix 1). It should not therefore be surprising that they would want to celebrate, or at least acknowledge, their close ties in some form. This was achieved in part through the inclusion of a livery collar on their memorials. But the collars signified other shared facets, not least service to the Yorkist king. Indeed, in some cases it becomes apparent that a personal bond was nurtured with Edward IV.

Royal service and favour

The Herbert affinity are a conspicuous presence among the exemptions from the 1467 Act of Resumption. Among those not required to surrender their royal grants of land were Thomas Herbert and his son Thomas, esquires of the body; Sir Richard Herbert, 'our well beloved knight'; William Herbert, esquire; Sir Roger Vaughan; 'our most trusty and well-beloved'; Thomas Vaughan, esquire (son of Watkin Vaughan, d. 1456); and another Thomas Vaughan, yeoman of the crown.[66] The strong household connection within the affinity is immediately apparent. The inclusion of livery collars on the effigies of Sir Richard Herbert at Abergavenny and Thomas Vaughan at Kington supports the theory that members of the royal household were awarded them.[67] Although we know that the earl of Pembroke, an eminent member of Edward IV's household as a king's knight, was the recipient of several collars, it is not clear whether he was depicted wearing one on his tomb effigy as it is no longer extant. In an inventory of the goods of Pembroke's son Sir Walter Herbert (d. 1507), found at Raglan Castle after his death, 'two slender collers of cours gold enameled' were listed among the items. It is likely that these were livery collars. Sir Walter continued the family's close association with the royal household, serving as knight of the body to Henry VII.[68]

The Welsh poet Lewis Glyn Cothi praised Herbert's rise to success, accentuating his association with the king and elevating the earl to almost mythological proportions in the process:

> Edward is a Charlemagne, by St Martin's grace!
> Herbert is Rolando, the liberal one
> Edward is like Arthur, as it beseems him
> Herbert like Julius Caesar with his black spear.

---

[66] *PROME*, Edward IV, Parliament of June 1467 to June 1468, mems. 6–20.
[67] See above, pp. 43–6.
[68] *CPR 1494–1509*, p. 603; NLW, Badminton Deeds, 347.

Glyn Cothi goes on to affirm that Herbert, Edward's 'master-lock', will 'keep all the men with the crown'.[69] Guto'r Glyn also celebrated the inseparable bond between Herbert and his king: 'Edward and his supporter, Herbert, are united as one. He is his limb and his elbow, his arm and his foot whenever a battle if fought. In the council he is consulted on all matters.'[70] The message could not be more explicit: not only did the earl provide the practical military strength that brought Edward to the throne, but he was also an intimate associate of the king, giving advice whenever required.

In an era in which royal household connections were an efficacious means of securing patronage, it would be natural that the earl's kin shared in his favour with the house of York.[71] His brother Thomas was a servant of Richard, duke of York, with whom he fought in France. Alongside his father Sir William ap Thomas and Sir Henry Wogan, he was also a member of Humphrey, duke of Gloucester's retinue and was one of those arrested on his death.[72] He was closely involved with his brother in the disturbances in the Marches in the 1450s, and was included in the pardons issued to many of his Herbert and Vaughan kin in June 1457 and June 1460. An esquire of the body to Edward IV in 1461, Thomas enjoyed the favour of the king, sitting on various commissions, many with his Herbert and Vaughan kin, and receiving various offices and grants throughout the 1460s, the majority associated with Gloucestershire and Herefordshire.[73] In September 1462 he was selected to travel to Spain with Thomas Kent and Peter Taster on an ultimately fruitless ambassadorial mission for discussions with Henry the Impotent.[74] An intriguing link with the Fitzherberts of Derbyshire was fostered when Thomas Herbert and John Fitzherbert were granted 'Le Holynherst' and 'Prince Fee' in Derbyshire in 1461, confirmed for life in 1465.[75] The two may have become acquainted through their service to the king. It is possible that the Herbert family, in an attempt to promote their Anglo Norman heritage by extending their history back to the Conquest, encouraged the belief that the Fitzherberts were their progenitors.

John Herbert, possibly a brother but more likely a cousin of the first earl, was also involved in several commissions, many of which involved other members of his family. In addition he was a prominent member of the prince of Wales's

---

[69] NLW, 6512, 1C, fols. 5–7; Davies and Jones (eds), *Gwaith Lewis Glyn Cothi*, p. 63.
[70] Williams and Williams (eds), *Gwaith Guto'r Glyn*, p. 136.
[71] For a detailed discussion of the various members of the family who served the house of York see Thomas, 'The Herberts', pp. 221–77.
[72] Harvey (ed.), *Itineraries*, p. 341; J. Gairdner (ed.), *Three Fifteenth Century Chronicles*, Camden Society, New Series, 28 (London, 1880), p. 65.
[73] CPR 1452–61, pp. 367, 594; CPR 1461–67, pp. 8, 15, 30, 38, 65, 74, 99, 151, 197, 424, 523; CPR 1467–77, p. 24.
[74] Scofield, *Edward the Fourth*, i, pp. 260–1.
[75] CFR 1461–71, p. 50; CPR 1461–67, pp. 422–3. See above, p. 111.

council in the 1470s, and served as deputy chamberlain to the earl of Huntingdon in south Wales in 1472 and 1475, and as deputy justiciar in 1475.[76] Several other Herberts also served the Yorkists. William Herbert, esquire, possibly half-brother to the first earl, became the constable of Cardigan Castle in August 1461, and as the king's servitor was appointed escheator of Caernarvon in 1464. It was probably the same William who was deputy chamberlain of south Wales between 1465 and 1468. A William Herbert served as treasurer to the earldom of Pembroke in the mid-1460s, and was receiver of Haverfordwest lordship between 1472 and 1475.[77] William Herbert (d. c. 1518), son of Sir Richard (d. 1469) and esquire of the body to Richard III, received an annuity of 40 marks for his services against the duke of Buckingham in 1483. He may well be the same William Herbert who served as secretary to the prince of Wales.[78]

Sir Richard Herbert, whose principal residence was Coldbrook House near Abergavenny, was an early adherent to the Yorkist cause, along with his older brother. He was connected with the duke of York during the mid-1450s, and was closely associated with the earl of Warwick by 1460.[79] His services towards Edward, earl of March, continued after his accession to the throne. His inclusion in various commissions during the early 1460s, many alongside his brothers William and Thomas, secured his position as a pre-eminent political figure in south Wales. He was included in the September 1461 commission to take custody of the Buckingham lands, in June 1463 he and his brother were instructed to receive various rebels in Wales, and he sat on the *oyer* and *terminer* sessions in north Wales in 1467 and 1468, alongside his brothers William and Thomas and Sir Roger Vaughan. He was also militarily active. In May 1462, a force of 200 men commanded by Herbert and Vaughan secured the surrender of Carreg Cennen Castle, after a hard-fought defence from the garrison,[80] and as we have seen he was instrumental in the brutal campaign in north Wales in 1468. In addition to his roles in the lordship of Newport, he served as deputy justiciar of south Wales under his brother, sitting on the great sessions of Carmarthenshire and Cardiganshire in 1464 and 1466.[81] In February 1462 his estates were augmented with the confiscated lands of Sir John Skydmore and Thomas Fitzharry in Herefordshire,

---

[76] Evans, *Wars of the Roses*, pp. 135, 228; CPR 1461–67, p. 30; CPR 1467–77, pp. 54, 288; Griffiths, *Principality of Wales*, pp. 158–9, 186–8.
[77] CPR 1461–67, pp. 42, 340; NLW, Badminton Deeds, 1501, 1502, 1503; Badminton Manorial, 1564; Griffiths, *Principality of Wales*, pp. 186–8.
[78] His cousin, William Raglan, was granted an annuity of £20: Harleian 433, i, pp. 94–5, 109, 143, 190, 275; TNA, DL 42/20, fol. 10; Somerville, *History of the Duchy*, p. 646.
[79] PL, iii, pp. 245–6.
[80] CPR 1461–67, pp. 100, 280; CPR 1467–77, pp. 54, 102; Griffiths, *Sir Rhys ap Thomas*, p. 28.
[81] Griffiths, *Principality of Wales*, pp. 156, 540.

Gloucestershire, Shropshire and Wales. Three years later he received additional Skydmore lands in Herefordshire, including the manor of Grove.[82]

Thomas Vaughan's younger brother Sir Roger (d. 1471) is more conspicuous in the records than his sibling, perhaps because Herbert and the king saw him as a more effective administrator and military commander.[83] Along with the Herberts, Vaughan developed early ties with the duke of York, serving as his receiver at Builth during the early 1440s.[84] In March 1464 Vaughan, alongside John Donne, crushed a Lancastrian force at Dryslwyn for which they were richly rewarded. The estates supplemented those in the West Country which had been granted to Vaughan in 1462.[85] He sat on a multitude of commissions alongside the Herberts throughout the 1460s, although he appears to have maintained closer ties with the earl of Warwick than his kin. As late as the summer of 1468 he witnessed a charter to Neath Abbey, alongside the earl, in his capacity as Warwick's chancellor of Cardiff.[86] These connections may explain his apparent lack of involvement at Edgecote. If he had been involved, he managed to escape punishment. The links with the Kingmaker did not appear to be detrimental to his relationship with the king. After the battle, Vaughan was entrusted with several offices in Wales, including the constableship of Cardigan Castle.[87] After the battle of Tewkesbury in 1471, Vaughan was sent by Edward to confront Jasper Tudor, who had once again escaped the king's clutches by retreating to Chepstow Castle. However, the plan dramatically backfired and Vaughan was captured and executed by Tudor.[88]

In an ode to Watkin Vaughan, son of Sir Roger, Lewis Glyn Cothi urged the family to remain loyal to Edward IV.[89] They adhered to the poet's advice. Led most notably by Thomas (d. 1493), another of Sir Roger's sons, the family continued to serve the Yorkists in household and administrative roles during the 1470s and 1480s.[90] When the duke of Buckingham rebelled against Richard III in October 1483, Thomas chose not to support his lord but, along with his relatives, raided Buckingham's residence, Brecon Castle, apparently under the instructions of the king. For this act he was granted the stewardship of Brecon.

---

[82] *CPR 1461–67*, pp. 77, 372.
[83] He did not die at Edgecote: H.F.J. Vaughan, 'The Vaughans of Herefordshire', in C. Reade, *Memorials of Old Herefordshire* (London, 1904), pp. 79–94, at p. 85.
[84] Johnson, *Richard of York*, p. 239.
[85] *CPR 1461–67*, pp. 76–7.
[86] *CPR 1467–77*, pp. 54, 57, 58, 102; W. de Gray Birch, *A History of Neath Abbey* (Neath, 1902), pp. 138, 321–31.
[87] *CPR 1467–77*, p. 183.
[88] R. Merrick, *A Book of Glamorganshire's Antiquities by Rice Merrick, Esq. 1578* (Broadway, 1825), p. 34.
[89] Davies and Jones (eds), *Gwaith Lewis Glyn Cothi*, pp. 51–7.
[90] *CPR 1476–85*, p. 222; *Harleian 433*, i, pp. 95, 137, 196, 197, 280, 285; ii, pp. 25, 123; iii, p. 154; Griffiths, *Principality of Wales*, p. 252.

Watkin Vaughan, (d. 1504), son of Thomas (d. 1469), was also made steward and receiver of Huntington by the earl of Huntington after Buckingham's lands were forfeited. Whether Thomas's actions against Buckingham were motivated more by loyalty to his king or by local grievances cannot be ascertained, although judging by the family's past service to the Yorkist regime it appears a degree of genuine duty to the king was involved. In April 1486 Vaughan rebelled against Henry Tudor. Lingering tensions between the two families may have been at the forefront of this action, particularly after Jasper Tudor's earlier beheading of Vaughan's father.[91] The family had apparently remained loyal to the house of York; many did not join Henry Tudor in 1485, and they were evidently not easily won over by the new regime.

A marriage between such geographically distant families as the Herberts and Griffiths would perhaps be surprising for gentry families but, alongside the Herberts, William Griffith was a prominent member of the Yorkist household. The marriage may therefore have been a result of a relationship between the two families which developed through this link. Griffith served as marshal to both Edward IV and Richard III, and was a gentleman usher to the former. In 1483 he was made chamberlain of north Wales by Richard III, a role taken over by his son, another William, after his death.[92] Richard's favour towards Griffith parallels that which he showed to the Vaughan family. Griffith was an early, possibly the first, retainer of William, Lord Hastings, the indenture dating from 6 November 1461.[93] Initially, therefore, his duties and connections would have been forged around this affinity, rather than William Herbert's in the south of Wales. However, their paths would have crossed more frequently after Herbert's remit was extended into the north of Wales in the mid-1460s.

National sentiment

Pembroke and his brother Sir Richard were treated by some as national heroes, martyrs to their nation and their king, particularly by the poets who sung numerous elegies for the brothers and their comrades. Ieuan Deulwyn lamented the loss of a Welsh hero in Sir Richard, in a battle that constituted a national calamity.[94] In his elegy to Thomas Vaughan, Lewis Glyn Cothi reflected on the 'great slaughter to great Cambria' in the battle, urging his three sons to take revenge on the treacherous English. In a fitting reference to the political turmoil of the time, he also refers to the various battle cries of the participants: 'Some,

[91] *Harleian 433*, i, p. 139; Pugh, *Marcher Lordships*, pp. 241, 298.
[92] *CPR 1476–85*, p. 18; *Harleian 433*, ii, p. 90; T.A. Glenn, *The Family of Griffith of Garn and Plasnewydd in the County of Denbigh* (London, 1934), pp. 195, 208b.
[93] Dunham, pp. 119, 123.
[94] I. Williams (ed.), *Casgliad O Waith Ieuan Deulwyn*, Bangor Welsh MSS Society, iv (Bangor, 1909), pp. 54–6, 93–4.

Herbert! Some, our Edward! / Earl Warwick! Others, Harry!'[95] It is noteworthy that some evidently thought they were fighting for the restoration of Henry VI, despite this not being Warwick's intent. It may however have proved useful in persuading some to fight against the royalist army at the battle.

Poets such as Guto'r Glyn and Lewis Glyn Cothi, themselves no lovers of the English, praised the Herberts' close connections with, and staunch loyalty to, Edward IV. After all, Guto stated that, despite the hatred he engendered in England, the earl of Pembroke's principal goal at the battle was to protect his king from the earl of Warwick.[96] Particularly for Guto, Edward and Herbert were potential healers of a factionalism which had existed in Wales since the rebellion of Owain Glyndŵr. But how was Herbert's potential as unifier of the Welsh reconciled with his close links with the English crown? Quite simply, the king, through his Mortimer descent, was seen as 'Welsh'. Some of those who fought for Edward at Edgecote believed that the ancient prophecy that the descendants of the Britons would finally secure the sovereignty of England would finally be delivered.[97] Though this was not to be, in the aftermath of the battle some poets urged their compatriots to support their king, reminding them that he had descended 'from the trunk of old stocks'.[98] For the more realistic Guto, however, the British prophecy had less appeal, his main concern being to plead with Edward to release the nation from its oppression.[99] Edward was, after all, their king, and the fact that he had Welsh blood in his veins added more pertinence. The articulation of loyalty to the king would be reflected in the appearance of Yorkist livery collars on several of the tombs of the deceased.

Other poets eulogised Sir Richard Herbert for his generous hospitality, physical prowess, and leadership, bravery and strength on the battlefield.[100] He was seen as a national hero, perhaps more so than his older brother: there could, after all, only be one soul of the Welsh nation. As with the earl, Sir Richard's exploits for his country are paired with commendations of his loyalty to Edward IV, the 'kingly Welshman'. He is described by Lewis Glyn Cothi as Edward's ally, his seal in the royal councils.[101]

The poets, it should be kept in mind, were very much singing for their supper. Travelling from court to court and singing for their subsistence, whether that was money, a fresh horse or food for the night, they would be expected to eulogise

---

[95] Davies and Jones (eds), *Gwaith Lewis Glyn Cothi*, pp. 16–19, 24.
[96] Evans, *Wars of the Roses*, pp. 174–5.
[97] Riley (ed.), *Croyland*, pp. 446–7.
[98] W.L. Richards (ed.), *Gwaith Dafydd Llwyd o Fathafarn* (Cardiff, 1964), pp. 73–4; translation in Williams, *Renewal and Reformation*, p. 211.
[99] Williams and Williams (eds), *Gwaith Guto'r Glyn*, pp. 157–9.
[100] 'I Syr Rhisiart Herbart', in Davies and Jones (eds), *Gwaith Lewis Glyn Cothi*, pp. 65–9; translation in NLW, 6512, 1C, fols. 9–13.
[101] NLW, 6512, 1C, fols. 9–12.

their hosts. Although Guto has been described as fostering Yorkist sympathies, and others such as Dafydd Llwyd labelled as Lancastrian, the majority of the poets were pragmatic in their approach. It was natural that they would secure as wide a range of patrons as possible, resulting in them singing for supporters of both factions.[102] Their regrettably under-utilised work has a lot to offer the historian. The content of their songs and poems is a reflection of the tastes of the Welsh gentry. More importantly, they are a direct illustration of how their local patrons wished to be portrayed, in the case of the Herberts and Vaughans, as loyal subjects and politically active supporters of the house of York. The fact that the king himself had Welsh blood, albeit rather diluted, running through his veins aided the causes of both the Herberts and their poets, who were particularly successful in pairing the two themes. For the Herberts, the poets' panegyric was another medium, alongside artwork and tomb sculpture, in which to express their associations with the king. They were particularly adept at utilising a variety of artistic forms for their own political agenda.

After the death of Edward IV, the poets turned to Henry Tudor. Unfortunately, despite his greater propensity to appeal to his Welsh roots, particularly to win support in 1485, their dreams were dashed. As Edward before him, Henry failed to transform the fortunes of the Welsh nation and bring them to the forefront of the English polity.

The monuments

William Herbert, earl of Pembroke (d. 1469), Tintern Abbey (Monmouthshire), no extant tomb

There are ambiguities in the earl's will and codicil regarding his intended resting place. In his will of 16 July 1469 Herbert requested to be buried at Abergavenny, close to his stronghold at Raglan and resting place of his father, 'in the ile in the arch between my fathers chapple and the high altar of the said priory, somewhere neare unto the said altar, thereby neare to my father's tombe; and the tombe to be of the same height as my father's and somewhat more'. The chancel and his father's chapel were also to be extended eastwards.[103] However, he later adds, 'at my tomb at Tinterne two priests yearly to befound till mine entombe be builded there', and later still: 'Item, where I have strucken out there I purposed to ly at the priory of Bergaveny, I will ly in the church of Tintern, and my wife in the same tomb with me.' He asks for his lands in Abergavenny, alongside his salt

---

[102] H. Fulton, 'Guto'r Glyn and the Wars of the Roses', in D.F. Evans, B.J. Lewis and A.P. Owen (eds), *Gwalch Cywyddau Gwŷr: Essays on Guto'r Glyn and Fifteenth-Century Wales* (Aberystwyth, 2013), pp. 53–68.
[103] *HP*, p. 55.

kept in store at Chepstow, to be sold for the erection of his tomb and chapel at Tintern, and to build new cloisters at the abbey.[104] Either the earl anticipated the erection of two tombs, one at Abergavenny and one at Tintern, or his intentions altered during the course of the will's composition. If this was the case, perhaps the incoherency of the will is a reflection of the earl's state of mind at the time. Herbert added a codicil on 27 July 1469, shortly before his execution. Here his intentions are clearer; he plans to be interred at Abergavenny:

> Item, I to [be] buried in the priory of Bergavenny undre charge bytwene my fader's toumbe and ye chauncell, and the cost þat shuld have be [at] Tyntaurn to be set uppon the chauncell as my confessor maister John Dezman shall say ... Item þat maister John Dezman have £20 to remembre me, and £20 to the Grey freres wher my body shall lygh and þat my body be sent fore home in alle hast secretely by maister Leison and certeyn freres with him.[105]

However, after his execution at Northampton, William Herbert's body was taken to Tintern Abbey and buried 'in ye quire before ye high aulter'.[106] The earl was patron of the abbey as lord of Chepstow, and his interment there continued a tradition of the abbey as the favoured burial place of the earls of Pembroke.[107] Though there is no trace of the tomb today, an illustration in the *Herbertorum Prosapia* apparently provides an insight into its appearance (Plate 9). The effigies of the earl and his wife, both wearing coronets, are depicted on a tomb chest, the panels of which feature six daughters and three sons above their respective coats of arms. An inscription is depicted on the bottom of the tomb. Hitherto, the drawing has been accepted as an accurate reproduction of the original tomb.[108] However, there are problems with this interpretation. Firstly, the monument had disappeared by the seventeenth century, evidently when the abbey was suppressed in the previous century.[109] As the *Herbertorum Prosapia* is a copy of an original manuscript written earlier in the seventeenth century, it is unlikely that the author of the original or of the copy saw the tomb in its original state. There may have been an earlier reproduction of the tomb on which the illustration was based, but if one examines the effigies it is apparent that they are depicted

---

[104] *HP*, pp. 57–8. There is no evidence that any words were deleted earlier in the will.
[105] TNA, PROB 11/5, fol. 216r.
[106] From William Fellows's 1530 visitation of Tintern Abbey, which also details the location of the tombs of Herbert's sons. The bodies of his heir William, earl of Huntingdon, and his brother Sir George Herbert lay in a single tomb to the north of their father, and Sir Walter Herbert was buried in the chapel of St John the Baptist on the north side of the church: London, College of Arms, MS H.8, fols. 4v–5r.
[107] W. Coxe, *An Historical Tour in Monmouthshire* (London, 1801), p. 375; O.B. Craster, *Tintern Abbey* (London, 1956), p. 6.
[108] P. Lord, *The Visual Culture of Wales: Medieval Vision* (Cardiff, 2003), p. 262, Figure 413.
[109] J.M. Shuttleworth (ed.), *The Life of Edward, First Lord Herbert of Cherbury, Written by Himself* (London, 1976), p. 6.

anachronistically, a not uncommon practice by the antiquaries of the seventeenth and eighteenth centuries. The beards sported by the male effigies and the details of the armour are more appropriate to the Elizabethan period than the late fifteenth century. We must therefore accept that the drawing may be nothing more than the product of the illustrator's imagination. Further doubts are cast if one compares the drawing of Sir Richard Herbert of Coldbrook's monument at Abergavenny to the extant tomb. It bears little resemblance to the actual monument. Among several inaccuracies, the addition of a shield is extraneous. Although we have no idea as to whether Herbert's tomb effigy was depicted wearing a Yorkist livery collar, we do at least know that he was given several. In his will he refers to his 'garters and collars of gold', which are differentiated from his other 'wearing chaines'. All were bequeathed to his son Lord Dunster.[110]

Sir Richard Herbert (d. 1469), St Mary's Priory Church, Abergavenny (Monmouthshire)

The recumbent alabaster effigies of Sir Richard and his wife Margaret, daughter of Thomas ap Griffith, lie on a tomb chest under the arch between the north side of the Herbert chapel and the south side of the chancel. The tomb may have been commissioned by Margaret after her husband's death. It has been damaged over time (Sir Richard's right arm is virtually all missing), although the Herbert tombs were intact when Richard Symonds saw them in September 1645. It is therefore likely that they were damaged after the siege of Raglan Castle in August 1646. Restorations and reconstructions have been undertaken, particularly to the tomb chest, the most recent being in the mid-1990s.[111]

We are blessed with an abundance of antiquarian notes on the Herbert monuments at Abergavenny. Thomas Churchyard's 1587 poem, 'The Worthines of Wales', noted the heraldry on Sir Richard's 'sumptuous tombe', most of which has now gone, and Symonds described the effigy as sporting black hair.[112] In his 'General Topography', Richard Gough stated that the effigy of Sir Richard had no livery collar.[113] However, this appears to have been an oversight on Gough's part. John Carter's drawings of the effigy in 1801, contemporaneous with Gough, includes a detailed illustration of the collar of suns and roses (Figure 9), and the collar's presence is confirmed by another drawing in William Coxe's *An*

---

[110] *HP*, p. 57.
[111] V. Rock, 'The Medieval Monuments at St Mary's Priory Church, Abergavenny, Gwent', *Medieval Life*, 3 (1995), 17–24, at 21–2; P. Lindley, 'A Restoration Restoration? The Herbert Monuments at Abergavenny', in his *Tomb Destruction and Scholarship*, pp. 199–236; BL, Harleian MS 944, fols. 18v–25v, at 22r–22v; C.E. Long (ed.), *Diary of the Marches of the Royal Army during the Great Civil War* (London, 1859), p. 236.
[112] O. Morgan, *Some Account of the Ancient Monuments in the Priory Church, Abergavenny* (Newport, 1872), pp. 15–18.
[113] Bodleian Library, MS 33, fols. 172r–v, in Lindley, 'A Restoration Restoration?' pp. 233–4.

Historical Tour in Monmouthshire.[114] Though the tomb was covered in Edward Blore's 'Monumental Remains', his 1855 drawing was taken from the north side of the tomb, all but obscuring Sir Richard's effigy.[115] Examining the tomb, there is no evidence that the collar was a later addition, and it appears to be contemporaneous with the rest of the effigy.

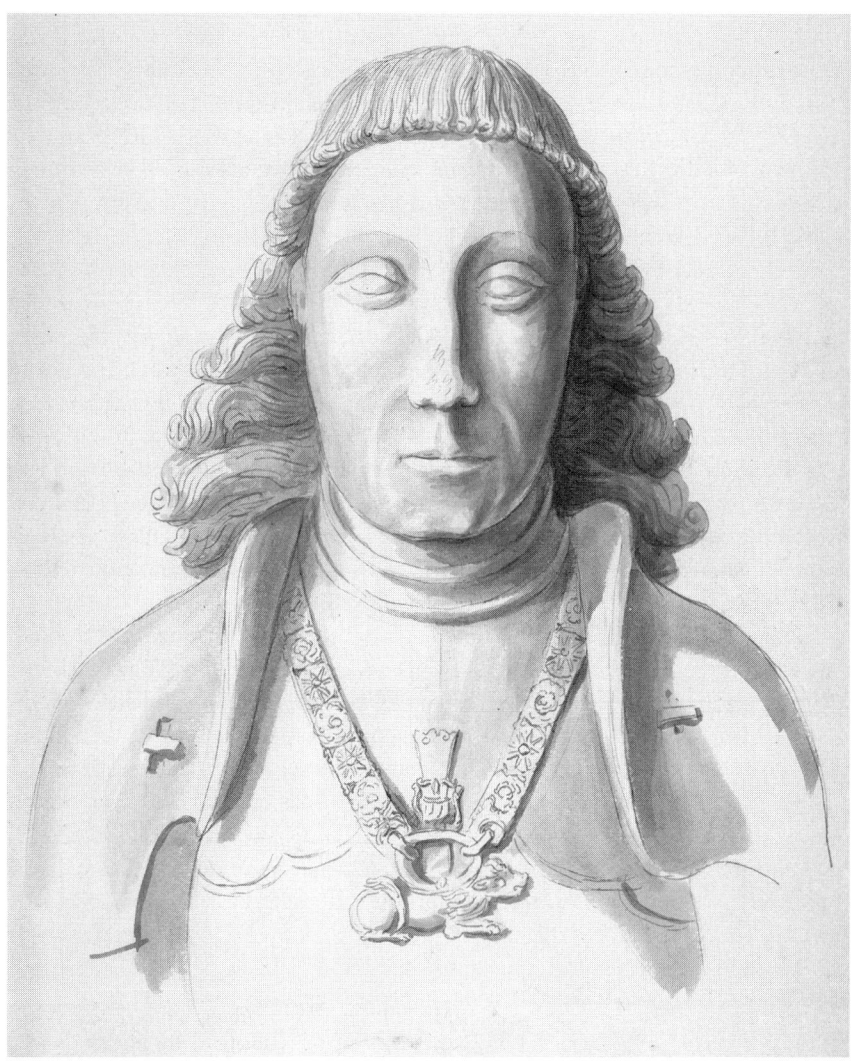

Figure 9. John Carter's drawing of Sir Richard Herbert's tomb effigy (1469).

[114] BL, Additional MS 29938, fol. 74r; Coxe, *Monmouthshire*, opposite p. 188.
[115] BL, Additional MS 42009, fol. 89r.

?Sir Richard Herbert (c. 1470–80), St Nicholas's, Montgomery (Montgomeryshire)

The alabaster military effigy, with no extant tomb chest, lies on the floor of the south transept in the Lymore chapel. The effigy appears to have been painted at some stage, giving the alabaster a dark appearance. The effigy wears a Yorkist livery collar of suns and roses with a lion of March pendant.

There is a degree of doubt as to whom this effigy represents, although it can be confidently identified as a member of the Herbert family. The family had a clear connection with Montgomery Castle. William Herbert was made steward of Montgomery in 1467, and his brother Sir Richard was also linked with the castle: one of his sons, Sir Richard (d. 1539) resided there.[116] It was to this individual that Edward, Lord Herbert of Cherbury, attributed the effigy. Writing in the early seventeenth century, he reported that his great grandfather 'lyeth buried ... in Montgomery; the upper Monument of the two placed in the Chancell being erected for him'. Evidently the effigy, along with a fourteenth-century military figure which it sits beside, has been moved since the seventeenth century. Although little else has been written on the effigy, later scholarly attention has subscribed to this view.[117] There are, however, serious flaws to this argument. Firstly, it is unlikely that an individual who was born in 1468 and died in 1539 would wear a Yorkist collar. Too young to have served the house of York, Sir Richard's career was spent serving Henry VIII's regime.[118] There are no Yorkist collars on English and Welsh tomb effigies dating from the sixteenth century. If the effigy is unlikely to represent Sir Richard, then who exactly does it commemorate? The presence of the collar and the lion pendant indicates service to Edward IV, and the long flowing hair is suggestive of a date of at least 1480. There are the remains of a clawed foot on the crest of the helm which may be the wyvern crest used by the Herberts. As it appears that the Herbert family were associated with Montgomery before Sir Richard (d. 1539), it is possible that the effigy represents one of the numerous sons of the earl of Pembroke, rather than the offspring of his brother Sir Richard of Coldbrook.

Thomas Vaughan (d. 1469), St Mary's, Kington (Herefordshire)

The alabaster effigies of Vaughan and his wife Ellen 'Gethin' lie on an altar tomb between the north side of the south chapel, erected by Vaughan, and the chancel. He wears a thin collar of suns and roses with a cross pendant. The tomb chest and effigies have been heavily restored, including the faces of both effigies,

---

[116] Shuttleworth (ed.), *Life*, p. 4.
[117] Shuttleworth (ed.), *Life*, p. 5; 'On the Two Recumbent Figures in Montgomery Church', in *Collections Historical and Archaeological Relating to Montgomeryshire and Its Borders*, Powysland Club Collections, 6 (1873), pp. 207–14.
[118] Bartrum, *Welsh Genealogies*, v, p. 786; Shuttleworth (ed.), *Life*, pp. 4–5.

the legs of Vaughan and the hands of his wife. The major restorative work was undertaken in the 1840s at a cost of £70. A lion that once rested at the feet of Vaughan was removed during these restorations, 'because it accorded not with the rest of the work'. The tomb has evidently been moved since 1847, when it was situated in the south-east corner of the south chapel.[119]

Unusually, we have a contemporary, albeit characteristically cryptic, description of the tomb, from Lewis Glyn Cothi's elegy. The monument, we are told, was erected by Vaughan's widow and cost more than the walls of a castle. The great 'pillars' of white alabaster are vividly described, as is the 'golden head' of Vaughan. The tomb chest was also richly gilded.[120] An inscription was placed above the tomb featuring the names of Thomas and Ellen and their descendants. This was subsequently added to until 1745, and in 1842 it was replaced by a stone slab.[121]

Sir Henry Wogan (d. 1475), Scolton Manor Museum (Pembrokeshire)

The damaged alabaster effigies of Sir Henry, from the Wiston branch of the Wogan family, and his wife Margaret, daughter of Sir William ap Thomas and sister to the earl of Pembroke, are now kept at Scolton Manor Museum (Figure 10). Henry has long curly hair, and wears a suns and roses collar with a lion pendant about his neck. The tomb originally resided under an elaborate canopy in the south side of the now ruined Commandery church at Slebech. Part of the canopy was illustrated in a selection of drawings by John Carter in 1803, which also included a bird's-eye view of the effigies and details of Henry's livery collar.[122] Although the 'collar of Roses' was noted by the antiquary George Owen during the 1590s,[123] it has been misinterpreted in the past as a collar of the Order of the Golden Fleece, leading some to wrongly identify the effigy of Henry as that of Roger Barlow (d. 1558), to whom the Commandery was conveyed in 1546.[124]

---

[119] Historical Monuments Commission, *An Inventory of the Historical Monuments in Herefordshire*, 3 vols (London, 1931–34), iii, p. 90; R.W.B., 'On the Family of Vaughan of Hergest', *Archaeologia Cambrensis*, 26 (1871), 23–34; W.J. Rees, 'Account of the Restored Tomb in Kington Church, 1847', *Archaeologia Cambrensis*, 3 (1848), 60–5. For a description of the tomb before the restorations see Richard Parry's *The History of Kington* (Kington, 1845), p. 98.

[120] 'Marwnad arall ar Thomas ab Rhosser', in Davies and Jones (eds), *Gwaith Lewis Glyn Cothi*, pp. 20–3. We are also told that Richard, one of Thomas's sons, had a monument in the church. This has now disappeared.

[121] Parry, *Kington*, p. 101; R.W.B., 'Vaughan of Hergest', 25.

[122] BL, Additional MS 29940, fols. 157r–158r.

[123] BL, Egerton MS 2586, fol. 337v.

[124] R. Fenton, *A Historical Tour through Pembrokeshire* (Brecknock, 1811), pp. 160–2. For the correct identification see E. Laws and E.H. Edwards, 'Monumental Effigies, Pembrokeshire', *Archaeologia Cambrensis*, 66 (1911), 349–80, at 371–80; F. Jones, 'Some Slebech Notes', *National Library of Wales Journal*, 7 (1951), 199–204.

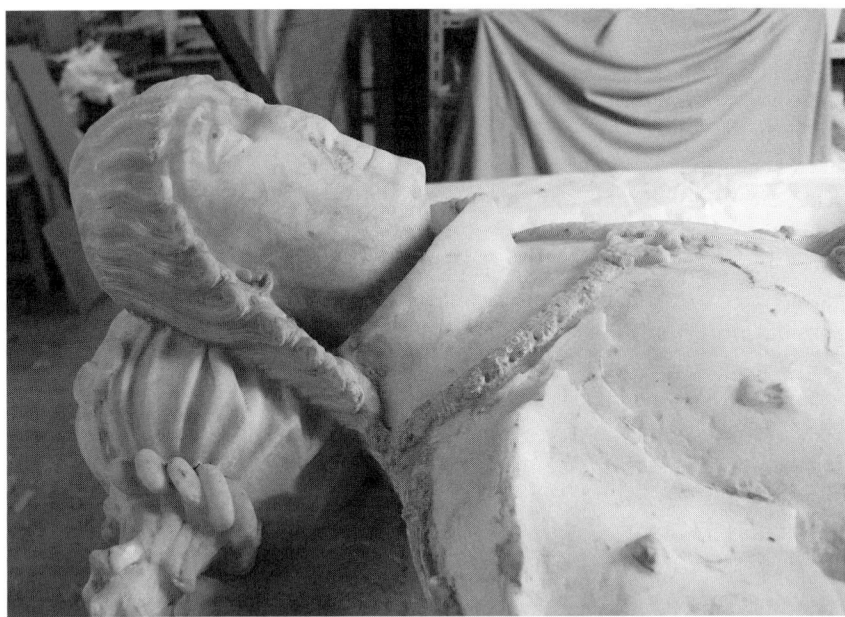

Figure 10. Scolton Manor Museum (Pembrokeshire).
Sir Henry Wogan (d. 1475).

William Griffith (d. c. 1483), St Tegai's, Llandegai (Gwynedd)

The recumbent alabaster effigies of William Griffith of Penrhyn and his unidentified wife lie on a tomb chest at the west end of the south side of the church. He wears a thin collar of suns and roses, she a choker collar of roses with a rose pendant. His pendant is too worn to be identified. The tomb dates from the early 1480s and is similar in appearance to the effigy of Sir John Saville at Thornhill.[125]

Conclusions

A group of alabaster tombs dating from the 1490s and early sixteenth century, possibly products of the same workshop, have recently attracted the attention of scholars of church monuments. They commemorate Sir John Morgan (d. 1493) at St Woolos Cathedral, Richard Herbert of Ewyas (d. 1510) at Abergavenny, and David Mathew (d. before 1470), Sir William Mathew (d. 1528) and Christopher Mathew (d. c. 1531) in Llandaff Cathedral.[126] As was the case with the

---

[125] Gardner, *Alabaster Tombs*, p. 103; plates 64, 234.
[126] R. Biebrach, '"Our Ancient Blood and Our Kings": Two Early Sixteenth-Century Heraldic Tombs in Llandaff Cathedral, Wales', *Church Monuments*, 24 (2009), 73–88, esp. 76–81; R.

individuals analysed in this chapter, those commemorated were connected through kinship and royal service. They also feature a livery collar, this time the SS collar adopted by the Tudors.[127] They therefore share similarities with the individuals and their memorials which form the basis of this chapter, and can be considered the next generation of gentry monuments, their tombs similarly being an expression of group solidarity. They can be interpreted alongside a wider introduction of Tudor iconographical motifs in Wales during the late fifteenth and early sixteenth centuries. Tudor imagery, not least the red dragon favoured by Henry VII, appeared in artwork, on church fittings and in stained glass during Tudor's reign. Examples can be seen at St David's Cathedral and, interestingly, the Herbert mausoleum at Abergavenny.[128] Perhaps here we have an example of a conscious insertion of the Tudor narrative in order to neutralise, as it were, a cultural narrative associated with the previous regime. It can be safely assumed that the tombs featuring SS collars were influenced by the style and aesthetics of the tombs of Herbert's affinity, and were perhaps deliberately copying their forebears who had died several decades before. Through the adoption of a similar form of monument and a livery collar, albeit the SS collar, continuity of lineage, royal service and loyalty was being emphasised. Yet there are subtle differences, in particular the fact that many of the individuals analysed in this case study died in battle. An element of comradeship, expressed through the shared depiction of the Yorkist collar of suns and roses, is unique to the individuals studied here.

They were, therefore, very much part of a tight affinity. The extensive group of retainers and allies built up by William Herbert constituted a close-knit, politically active affinity from at least the mid-1450s, until its demolition in 1469. Even after Edgecote, the association between many of the families continued. This is not necessarily surprising, nor unique. Affinities from the period became accustomed to surviving the death of their lord and continuing their local relationships, which in many cases had existed for decades. We have previously seen how members of the Hastings affinity switched their services *en masse* to the duke of Buckingham after their former lord's execution in 1483. On the whole, the Herberts and their kin found little difficulty in at least tacitly supporting Henry

---

Biebrach, 'Conspicuous by Their Absence: Rethinking Explanations for the Lack of Brasses in Medieval Wales', *TMBS*, 18 (2009), 36–42, at 41–2.

[127] The effigy of David Mathew wears a collar of S-shaped links, rather than a livery collar. Mathew was a contemporary and a relation of the earl of Pembroke. He was also a prominent Yorkist, being Edward IV's standard-bearer at the battle of Towton. He died before Edgecote. His effigy may be retrospective, dating from *c.* 1500, although this is open to question. I am grateful to Dr Rhianydd Biebrach for her thoughts on the Mathew tombs.

[128] See J. Morgan-Guy, 'Arthur, Harri Tudor and the Iconography of Loyalty in Wales', in S.J. Gunn and L. Monckton (eds), *Arthur Tudor, Prince of Wales: Life, Death and Commemoration* (Woodbridge, 2009), pp. 50–63.

Tudor in 1485 (Sir Walter Herbert probably openly), although members of the Vaughan family continued to trouble the new regime for some time. Whether this was due to lingering Yorkist sympathies, or local grievances with the Tudor family, cannot be fully ascertained. But until the battle of Edgecote the affinity was conspicuous in its durable active support, particularly militarily, for Richard, duke of York, and then for his son Edward IV. In this respect they can be contrasted to the Derbyshire group examined in the previous chapter, the majority of whom apparently eschewed explicit political support for either side in the wars. The surviving relationship between the families of the deceased after the battle of Edgecote ensured that the Yorkist collars on their relatives' tombs were a lasting testament to their bonds.

Although there are examples of SS collars on church monuments in Wales which pre-date the Wars of the Roses period,[129] there is a distinct break in collared tombs from c. 1450, until a relative proliferation of examples appears after the battle of Edgecote in 1469. The same situation is discernible in Herefordshire, there being several examples of earlier SS collars such as that featured on the tomb effigy of Sir Roger Vaughan (d. 1415) at St Andrew's, Bredwardine, although Thomas Vaughan's tomb at Kington is the only surviving memorial to feature a livery collar from the Wars of the Roses period.[130] All those memorials in Wales from the Wars of the Roses period which feature a collar were linked, and all wear the Yorkist collar of suns and roses.[131] Whilst allowing for the fact that there may have been additional monuments which have since been destroyed, the evidence from extant tombs indicates that the use of the Yorkist livery collar on tombs in the region was an original and conscious act by the individuals commemorated or, more likely, their families. The same originality was exemplified with the first extant examples of the Yorkist collar in manuscript form, in the *Troy Book* commissioned by William Herbert in the early 1460s. As the Welsh poets attempted to construct a legend of Welsh bravery and loyalty

[129] Sir William ap Thomas at Abergavenny and Sir Rowland Bulkeley (c. 1450) at St Mary's and St Nicholas's, Beaumaris (Anglesey). An alternative identification for this tomb is Sir William Bulkeley (d. 1490).

[130] A brass dating from c. 1470 in All Saints' Church, Clehonger, thought to represent a Lady Aubrey, depicts a collar of roses, but no suns: H. Haines, 'The Monumental Brasses of the Cathedral and County of Hereford', *Journal of the British Archaeological Association*, 27 (1871), 85–99, 198–203, 341, at 198.

[131] The only relevant brass from the period commemorates Sir Hugh Johnys (d. c. 1485) and his wife Maud at St Mary's, Swansea. It does not feature a collar. Johnys had connections with both Edward IV and Henry Tudor. He was admitted to the Poor Knights of Windsor in 1468. The brass is retrospective, dating twenty years after his death: W.R.B. Robinson, 'Sir Hugh Johnys: A Fifteenth-Century Welsh Knight', *Morgannwg: Transactions of the Glamorgan Local History Society*, 14 (1970), 5–34; J.M. Lewis, *Welsh Monumental Brasses* (Cardiff, 1974), pp. 42–3. In addition, the virtually identical tombs of Thomas White (1482) and his son John (c. 1490), are situated in St Anne's Chapel in St Mary's, Tenby. They are depicted as civilians, and neither wears a livery collar.

to the king through their own cultural articulation, so too did the inclusion of a livery collar on the effigies of those commemorated. An affinity built around intimate bonds of kinship, geographical proximity, royal service and military and political unanimity was left to posterity.

Conclusion

In his *Regement of Princes*, Thomas Hoccleve reflected on the efficacy of church images in prompting the viewer to meditate on their subject matter:

> When the images they beholden & seen;
> Where often unsight of them causith restraints
> Of thoughts good: when a thing depaint is,
> Or entailed, if men take of it heed,
> Thought of the likeness, it will in him breed.[1]

The essential purpose of an image is to engender a response; the viewer is encouraged to reflect on why the image is there, and what purpose it carries. In addition, Hoccleve considered the similitude of images. In most cases they are intended as reflections of a reality. Although the poet is primarily concerned with devotional works, the image and response process he is describing was applicable to all images, sacred and secular. When the viewer beheld a tomb effigy or memorial brass, for example, they were encouraged to contemplate all the details. Armour, heraldry, representations of spouses and children, religious iconography and, if one was present, a livery collar, were all included for a reason. Collars in particular were not simply fashion accessories added at a whim. Placed on the most visually prominent part of the body, hung around the neck with a pendant of the lord's badge resting against the heart – a particularly appropriate symbolic position – they were designed to catch the eye. This was not only applicable to the collar's appearance on tombs; the artefact was also a significant aspect of the recipient's life.

The collar was an integral and significant aspect of the political and cultural lives of hundreds, if not thousands of individuals: so significant, in fact, that a correspondent of the Pastons deemed it necessary to mention that a visitor was wearing one. It associated the recipient with the donor who, as a result of the legislation of the beginning of the fifteenth century, was frequently the king or a member of the royal family, thus bestowing an element of prestige on the individual who wore the item. At the same time the collar served to proclaim the authority and worship of the crown: a symbiosis was at work.

---

[1] Thomas Hoccleve, *Works*, ed. F. Furnivall, 3 vols (London, 1892–97), iii, p. 180, stanza 715.

How should we judge the collar's significance? Hitherto, the item has been referred to by historians, but not always given due scholarly reflection. This is surprising considering its pervasive presence from the late fourteenth century onwards. Not only is the collar depicted on a multitude of extant church monuments, but it is also referred to in other contemporary sources, from works of art and sculpture to documentary accounts such as probate records, parliamentary proceedings and literature. Through an analysis and appraisal of the livery collar this study has, it is hoped, contributed to our understanding of the utility of visual and material culture, the nature of political conviction, the character of royal authority and the construction and expression of group identities in late medieval England.

A salient theme of the book has been the extent to which the livery collar was utilised to articulate one's identity as part of a group. On its broadest level this could mean the recipient's membership of an 'elite' culture. A degree of honour was bestowed on this large corpus of individuals who were connected to the king, and each other, through their collars. In addition it could, of course, associate the wearer with the Lancastrian or Yorkist dynasties; in some cases it could therefore have strong political resonances. In the localities, the collar could be employed on church monuments by a close-knit group of individuals and their families associated through bonds of kinship, tenure and office, in order to reflect their intimate ties. As we have been concerned with the motivations which lay behind the distribution and depiction of the collar, some of which may appear contradictory, two broad strands of enquiry have been followed: the motivations which lay behind the donor giving the collar; and the various ways in which the item was interpreted and 'used' by the recipients.

During the last decade much has been written on the role of church monuments as expressions of group identity, one example being Saul's study of the Cobham family's adoption of a similar style of memorial brass to stress familial bonds and continuity.[2] I have treated the livery collar in a similar manner. Here we have an example of a visual artefact deliberately distributed and appropriated as a means of demonstrating and strengthening group identity. The appearance of the collar on memorials was therefore one, apparently permanent, medium in which group identity and solidarity were expressed. The role of agency in commissioning and producing visual and material works of art during the late medieval period has been an important facet here. With regard to specific details added to sculpture, the case of the livery collar suggests that the majority were included at the request of the individual, or in some cases their families. While workshop stock items would provide a basic model on to which other elements were appended, it is suggested that details such as the collar were requested as they helped to reflect the realities, perhaps in some cases to reconstruct the

---

[2] See Saul, *Death, Art and Memory*.

realities, of the commemorated. They helped assemble an individual's story. In some instances there may, of course, have been an element of retrospective manipulation of history on the part of those who commissioned the tombs. That is not to say that the commemorated did not receive a collar; in the majority of instances they undoubtedly did. It is also not suggested that the motivations differed: the representation of a collar served the need to be seen as part of a group. Those commissioning such an expensive piece of work as a church monument involved themselves in various stages of its production. Although there are few extant tomb contracts from the late medieval period, it is evident that, in addition to plans for the proposed tomb, many considerations were discussed face to face with the workshop.

This study has appraised the political significance of the livery collar, and through it the nature of the political identity of landed society during the second half of the fifteenth century, the period associated with the Wars of the Roses. Today, when an individual or group makes the decision to wear a common badge, it is not infrequently to express some form of political (or religious) statement or association. In some areas of the world there are of course questions over the extent to which this is done voluntarily, but on the whole it can be argued that it is a choice. Perhaps because of this, historians have tended to assume the same motivations were at play when one took the decision to depict a Lancastrian or Yorkist livery collar, particularly on one's church monument. It has hitherto been assumed that those individuals who are depicted wearing a collar in works of art or on monuments were politically active adherents to either the house of Lancaster or that of York. This was not always the case: livery collars did not necessarily denote Yorkist or Lancastrian sympathies.

It is hoped that this study has contributed to our understanding of the use of the visual medium in expressing political and other identities during the period. It has considered the interconnectivity between thinking and practising politics during the fifteenth century, particularly during the Wars of the Roses. The livery collar, frequently considered the single most important form of political expression during the period, was a more nuanced vehicle for expression. Politics was not simply about dynastic rivalry and association, or switching sides. For some, local kinship, tenure and office-holding amalgamated with politics. Indeed, for some, kinship and tenure *were* politics: this could even be the case with groups who unquestionably placed a degree of political meaning in the livery collar, such as the Herbert affinity in Wales. The most salient 'politics' for some was the desire to form and express bonds of connectedness, and this did not necessarily have to be in the form of what we today call political affiliation. Individuals and groups were affected by degrees of allegiance and influence, and decisions were made depending on geographical nuances. Paradoxically, a study of a seemingly overtly political artefact encourages us to question exactly how much politics meant to contemporaries during a civil war.

Collars can, however, be used to inform us of the political climate, or how the political climate was interpreted at a local level. We have witnessed Henry Fotherby bequeathing his collar 'of the lord king Henry VI' to his son John in his will in February 1471.³ As the will was made during the Readeption of 1470–71 the reference to Henry as king was correct, Fotherby was indeed leaving the king's collar as a bequest. Perhaps this particular collar dated from before 1461 when Henry was deposed. Alternatively, this may be one example of a Lancastrian SS collar which was possibly reintroduced during the Readeption. It may also be the case that Fotherby was, or had been, a Lancastrian supporter, the reference to 'the lord king Henry' being an expression of his loyalty to the king. Every such reference to a collar can help unveil insights into the individual's world, and help us to ask questions concerning the wider political climate.

In some cases livery collars can tell us something of the political persuasion of individuals and their families. We have seen examples of William Herbert's affinity being depicted wearing suns and roses collars on their tombs to demonstrate their commitment to the Yorkist dynasty. In some cases there were complexities involved in the depiction of a collar. Take, for example, the now lost effigy of Ralph Neville, earl of Westmorland, at Brancepeth.⁴ It featured a Yorkist collar of suns and roses, and included a rare extant example of the boar pendant of Richard III. Yet the earl was no staunch Yorkist. How then can we explain the presence of the collar on his tomb effigy? As it is unlikely that he did not receive a collar – his positon as an earl probably ensured that he did – its inclusion may have been at the behest of his nephew, the third earl, who had been associated with King Richard as duke of Gloucester and was hoping for his family's fortunes, for so long eclipsed by the younger Neville line, to be revived under the new king. The livery collar can, therefore, be used to develop a more nuanced understanding of an individual's political position and circumstances. Conversely, a detailed investigation into the individual and their family's political, social and cultural contexts can provide more accurate and detailed explanations for the appearance of their collar.⁵ It should be kept in mind that the political lives of landed society were nuanced, at times complicated, and developed through a variety of contexts.⁶

In contrast to overt political expression, was the appearance of the livery collar on church monuments perhaps used to express crown service, whether that was to the Lancastrian or Yorkist king? There is a conspicuous lack of SS

---

³ Lincoln Cathedral Library, Dean and Chapter, A/2/35, fol. 131v.
⁴ See above, p. 23.
⁵ For an example of re-identifying a tomb effigy through a consideration of the livery collar, see M. Ward, 'The Tomb of "The Butcher"? The Tiptoft Monument in the Presbytery of Ely Cathedral', *Church Monuments*, 27 (2012), 22–37.
⁶ M. Mercer, *The Medieval Gentry: Power, Leadership and Choice during the Wars of the Roses* (London and New York, 2010), especially chapter 3.

collars dating from 1461 to 1485, and after Bosworth the appearance of the Yorkist suns and roses collar declines rapidly. Individual circumstances may help explain the lingering presence of some examples,[7] but, in the years after 1485, perhaps the new Tudor regime was willing to accept that the collar had, in some cases, denoted service to a king, rather than explicitly stating the political conviction of the individual commemorated. The vast majority of Yorkist collars date from the Yorkist period, and the return to Tudor SS collars after 1485 does suggest that the inclusion of the opposing regime's collar was perhaps deemed risky, but that does not mean that their inclusion on a church monument always equated to an expression of political loyalty. After all, was it at all clear that after 1461 or 1471 the civil wars would continue? More pertinent may have been an acknowledgement of the individual's association to the crown, and the prestige that accompanied this. Although the SS collar may have originally been introduced to help build up the Lancastrian affinity, therefore serving a political purpose to an extent, after the legislation of the beginning of the fifteenth century the collar became increasingly associated with the crown. In some cases the desire to express royal service evidently overrode the desire to express one's political position. Collar wearers were, of course, in some way connected to the crown. In some cases they will have fought and died for Lancaster or York, or for a lord who was attached to either regime. But other recipients were more loosely connected to the donor, as we have seen in Derbyshire. It is therefore perhaps a step too far to assume that all collar wearers were members of the royal household, and perhaps even too far to suggest that all were members of the king's extended affinity.

Functioning in a similar way to coinage, the livery collar 'circulated' the crown, or at least a symbol of the crown, throughout the kingdom and beyond. In addition to those worn by the living, the appearance of several hundred richly gilded collars on tombs and memorial brasses and in stained glass, across the kingdom and on the continent, would have served to benefit the king. They were tangible reminders of the stretch of his royal power and dignity, and they certainly attracted the attention of contemporaries. For this reason they were utilised as diplomatic tools, particularly in the princely courts of Europe. A gift of a lavish collar demonstrated the 'love' between rulers, and was frequently used to cement alliances. The composition of the collar also added something to the mystical nature and allure of kingship. As no image of the person of the king was present on the collar, it at once brought the majesty and authority of the crown into the communities, whilst also depersonifying the king as an individual. The crown was therefore ever present, but only at a distance. Although the devices used on both Lancastrian and Yorkist collars would have been recognised by the majority of the populace, a lack of easily accessible portraits of the king may have

---

[7] Such as Sir Henry Pierrepont: see above, p. 124.

enhanced its effectiveness in promoting the authority and dignity of the crown, or at least the dynasty, as opposed to an individual ruler.[8]

In the localities, and with particular reference to the appearance of the livery collar on church monuments, the prosopographies in the final two chapters of the book have revealed that the item could be utilised differently by its recipients, often determined by local contexts. Again, the suggestion is that in some cases the political significance of the collar was not the primary motive behind its depiction. For those individuals in the south of Wales and Herefordshire, closely associated through the Herbert affinity and their participation and, in many cases, deaths fighting for Edward IV at the battle of Edgecote in 1469, the collar represented shared political conviction in the Yorkist claim to the throne. They clearly lived and died fighting for a cause. In Derbyshire, however, the appearance of the collar was a manifestation of the respective families' mutual pride in their long-standing service to the honour of Tutbury. It should be recalled that it is unlikely that the majority fought for either side in the wars. There is, however, one apparently constant and striking trend: where clusters of collars on church monuments appear, as in Wales and Derbyshire, the commemorated were all closely related. Further links, particularly between in-laws, can be found throughout the country, one example being the Yorkist collars on the effigies of Sir William Gascoigne (d. 1461–65) at Harewood, and Sir John Saville (d. 1481) at Thornhill, both in West Yorkshire. There is therefore a strong kinship element to the decision by individuals to depict a collar on their tomb. The significance of kinship in determining the appearance of a collar on tombs is supported by family bequests of the item. We have witnessed several examples of the collar being passed down to family members, in some cases over three generations, as was the case with the Reresbie family.[9] It therefore appears that familial identity was sometimes more relevant to the commemorated and their families than political statements.

To bring this study to a conclusion, one final source will be examined. Fittingly it is a piece of art, and in many ways it neatly encapsulates the collar's purpose and effect. It is a miniature from the Military Ordinance of Charles the Bold (1475), depicting the duke appointing his captains (Plate 10). All the characters in the composition are portrayed as distinct. All wear different clothing and have idiosyncratic features; there appears to have been an attempt at portraiture. But one immediately noticeable item links Charles and his courtiers sitting on the left of the painting. They all wear gold collars of the duke's Order of the Golden Fleece. Not only that, but they all wear virtually identical collars;

---

[8] The Yorkist kings in particular would have been identified through the adoption of their individual badges (the white lion of March for Edward IV and the white boar for Richard III) as pendants on their collars.

[9] See above, p. 33.

there does not appear to have been an attempt to discern rank through their composition. Although the duke is naturally the focus, the courtiers are able to share something of his dignity and majesty through wearing his collar. They are at once subservient to him, yet they are, for this moment at least, virtually his equals. But the most striking observation is the most obvious. They are associated with each other through the visual artefact: they are clearly a group. It is this function of the collar which was perhaps most salient to contemporaries, and it is a role we must acknowledge. If anything can be taken from this study, it is that groups and association mattered, and if they were articulated through the visual medium, in many cases for posterity on a church monument, then they were all the more effective. The hundreds of examples that are still with us today are testament to the prominence, influence and importance of the livery collar in late medieval England.

APPENDIX 1

Genealogies

Fitzherbert of Norbury

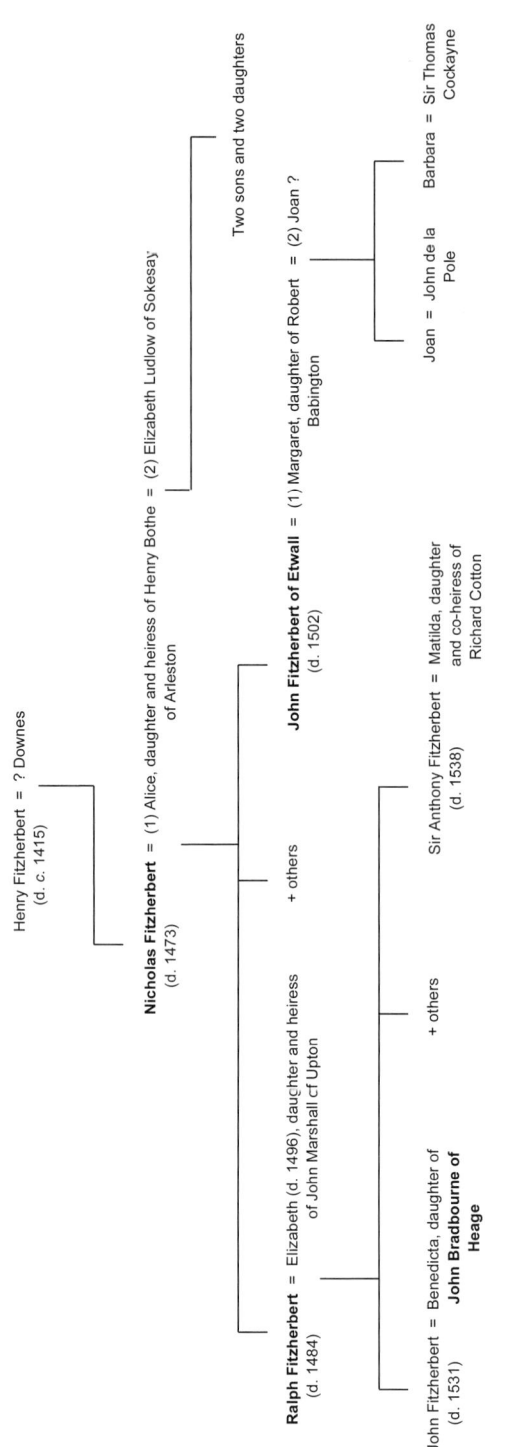

Bold = livery collar on monument

Cockayne of Ashbourne and Pooley

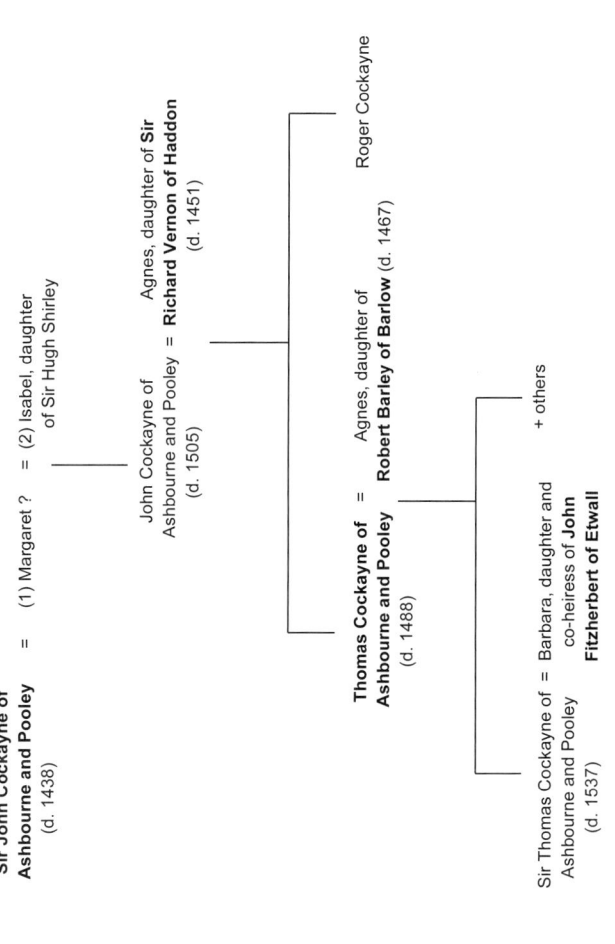

Barley of Barlow

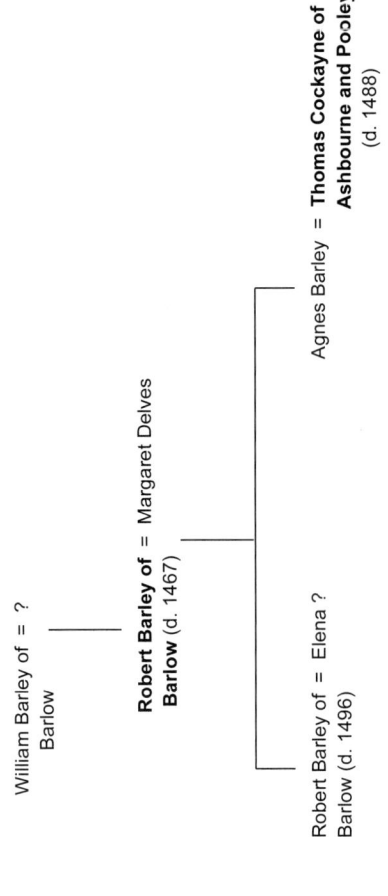

Pedigree recorded in the College of Arms, printed in Barlow, *Barlow Family Records*, p. 16.

Bothe of Arleston and Sawley

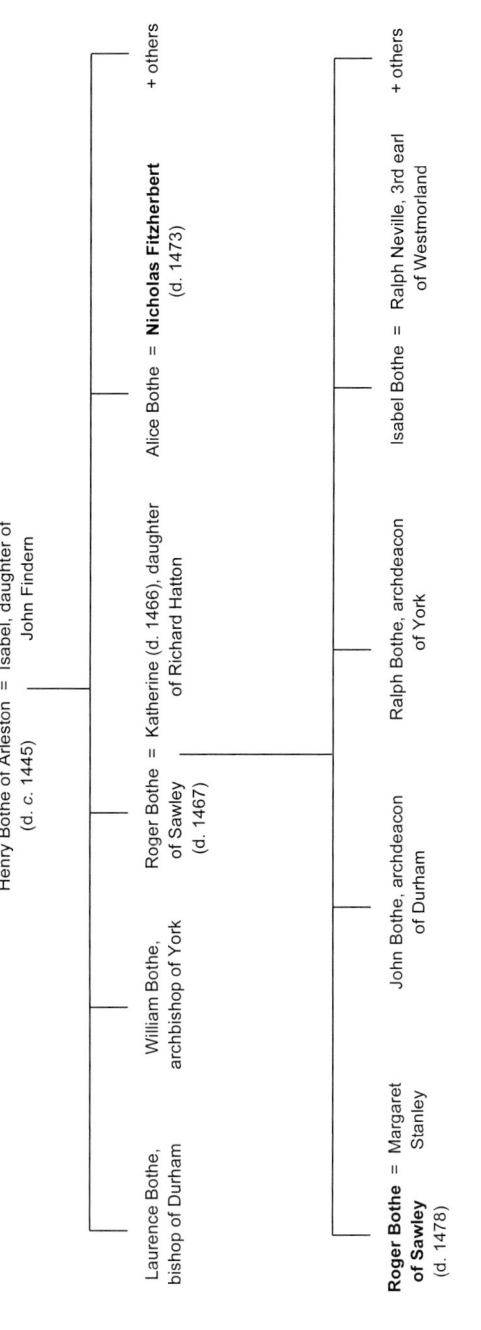

Bradbourne

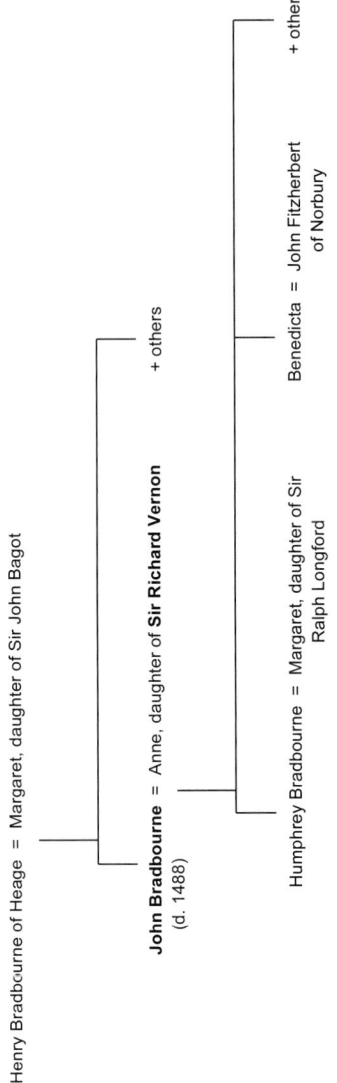

Henry Bradbourne of Heage = Margaret, daughter of Sir John Bagot

John Bradbourne = Anne, daughter of **Sir Richard Vernon**
(d. 1488)

+ others

Humphrey Bradbourne = Margaret, daughter of Sir Ralph Longford

Benedicta = John Fitzherbert of Norbury

+ others

Fraunceys and Montgomery

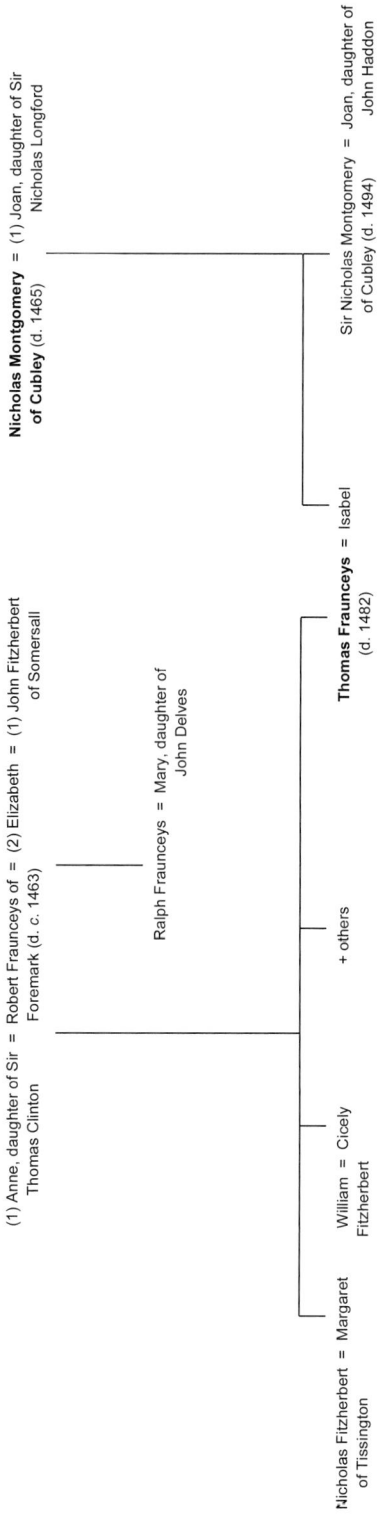

Pole of Radbourne

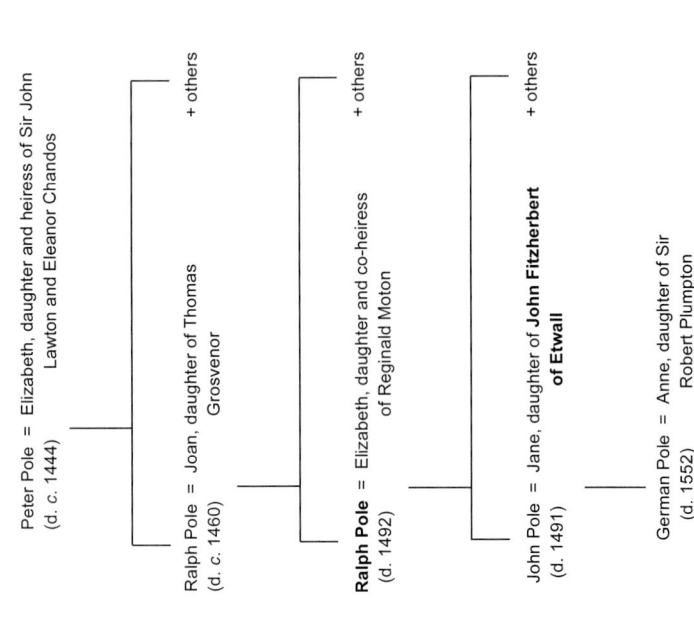

Peter Pole = Elizabeth, daughter and heiress of Sir John
(d. c. 1444)   Lawton and Eleanor Chandos

Ralph Pole = Joan, daughter of Thomas   + others
(d. c. 1460)   Grosvenor

Ralph Pole = Elizabeth, daughter and co-heiress   + others
(d. 1492)   of Reginald Moton

John Pole = Jane, daughter of **John Fitzherbert**   + others
(d. 1491)   **of Etwall**

German Pole = Anne, daughter of Sir
(d. 1552)   Robert Plumpton

Curzon of Kedleston and Kniveton of Mercaston

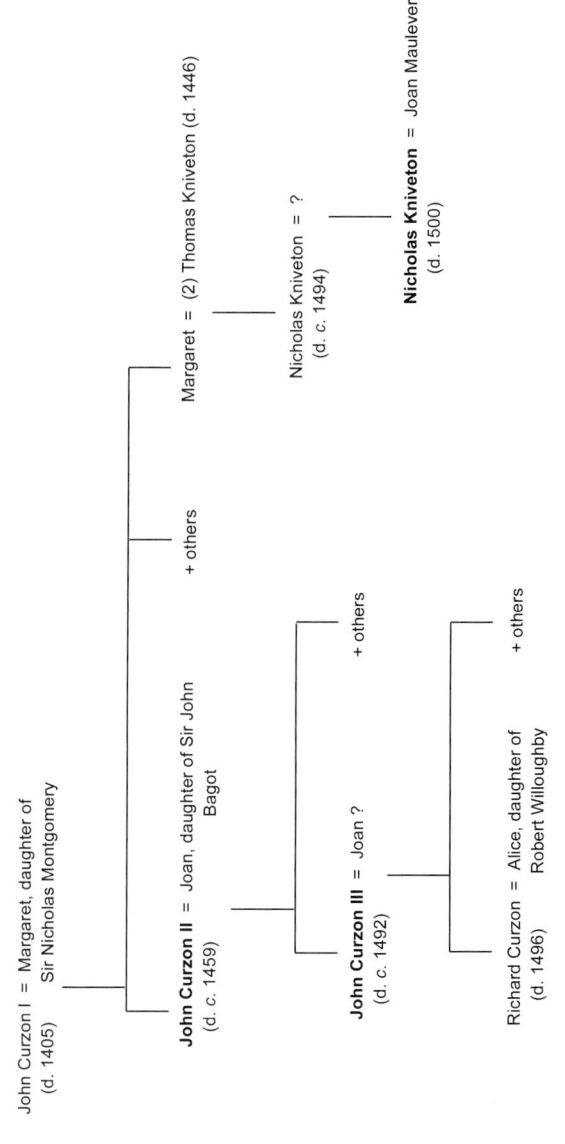

Vernon of Haddon

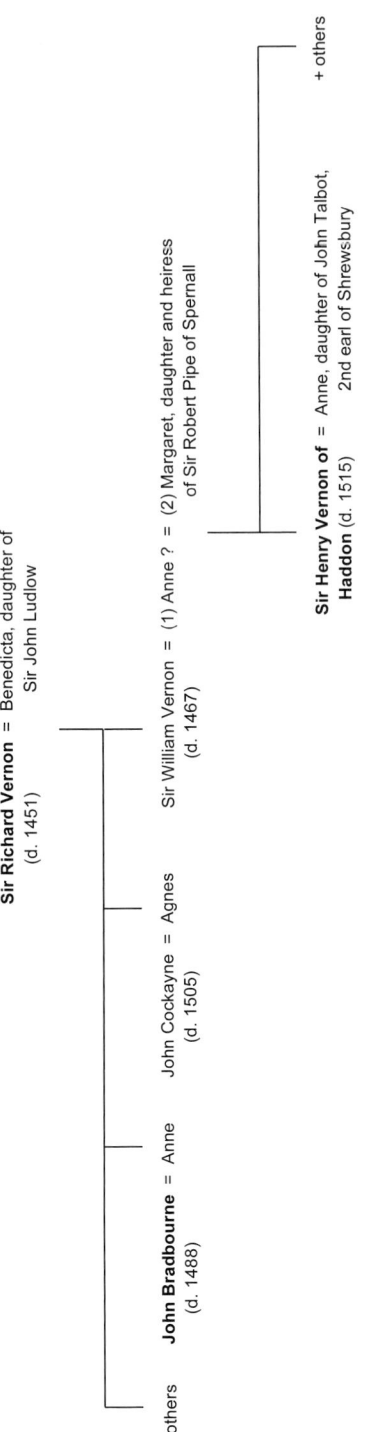

Sir Richard Vernon = Benedicta, daughter of
(d. 1451)   Sir John Ludlow

+ others

John Bradbourne = Anne
(d. 1488)

John Cockayne = Agnes
(d. 1505)

Sir William Vernon = (1) Anne ? = (2) Margaret, daughter and heiress
(d. 1467)   of Sir Robert Pipe of Spernall

Sir Henry Vernon of = Anne, daughter of John Talbot,   + others
Haddon (d. 1515)   2nd earl of Shrewsbury

Herbert of Raglan and Vaughan of Bredwardine

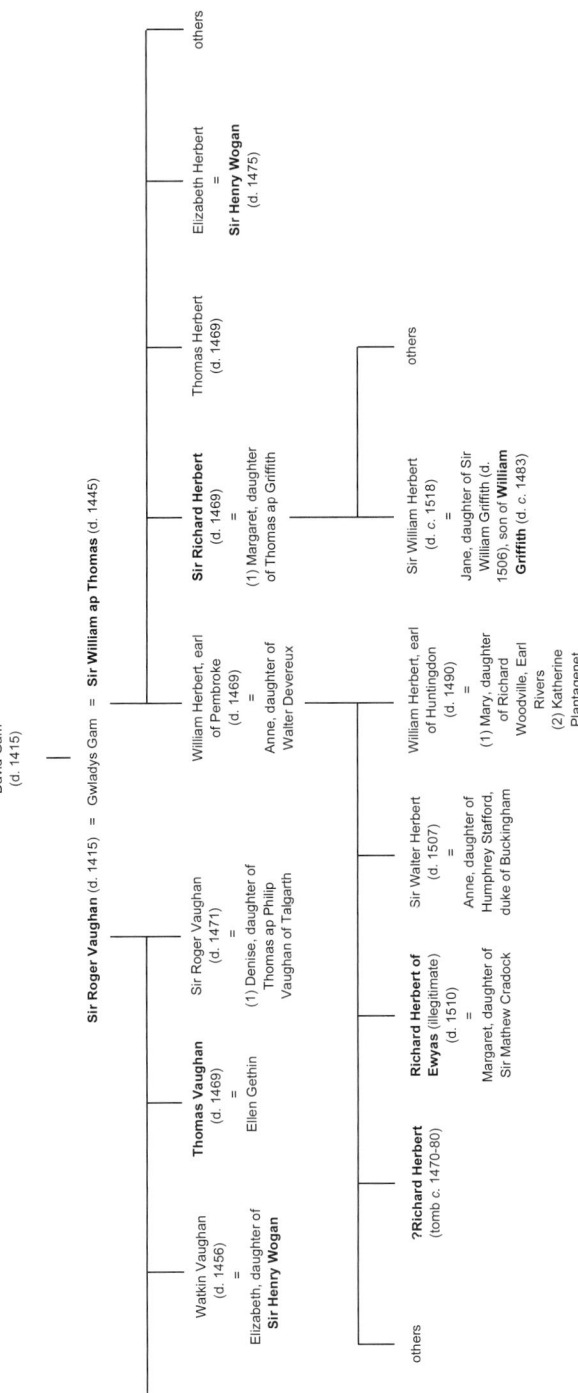

A variety of sources have been consulted to compile this pedigree: BL, Egerton MS 2586 (George Owen's Welsh Pedigrees, 1590–1603); NLW, MS 1449 (Pedigrees of Carmarthenshire, Cardiganshire and Pembrokeshire Families); NLW, Castell Gorford MS, 7 (The Golden Grove books); NLW, MS 4517 (R. Thomkins's Herbert Family Pedigree); NLW, MS 16920F; 16921E (Herbert pedigrees); Bartrum, *Welsh Genealogies*; J.E. Griffiths, *Pedigrees of Anglesey and Carnarvonshire Families with Their Collateral Branches in Denbighshire, Merionethshire* (Horncastle, 1914); Clark, *Limbus Patrum*; M.P. Siddons (ed. and trans.), *Visitation of Herefordshire 1634*, Harleian Society, New Series, 15 (London, 2002); S.R. Meyrick (ed.), *Heraldic Visitations of Wales and Part of the Marches between the Years 1586 and 1613, by Lewys Dwnn*, 2 vols (Llandovery, 1846).

APPENDIX 2

Livery Collars on Church Monuments in England, Wales and Ireland to *c*. 1540

Compiled using C.E.J. Smith's list as a basis, with additions and revisions by the present author.

Bedfordshire

Aspley Guise	Brass	Sir John Guise (1501)	SS
Bromham	Brass	Thomas Widville (1435)	SS
Cockayne Hatley	Brass	John Cockayne (c. 1430)	Abraded
Houghton Regis	Effigy	Sir John Sewell (1433)	Knots
Turvey	Effigy	Sir John Mordaunt (1506)	SS

Berkshire

Aldermaston	Effigy	Sir George Forster (1526)	SS
Burghfield	Effigy	Richard Neville, earl of Salisbury (1460)	Yorkist
Faringdon	Brass	Thomas Faryndon (1396)	Abraded
	Effigy	Sir Thomas Unton (1533)	SS
Windsor, St George's Chapel	Effigy	George Manners, Lord Ros (1513)	SS

Buckinghamshire

Bletchley	Effigy	Richard, Lord Grey of Wilton (1442)	SS
Great Missenden	Brass (lost)	John Iwardby (1436)	SS
Lillingstone Lovell	Brass	Thomas Clarell (1471)	Yorkist
Taplow	Brass	Richard Manfeld (1455)	Abraded

Cambridgeshire

Burrough Green	Effigy	John de Burgh (c. 1370)	SS

	Effigy	Sir John Ingoldesthorpe (1420)	SS
Ely Cathedral	Effigy	John, Lord Tiptoft (1443)	SS
Isleham	Brass	Sir John Bernard (1451)	SS
Cheshire			
Acton	Effigy	Sir William Mainwearing (1399)	SS
Barthomley	Effigy	Sir Robert Foulshurst (1389)	SS
Cheadle	Effigy	Sir John Hondford (1461)	SS
	Effigy	Sir John Hondford (1473)	SS
Chester, St Mary's	Effigy (lost)	Sir Adam Troutbeck	SS
	Effigy (lost)	Lady Troutbeck	SS
	Effigy (lost)	Member of Troutbeck family	SS
Macclesfield, St Michael's	Effigy	Member of Downes family (1475)	SS
	Effigy	Sir John Savage (1449)	SS
	Effigy	Sir John Savage (1495)	Yorkist
	Effigy	Katherine Savage	Yorkist?
	Effigy	Sir John Savage (1528)	SS
Malpas	Effigy	Sir Randle Brereton (1522)	SS
Mottram in Longendale	Effigy	Sir John Lovell (1408)	SS
	Effigy	Lady Lovell	SS
Over Peover	Effigy	Sir John Mainwearing (1410)	SS
	Effigy	Johanna Mainwearing	SS
	Effigy	Sir Randle Mainwearing (c. 1456)	SS
Cornwall			
Callington	Effigy	Lord Willoughby de Broke (1503)	Garter
Duloe	Effigy	Sir John Colshull (1415)	SS
Quethiock	Brass	Edward Kyngdon (1415)	Crown
Cumberland			
Crosthwaite	Effigy	Sir John Derwentwater (c. 1509)	Livery?
Greystoke	Effigy	John, Baron Greystoke (1436)	SS
Millom	Effigy	Sir John Hudleston (1494)	Yorkist
	Effigy	Joan Hudleston	Yorkist?
Wetheral	Effigy	Sir Richard Salkeld (1515)	SS/Roses
	Effigy	Jane Salkeld	SS/Roses

Workington	Effigy	Sir Christopher Curwen (1450)	SS
Derbyshire			
Ashbourne	Effigy	Edmund Cockayne (1403)	SS
	Effigy	Sir John Cockayne (1438)	SS
	Effigy	John Bradbourne (1488)	Yorkist
Aston-on-Trent	Effigy	Lady Hunt (temp. Henry IV)	SS
Bakewell	Effigy	Sir Thomas Wendesley (1403)	SS
Barlow	Incised slab	Robert Barley (1467)	Yorkist
Cubley	Effigy	Sir Nicholas Montgomery (1465)	Yorkist
Duffield	Effigy	Sir Roger Mynors (1536)	SS
Kedleston	Effigy	John Curzon (d. c. 1459)	SS
	Effigy	John Curzon (d. c. 1492)	SS
Longford	Effigy	Sir Nicholas Longford (1385)	SS
	Effigy	Sir Nicholas Longford (1429)	SS
Mugginton	Brass	Nicholas Kniveton (1500)	SS
Norbury	Effigy	Nicholas Fitzherbert (1473)	Yorkist
	Weeper	John Fitzherbert?	Yorkist
	Weeper	Ralph Fitzherbert?	Yorkist
	Effigy	Ralph Fitzherbert (1484)	Yorkist
Radbourne	Effigy	Ralph Pole (1492)	SS
Repton	Effigy	Thomas Fraunceys (c. 1482)	Yorkist
Sawley	Brass	Robert Bothe (1478)	Yorkist
Sutton Scarsdale	Incised slab	John Foljambe (1499)	Abraded
Tideswell	Effigy	Sir Thurstan de Bower (1423)	SS
Youlgreave	Effigy	Thomas Cockayne (1488)	Yorkist
Devon			
Modbury	Effigy	Sir John Champernowne	Yorkist?
Tamerton Foliot	Effigy	Member of Gorges family	SS
Dorset			
Marnhull	Effigy	John Carent (1478)	Yorkist
Melbury Sampford	Effigy	John Browning (1467)	Yorkist
	Effigy	William Browning (1467)	Yorkist
Netherbury	Effigy	Member of Moor family (c. 1480)	SS
Puddletown	Effigy	Thomas Martyn (1470)	Yorkist

Thorncombe	Brass	Sir Thomas Brook (1415)	SS
	Brass	Joan Brook (1437)	SS
Wimborne Minster	Effigy	John Beaufort, duke of Somerset (1444)	SS
	Effigy	Margaret Beaufort	SS
Durham			
Brancepeth	Effigy (lost)	Ralph Neville, earl of Westmorland (1484)	Yorkist
	Effigy (lost)	Elizabeth Neville	Yorkist
Redmarshall	Effigy	Thomas de Langton (1440)	SS
Staindrop	Effigy	Ralph Neville, earl of Westmorland (1425)	SS
	Effigy	Margaret Stafford	SS
	Effigy	Joan Beaufort	SS
Essex			
Dunmow Priory	Effigy	Joan Devereux (1409)	SS
	Effigy	Walter, Lord Fitzwalter (1432)	SS
	Effigy	Lady Fitzwalter	Yorkist?
Little Bentley	Brass	Sir William Pyrton (1490)	SS
Little Easton	Brass	Henry Bourchier, earl of Essex (1483)	Yorkist
	Brass	Isabella Bourchier	Yorkist
Little Horkesley	Brass	Sir Thomas Swynborne (1412)	SS
Roydon	Brass	Thomas Colte (1471)	Yorkist
	Brass	Joan Colte	Yorkist
Wethersfield	Effigy	Ann Tyrell (1482)	Yorkist
Wormingford	Brass	Thomas Bowden (c. 1460)	Abraded
Gloucestershire			
Berkeley	Effigy	James, Lord Berkeley (1463)	Yorkist
	Effigy	James Berkeley (1490)	Yorkist
Bristol, Lord Mayor's Chapel	Effigy	Sir Maurice Berkeley (1464)	Yorkist
Gloucester Cathedral	Effigy	Thomas Bridges (1410)	SS
	Effigy	Lady Bridges	SS
Icomb	Effigy	Sir John Blaket (1431)	SS?

Mangotsfield	Effigy	John Blount (1444)	SS
Wotton-under-Edge	Brass	Thomas, Lord Berkeley (1417)	Mermaids

Hampshire

Christchurch	Effigy	Sir John Chideock (1446)	SS
Godshill, Isle of Wight	Effigy	Sir John Leigh (1529)	SS

Herefordshire

Bredwardine	Effigy	Sir Roger Vaughan (1415)	SS
Clehonger	Brass	Lady of Aubrey family (1470)	Yorkist?
Eye	Effigy	Sir Richard Cornewall (1540)	SS
	Effigy	Sir Rowland Cornewall (1520)	SS
Hereford Cathedral	Brass	Isabel Delamere (1435)	SS
Kington	Effigy	Thomas Vaughan (1469)	Yorkist
Ledbury	Brass	Thomas Caple (1490)	SS
Weobley	Effigy	Sir Walter Devereux (1402)	SS
	Effigy	Sir John Marbury (1437)	SS
	Effigy	Alice Marbury	SS

Hertfordshire

Aldbury	Effigy	Sir Robert Whittingham (1471)	SS
	Effigy	Lady Whittingham	SS
Benington	Effigy	Sir Edward Benstead (1432)	SS
Broxbourne	Brass	Sir John Say (1478)	Yorkist
Digswell	Brass	John Peryent (1415)	SS
	Brass	Joan Peryent	SS
Little Munden	Effigy	Sir Philip Thornbury (1457)	SS
St Albans Cathedral	Brass	Sir Anthony Grey (1480)	Yorkist
Sandon	Brass	John Fitzgeffrey (1480)	Livery
Sawbridgeworth	Brass	John Leventhorpe (1433)	Abraded
	Brass	John Chauncey (1479)	Abraded

Kent

Ash	Effigy	John Septvans (1458)	SS
Barham	Brass	John Digges (c. 1455)	Abraded
Bobbing	Brass	Sir Arnold Savage (1420)	SS
Canterbury Cathedral	Effigy	John Beaufort, earl of Somerset (1410)	SS

	Effigy	Thomas, duke of Clarence (1421)	SS
	Effigy	Joan, queen of Henry IV (1437)	SS
Gillingham, St Mary's	Brass (lost)	John Bamme (1488)	SS?
Little Chart	Effigy	Sir John Darell (1509)	SS
Minster-in-Sheppey	Effigy	Sir John Cheyne (1475)	Yorkist
Teynham	Brass	John Frogenhall (1444)	SS
Thanet	Brass	Nicholas Manston (1444)	SS
Lancashire			
Clitheroe	Effigy	Thomas Radcliffe (c. 1460)	Yorkist
	Effigy	Lady Radcliffe	Yorkist
Ormskirk	Effigy	Thomas Stanley, earl of Derby (1504)	SS
Warrington	Effigy	Sir John Boteler (1463)	Yorkist?
	Effigy	Lady Boteler	Yorkist?
Leicestershire			
Ashby-de-la-Zouche	Effigy	Member of Hastings family	SS
Bottesford	Effigy	John, Lord Rous (1421)	SS
	Effigy	William, Lord Rous (1414)	SS
Castle Donington	Effigy	Robert Hazelrigg (1529)	SS
Gaddesby	Effigy	Member of Segrave family (1520)	SS
Leicester, Trinity Hospital	Effigy	Mary Harvey (temp. Henry IV)	SS
Noseley	Incised slab	Unidentified lady (c. 1406)	SS
Thurmaston	Effigy	John Turville (c. 1509)	SS
	Effigy	Lady Turville	SS
Lincolnshire			
Broughton	Effigy	Sir Henry Redford (1409)	SS
	Effigy	Lady Redford	SS
Great Grimsby	Incised slab	Unidentified civilian (c. 1410)	SS
Gunby	Brass	Sir Thomas Massingberd (1405)	SS
	Brass	Joanna Massingberd	SS
Lincoln Cathedral	Tomb chest	Joan Neville (1440)	SS
Stamford, St Mary's	Effigy	Sir David Philip (1506)	SS
	Effigy	Anne Philip	SS

APPENDIX 2: LIVERY COLLARS ON CHURCH MONUMENTS 205

Uffington	Effigy	Member of Badlesmere family (c. 1450)	SS
Wellingore	Effigy	Sir Richard Buslingthorpe (1430)	SS

London

Bishopsgate	Brass	Robert Rochester (1514)	SS
	Effigy	Sir John Crosby (1475)	Yorkist
	Effigy	Agnes Crosby	Yorkist
Shoreditch	Effigy	Sir John Elrington (1483)	Yorkist
	Effigy	Lady Elrington	Yorkist
	Effigy	Sir Simon Burley (1387)	SS
Southwark Cathedral	Effigy	John Gower (1408)	SS
Tower of London	Effigy	Sir Richard Chomondley (1544)	SS
Westminster Abbey	Brass	Sir John Golafre (1396)	Broomcod

Middlesex

Northolt	Brass	Henry Rowdell (1452)	Abraded

Norfolk

Ashwellthorpe	Effigy	Sir Edmund Thorpe (1417)	SS
	Effigy	Joan Thorpe	SS
Burnham Thorpe	Brass	Sir William Calthorpe (1420)	SS
	Brass	Lady Isabella Delamere (1421)	SS
Erpingham Gate	Sculpture	Sir Thomas Erpingham (1428)	SS
Holme-next-the-Sea	Brass	Henry Notingham (1405)	Livery
Raveningham	Brass	Margaret Willoughby (1483)	Yorkist
Rougham	Brass	Sir William Yelverton (1472)	Yorkist
Shernborne	Brass	Sir Thomas Shernborne (1458)	SS
Sloley	Sculpture	Oliver Groos (1438)	SS
Stokesby	Brass	Edmund Clere (1488)	Yorkist?
Stradsett	Brass	Thomas Lathe (1418)	SS?

Northamptonshire

Blakesley	Brass	Matthew Swetenham (1416)	SS?
Cranford	Brass	Maude Fossebrooke (1418)	SS
Deene	Effigy	Sir Robert Brudenell (1531)	SS
Dodford	Effigy	Sir John Cressey (1444)	SS
Fawsley	Effigy	Sir Richard Knightley (1534)	SS

	Weeper	Son of Sir Richard Knightley	SS
Great Addington	Effigy	Sir Henry Vere (1516)	SS
Greens Norton	Effigy	Sir Thomas Greene (1437)	SS
	Effigy	Philippa Greene	SS
Lowick	Effigy	Edmund Stafford, earl of Wiltshire (1499)	SS
	Effigy	Ralph Grene (1418)	SS
Marholm	Effigy	Sir John de Wittelbury (1410)	SS
Spratton	Effigy	Sir John Swinford (1371)	SS
Upton	Effigy	Sir Richard Knightley (1537)	SS
	Effigy	Jane Knightley	SS
Northumberland			
Chillingham	Effigy	Sir Ralph Grey (1443)	SS
Nottinghamshire			
Aston-by-Trent	Effigy	Lady of Hunt family (temp. Henry IV)	SS
Holme Pierrepont	Effigy	Sir Henry Pierrepont (1499)	Yorkist
Hoveringham	Effigy	Sir Robert Goushill (1403)	SS
Ratcliffe-on-Soar	Effigy	Ralph Sacheverell (1539)	SS
Sutton Bonington	Effigy	Thomas Staunton (c. 1486)	Yorkist
Uffington	Effigy	William de Albini	SS
Whatton	Effigy	Sir Adam de Newmarch (c. 1380)	SS
Worksop Priory	Effigy	Sir Thomas Neville (1406)	SS
	Effigy	Joan Neville	SS
Oxfordshire			
Adderbury	Brass	Unidentified knight (c. 1460)	SS?
Broughton	Effigy	Elizabeth Wykeham (early fifteenth century)	SS
	Effigy	Lord Say and Sele (1471)	Yorkist
Chinnor	Brass (lost)	Unidentified civilian (1480)	Livery
Dorchester	Brass	Sir John Drayton (1417)	SS
Great Tew	Brass	John Wylcotes (1422)	SS?
Minster Lovell	Effigy	William, Lord Lovell (1455)	Yorkist?
North Aston	Effigy	Sir John Anne (1490)	SS
North Leigh	Effigy	Sir William Wilcote (1411)	SS

	Effigy	Elizabeth Wilcote (1442)	SS
	Brass	Thomas Beckingham (1431)	SS?
Stanton Harcourt	Effigy	Sir Robert Harcourt (1470)	Yorkist
	Effigy	Sir Robert Harcourt (1503)	SS
Rutland			
Burley	Effigy	Unidentified knight (late fifteenth century)	Yorkist
	Effigy	Unidentified lady	Yorkist
Exton	Effigy	Sir John Harrington (1524)	SS
Little Casterton	Brass	Sir Thomas Burton (1381)	SS
Shropshire			
Chetwynd	Effigy (lost)	Member of Pigott family (temp. Henry VI)	SS
Kinlet	Effigy	Sir Humphrey Blount (1478)	Yorkist
	Effigy	Sir John Blount (1531)	SS
Shrewsbury, St Mary's	Brass	Nicholas Stafford (1471)	Yorkist
Tong	Effigy	Sir Richard Vernon (1451)	SS
	Effigy	Benedicta Vernon	SS
	Effigy	Sir Richard Vernon (1517)	SS
	Effigy	Sir Henry Vernon (1515)	SS
Whitchurch	Effigy	Gilbert, Lord Talbot (1418)	SS
Somerset			
Backwell	Effigy	Sir Walter Rodney (1467)	Yorkist
Chew Magna	Effigy	Sir John St Loe (1443)	SS
	Effigy	Agnes St Loe	SS
Dunster	Effigy	Sir Hugh Luttrell (1428)	SS
Hutton	Brass	John Payne (1496)	SS?
Ilton	Effigy	Lady of Wadham family (1470)	Yorkist?
Long Ashton	Effigy	Lady Choke (c. 1470)	Yorkist
North Cadbury	Effigy	William Botreaux (1391)	SS
Nunney	Effigy	John Delamere (1440)	SS
Porlock	Effigy	Sir John Harrington (1417)	SS
Rodney Stoke	Effigy	Sir Thomas Rodney (1470)	Yorkist
Yatton	Effigy	Sir John Newton (1485)	SS
	Effigy	Sir Richard Newton (1449)	SS

		Effigy	Emmota Newton (1475)	SS
Staffordshire				
Burslem		Brass	Unidentified knight (c. 1420)	SS
Dudley		Effigy (lost)	Unidentified Garter knight	SS
		Effigy (lost)	Unidentified knight	SS
		Effigy	Unidentified lady	SS
Elford		Effigy	Sir Thomas Arderne (1391)	SS
		Effigy	Matilda Arderne	SS
		Effigy	William Staunton (1450)	SS
		Effigy	Sir William Smythe (1525)	SS
Kinver		Effigy	John Hampton (c. 1472)	SS
Leigh		Effigy	Sir John Ashenhurst (1523)	Roses
Patshull		Effigy	Sir Richard Astley (1532)	SS
Tamworth		Effigy	Sir John Ferrers (1512)	SS
Suffolk				
Barsham		Brass	Sir Robert Suckling (1415)	SS
Bures		Effigy	Richard de Vere, earl of Oxford (1417)	SS
		Effigy	Alice de Vere (1452)	Florets
Bury St Edmunds, St Mary's		Tomb chest	John Baret (1467)	SS
		Brass	Jankyn Smith (1481)	Yorkist
Chilton		Effigy	Anne Crane (1500)	SS
Dennington		Effigy	William, Lord Bardolph (1441)	SS
		Effigy	Lady Bardolph (1445)	SS
Holbrook		Brass	Sir Gilbert Debenham (1493)	Yorkist
Mildenhall		Brass	Thomas Hethe (1390)	Branches
Sotterley		Brass	Ann Playters	SS
Wrentham		Brass	Ela Bowet (1400)	SS
Surrey				
Carshalton		Brass	Margaret Gaynesford (c. 1498)	Yorkist
Cheam		Brass	John Yerde (1449)	Abraded
Horley		Brass	Unidentified lady of Salmon family (1420)	SS?
Shere		Brass	Edward de la Hale (1431)	SS

APPENDIX 2: LIVERY COLLARS ON CHURCH MONUMENTS

Sussex

Arundel	Effigy	Thomas, earl of Arundel (1416)	SS
	Brass	Agnes Salmon (1418)	SS
	Brass	Thomas Salmon (1430)	SS
	Effigy	John Fitzalan, earl of Arundel (1435)	SS
	Effigy	Joan Neville (1462)	Yorkist
	Brass	John Threel (1465)	Yorkist
Easebourne	Effigy	Sir David Owen (1542)	SS
Hurstmonceux	Effigy	Thomas, Lord Hoo (1455)	SS
	Effigy	Sir Thomas Hoo (1486)	SS
Lewes	Brass	Unidentified member of Warrenne family (c. 1430)	SS
	Effigy	Sir Edward Dalyngrigge (c. 1390)	SS
Stopham	Brass	Richard Barttelot (1462)	Yorkist?
Trotton	Brass	Thomas Camoys (1419)	SS
	Brass	Elizabeth Camoys	SS

Warwickshire

Astley	Effigy	Edward, Lord Ferrers (1457)	SS
	Effigy	Elizabeth L'Isle (1483)	Yorkist
Aston	Effigy	Sir Thomas Erdington (1433)	SS
	Effigy	Joan Harcourt (1416)	SS
	Effigy	Sir William Harcourt (1462)	Yorkist
	Effigy	Sir William Holte (1518)	SS
Baginton	Brass	Sir William Bagot (1407)	SS
	Brass	Margaret Bagot	SS
Coleshill	Effigy	Sir Simon Digby (1519)	SS
Compton Verney	Brass	Richard Vernon (1536)	Crown
Compton Wynyates	Effigy	Sir William Compton (1528)	SS
Emscote	Brass (lost)	John Hugford (1485)	Hearts?
	Brass (lost)	Thomas Hugford	Hearts?
Upper Shuckburgh	Brass	Thomas Shukburgh (1549)	Crown
Warwick, St Mary's	Effigy (lost)	Margaret Peito (temp. Edward III)	SS
	Brass	Thomas de Beauchamp (1406)	Ragged staffs

APPENDIX 2: LIVERY COLLARS ON CHURCH MONUMENTS

Wellesbourne Hastings	Brass	Sir Thomas le Strange (1426)	SS
Wootton Wawen	Effigy	John Harewell (1428)	Florets
Westmorland			
Kirkby Lonsdale	Effigy	Edward Middleton (fifteenth century)	SS?
Wiltshire			
Bromham	Effigy	Sir Roger Tocotes (1492)	SS
Salisbury Cathedral	Effigy	Sir John Cheney (1509)	SS
	Effigy	Robert, Lord Hungerford (1459)	SS
	Brass (lost)	Walter, Lord Hungerford (1449)	SS
Worcestershire			
Bromsgrove, St John the Baptist's	Effigy	Sir Humphrey Stafford (1450)	SS
	Effigy	Sir John Talbot (1501)	SS
Dudley, St Edmund's	Effigy (lost)	Unidentified Garter knight	SS
	Effigy (lost)	Unidentified knight	SS
	Effigy (lost)	Unidentified lady	SS
Fladbury	Brass	Edward Peytoo (1458)	Abraded
Kidderminster, St Mary's	Brass	Walter Cokesey (1407)	SS
	Brass	Sir John Phelip (1415)	SS
	Effigy	Sir Hugh Cokesay (1445)	SS
Martley	Effigy	Sir Hugh Mortimer (c. 1459)	Yorkist
Stanford-on-Teme	Effigy	Sir Humphrey Selway (1493)	SS
Yorkshire			
Barmston	Effigy	William Monceux (1446)	SS
Brandesburton	Brass	Lora St Quinton (1398)	SS?
Burton Agnes	Effigy	Sir Walter Griffith (1481)	SS
	Effigy	Joan Griffith (1481)	SS
Croft	Tomb	Sir Richard Clervaux (1490)	SS
Darfield	Effigy	Sir John Bosevile (1410)	SS
Escrick	Effigy	Sir Roger Lascelles (c. 1450)	SS
	Effigy (lost)	Lady Lascelles	SS
Giggleswick	Effigy	Sir Richard Tempest (1488)	SS

APPENDIX 2: LIVERY COLLARS ON CHURCH MONUMENTS

Halsham	Effigy	Sir John Constable (1407)	SS
Harewood	Effigy	Sir William Gascoigne (d. 1461–65)	Yorkist
	Effigy	Sir William Gascoigne (1487)	SS
	Effigy	Sir Edward Redman (1510)	SS
	Effigy	Sir Richard Redman (1426)	SS
	Effigy	Sir William Ryther (1425)	SS
Harpham	Brass	Thomas de St Quinton (1445)	SS?
Helmsley	Brass	Thomas, Lord de Ros (1465)	Yorkist
Methley	Effigy	Sir Robert Waterton (1424)	SS/crowns
	Effigy	Cecily Waterton	SS
Owston	Brass	Robert Hatfield (1417)	SS
	Brass	Ade Hatfield	SS
Pickering, St Peter's and St Paul's	Effigy	Sir David Rowcliffe (1407)	SS
	Effigy	Margaret Rowcliffe	SS
	Effigy	Unidentified knight	SS
Ripon Cathedral	Effigy	Sir Thomas de Markenfield (fourteenth century)	Palings
Routh	Brass	Sir John Routh (1410)	SS
	Brass	Agnes Routh	SS
Ryther	Effigy	Sir William Ryther (1475)	Yorkist
Selby Abbey	Effigy	John, Lord Darcy (1411)	SS
South Cave	Effigy (lost)	Sir Henry Lound (1426)	SS
South Cowton	Effigy	Sir Richard Conyers (1493)	SS
Swine	Effigy	Sir Robert Hilton (1410)	SS
	Effigy	Constance Hilton	SS
Thornhill	Effigy	Sir John Saville (1481)	Yorkist
Tickhill	Effigy	Sir Thomas Fitzwilliam (1495)	SS
Wadworth	Effigy	Sir Edmund Fitzwilliam (1430)	SS
Wentworth	Effigy	Sir William Gascoigne (1460)	SS
West Tanfield	Effigy	Sir John Marmion (1386)	SS
York Minster	Sculpture	Henry IV	SS
	Sculpture	Henry V	SS
Wales			
Abergavenny	Effigy	Sir William ap Thomas (1445)	SS

	Effigy	Richard Herbert (1510)	SS
	Effigy	Sir Richard Herbert (1469)	Yorkist
Beaumaris	Effigy	Sir Rowland Bulkeley (mid-fifteenth century)	SS
Carmarthen	Effigy	Sir Rhys ap Thomas (1525)	Florets
Llandaff Cathedral	Effigy	Christopher Mathew (d. c. 1531)	SS
	Effigy	Sir David Mathew (1470)	SS?
	Effigy	Sir William Mathew (1528)	SS
Llandegai	Effigy	William Griffith (d. 1483)	Yorkist
Montgomery	Effigy	Sir Richard Herbert (1470–80)	Yorkist
Newport	Effigy	John Morgan (d. 1493)	SS
Ruabon	Effigy	John ap Ellis Eyton (1526)	SS
Scolton Manor	Effigy	Sir Henry Wogan (1475)	Yorkist

Ireland

Dublin, St Audeon's	Effigy	Sir Roland FitzEustace (c. 1482)	Yorkist
Lusk	Effigy	James Bermingham (sixteenth century?)	Yorkist

Bibliography

Manuscripts

Aberystwyth, National Library of Wales

Alice M. Dixon Collection
Badminton Deeds
Badminton Manorial
Castell Gorford MSS
Eaton Evans and Williams Collection
Llangibby MSS
MS 1449, Pedigrees of Carmarthenshire, Cardiganshire and Pembrokeshire families
MS 4517, Herbert family pedigree
MS 6512, 1C, English translations of the work of Lewis Glyn Cothi
MS 16920F, 16921E, Herbert pedigrees
Peniarth Estate MSS
Picton Castle MSS
Powis Castle Deeds
Tredegar MSS

Cardiff Central Library

Philipps MS, 5:7, The *Herbertorum Prosapia*

Derby Local Studies Library

Brookhill Hall Collection
Derbyshire Deeds
DL84, Stephen Glover papers
MS 6341, Chaloner's 1615 compilation of the heralds' visitations of Derbyshire in 1569 and 1611
Mundy MS
Sir Edward Every Deeds

Free Library of Philadelphia

MS Lewis, E 210, Edward IV Roll

Lichfield Record Office

B/A/1/13, Bishops' Registers
B/C/10ii, Bishops' Registers, supplementary

Lincoln Cathedral Library
A/2/35, Dean and Chapter records

Lincoln, Lincolnshire Archives Office
I, L1/3/1, Corporation of Lincoln Registers, The White Book

London, British Library
Additional Charters, 1816
Additional MS 18850, 29938, 29940, 30946, 31835, 36619, 42009, 48976, 71474
Arundel 66
Cotton MS Vespasian F VIII
Egerton Charters, 7358
Egerton MS 2586
Harleian MS 911, 944, 1096
Harley MS 545, 3606, 3607, 4431, 6291, 7353
Lansdowne MS 874
Royal 11 E II
Royal 14 E IV
Royal 15 E IV
Royal 18 D II
Royal 19 A V
Royal 19 E V
Sloane Charters

London, College of Arms
MS H.8, William Fellows's 1530 visitation of Tintern Abbey

London, The National Archives
C 131, Chancery, Extents for Debts
C 140, Chancery, Inquisitions Post Mortem
CP 25, Court of Commons Pleas, Feet of Fines
DL 28, Duchy of Lancaster, Various Accounts
DL 29, Duchy of Lancaster, Accounts of Auditors, Receivers, Feodaries and Ministers
DL 37, Duchy of Lancaster, Chancery Rolls
DL 41, Duchy of Lancaster, Miscellanea
DL 42, Duchy of Lancaster, Miscellaneous Books
E 36, Exchequer, Treasury of the Receipt, Miscellaneous Books
E 101, Exchequer, Various Accounts
E 154, Exchequer, King's Remembrancer and Treasury of the Receipt, Inventory of Goods and Chattels
E 159, Exchequer, King's Remembrancer, Memoranda Rolls and Enrolment Books
E 403, Exchequer of Receipt, Issue Rolls and Registers
E 404, Exchequer of Receipt, Warrants for Issues
KB 9, King's Bench, Ancient Indictments
KB 29, King's Bench, Controlment Rolls
KB 149, King's Bench, Plea Side, Cedule Files
PROB 11, Prerogative Court of Canterbury Wills

SC 8, Special Collections, Ancient Petitions
STAC 2, Star Chamber Proceedings, Henry VIII

London, Westminster Abbey

Muniments, 6625, 6646

Matlock, Derbyshire Record Office

D31, Glossop and Wirksworth papers
D231, Okeover papers
D239, Fitzherbert of Tissington papers
D2375, Harpur Crewe papers
D5236, Every of Egginton papers

Norwich, Norfolk Record Office

DCN 40/11, Norwich Sacrist's Register

Nottingham, Nottinghamshire Archives

DD/P, Portland of Welbeck, deeds and estate papers

Oxford, Bodleian Library

Digby MS 82, list of the badges of supporters of the House of York
MS.Eng.misc.d.227, John Blount's translation of *De Studio Militari*
MS 33, Richard Gough's 'General Topography'

Oxford, Merton College

MS 297B, The Statutes of England

Oxford, St John's College

MS 179, Sarum Breviary

Prendergast, Haverfordwest, Pembrokeshire Record Office

HDX/337/42, Wogan family documents

Stafford Record Office

D641, Stafford family papers
D(W)1734, Paget papers

Stafford, William Salt Library

S. Ms. 459/3, transcripts of medieval deeds

Swynnerton Park

Swynnerton MSS

University of Nottingham

Manuscripts and Special Collections, Middleton Collection, Mi 5/168/34, contract for the brass of Richard Willoughby

University of York, Borthwick Institute for Archives

Archbishops Register, 23

Printed primary sources

Babington, C. and Lumby, J.R. (eds), *Polychronicon Ranulphi Higden Monachi Cestrensis, together with the English translation by John Trevisa*, 9 vols (1865–86).

Bedells, J. (ed.), *The Visitation of the County of Huntingdon 1684 made by Sir Henry St. George, Knight, Clarenceux King of Arms*, Harleian Society, New Series, 13 (London, 2000).

Bentley, S., *Excerpta Historica, or, Illustrations of English History* (London, 1831).

Boatwright, L., Habberjam, M. and Hammond, P. (eds), *The Logge Register of PCC Wills, 1479 to 1486*, 2 vols (Knaphill, 2008).

Bruce, J. (ed.), *Historie of the Arrivall of King Edward IV*, Camden Society, 1st Series, 1 (1838).

Calendar of Charter Rolls Preserved in the Public Record Office, 6 vols (London, 1903–27).

Calendar of Close Rolls Preserved in the Public Record Office, 1441–85, 6 vols (London, 1933–54).

Calendar of Fine Rolls Preserved in the Public Record Office, 1452–1509, 4 vols (London, 1911–62).

Calendar of Inquisitions Miscellaneous, Chancery, Preserved in the Public Record Office, 7 vols (London, 1916–68).

Calendar of Inquisitions Post Mortem and Other Analogous Documents Preserved in the Public Record Office, Henry VII, 3 vols (London, 1898–1955).

Calendar of Patent Rolls Preserved in the Public Record Office, 1370–1509, 25 vols (London, 1895–1916).

Carpenter, C. (ed.), *Kingsford's Stonor Letters and Papers 1290–1483* (Cambridge, 1996).

Clark, G.T., *Cartae et Alia Munimenta quae ad Dominium de Glamorgancia pertinent*, 6 vols (Cardiff, 1910).

Clark, G.T., *Limbus Patrum Morganiae et Glamorganiae* (London, 1886).

Commynes, P. de, *Philippe de Commynes: The Reign of Louis XI 1461–83*, ed. and trans. M. Jones (London, 1972).

Cooper, C.H., *Annals of Cambridge*, 5 vols (1842–1908).

Danter, J., *A Merrie Pleasant and Delectable Historie betweene King Edward the Fourth and a Tanner of Tamworth* (London, 1596).

Davies, J.S., *An English Chronicle of the Reigns of Richard II, Henry IV, Henry V, and Henry VI*, Camden Society, 1st Series, 64 (1856).

Davies, R. (ed.), *Extracts from the Municipal Records of the City of York, during the Reigns of Edward IV, Edward V and Richard III* (London, 1843).

Davies, W. and Jones, J. (eds), *Gwaith Lewis Glyn Cothi* (Oxford, 1837).

Davis, N. (ed.), *Paston Letters and Papers of the Fifteenth Century*, 2 vols (1971–76).

Devlin, M.A. (ed.), *The Sermons of Thomas Brinton, Bishop of Rochester (1373–1389)*, Camden Society, 3rd Series, 85–6 (London, 1954).

Devon, F., *Issue Rolls of the Exchequer; being a Collection of Payments Made out of His Majesty's Revenue, from King Henry III to King Henry VI Inclusive* (London, 1837).

Dillon, V. and St John Hope, W.H. (eds), *Pageant of the Birth Life and Death of Richard Beauchamp Earl of Warwick K.G. 1389–1439* (London, 1914).

BIBLIOGRAPHY

Dudley, E., *The Tree of Commonwealth*, ed. D.M. Brodie (Cambridge, 1948).
Edwards, D.G. (ed.), *Derbyshire Wills Proved in the Prerogative Court of Canterbury 1393–1574*, Derbyshire Record Society, 26 (Chesterfield, 1998).
Ellis, H. (ed.), *Original Letters Illustrative of English History*, 1st Series, 3 vols (London, 1824).
Fortescue, J., *The Governance of England*, ed. C. Plummer (Oxford, 1885).
Gairdner, J. (ed.), *The Historical Collections of a Citizen of London in the Fifteenth Century*, Camden Society, New Series, 17 (London, 1876).
Gairdner, J. (ed.), *The Paston Letters A.D. 1422–1509*, Complete Library edn, 6 vols (London, 1904).
Gairdner, J. (ed.), *Three Fifteenth Century Chronicles*, Camden Society, New Series, 28 (London, 1880).
Galbraith, V.H. (ed.), *The Anonimalle Chronicle 1333 to 1381*, Rolls Series (Manchester, 1927).
Genet, J.P. (ed.), *Four English Political Tracts of the Later Middle Ages*, Camden Society, 4th Series, 18 (London, 1977).
Giles, J.A., *The Chronicles of the White Rose of York*, 2nd edn (London, 1845).
Given-Wilson, C. (ed. and trans.), *The Chronicle of Adam Usk, 1377–1421* (Oxford, 1997).
Given-Wilson, C. (ed. and trans.), *Chronicles of the Revolution, 1397–1400* (Manchester, 1993).
Given-Wilson, C., Brand, P., Curry, A., Horrox, R., Martin, G., Ormrod, M. and Phillips, S. (eds), *The Parliament Rolls of Medieval England, 1275–1504* (Leicester, 2005).
Glover, C. and Riden, P. (eds), *William Woolley's History of Derbyshire*, Derbyshire Record Society, 4 (Chesterfield, 1981).
Hall, E., *Chronicle*, ed. H. Ellis (London, 1809).
Hall, E., *The Union of the Two Noble Families of Lancaster and York* (Menston, 1970).
Halliwell, J.O. (ed.), *A Chronicle of the First Thirteen Years of the Reign of King Edward the Fourth, by John Warkworth*, Camden Society, 1st Series, 10 (London, 1839).
Harvey, J.H. (ed.), *William Worcestre Itineraries* (Oxford, 1969).
Hearne, T. (ed.), *Historia Regum Angliae* (Oxford, 1745).
Hector, L.C. and Harvey, B.F. (eds), *The Westminster Chronicle, 1381–1394* (Oxford, 1982).
Hingeston, F.C. (ed.), *The Chronicle of England by John Capgrave*, Rolls Series (London, 1858).
Historical Manuscripts Commission, *The Cartulary of Tutbury Priory*, ed. A. Saltman (London, 1962).
Historical Manuscripts Commission, *The Manuscripts of His Grace the Duke of Rutland, K.G. Preserved at Belvoir Castle*, 4 vols (London, 1888–1905).
Historical Manuscripts Commission, *Report on the MSS of the Late Reginald Rawdon Hastings, Esq., The Manor House, Ashby de la Zouche*, 4 vols (1928–42).
Hoccleve, T., *Works*, ed. F. Furnivall, 3 vols (London, 1892–97).
Horrox, R. and Hammond, P.W. (eds), *British Library Harleian Manuscript 433: Register of Grants for the Reigns of Edward V and Richard III*, 4 vols (Upminster and London, 1979–83).
Jeayes, I.H., *Descriptive Catalogue of the Charters and Muniments in the Possession of Reginald Walkelyne Chandos-Pole Esq., at Radbourne Hall* (London, 1896).
Jeayes, I.H., *Descriptive Catalogue of Derbyshire Charters in the Public and Private Libraries and Muniment Rooms* (London and Derby, 1906).

Jefferson, L. (ed.), *Wardens' Accounts and Court Minute Books of the Goldsmiths' Mistery of London 1334-1446* (Woodbridge, 2003).
Jolliffe, J. (ed. and trans.), *Froissart's Chronicles* (London, 1967).
Kekewich, M., Richmond, C., Sutton, A.F., Visser-Fuchs, L. and Watts, J.L. (eds), *The Politics of Fifteenth Century England: John Vale's Book* (Stroud, 1995).
Kingsford, C.L., *Chronicles of London* (Oxford, 1905).
Kingsford, C.L. (ed.), *The Stonor Letters and Papers 1290-1483*, Camden Society, 3rd Series, 29-30, 2 vols (London, 1919).
Letts, M. (ed.), *The Travels of Leo of Rozmital through Germany, Flanders, England, France, Spain, Portugal and Italy, 1465-1467* (Cambridge, 1957).
List of Sheriffs for England and Wales, PRO Lists and Indexes, 9 (London, 1898).
Long, C.E. (ed.), *Diary of the Marches of the Royal Army during the Great Civil War* (London, 1859).
Luders, A. (ed.), *The Statutes of the Realm*, 11 vols (London, 1810-25).
Macaulay, G.C., *The Complete Works of John Gower*, 4 vols (Oxford, 1899-1902).
Mandrot, B. de (ed.), *Mémoires de Philippe de Commynes*, 2 vols (Paris, 1901-3).
Martorell, J. and de Galba, M.J., *Tirant lo Blanc*, ed. and trans. D.H. Rosenthal (New York and London, 1984).
Merrick, R., *A Book of Glamorganshire's Antiquities by Rice Merrick, Esq. 1578* (Broadway, 1825).
Meyrick, S.R. (ed.), *Heraldic Visitations of Wales and Part of the Marches between the Years 1586 and 1613, by Lewys Dwnn*, 2 vols (Llandovery, 1846).
Myers, A.R. (ed.), *English Historical Documents: 1327-1485* (1969).
Myers, A.R. (ed.), *The Household of Edward IV: The Black Book and the Ordinance of 1478* (Manchester, 1959).
Nasmith, J. (ed.), *Itineraria Symonis Simeonis et Willelmi de Worcestre* (Cambridge, 1778).
Nichols, J.G. (ed.), *The Boke of Noblesse* (London, 1860).
Nicolas, N.H., *Privy Purse Expenses of Elizabeth of York: Wardrobe Accounts of Edward the Fourth* (London, 1830).
Nicolas, N.H. (ed.), *Proceedings and Ordinances of the Privy Council of England*, 7 vols (London, 1834-37).
Owen, H. (ed.), *A Calendar of the Public Records relating to Pembrokeshire*, Cymmrodorion Record Series, 3 vols (London, 1911-18).
'Pardon to Rhys ap Griffith ap Aron, of Peniarth, and Others', *Archaeologia Cambrensis*, 15 (1860), 309-12.
Pronay, N. and Cox, J. (eds), *The Crowland Chronicle Continuations 1459-1486* (London, 1986).
Pugh, T.B. (ed.), *The Marcher Lordships of South Wales 1415-1536, Select Documents* (Cardiff, 1963).
Raine, J. and Clay, J.W. (eds), *Testamenta Eboracensia, or, Wills registered at York*, Surtees Society, 6 vols (London, 1836-1902).
Richards, W.L. (ed.), *Gwaith Dafydd Llwyd o Fathafarn* (Cardiff, 1964).
Riden, P. and Blair, J. (eds), *Records of the Borough of Chesterfield and Related Documents 1204-1835* (Chesterfield, 1980).
Riley, H.T. (ed.), *Ingulph's Chronicle of the Abbey of Croyland* (London, 1854).
Robbins, R.H. (ed.), *Historical Poems of the Fourteenth and Fifteenth Centuries* (New York, 1959).

Rymer, T., *Foedera conventiones, literae, et cujuscunque generis acta publica, inter reges Angliae*, 20 vols (London, 1704–35).
Sawbridge, G., Rawlins, W. and Roycroft, S., *La premiere part des ans du Roy Henry le VI* (London, 1679).
Shuttleworth, J.M. (ed.), *The Life of Edward, First Lord Herbert of Cherbury, Written by Himself* (London, 1976).
Siddons, M.P. (ed. and trans.), *Visitation of Herefordshire 1634*, Harleian Society, New Series, 15 (London, 2002).
Skeat, W.W. (ed.), *The Vision of William concerning Piers the Plowman in Three Parallel Texts*, 2 vols (Oxford, 1886).
Sneyd, C.A. (ed. and trans.), *A Relation, or rather True Account, of the Island of England ... about the Year 1500* (London, 1847).
Stapleton, T. (ed.), *Plumpton Correspondence*, Camden Society, 1st Series, 4 (1839).
Starkey, D. (ed.), *The Inventory of King Henry VIII* (London, 1998).
Steele, R.R. (ed.), *Three Prose Versions of the Secreta Secretorum*, Early English Text Society, Extra Series, 74 (London, 1898).
Stenton, D.M., *Rolls of the Justices in Eyre for Yorkshire in 3 Henry III*, Selden Society, 56 (1937).
Stevenson, J. (ed.), *Letters and Papers Illustrative of the Wars of the English in France during the Reign of Henry VI*, Rolls Series, 2 vols in 3 (London, 1861–64).
Stow, G.B. (ed.), *Historia Vitae et Regni Ricardi Secundi* (Philadelphia, PA, 1977).
Stow, J., *The Annales or Generall Chronicle of England* (London, 1600).
Stratford, J., *The Bedford Inventories* (London, 1993).
Sutton, A.F. and Hammond, P.W. (eds), *The Coronation of Richard III: The Extant Documents* (Gloucester and New York, 1983).
Thomas, A.H. and Thornley, I.D. (eds), *The Great Chronicle of London* (London, 1938).
Thompson, E.M. (ed.), *Chronicon Angliae ab anno domini 1328 usque ad annum 1388* (London, 1874).
Tymms, S. (ed.), *Wills and Inventories from the Register of the Commissary of Bury St. Edmunds and the Archdeacon of Sudbury*, Camden Society, Original Series, 49 (London, 1850).
Vegetius Renatus, F., *Knyghthode and Bataile*, ed. R. Dybosky and Z.M. Arend, Early English Text Society, Original Series, 201 (London, 1936).
Vinaver, E. and Field, P.J.C. (eds), *The Works of Sir Thomas Malory*, 3rd edn (Oxford, 1990).
Wagner, A., Barker, N. and Payne, A. (eds), *Medieval Pageant: Writhe's Garter Book: The Ceremony of the Bath and the Earldom of Salisbury Roll* (London, 1993).
Walther, H., *Initia carminum ac versuum Medii Aevi posterioris Latinorum*, 5 vols (Göttingen, 1959).
Waurin, J. de, *Recueil des chroniques et anchiennes istoires de la Grant Bretaigne*, ed. W. Hardy, Rolls Series (1891).
Weaver, J.R.H. (ed.), *Some Oxfordshire Wills Proved in the Prerogative Court of Canterbury, 1393–1510* (1958).
Weever, J., *Ancient Funerall Monuments* (London, 1631).
Williams, I. (ed.), *Casgliad O Waith Ieuan Deulwyn*, Bangor Welsh MSS Society, iv (Bangor, 1909).
Williams, I. and Williams, J.L. (eds), *Gwaith Guto'r Glyn* (Cardiff, 1939).

Wright, T., *Political Poems and Songs Relating to English History*, 2 vols (London, 1859–61).
Wright, T. (ed.), *The Vision and Creed of Piers Plowman*, 2 vols (London, 1856).
Wrottesley, G., 'Extracts from the Plea Rolls, 34 Henry VI to 14 Edward IV', *Staffordshire Historical Collections*, New Series, 4 (1901), 93–212.
Wrottesley, G., 'Extracts from the Plea Rolls, Temp. Edward IV, Edward V and Richard III', *Staffordshire Historical Collections*, New Series, 6, Part I (1903), 89–164.

Secondary sources

Acheson, E., *A Gentry Community, Leicestershire in the Fifteenth Century, c. 1422–c. 1485* (Cambridge, 1992).
Alamo, E.V. del, and Pendergast, C.S. (eds), *Memory and the Medieval Tomb* (Aldershot, 2000).
Althoff, G., *Family, Friends and Followers: Political and Social Bonds in Early Medieval Europe*, trans. C. Carroll (Cambridge, 2004).
'An Agreement for the Construction of a Tomb in Wollaton Church, 1515', in J.H. Hodson, P.A. Kennedy and V.W. Walker (eds), *A Nottinghamshire Miscellany* (Nottingham, 1962), pp. 1–2.
Anglo, S., *Images of Tudor Kingship* (London, 1992).
Angus-Butterworth, L.M., *Old Cheshire Families and Their Seats* (Manchester, 1932).
Arthurson, I., *The Perkin Warbeck Conspiracy 1491–1499* (Stroud, 1994).
Ashdown-Hill, J., 'The Red Rose of Lancaster?' *The Ricardian*, 10 (1996), 406–20.
Astell, A.W., *Political Allegory in Late Medieval England* (Ithaca, NY, and London, 1999).
Aston, M., 'The Use of Images', in R. Marks and P. Williamson (eds), *Gothic: Art for England 1400–1547* (London, 2003), pp. 68–75.
Attreed, L.C., 'An Indenture between Richard Duke of Gloucester and the Scrope Family of Masham and Upsall', *Speculum*, 58 (1983), 1018–25.
Axon, E., 'The Family of Bothe (Booth) and the Church in the 15th and 16th Centuries', *Transactions of the Lancashire and Cheshire Antiquarian Society*, 53 (1938), 32–82.
Ayres, E.A., 'Parliamentary Representation in Derbyshire and Nottinghamshire in the Fifteenth Century', University of Nottingham, unpublished MA thesis (1956).
Badham, S., 'Monumental Brasses: The Development of the York Workshops in the Fourteenth and Fifteenth Centuries', in C. Wilson (ed.), *Medieval Art and Architecture in the East Riding of Yorkshire*, British Archaeological Association Conference for the Year 1983, 9 (Leeds, 1989), pp. 165–85.
Badham, S., 'Patterns of Patronage: Brasses to the Cromwell–Bourchier Kinship Group', *Transactions of the Monumental Brass Society*, 17 (2007), 423–52.
Badham, S., 'Status and Salvation: The Design of Medieval English Brasses and Incised Slabs', *Transactions of the Monumental Brass Society*, 15 (1996), 413–65.
Badham, S. and Oosterwijk, S., '"Cest endenture fait parentre": English Tomb Contracts of the Long Fourteenth Century', in S. Badham and S. Oosterwijk (eds), *Monumental Industry: The Production of Tomb Monuments in England and Wales in the Long Fourteenth Century* (Donington, 2010), pp. 187–236.
Badham, S. and Oosterwijk, S., 'Introduction', in S. Badham and S. Oosterwijk (eds), *Monumental Industry: The Production of Tomb Monuments in England and Wales in the Long Fourteenth Century* (Donington, 2010), pp. 1–11.

Bagnall-Oakeley, M.E., 'On the Monumental Effigies of the Family of Berkeley', *Transactions of the Bristol and Gloucestershire Archaeological Society*, 15 (1892), 89–102.
Banks, R.W., 'On the Family of Vaughan of Hergest', *Archaeologia Cambrensis*, 26 (1871), 23–34.
Bark, G.M., 'A London Alabasterer in 1421', *Antiquaries Journal*, 29 (1949), 89–91.
Barker, J., 'Monuments and Marriage in Late Medieval England: Origins, Function and Reception of Double Tombs', Courtauld Institute of Art, unpublished PhD thesis, 2 vols (2015).
Barlow, M., *Barlow Family Records* (London and Derby, 1932).
Barnard, F.P. (ed.), *Edward IV's French Expedition of 1475: The Leaders and Their Badges* (Oxford, 1925).
Barr, H. (ed.), *The Piers Plowman Tradition* (London, 1993).
Barth, F. (ed.), *Ethnic Groups and Boundaries: The Social Organization of Culture Difference*, 2nd edn (Long Grove, IL, 1998).
Barthes, R., *Elements of Semiology*, trans. A. Lavers and C. Smith (London, 1967).
Bartrum, P.C., *Welsh Genealogies AD 1400–1500*, 18 vols (Aberystwyth, 1983).
Bateman, T., *Vestiges of the Antiquities of Derbyshire, and the Sepulchral Usages of Its Inhabitants, from the Most Remote Ages to the Reformation* (London, 1848).
Bayliss, J., 'An Indenture for Two Alabaster Effigies', *Church Monuments*, 16 (2001), 22–9.
Bean, J.M.W., *From Lord to Patron* (Manchester, 1989).
Bellamy, J.G., *Bastard Feudalism and the Law* (1989).
Beltz, G.F., 'Notices Relating to the Ancient "Collars of the King's Livery", and, in Particular, Those which are still Denominated "Collars of SS"', *Retrospective Review*, 16 (1828), 500–10.
Bennet, H.S., *The Pastons and Their England* (Cambridge, 1932).
Bennett, J.A.W., 'The Date of the B-Text of Piers Plowman', *Medium Ævum*, 12 (1943), 55–64.
Bertelli, S., *The King's Body: Sacred Rituals of Power in Medieval and Early Modern Europe* (University Park, PA, 2001).
Bertram, J. (ed.), *Monumental Brasses as Art and History* (Stroud, 1996).
Bestard-Camps, J., *What's In a Relative? Household and Family in Formentera*, trans. R. Pitt (Oxford and New York, 1991).
Beverley Smith, J. and Pugh, T.B., 'The Lordship of Gower and Kilvey in the Middle Ages', in T.B. Pugh (ed.), *Glamorgan County History, III, The Middle Ages* (Cardiff, 1971), pp. 205–65.
Biddle, M., 'The Hanging of the Round Table', in M. Biddle (ed.), *King Arthur's Round Table: An Archaeological Investigation* (Woodbridge, 2000), pp. 393–424.
Biddle, M., Clayre, B. and Morris, M., 'The Setting of the Round Table: Winchester Castle and the Great Hall', in M. Biddle (ed.), *King Arthur's Round Table: An Archaeological Investigation* (Woodbridge, 2000), pp. 59–101.
Biebrach, R., 'Conspicuous by Their Absence: Rethinking Explanations for the Lack of Brasses in Medieval Wales', *Transactions of the Monumental Brass Society*, 18 (2009), 36–42.
Biebrach, R., '"Our Ancient Blood and Our Kings": Two Early Sixteenth-Century Heraldic Tombs in Llandaff Cathedral, Wales', *Church Monuments*, 24 (2009), 73–88.
Bigsby, R., *Historical and Topographical Description of Repton, in the County of Derby* (London, 1854).

Binski, P., *Medieval Death: Ritual and Representation* (London, 1996).
Birrell, J.R., 'The Honour of Tutbury in the Fourteenth and Fifteenth Centuries', University of Birmingham, unpublished MA thesis (1962).
Blair, J., 'Henry Lakenham, Marbler of London, and a Tomb Contract of 1376', *Antiquaries Journal*, 60 (1980), 66–74.
Blanchard, I.S.W., *The Duchy of Lancaster's Estates in Derbyshire 1485–1540*, Derbyshire Archaeological Society Record Series, 3 (1971, for 1967).
Blanchard, I.S.W., 'Economic Change in Derbyshire in the late Middle Ages, 1272–1540', University of London, unpublished PhD thesis (1967).
Bond, S.M. (ed.), *The Monuments of St. George's Chapel, Windsor Castle* (Windsor, 1958).
Bourdieu, P., 'The Forms of Capital', in J.G. Richardson (ed.), *Handbook of Theory and Research for the Sociology of Education* (New York, 1986), pp. 241–58.
Bourdieu, P., *Outline of a Theory of Practice* (New York, 1977).
Bowyer, L.J., *The Ancient Parish of Norbury* (Ashbourne, 1953).
Brodrick, A. and Darrah, J., 'The Fifteenth Century Polychromed Limestone Effigies of William Fitzalan, 9th Earl of Arundel, and His Wife Joan Nevill, in the Fitzalan Chapel, Arundel', *Church Monuments*, 1 (1986), 65–94.
Brown, E.A.R., 'Ritual Brotherhood in Western Medieval Europe', *Traditio*, 52 (1997), 357–81.
Burgess, C., '"A Fond Thing Vainly Invented": An Essay on Purgatory and Pious Motive in Late Medieval England', in S.J. Wright (ed.), *Parish, Church and People: Local Studies in Lay Religion, 1350–1750* (London, 1988), pp. 56–84.
Burckhardt, J., *The Civilization of the Renaissance in Italy*, 6th edn (London, 1960).
Burke, P., *The Fabrication of Louis XIV* (New Haven, CT, and London, 1992).
Bynum, C.W., *Christian Materiality: An Essay on Religion in Late Medieval Europe* (New York, 2011).
Calhoun, J.C., 'Community: Towards a Variable Conceptualization for Comparative Research', *Social History*, 5 (1980), 105–29.
Cameron, A., 'The Giving of Livery and Retaining in Henry VII's reign', *Renaissance and Modern Studies*, 18 (1974), 17–35.
Campbell, S.J., 'Introduction', in S.J. Campbell (ed.), *Artists at Court: Image-Making and Identity, 1300–1550* (Boston, 2004), pp. 1–13.
Carpenter, C., 'The Beauchamp Affinity: A Study of Bastard Feudalism at Work', *English Historical Review*, 95 (1980), 514–32.
Carpenter, C., 'The Duke of Clarence and the Midlands: A Study in the Interplay of Local and National Politics', *Midland History*, 11 (1986), 23–48.
Carpenter, C., 'Gentry and Community in Medieval England', *Journal of British Studies*, 33 (1994), 340–80.
Carpenter, C., 'Introduction: Political Culture, Politics and Cultural History', in L. Clark and C. Carpenter (eds), *The Fifteenth Century, IV: Political Culture in Late Medieval Britain* (Woodbridge, 2004), pp. 1–19.
Carpenter, C., *Locality and Polity: A Study of Warwickshire Landed Society, 1401–1499* (Cambridge, 1992).
Carpenter, C., *The Wars of the Roses: Politics and the Constitution in England, c. 1437–1509* (Cambridge, 1997).
Carrington, A. and Andrew, W.J., 'A Lancastrian Raid in the Wars of the Roses', *Derbyshire Archaeological Journal*, 34 (1912), 33–49.

Carsten, J., 'Introduction: Cultures of Relatedness', in J. Carsten (ed.), *Cultures of Relatedness: New Approaches to the Study of Kinship* (Cambridge, 2000), pp. 1–36.
Castor, H., *The King, the Crown, and the Duchy of Lancaster* (Oxford, 2000).
Chartier, R., *Cultural History: Between Practices and Representations*, trans. L.G. Cochrane (Cambridge, 1988).
Cheetham, F., *Alabaster Images of Medieval England* (Woodbridge, 2003).
Cherry, M., 'The Courtenay Earls of Devon: The Formation and Disintegration of a Late-Medieval Aristocratic Affinity', *Southern History*, 1 (1979), 71–97.
Chrimes, S.B., *English Constitutional Ideas in the Fifteenth Century* (Cambridge, 1936).
Clark, G., *Symbols of Excellence: Precious Materials as Expressions of Status* (Cambridge, 1986).
Clercq, W. de, Dumolyn, J. and Haemers, J., '"Vivre Noblement": Material Culture and Elite Identity in Late Medieval Flanders', *Journal of Interdisciplinary History*, 38 (2007), 1–31.
Cockayne, A.E., *Cockayne Memoranda: Collections towards a Historical Record of the Family of Cockayne* (Congleton, 1869).
Cohen, A.P., *The Symbolic Construction of Community* (London and New York, 1985).
Collections Historical and Archaeological Relating to Montgomeryshire and Its Borders, Powys-land Club Collections, 6 (1873).
Compton Reeves, A., 'Some of Humphrey Stafford's Military Indentures', *Nottingham Medieval Studies*, 16 (1972), 80–91.
Coss, P., 'An Age of Deference', in R. Horrox and W.M. Ormrod (eds), *A Social History of England 1200–1500* (Cambridge, 2006), pp. 31–73.
Coss, P., 'Aspects of Cultural Diffusion in Medieval England: The Early Romances, Local Society and Robin Hood', *Past & Present*, 108 (1985), 35–79.
Coss, P.R., 'Bastard Feudalism Revised', *Past & Present*, 125 (1989), 27–64.
Coss, P., 'Knighthood, Heraldry and Social Exclusion in Edwardian England', in P. Coss and M. Keen (eds), *Heraldry, Pageantry and Social Display in Medieval England* (Woodbridge, 2002), pp. 39–68.
Cox, J.C., 'Forestry', in W. Page (ed.), *The Victoria County History of the County of Derby*, 2 vols (London, 1905–7), i, pp. 397–426.
Cox, J.C., *Memorials of Old Derbyshire* (London, 1907).
Cox, J.C., 'Norbury Manor House and the Troubles of the Fitzherberts', *Derbyshire Archaeological Journal*, 7 (1885), 221–59.
Cox, J.C., *Notes on the Churches of Derbyshire*, 4 vols (Chesterfield and London, 1875).
Cox, J.C., 'Political History', in W. Page (ed.), *The Victoria County History of the County of Derby*, 2 vols (London, 1905–7), ii, pp. 93–160.
Coxe, W., *An Historical Tour in Monmouthshire* (London, 1801).
Crane, S., *The Performance of Self: Ritual, Clothing and Identity during the Hundred Years War* (Philadelphia, PA, 2002).
Craster, O.B., *Tintern Abbey* (London, 1956).
Crawford, A., *Yorkist Lord: John Howard, Duke of Norfolk, c. 1425–1485* (London and New York, 2010).
Crease, J., '"Not Commonly Reputed or Taken for a Saincte": The Output of a Northern Workshop in the Late Fourteenth and Early Fifteenth Centuries', in S. Badham and S. Oosterwijk (eds), *Monumental Industry: The Production of Tomb Monuments in England and Wales in the Long Fourteenth Century* (Donington, 2010), pp. 136–60.

Crossley, F., *English Church Monuments 1150–1550* (London, 1921).
Crouch, D., Carpenter, D.A. and Coss, P., 'Debate: Bastard Feudalism Revised', *Past & Present*, 131 (1991), 165–203.
Dahmus, J., *William Courtenay Archbishop of Canterbury, 1381–1396* (London, 1966).
Davies, R.R., 'Presidential Address: The Peoples of Britain and Ireland, 1100–1400: II. Names, Boundaries and Regnal Solidarities', *Transactions of the Royal Historical Society*, 6th series, 5 (1995), 1–20.
Davies, R.R., 'Richard II and the Principality of Chester 1397–9', in F.R.H. Du Boulay and C.M. Barron (eds), *The Reign of Richard II: Essays in Honour of May McKisack* (London, 1971), pp. 256–79.
Davis, I., 'Introduction', in I. Davis, M. Müller and S. Rees Jones (eds), *Love, Marriage, and Family Ties in the Later Middle Ages* (Turnhout, 2003), pp. 1–13.
Denton, J., 'The East-Midland Gentleman, 1400–1530', Keele University, unpublished PhD thesis (2006).
Denton, J., 'Genealogy and Gentility: Social Status in Provincial England', in R. Radulescu and E.D. Kennedy (eds), *Broken Lines: Genealogical Literature in Late-Medieval Britain and France* (Turnhout, 2009), pp. 143–58.
Denton, J., 'Image, Identity and Gentility: The Woodford Experience', in L. Clark (ed.), *The Fifteenth Century*, V: *'Of Mice and Men': Image, Belief and Regulation in Late Medieval England* (Woodbridge, 2005), pp. 1–18.
Devine, M., 'The Lordship of Richmond in the Later Middle Ages', in M. Prestwich (ed.), *Liberties and Identities in the Medieval British Isles* (Woodbridge, 2008), pp. 98–110.
Dinn, R., '"Monuments Answerable to Mens Worth": Burial Patterns, Social Status and Gender in Late Medieval Bury St Edmunds', *Journal of Ecclesiastical History*, 46 (1995), 237–55.
Dockray, K., 'Sir Marmaduke Constable of Flamborough', *The Ricardian*, 5 (1979–81), 262–7.
Dodd, G., 'A Parliament Full of Rats? *Piers Plowman* and the Good Parliament of 1376', *Historical Research*, 79 (2006), 21–49.
Downing, M., *Military Effigies of England and Wales*, 8 vols (Shrewsbury, 2010–13).
Du Boulay, F.R.H., *An Age of Ambition, English Society in the Late Middle Ages* (London, 1970).
Duby, G., 'The Diffusion of Cultural Patterns in Feudal Society', *Past & Present*, 39 (1968), 3–10.
Duffy, M., *Royal Tombs of Medieval England* (Stroud, 2003).
Duffy, M., 'Two Fifteenth-Century Effigies in Burghfield Church and the Montagu Mausoleum at Bisham (Berkshire)', *Church Monuments*, 25 (2010), 58–84.
Dugdale, W., *The Antiquities of Warwickshire* (London, 1656).
Duggan, A.J., 'Introduction', in A.J. Duggan (ed.), *Nobles and Nobility in Medieval Europe: Concepts, Origins, Transformations* (Woodbridge, 2000), pp. 1–14.
Düll, S., Luttrell, A. and Keen, M., 'Faithful unto Death: The Tomb Slab of Sir William Neville and Sir John Clanvowe, Constantinople 1391', *Antiquaries Journal*, 71 (1991), 174–90.
Dunham, W.H., *Lord Hastings' Indentured Retainers 1461–1483*, Transactions of the Connecticut Academy of Arts and Sciences, 39 (1955, reprinted 1970).
Eco, U., *A Theory of Semiotics* (Bloomington, IN, 1976).
Edwards, R., 'King Richard's Tomb at Leicester', *The Ricardian*, 3 (1975), 8–9.

Emery, A., 'Late-Medieval Houses as an Expression of Social Status', *Historical Research*, 78 (2005), 140–61.

Erickson, P. and Hulse, C., 'Introduction', in P. Erickson and C. Hulse (eds), *Early Modern Visual Culture: Representation, Race, and Empire in Renaissance England* (Philadelphia, 2000), pp. 1–14.

Esdaile, K., *English Monumental Sculpture since the Renaissance* (London, 1927).

Evans, H.T., *Wales and the Wars of the Roses* (Cambridge, 1915).

Fenton, R., *A Historical Tour through Pembrokeshire* (Brecknock, 1811).

Finch, J., *Church Monuments in Norfolk before 1850: An Archaeology of Commemoration*, British Archaeological Reports, 317 (Oxford, 2000).

Firth, R., 'Spiritual Aroma: Religion and Politics', *American Anthropologist*, 83 (1981), 582–601.

Fleming, P., 'Politics', in R. Radulescu and A. Truelove (eds), *Gentry Culture in Late Medieval England* (Manchester and New York, 2005), pp. 50–62.

Fletcher, D., 'The Lancastrian Collar of Esses: Its Origins and Transformations down the Centuries', in J.L. Gillespie (ed.), *The Age of Richard II* (Stroud and New York, 1997), pp. 191–204.

Fletcher, J.M.J., 'Sir Sampson Meverell of Tideswell, 1388–1462', *Derbyshire Archaeological Journal*, 30 (1908), 1–22.

Foss, E., 'Hackington, or St. Stephen's, Canterbury. Collar of SS', *Archaeologia Cantiana*, 1 (1858), 73–93.

Freeberg, D., *The Power of Images: Studies in the History of Theory and Response* (Chicago and London, 1989).

Friar, S., 'Livery Collars on Late-Medieval English Church Monuments: A Survey of the South-Western Counties and Some Suggestions for Further Study', University of Southampton, unpublished MPhil dissertation (2000).

Fulton, H., 'Guto'r Glyn and the Wars of the Roses', in D.F. Evans, B.J. Lewis and A.P. Owen (eds), *Gwalch Cywyddau Gwŷr: Essays on Guto'r Glyn and Fifteenth-Century Wales* (Aberystwyth, 2013), pp. 53–68.

Gardner, A., *Alabaster Tombs of the Pre-Reformation Period in England* (Cambridge, 1940).

Geertz, C., *The Interpretation of Cultures* (New York, 1973).

Gendzel, G., 'Political Culture: Genealogy of a Concept', *Journal of Interdisciplinary History*, 28 (1997), 225–50.

Gibson, J.P., 'A Defence of the Proscription of the Yorkists in 1459', *English Historical Review*, 26 (1911), 512–25.

Gilderdale Scott, H., '"This Little Westminster": The Chantry-Chapel of Sir Henry Vernon at Tong, Shropshire', *Journal of the British Archaeological Association*, 158 (2005), 46–81.

Gillingham, J.B., 'Crisis or Continuity? The Structure of Royal Authority in England, 1369–1422', in R. Schneider (ed.), *Das spätmittelalterliche Königtum im europäischen Vergleich* (Sigmaringen, 1987), pp. 59–80.

Gittos, B. and M., 'Motivation and Choice: The Selection of Medieval Secular Effigies', in P. Coss and M. Keen (eds), *Heraldry, Pageantry and Social Display in Medieval England* (Woodbridge, 2002), pp. 143–67.

Given-Wilson, C., *The Royal Household and the King's Affinity: Service, Politics and Finance in England 1360–1413* (New Haven, CT, and London, 1986).

Glenn, T.A., *The Family of Griffith of Garn and Plasnewydd in the County of Denbigh* (London, 1934).
Goodall, J.A., 'Heraldry Depicted on Brasses', in J. Bertram (ed.), *Monumental Brasses as Art and History* (Stroud, 1996), pp. 47–55.
Goodman, A. and Gillespie, J. (eds), *Richard II: The Art of Kingship* (Oxford and New York, 1999).
Gordon, D., *The Wilton Diptych* (London, 1993).
Gough, R., *Sepulchral Monuments of Great Britain*, 2 vols (London, 1786–96).
Gough Nichols, J., 'On Collars of the Royal Livery', *Gentleman's Magazine*, 18 (February, 1842), 157–61; 18 (March, 1842), 250–8; 18 (April, 1842), 378–80; 18 (May, 1842), 477–85; 18 (October, 1842), 353–60; 18 (December, 1842), 595–7.
Grassby, R., 'Material Culture and Cultural History', *Journal of Interdisciplinary History*, 35 (2005), 591–603.
Gray Birch, W. de, *A History of Neath Abbey* (Neath, 1902).
Green, F., 'The Wogans of Pembrokeshire', *West Wales Historical Records*, 6 (1916), 169–232.
Gregory, C.A., *Gifts and Commodities* (London, 1982).
Griffiths, J.E., *Pedigrees of Anglesey and Carnarvonshire Families with Their Collateral Branches in Denbighshire, Merionethshire* (Horncastle, 1914).
Griffiths, R.A., 'Herbert, William, first earl of Pembroke (c. 1423–1469)', *Oxford Dictionary of National Biography*, Oxford University Press, 2004; online edn, 2008 (www.oxforddnb.com/view/article/13053, accessed 12 May 2012).
Griffiths, R.A., 'Introduction', in R.A. Griffiths (ed.), *Patronage, the Crown and the Provinces in Later Medieval England* (Gloucester, 1981), pp. 9–14.
Griffiths, R.A., 'Local Rivalry and National Politics: The Percies, the Nevilles, and the Duke of Exeter, 1452–55', *Speculum*, 43 (1968), 589–632.
Griffiths, R.A., 'Lordship and Society in the Fifteenth Century', in R.A. Griffiths (ed.), *The Gwent County History*, 5 vols (Cardiff, 2004–13), ii, pp. 241–79.
Griffiths, R.A., *The Principality of Wales in the Later Middle Ages: The Structure of Personnel and Government, I. South Wales, 1277–1536* (Cardiff, 1972).
Griffiths, R.A., *Sir Rhys ap Thomas and his Family: A Study in the Wars of the Roses and Early Tudor Politics*, 2nd edn (Cardiff, 2014).
Gross, A., 'Langland's Rats: A Moralist's Vision of Parliament', *Parliamentary History*, 9 (1990), 286–301.
Grössinger, C., 'Questioning Signs and Symbols: Their Meaning and Interpretation', in J. Cherry and A. Payne (eds), *Signs and Symbols: Proceedings of the 2006 Harlaxton Symposium*, Harlaxton Medieval Studies, XVIII (Donington, 2009), pp. 180–91.
Grummitt, D., 'Public Service, Private Interest and Patronage in the Fifteenth-Century Exchequer', in L. Clark (ed.), *The Fifteenth Century, III: Authority and Subversion* (Woodbridge, 2003), pp. 149–62.
Haigh, P.A., '…*Where Both the Hosts Fought*…' *The Rebellions of 1469–1470 and the Battles of Edgecote and Lose-Cote-field* (Heckmondwicke, 1997).
Haines, H., *Manual of Monumental Brasses*, 2 vols (London, 1861).
Haines, H., 'The Monumental Brasses of the Cathedral and County of Hereford', *Journal of the British Archaeological Association*, 27 (1871), 85–99.
Hampton, W.E., *Memorials of the Wars of the Roses* (Upminster, 1979).

Harris, B.J., 'Defining Themselves: English Aristocratic Women, 1450–1550', *Journal of British Studies*, 49 (2010), 734–52.
Harriss, G.L., 'The Dimensions of Politics', in R.H. Britnell and A.J. Pollard (eds), *The McFarlane Legacy, Studies in Late Medieval Politics and Society* (Stroud and New York, 1995), pp. 1–20.
Harriss, G.L., 'Introduction', in K.B. McFarlane, *England in the Fifteenth Century: Collected Essays* (London, 1981), pp. ix–xxvii.
Harriss, G.L., 'The King and His Subjects', in R. Horrox (ed.), *Fifteenth-Century Attitudes: Perceptions of Society in Late Medieval England* (Cambridge, 1994), pp. 13–28.
Harriss, G., 'Political Society and the Growth of Government in Late Medieval England', *Past & Present*, 138 (1993), 28–57.
Hartshorne, A., 'The Gold Chains, the Pendants, the Paternosters and the Zones of the Middle Ages, the Renaissance, and Later Times', *Archaeological Journal*, 66 (1909), 77–102.
Hartshorne, A., 'Notes on Collars of SS', *Archaeological Journal*, 39 (1882), 376–83.
Hartshorne, A., *The Recumbent Monumental Effigies in Northamptonshire* (London, 1876).
Harvey, I.M.W., *Jack Cade's Rebellion of 1450* (Oxford, 1991).
Harwood, T., *A Survey of Staffordshire: Containing the Antiquities of that County by Sampson Erdeswick, Esq.* (Westminster, 1820).
Hayward, M., *Dress at the Court of King Henry VIII* (Leeds, 2007).
Hemp, W.J., 'A Late Fifteenth Century Incised Slab at Bruges with a Collar of Suns and Roses in Brass', *Transactions of the Monumental Brass Society*, 6 (1913), 320–5.
Henderson, V.K., 'Retrieving the "Crown in the Hawthorn Bush": The Origins of the Badges of Henry VII', in D. Biggs, S.D. Michalove and A. Compton Reeves (eds), *Traditions and Transformations in Late Medieval England* (Leiden, 2001), pp. 237–59.
Herbert, A., 'Herefordshire, 1413–61: Some Aspects of Society and Public Order', in R.A. Griffiths (ed.), *Patronage, the Crown and the Provinces in Later Medieval England* (Gloucester, 1981), pp. 103–22.
Herman, B., *The Stolen House* (Charlottesville, VA, and London, 1992).
Hicks, M., 'The 1468 Statute of Livery', *Historical Research*, 64 (1991), 15–28.
Hicks, M., *Bastard Feudalism* (London and New York, 1995).
Hicks, M.A., 'Edward IV, the Duke of Somerset and Lancastrian Loyalism in the North', *Northern History*, 20 (1984), 23–37.
Hicks, M., *English Political Culture in the Fifteenth Century* (London and New York, 2002).
Hicks, M., *False, Fleeting, Perjur'd Clarence: George, Duke of Clarence 1449–78* (Gloucester, 1980).
Hicks, M.A., *The Wars of the Roses* (New Haven, CT, and London, 2010).
Hicks, M., *Warwick the Kingmaker* (Oxford, 1998).
Hillyard, D., 'Stanton by Bridge: Some Early Incumbents', *Derbyshire Archaeological Journal*, 66 (1946), 40–7.
Historical Monuments Commission, *An Inventory of the Historical Monuments in Herefordshire*, 3 vols (London, 1931–34).
The History and Topography of Ashbourn, the Valley of the Dove, and the Adjacent Villages (no author, Ashbourne, 1839).
Horrox, R., 'Personalities and Politics', in A.J. Pollard (ed.), *The Wars of Roses* (Basingstoke, 1995), pp. 89–109.
Horrox, R., *Richard III: A Study of Service* (Cambridge, 1989).

Horrox, R., 'Urban Patronage and Patrons in the Fifteenth Century', in R.A. Griffiths (ed.), *Patronage, the Crown and the Provinces in Later Medieval England* (Gloucester, 1981), pp. 145–66.
Hunt, J., *Irish Medieval Figure Sculpture, 1200–1600*, 2 vols (Dublin, 1974).
Jacob, E.F., *Essays in Later Medieval History* (Manchester, 1968).
Jacob, E.F., *The Fifteenth Century, 1399–1485* (Oxford, 1961).
James, L., 'York and Lancaster, a Study of Collars', *Transactions of the Monumental Brass Society*, 10 (1968), 454–7.
Jeavons, S.A., 'The Church Monuments of Derbyshire, the Sixteenth and Seventeenth Centuries, Part 1', *Derbyshire Archaeological Journal*, 84 (1964), 52–80.
Jenkins, C.K., 'Collars of SS: A Quest', *Apollo*, 49 (1949), 60–2.
Jewitt, L., 'The Booths or Bothes, Archbishops and Bishops, and the Derbyshire Family to which They Belonged', *The Reliquary*, 25 (1884–85), 33–40.
Johnson, P.A., *Duke Richard of York 1411–1460* (Oxford, 1988).
Jones, F., 'Some Slebech Notes', *National Library of Wales Journal*, 7 (1951), 199–204.
Jones, R.W., *Bloodied Banners: Martial Display on the Medieval Battlefield* (Woodbridge, 2010).
Jordanova, L., *The Look of the Past: Visual and Material Evidence in Historical Practice* (Cambridge, 2012).
Jourdain, F., 'The Heraldic Stained Glass in Ashbourne Church, Derbyshire', *Derbyshire Archaeological Journal*, 3 (1881), 90–4.
Keen, M.H., 'Brotherhood in Arms', *History*, xlvii (1962), 1–17.
Keen, M., 'Introduction', in P. Coss and M. Keen (eds), *Heraldry, Pageantry and Social Display in Medieval England* (Woodbridge, 2002), pp. 1–16.
Keen, M., *Origins of the English Gentleman* (Stroud, 2002).
Kemp, B., *English Church Monuments* (London, 1980).
Kennedy, K.E., 'Retaining Men (and a Retaining Woman) in *Piers Plowman*', *Yearbook of Langland Studies*, 20 (2006), 191–214.
Kent, J.P.C., 'Monumental Brasses: A New Classification of Military Effigies, c. 1360–c. 1485', *Journal of the British Archaeological Association*, 12 (1949), 70–97.
Kenyon, J.R., *Raglan Castle* (Cardiff, 2003).
King, D., 'The Indent of John Aylward: Glass and Brass at East Harling', *Transactions of the Monumental Brass Society*, 18 (2011), 251–67.
King, P., 'The English Cadaver Tomb in the Late Fifteenth Century: Some Indications of a Lancastrian Connection', in J.H.M. Taylor (ed.), *Dies Illa, Death in the Middle Ages: Proceedings of the 1983 Manchester Colloquium* (Liverpool, 1984), pp. 45–57.
Kingsford, C.L., *English Historical Literature in the Fifteenth Century* (Oxford, 1913).
Kinsey, R.C., 'Legal Service, Careerism and Social Advancement in Late Medieval England: The Thorpes of Northamptonshire, c. 1200–1391', University of York, unpublished PhD thesis (2009).
Kirke, H., 'Sir Henry Vernon of Haddon', *Derbyshire Archaeological Journal*, 42 (1920), 1–17.
Lachaud, F., 'Liveries of Robes in England, c. 1200–c. 1330', *English Historical Review*, 111 (1996), 279–98.
Lack, W., Stuchfield, H.M. and Whittemore, P., *The Monumental Brasses of Derbyshire* (London, 1999).

Lander, J.H., 'Lead Mining', in W. Page (ed.), *The Victoria County History of the County of Derby*, 2 vols (London, 1905–7), ii, pp. 323–48.
Lander, J.R., *Crown and Nobility, 1450–1509* (London, 1976).
Lang, T., 'Medical Recipes from the Yorkist Court', *The Ricardian*, 20 (2010), 94–102.
Lawrance, H. and Routh, T.E., 'Derbyshire Military Effigies, III', *Derbyshire Archaeological Journal*, 48 (1926), 37–50.
Lawrance, H. and Routh, T.E., 'Medieval Military Effigies in Derbyshire, II', *Derbyshire Archaeological Journal*, 47 (1925), 137–51.
Laws, E. and Edwards, E.H., 'Monumental Effigies, Pembrokeshire', *Archaeologia Cambrensis*, 66 (1911), 349–80.
Lethbridge Farmer, R., 'Chellaston Alabaster', *Derbyshire Archaeological Journal*, 38 (1916), 135–46.
Lévi-Strauss, C., *The Elementary Structures of Kinship* (London, 1949).
Lewis, J.M., *Welsh Monumental Brasses* (Cardiff, 1974).
Lewis, P.S., 'Decayed and Non-Feudalism in Later Medieval France', *Bulletin of the Institute of Historical Research*, 37 (1964), 157–84.
Lewis, W.G., 'The Exact Date of the Battle of Banbury, 1469', *Bulletin of the Institute of Historical Research*, 55 (1982), 194–6.
Lightbown, R.W., *Mediaeval European Jewellery* (London, 1992).
Lindley, P., 'Introduction: Secular Sculpture 1300–1550', in P. Lindley and T. Frangenberg (eds), *Secular Sculpture 1300–1550* (Stamford, 2000), pp. 1–9.
Lindley, P., *Tomb Destruction and Scholarship: Medieval Monuments in Early Modern England* (Donington, 2007).
Llewellyn, N., *The Art of Death: Visual Culture in the English Death Ritual c. 1500–c. 1800* (London, 1991).
Lloyd, S.D., 'The Lord Edward's Crusade, 1270–2: Its Setting and Significance', in J. Gillingham and J.C. Holt (eds), *War and Governance in the Middle Ages: Essays in Honour of J.O. Prestwich* (Woodbridge, 1984), pp. 120–33.
Lord, P., *The Visual Culture of Wales: Medieval Vision* (Cardiff, 2003).
Luckett, D., 'Patronage, Violence and Revolt in the Reign of Henry VII', in R.E. Archer (ed.), *Crown, Government and People in the Fifteenth Century* (Stroud and New York, 1995), pp. 145–60.
Lutkin, J., 'Luxury and Display in Silver and Gold at the Court of Henry IV', in L. Clark (ed.), *The Fifteenth Century, IX: English and Continental Perspectives* (Woodbridge, 2010), pp. 155–78.
Luxford, J., 'The Hastings Brass at Elsing: A Contextual Analysis', *Transactions of the Monumental Brass Society*, 18 (2011), 193–211.
Lysons, D. and S., *Derbyshire* (London, 1817).
Macklin, H.W., *The Brasses of England* (London, 1907).
Maddern, P., '"Best Trusted Friends": Concepts and Practices of Friendship among Fifteenth-Century Norfolk Gentry', in N. Rogers (ed.), *England in the Fifteenth Century: Proceedings of the 1992 Harlaxton Symposium*, Harlaxton Medieval Studies, IV (Stamford, 1994), pp. 100–17.
Marks, R., 'The Glazing of Fotheringhay Church and College', *Journal of the British Archaeological Association*, 131 (1978), 79–109.
Marks, R., 'Yorkist–Lancastrian Political and Genealogical Propaganda in the Visual Arts', *Family History*, 12 (1982), 149–66.

Martindale, A., 'Patrons and Minders: The Intrusion of the Secular into Sacred Spaces in the Late Middle Ages', in D. Wood (ed.), *The Church and the Arts* (Oxford, 1995), pp. 143–78.
Mauss, M., *The Gift* (London, 1925).
McFarlane, K.B., 'Bastard Feudalism', *Bulletin of the Institute of Historical Research*, 20 (1945), 161–80.
McFarlane, K.B., *The Nobility of Later Medieval England* (Oxford, 1973).
Mead, G.H., *Mind, Self and Society*, ed. Charles Morris (Chicago, 1934).
Mercer, M., 'Lancastrian Loyalism in the South-West: The Case for the Beauforts', *Southern History*, 19 (1997), 42–60.
Mercer, M., *The Medieval Gentry: Power, Leadership and Choice during the Wars of the Roses* (London and New York, 2010).
Mertes, K., 'Aristocracy', in R. Horrox (ed.), *Fifteenth Century Attitudes: Perceptions of Society in Late Medieval England* (Cambridge, 1994), pp. 42–60.
Metcalfe, W.C., 'Pedigrees Contained in the Visitations of Derbyshire, 1569 and 1611', *The Genealogist*, New Series, 7 (1891), 1–16; 65–80; 129–44; 225–32.
Moreton, C.E., 'A Social Gulf? The Upper and Lesser Gentry of Later Medieval England', *Journal of Medieval History*, 17 (1991), 255–62.
Morgan, D.A.L., 'The Individual Style of the English Gentleman', in M. Jones (ed.), *Gentry and Lesser Nobility in Late Medieval Europe* (Gloucester, 1986), pp. 15–35.
Morgan, D.A.L., 'The King's Affinity in the Polity of Yorkist England', *Transactions of the Royal Historical Society*, 23 (1973), 1–25.
Morgan, N., 'An SS Collar in the Devotional Context of the Shield of the Five Wounds', in J. Stratford (ed.), *The Lancastrian Court: Proceedings of the 2001 Harlaxton Symposium*, Harlaxton Medieval Studies, XIII (Donington, 2003), pp. 147–62.
Morgan, N., 'The Monograms, Arms and Badges of the Virgin Mary in Late Medieval England', in J. Cherry and A. Payne (eds), *Signs and Symbols: Proceedings of the 2006 Harlaxton Symposium*, Harlaxton Medieval Studies, XVIII (Donington, 2009), pp. 53–63.
Morgan, O., *Some Account of the Ancient Monuments in the Priory Church, Abergavenny* (Newport, 1872).
Morgan-Guy, J., 'Arthur, Harri Tudor and the Iconography of Loyalty in Wales', in S.J. Gunn and L. Monckton (eds), *Arthur Tudor, Prince of Wales: Life, Death and Commemoration* (Woodbridge, 2009), pp. 50–63.
Mortimer, I., *The Fears of Henry IV* (London, 2008).
Murphy, R., *Social Closure: The Theory of Monopolization and Exclusion* (Oxford 1988).
Myers, A.R., 'The Household of Queen Elizabeth Woodville, 1466–7', *Bulletin of the John Rylands Library*, 50 (1967–68), 207–35; 443–81.
Myers, A.R., 'The Jewels of Queen Margaret of Anjou', *Bulletin of the John Rylands Library*, 42 (1959), 113–31.
Norris, M., 'An Analysis of Style in Monumental Brasses', in J. Bertram (ed.), *Monumental Brasses as Art and History*, (Stroud, 1996), pp. 103–31.
Norris, M., *Monumental Brasses: The Craft* (London, 1978).
Norris, M., *Monumental Brasses: The Memorials*, 2 vols (London, 1977).
Offer, A., 'Between the Gift and the Market: The Economy of Regard', *Economic History Review*, 50 (1997), 450–76.
Ogden, C.K. and Richards, I.A., *The Meaning of Meaning* (London, 1923).

Ormerod, G., *The History of the County Palatine and City of Chester*, 3 vols (London, 1819).
Ostrom, T., '"And He Honoured that Hit Hade Euermore After": The Influence of Richard II's Livery System on *Sir Gawain and the Green Knight*', University of Florida, unpublished MA dissertation (2003).
Owen, G., *The Description of Penbrokshire*, 3 vols (1892–1906).
Palliser, D.M., 'Richard III and York', in R. Horrox (ed.), *Richard III and the North* (Hull, 1986), pp. 51–81.
Panofsky, E., *Tomb Sculpture: Its Changing Aspects from Ancient Egypt to Bernini* (London, 1964).
Parry, R., *The History of Kington* (Kington, 1845).
Patterson, A., '"The Face Divine": Identity and the Portrait from Locke to Chaucer', in S. McKee (ed.), *Crossing Boundaries: Issues of Cultural and Individual Identity in the Middle Ages and the Renaissance* (Turnhout, 1999), pp. 155–86.
Payling, S., *Political Society in Lancastrian England: The Greater Gentry of Nottinghamshire* (Oxford, 1991).
Peirce, C.S., *Collected Writings*, ed. C. Hartshorne, P. Weiss and A.W. Burks, 8 vols (Cambridge, 1931–58).
Petre, J., 'The Nevills of Brancepeth and Raby 1425–1499, Part II 1470–1499: Recovery and Collapse', *The Ricardian*, 6 (1982), 2–13.
Planché, J.R., 'On the Badges of the House of Lancaster', *Journal of the British Archaeological Association*, 6 (1851), 374–93.
Pollard, A.J., 'Introduction: Society, Politics and the Wars of the Roses', in A.J. Pollard (ed.), *The Wars of Roses* (Basingstoke, 1995), pp. 1–19.
Pollard, A.J., *North-Eastern England during the Wars of the Roses: Lay Society, War and Politics 1450–1500* (Oxford, 1990).
Pollard, A.J., 'Richard Clervaux of Croft: A North Riding Squire in the Fifteenth Century', *Yorkshire Archaeological Journal*, 50 (1978), 151–69.
Pollard, A.J., 'The Richmondshire Community of Gentry', in C. Ross (ed.), *Patronage, Pedigree and Power in Later Medieval England* (Gloucester, 1979), pp. 37–59.
Pollard, A.J., *The Wars of the Roses*, 2nd edn (Basingstoke, 2001).
Potter, J., *The Rose, A True History* (London, 2010).
Powell, E., 'After "After McFarlane": The Poverty of Patronage and the Case for Constitutional History', in D.J. Clayton, R.G. Davies and P. McNiven (eds), *Trade, Devotion and Governance: Papers in Late-Medieval History* (Stroud, 1994), pp. 1–16.
Powis, J., *Aristocracy* (Oxford, 1984).
Prown, J.D., *Art as Evidence: Writings on Art and Material Culture* (New Haven, CT, and London, 2001).
Pugh, T.B., 'The Magnates, Knights and Gentry', in S.B. Chrimes, C.D. Ross and R.A. Griffiths (eds), *Fifteenth Century England 1399–1509* (Manchester, 1972), pp. 86–128.
Pugh, T.B., 'The Marcher Lords of Glamorgan, 1317–1485', in T.B. Pugh (ed.), *Glamorgan County History, III, The Middle Ages* (Cardiff, 1971), pp. 167–204.
Purey-Cust, A.P., *The Collar of SS, A History and Conjecture* (Leeds, 1910).
R.W.B., 'On the Family of Vaughan of Hergest', *Archaeologia Cambrensis*, 26 (1871), 23–34.
Radulescu, R., 'Introduction', in R. Radulescu and A. Truelove (eds), *Gentry Culture in Late Medieval England* (Manchester and New York, 2005), pp. 1–4.
Radulescu, R., 'Literature', in R. Radulescu and A. Truelove (eds), *Gentry Culture in Late Medieval England* (Manchester and New York, 2005), pp. 100–18.

Ramsay, N., 'Alabaster', in J. Blair and N. Ramsay (eds), *English Medieval Industries* (London and Rio Grande, 1991), pp. 29–40.

Rawcliffe, C., *The Staffords, Earls of Stafford and Dukes of Buckingham, 1394–1521* (Cambridge, 1978).

Rawlins, R.R., *Churches and Chapels in the County of Derby*, 3 vols (1819–23).

Rees, W.J., 'Account of the Restored Tomb in Kington Church, 1847', *Archaeologia Cambrensis*, 3 (1848), 60–5.

Reuter, T., 'Nobles and Others: The Social and Cultural Expression of Power Relations in the Middle Ages', in A.J. Duggan (ed.), *Nobles and Nobility in Medieval Europe: Concepts, Origins, Transformations* (Woodbridge, 2000), pp. 85–98.

Reynolds, S., *Kingdoms and Communities in Western Europe 900–1300* (Oxford, 1984).

Richmond, C. and Kekewich, M.L., 'The Search for Stability, 1461–1483', in M. Kekewich, C. Richmond, A.F. Sutton, L. Visser-Fuchs and J.L. Watts (eds), *The Politics of Fifteenth Century England: John Vale's Book* (Stroud, 1995), pp. 43–72.

Rigby, S.H., *English Society in the Later Middle Ages: Class, Status and Gender* (Basingstoke and London, 1995).

Robinson, C.J., *Herefordshire Mansions and Manors* (London, 1872).

Robinson, W.R.B., 'Sir Hugh Johnys: A Fifteenth-Century Welsh Knight', *Morgannwg: Transactions of the Glamorgan Local History Society*, 14 (1970), 5–34.

Rock, V., 'The Medieval Monuments at St Mary's Priory Church, Abergavenny, Gwent', *Medieval Life*, 3 (1995), 17–24.

Roffey, S., *The Medieval Chantry Chapel: An Archaeology* (Woodbridge, 2007).

Rogers, N., 'Cambridgeshire Brasses', in C. Hicks (ed.), *Cambridgeshire Churches* (Stamford, 1997), pp. 303–19.

Rogers, N., '"Hic Iacet…": The Location of Monuments in Late Medieval Parish Churches', in C. Burgess and E. Duffy (eds), *The Parish in Late Medieval England: Proceedings of the 2002 Harlaxton Symposium*, Harlaxton Medieval Studies, XIV (Donington, 2006), pp. 261–81.

Roper, I.M., *The Monumental Effigies of Gloucestershire and Bristol* (Gloucester, 1931).

Rose, S., 'A Twelfth-Century Honour in a Fifteenth-Century World: The Honour of Pontefract', in L. Clark (ed.), *The Fifteenth Century, IX: English and Continental Perspectives* (Woodbridge, 2010), pp. 38–57.

Rosenthal, M.T., 'Cultures of Clothing in Later Medieval and Early Modern Europe', *Journal of Medieval and Early Modern Studies*, 39 (2009), 459–81.

Ross, C., *Edward IV* (London, 1974).

Routh, P.E., *Medieval Effigial Alabaster Tombs in Yorkshire* (Ipswich, 1976).

Routh, P., 'Richard Neville, Earl of Salisbury: The Burghfield Effigy', *The Ricardian*, 6 (1984), 417–23.

Routh, P. and Knowles, R., *The Medieval Monuments of Harewood* (Wakefield, 1983).

Rowney, I., 'The Curzons of Fifteenth-Century Derbyshire', *Derbyshire Archaeological Journal*, 103 (1983), 107–17.

Rowney, I., 'The Hastings Affinity in Staffordshire and the Honour of Tutbury', *Historical Research*, 57 (1984), 35–45.

Rubin, M., 'Identities', in R. Horrox and W.M. Ormrod (eds), *A Social History of England 1200–1500* (Cambridge, 2006), pp. 383–412.

Rubin, M., 'Religious Symbols and Political Culture in Fifteenth-Century England', in L. Clark and C. Carpenter (eds), *The Fifteenth Century, IV: Political Culture in Late Medieval Britain* (Woodbridge, 2004), pp. 97–110.
Rubin, M., 'Small Groups: Identity and Solidarity in the Late Middle Ages', in J. Kermode (ed.), *Enterprise and Individuals in Fifteenth Century England* (Stroud, 1991), pp. 132–50.
Ryde, C., 'Chellaston Standing Angels with Shields at Aston on Trent: Their Wider Distribution 1400–1450', *Derbyshire Archaeological Journal*, 113 (1993), 69–90.
Sadler, E.A., 'The Ancient Family of Cockayne and Their Monuments in Ashbourne Church', *Derbyshire Archaeological Journal*, 55 (1935), 14–39.
Sadler, E.A., 'The Family of Bradbourne and Their Monuments in Ashbourne Church', *Derbyshire Archaeological Journal*, 57 (1936), 113–24.
St John Hope, W.H., 'On the Early Working of Alabaster in England', *Archaeological Journal*, 61 (1904), 221–40.
Saul, N., 'The Commons and the Abolition of Badges', *Parliamentary History*, 9 (1990), 302–15.
Saul, N., 'The Contract for the Brass of Richard Willoughby (d. 1471) at Wollaton (Notts.)', *Nottingham Medieval Studies*, 50 (2006), 166–93.
Saul, N., *Death, Art and Memory in Medieval England: The Cobham Family and Their Monuments, 1300–1500* (Oxford, 2001).
Saul, N., *English Church Monuments in the Middle Ages: History and Representation* (Oxford, 2009).
Saul, N., *Knights and Esquires: The Gloucestershire Gentry in the Fourteenth Century* (Oxford, 1981).
Saul, N., *Richard II* (New Haven, CT, 1999).
Saul, N., *Scenes from Provincial Life: Knightly Families in Sussex, 1280–1400* (Oxford, 1986).
Saul, N., Mackman, J. and Whittick, C., 'Grave Stuff: Litigation with a London Tomb-Maker in 1421', *Historical Research*, 84 (2011), 572–85.
Scattergood, V.J., *Politics and Poetry in the Fifteenth Century* (London, 1971).
Scharf, G., 'A Note upon Collars', *Archaeologia*, 39 (1863), 265–71.
Scofield, C.L., *The Life and Reign of Edward the Fourth*, 2 vols (London, 1923).
Scott, J., *The Upper Classes: Property and Privilege in Britain* (London and Basingstoke, 1982).
Scott, R.F., 'On the Contracts for the Tomb of the Lady Margaret Beaufort, Countess of Richmond and Derby', *Archaeologia*, 66 (1915), 365–76.
Seward, B., *The Symbolic Rose* (New York, 1960).
Shaw, D.G., *Necessary Conjunctions: The Social Self in Medieval England* (New York and Basingstoke, 2005).
Shaw, S., *The History and Antiquities of Staffordshire*, 2 vols (London, 1798–1801).
Shaw, W.A., *The Knights of England*, 2 vols (London, 1916).
Sheppard Routh, P. and Knowles, R., 'The Markenfield Collar', *Yorkshire Archaeological Journal*, 62 (1990), 133–40.
Siddons, M.P., *Heraldic Badges in England and Wales*, 4 vols (Woodbridge, 2009).
Skeat, W.K., 'Souvent Me Souvient', *Christ's College Magazine* (Michaelmas Term, 1905), 1–5.
Skinner, Q.R.D., *The Foundations of Modern Political Thought*, 2 vols (Cambridge, 1978).

Skinner, Q.R.D., 'The Principles and Practice of Opposition: The Case of Bolingbroke vs. Walpole', in N. McKendrick (ed.), *Historical Perspectives: Studies in English Thought and Society in Honour of J.H. Plumb* (London, 1974), pp. 93–128.
Smith, A.D., *Derbyshire Landholdings in the Fifteenth Century, The Lay Subsidy of 1431* (privately published, 1999).
Smith, C.E.J., 'The Livery Collar', *Coat of Arms*, 8 (1990), 238–53.
Somerville, R., *History of the Duchy of Lancaster*, 2 vols (London, 1953–70).
Spencer, B., 'Fifteenth-Century Collar of SS and Hoard of False Dice with Their Container, from the Museum of London', *Antiquaries Journal*, 65 (1985), 449–51.
Spencer, B., *Pilgrim Souvenirs and Secular Badges* (London, 1998).
Stafford, P., Nelson, J.L. and Martindale, J., 'Introduction', in P. Stafford, J.L. Nelson and J. Martindale (eds), *Law, Laity and Solidarities: Essays in Honour of Susan Reynolds* (Manchester, 2001), pp. 1–11.
Stanford London, H., 'The Greyhound as Royal Beast', *Archaeologia*, 97 (1959), 139–63.
Stanford London, H., *Royal Beasts* (East Knoyle, 1956).
Starkey, D., 'The Age of the Household: Politics, Society and the Arts, c. 1350–c. 1550', in S. Medcalf (ed.), *The Later Middle Ages* (London, 1981), pp. 225–90.
Statham, M. and Badham, S., 'Jankyn Smith of Bury St. Edmunds and His Brass', *Transactions of the Monumental Brass Society*, 18 (2011), 227–50.
Steel, A.B., *The Receipt of the Exchequer 1377–1485* (Cambridge, 1954).
Stephenson, M., *A List of Monumental Brasses in the British Isles* (London, 1926).
Stets, J.E. and Burke, P.J., 'Identity Theory and Social Identity Theory', *Social Psychology Quarterly*, 63 (2000), 224–37.
Stone, L., *Sculpture in Britain: The Middle Ages* (Harmondsworth, 1955).
Storey, R.L., *The End of the House of Lancaster* (Stroud, 1986).
Storey, R.L., 'Gentleman-Bureaucrats', in C.H. Clough (ed.), *Profession, Vocation and Culture in Later Medieval England* (Liverpool, 1982), pp. 90–109.
Storey, R.L., 'Liveries and Commissions of the Peace 1388–90', in F.R.H. Du Boulay and C.M. Barron (eds), *The Reign of Richard II: Essays in Honour of May McKisack* (London, 1971), pp. 131–52.
Stothard, C.A., The *Monumental Effigies of Great Britain* (London, 1817–32).
Strathern, M., 'Qualified Value: The Perspective of Gift Exchange', in C. Humphrey and S. Hugh-Jones (eds), *Barter, Exchange and Value, An Anthropological Approach* (Cambridge, 1992), pp. 169–91.
Stringer, K., 'States, Liberties and Communities in Medieval Britain and Ireland (c. 1100–1400)', in M. Prestwich (ed.), *Liberties and Identities in the Medieval British Isles* (Woodbridge, 2008), pp. 5–36.
Sutton, A.F. and Visser-Fuchs, L., *The Royal Funerals of the House of York at Windsor* (Bury St Edmunds, 2005).
Swanson, J., *John of Wales: A Study of the Works and Ideas of a Thirteenth Century Friar* (Cambridge, 1989).
Thomas, D.H., 'The Herberts of Raglan as Supporters of the House of York in the Second Half of the Fifteenth Century', University of Wales, unpublished MA thesis (1967).
Thomas, D.H., *The Herberts of Raglan and the Battle of Edgecote 1469* (Enfield, 1994).
Tilley, J., *The Old Halls, Manors and Families of Derbyshire*, 4 vols (London, 1892–1902).
Toesca, I., 'Lancaster and Gonzaga: The Collar of SS at Mantua', in D. Chambers and J. Martineau (eds), *Splendours of the Gonzaga* (London, 1981), pp. 1–2.

Tolley, T., 'Visual Culture', in R. Radulescu and A. Truelove (eds), *Gentry Culture in Late Medieval England* (Manchester and New York, 2005), pp. 167–82.
Toulmin-Smith, L., *Expeditions to Prussia and the Holy Land made by Henry, Earl of Derby In the Years 1390–1 and 1392–3*, Camden Society, New Series, 52 (London, 1894).
Trexler, R.C., 'Introduction', in R.C. Trexler (ed.), *Persons in Groups: Social Behaviour as Identity Formation in Medieval and Renaissance Europe* (Binghamton, NY, 1985), pp. 3–16.
Tringham, N.J., 'Honour of Tutbury', in *The Victoria County History of the County of Stafford*, 14 vols (1908–2013), x, pp. 9–20.
Turbutt, G., *A History of Derbyshire*, 4 vols (Cardiff, 1999).
Vaughan, H.F.J., 'The Vaughans of Herefordshire', in C. Reade, *Memorials of Old Herefordshire* (London, 1904), pp. 79–94.
Virgoe, R., 'The Crown and Local Government: East Anglia under Richard II', in F.R.H. Du Boulay and C.M. Barron (eds), *The Reign of Richard II: Essays in Honour of May McKisack* (London, 1971), pp. 218–41.
Visser-Fuchs, L., 'The Garters and the Garter Achievements of Charles the Bold, Duke of Burgundy', *The Ricardian*, 23 (2013), 1–19.
Voloshinov, V.N., *Marxism and the Philosophy of Language* (New York, 1973).
Wagner, A.R., 'The Swan Badge and the Swan Knight', *Archaeologia*, 97 (1959), 127–38.
Walker, J.A. and Chaplin, S., *Visual Culture: An Introduction* (Manchester and New York, 1997).
Walker, S., 'Communities of the County in Later Medieval England', in M.J. Braddick (ed.), *Political Culture in Later Medieval England: Essays by Simon Walker* (Manchester, 2006), pp. 68–80.
Walker, S., *The Lancastrian Affinity, 1361–1399* (Oxford, 1990).
Walker, S., 'Lordship and Lawlessness in the Palatinate of Lancaster, 1370–1400', *Journal of British Studies*, 28 (1989), 325–48.
Ward, M., 'The Life and Death of Sir Henry Pierrepont, 1430–1499: A Search for Identity and Memorial', *The Ricardian*, 20 (2010), 80–93.
Ward, M., 'The Tomb of "The Butcher"? The Tiptoft Monument in the Presbytery of Ely Cathedral', *Church Monuments*, 27 (2012), 22–37.
Watts, J.L., *Henry VI and the Politics of Kingship* (Cambridge, 1996).
Watts, J.L., 'Ideas, Principles and Politics', in A.J. Pollard (ed.), *The Wars of Roses* (Basingstoke, 1995), pp. 110–33.
Watts, J., 'Looking for the State in Later Medieval England', in P. Coss and M. Keen (eds), *Heraldry, Pageantry and Social Display in Medieval England* (Woodbridge, 2002), pp. 243–67.
Watts, J.L., 'Polemic and Politics in the 1450s', in M. Kekewich, C. Richmond, A.F. Sutton, L. Visser-Fuchs and J.L. Watts (eds), *The Politics of Fifteenth Century England: John Vale's Book* (Stroud, 1995), pp. 3–42.
Wedgwood, J.C., *Collections for a History of Staffordshire* (1912).
Wedgwood, J.C. (ed.), *History of Parliament 1439–1509*, 2 vols (London, 1936–38).
Welch, E.S., *Art and Identity in Renaissance Milan* (New Haven, CT, and London, 1995).
Wells, P.S., *Image and Response in Early Europe* (London, 2008).
Westerhof, D., *Death and the Noble Body in Medieval England* (Woodbridge, 2008).

Westervelt, T., 'The Changing Nature of Politics in the Localities in the Later Fifteenth Century: William Lord Hastings and His Indentured Retainers', *Midland History*, 26 (2001), 96–106.

Wilkins, E., *The Rose-Garden Game* (London, 1969).

Williams, G., *Renewal and Reformation, Wales c. 1415–1642* (Oxford and New York, 1993).

Williams, I., 'Guto'r Glyn', *Welsh Biography Online*, 2009 (wbo.llgc.org.uk/en/s-GUTO-GLY-1440.html, accessed 18 May 2013).

Wilson-Lee, K., 'Dynasty and Strategies of Commemoration: Knightly Families in Late-Medieval and Early Modern Derbyshire, Part 1', *Church Monuments*, 25 (2010), 85–104.

Wilson-Lee, K., 'Dynasty and Strategies of Commemoration: Knightly Families in Late-Medieval and Early Modern Derbyshire, Part 2', *Church Monuments*, 26 (2011), 27–43.

Wilson-Lee, K., 'Representations of Piety and Dynasty: Late-Medieval Stained Glass and Sepulchral Monuments at Norbury, Derbyshire', *Derbyshire Archaeological Journal*, 131 (2011), 226–44.

Wilson-Lee, K., '"Their Final Blazon": Burial and Commemoration among the North Midland Nobility and Gentry, c. 1200–1536', University of London, unpublished PhD thesis, 2 vols (2009).

Wiltshire, M. and Woore, S., *Medieval Parks of Derbyshire: A Gazetteer with Maps, Illustrations and Historical Notes* (Ashbourne, 2009).

Winston-Allen, A., *Stories of the Rose: The Making of the Rosary in the Middle Ages* (University Park, PA, 1997).

Woodhouse, J.R., *Baldesar Castiglione: A Reassessment of* The Courtier (Edinburgh, 1978).

Woolf, D. and Jones, N.L., 'Introduction', in N.L. Jones and D. Woolf (eds), *Local Identities in Late Medieval and Early Modern England* (Basingstoke and New York, 2007), pp. 1–18.

Wright, S.M., *The Derbyshire Gentry in the Fifteenth Century*, Derbyshire Record Society, 8 (Chesterfield, 1983).

Wylie, J.H., *History of England under Henry the Fourth*, 4 vols (London, 1884–98).

Yeatman, J.P., *The Feudal History of the County of Derby*, 6 vols (London and Birmingham, 1886–1907).

Youngs, D., 'Cultural Networks', in R. Radulescu and A. Truelove (eds), *Gentry Culture in Late Medieval England* (Manchester and New York, 2005), pp. 119–33.

Index

Abergavenny (Monmouthshire) 153
    priory church of St Mary 81, 82, 100, 148, 152, 168–9, 170, 174, 176n
Aberystwyth Castle 152
Abrey, John 55
Acton (Cheshire), St Mary's church 103n
Adam of Usk 52, 56
Agard, family 128
    John 128
agency 5, 77, 80–4, 180
Agincourt, battle of (1415) 108, 158
alabaster 33, 81–2, 132, 173, 174
Aleyn, Sir John, mayor of London 32
Althoff, Gerd 95
angels 6, 55, 81–2, 137, 139, 141
Anglesey 157, 176n
Aphrodite 39
archaeology 10–11
architecture 5, 38, 85
    church 9
aristocracy 6, 12, 20, 69, 88–9, 90, 151
armour, representation of 11, 12, 91, 100, 139, 170
array, commissions of 88, 110, 115, 121
Arundel, Sussex 8n
Ash (Derbyshire) 111
Ashbourne (Derbyshire) 116, 126
    Bradbourne chantry 124
    St Oswald's church 67, 81n, 107, 116, 124, 125, 132, 137, 138, 143
Ashmole, Elias 139, 139n
Aubrey, Lady 176n

Bacchus 39
badge 6, 21, 21n, 22, 23, 26, 30, 35, 36, 38n, 39, 40, 40n, 52, 54, 57, 57n, 59, 60n, 62, 68n, 78, 114, 154, 173, 184n
    black bull 130
    crown 55, 61
    eagle's foot 62
    gorget 61

    portcullis 24, 24n, 33, 122, 141–2
    ragged staff 57n, 60
    star 60
    sun in splendour 24, 38, 39, 41, 42–3, 47, 60, 134
    whelk shell 68, 83
    white boar 23, 59, 60, 113, 133, 135, 182, 184n
Baginton (Warwickshire), St John the Baptist's church 20
Bagot, family
    Joan 141
    Sir William (d. 1407) 20
ballads 41, 72
Banbury (Oxfordshire) 150
Barantyn, Drugo 28
Baret, John (d. 1467)
    collars 31–2
    tomb 83, 102
Barley, family 115, 116, 123, 126, 144n
    Agnes 115, 116
    Richard (d. c. 1491) 81n, 131
    Robert (d. 1467) 107, 110, 115, 117, 118, 123, 130, 137, 144, 145
    Robert, son of Robert 115
    Roger (d. 1558) 173
Barlow (Derbyshire) 105
    hall 115
    St Lawrence's church 82, 107, 137
Barnet, battle of (1471) 60, 70
Barre, Sir John (d. 1483) 66
Barrett, Thomas, bishop of Annaghdown 28
Barthomley (Cheshire), St Bertoline's church 103n
Basle, Switzerland 35
Bassett, family 116
bastard feudalism 2, 13, 50, 61–7
Bate, Thomas 116
Baynard's Castle 154
Beauchamp, family
    Pageant 30

238 INDEX

Richard, earl of Warwick (d. 1439) 14, 30, 64, 67, 82, 160
Beaufort, family 24, 67, 141–2
    Edmund, 2nd duke of Somerset (d. 1455) 60n
    Henry, 3rd duke of Somerset (d. 1464) 89
    Margaret, countess of Richmond and Derby (d. 1509) 24n, 122
Beaumaris (Anglesey), St Mary's and St Nicholas's church 176n
Belgium 2
Berkeley (Gloucestershire), St Mary's church 23, 161
Berkeley, family 160
    Elizabeth, daughter of Thomas, Lord Berkeley 160
    Ellen, wife of Sir Maurice Berkeley 161
    James (d. 1452) 23, 161
    James, Lord Berkeley (d. 1463) 23, 160–1
    Sir Maurice (d. 1464) 161
    Sir Thomas of Coberley 161
    Thomas, Lord Berkeley 57n, 160
    William, earl of Nottingham 161
Bermingham, James 100
Bernard of Clairvaux 42
Bernardini, Jacopo 36
Billeswick, Bristol, Lord Mayor's Chapel 161
Billing, Thomas 63
Binski, Paul 10
Birchwood (Derbyshire) 109
Black Book, *see* Edward IV, household ordinances
Black Death 91
Blanche of Lancaster, wife of John of Gaunt 126
Blondell, Jacques 72
Blore, Edward 171
Blore Heath, battle of (1459) 108
Blount, family 108, 110
    Walter, Lord Mountjoy 108, 110, 127, 128, 145
Blount, John 1
Blythburgh (Suffolk), Holy Trinity church 99
Bohun, family 59
    Eleanor, duchess of Gloucester 59
    Mary 59
Bolingbroke (Lincolnshire) 103
Bonville, William Lord 74
Boothby, family 137
Bosworth, battle of (1485) 12, 74, 76, 106, 119, 122, 128, 143, 161, 183

Bothe, family 82, 109, 111, 112, 113, 126, 129, 130, 148
    Alice 109, 112, 134
    Anne of Dunham Massey 130
    Henry of Arleston 109, 112, 114, 134
    Isabel 113
    John 107, 110, 112
    John, bishop of Exeter 113
    Laurence, archbishop of York 113
    Roger I (d. 1467) 112
    Roger II (d. 1478) 107, 112, 113, 136
    William 107, 112, 112n, 127
    William, priest 112
Boulogne, siege of (1492) 143
Bourchier, family
    Henry, earl of Essex (d. 1483) 90, 104, 104n, 114
Bourdieu, Pierre 90–1
Bowet, Henry, archbishop of York (d. 1423) 93
Boyd, Thomas, 1st earl of Arran 90
Bradbourne, family 108, 113, 118, 123, 124–5, 126, 127
    Anne 114, 124–5
    Benedicta 110–11, 114
    Henry 114
    Humphrey, son of John (d. 1488) 114, 125, 129
    John (d. 1488) 81n, 107, 110, 114, 127, 137, 146,
Bradley (Derbyshire) 121, 124
Brancepeth (County Durham), St Brandon's church 23, 113, 161n, 182
Brecon (Powys) 151, 155, 159
    castle 165
Bredwardine (Herefordshire), St Andrew's church 176
Bridges, family 161
    Alice 161
    Thomas 161
Bridgwater (Somerset) 150
Bristol 150, 161
Broke, Sir Robert, chief justice of the Common Pleas 25
Bromsgrove (Worcestershire), St John the Baptist's church 23
Browning, family 137
    William (d. 1467) 105
Broxbourne (Hertfordshire), St Augustine's church 104
Bruges, Belgium, Hôpital St Josse 20n, 34, 100
Brut, chronicle 90
Builth (Powys) 157, 165

Bul, family
  Joos de (d. 1488) 20n, 34, 100
  Katherine de 34
Bulkeley, family
  Sir Rowland 176n
  Sir William (d. 1490) 176n
Bullock, family 123
Burckhardt, Jacob 84
Burdett, Thomas 137
Burghfield (Berkshire), St Mary's church 12
Burgundy 13, 34, 36, 92
Burscough Priory (Lancashire) 103
Burton-on-Trent 101, 132, 140
  abbey 126, 128
Bury St Edmunds 31, 101
  St Mary's church 31, 32, 102, 104, 105
Byrkhede, John (d. 1468) 38

Cade, Jack 71
Caernarvon (Gwynedd) 164
Caerleon (South Wales) 152, 157
Calais 60, 122, 144, 149
Caly, William, mercer 21
Cambridge 49, 101
Cambridgeshire 99
Canterbury Cathedral 8, 37, 40, 46, 135
  shrine of St Thomas 8
Cardiff 165
Cardigan Castle 164, 165
Cardiganshire 155, 164
Carmarthen Castle 152
Carmarthenshire 155, 164
Carpenter, Christine 13, 14, 15
Carreg Cennen Castle 164
Carshalton (Surrey), All Saints' church 46
Carter, John 170–1, 173
Castiglione, Count Baldesar (d. 1529) 100
Catherine of Valois
  tomb 99
Cawdrey, Richard 27
Caxton, William 90
  St Albans Chronicles 90
  The Booke of the Ordre of Chevalrye or Knyghthode 90
ceremony 5, 28, 30, 38, 95
Chabot, Jean of Emæl (d. 1496) 44
chains 21n, 123, 139, 143, 170
Chaloner, John 115
Chamberlain, Sir William 9
Chandos, family
  Elizabeth 119
  Sir John (d. 1370) 119

Charles the Bold, duke of Burgundy 34, 184
Charles VI, king of France 88
Charles VII, king of France 36
Charles, Nicholas 20
Charleton, Sir Thomas 27, 45
charters 15, 108, 120, 123, 165
Châteauvillain, Seigneur de 36
Chellaston (Derbyshire) 81–2, 101, 132
Cheney, Sir John (d. 1499) 24
Chepstow (Monmouthshire) 169
  castle 165
Cheshire 55–6, 59, 73, 103, 112, 124
Chesterfield (Derbyshire) 122, 123
  All Saints' church 123, 140
  guild of the Holy Cross 123
chivalry 87, 89, 94
Chorlegh, William, steward for
  Penwortham 55
Christomimesis 39
Church Broughton (Derbyshire) 109
Churchyard, Thomas 170
Clanvowe, Sir John 151
Clapham, John 150
Clarell, Thomas 83
Claverley (Salop), All Saints' church 25
Clehonger (Herefordshire), All Saints'
  church 176n
Clervaux, Richard 75
Clifford (Herefordshire) 40n, 157, 158
Clifford, Lord 59
Clifton (Derbyshire) 116
Clinton, Anne 118
clothing 37, 38, 54, 62, 85, 93, 124, 184
coats of arms 20, 37, 51, 75, 93, 100, 115, 116, 121,
  125, 131, 134, 140, 151, 155, 161, 169
Cobham, family 12, 180
  Sir Reginald (d. 1446) 8
Cockayne, family 67, 108, 110, 113, 117, 118, 121,
  123, 125, 126, 143, 144n, 145
  Isabel 117
  John (d. 1505) 110, 114, 115, 116, 117, 124, 125,
    137
  John of Bury Hatley 116
  Sir John (d. 1438) 107, 116, 117, 143, 144
  Sir Thomas (d. 1537) 116, 117
  Thomas (d. 1488) 81n, 107, 115, 116, 117, 129,
    137–8, 146
coinage 183
Coldbrook House, Abergavenny 164
Colebrook Ward (Derbyshire) 127
Colte, family 104
  Thomas 44

240   INDEX

Commines, Philippe de 60
Commons, parliamentary 50, 52, 53, 54, 55, 57, 58, 66, 71
Constable, Sir Marmaduke (d. 1520) 68
Constantinople 151
constructivism 4
Conyers, family 15
    Sir John 149
corbels 6
Corby 160
Cornwall 76, 100, 101
Cornwall, Cecily 130
Cotton, John, goldsmith 25
county community 14, 67, 86
Courtenay, family
    Thomas, earl of Devon (d. 1461) 74
    William, bishop of London and archbishop of Canterbury 51
courtiers 20, 43, 100, 155, 184–5
courts 11, 22, 22n, 25, 26, 34, 35, 46, 51, 57, 59, 62, 65, 66, 74, 88, 89, 92, 93, 111, 112, 123, 127, 153, 154, 161, 167, 183
Coventry 101, 115, 150, 157
Coxe, William 170–1
Crickhowell (Powys) 156
Croft Castle 135, 141
Croft, family 75
    Sir Richard (d. 1509) 135, 141
Cromwell, Ralph Lord 89, 124
Crossley, Frederick H. 9
Croxall (Staffordshire) 120, 129
Croyland Chronicle 40, 73, 76
Cubley (Derbyshire) 81n, 109, 118, 134
    St Andrew's church 107, 133, 139
Curzon, family 107, 110, 114, 120, 124, 125, 126
    John (d. 1405) 120
    John II (d. c. 1459) 119, 120, 121, 130
    John III (d. c. 1492) 24, 81n, 107, 110, 114, 120, 127, 128, 129, 140, 141, 146
    John of Croxall 129
    Margaret 121
    Richard (d. 1496) 120, 131
    Thomas of Croxall 129
    Thomasine, daughter of John II 130

Dafydd Llwyd 168
Dalby, Thomas, canon of York Minster 31
Darell, Sir John 83
Dartasso, Janico 58
Daubeney, William, clerk of the king's jewels 27–8
Davies, Rees 86

Debenham, Sir Gilbert 104–5
Della Croce, family 110
Delves, Margaret, daughter of Sir Henry Delves 137
Denbigh 157
Derby 115
Devereux, Walter, Lord Ferrers 152, 152n, 153, 154, 155
Dezman, John 169
Diddington (Huntingdonshire), St Lawrence's church 38
Digswell (Hertfordshire), St John's church 59
Dinas (Gwynedd) 157
dogs 50–4
Donne, family 151
    Donne Triptych 2, 46
    Elizabeth 2, 46
    Sir John (d. 1503) 2, 46, 154n, 165
Dorset 105, 137
dove 39
Dronfield (Derbyshire), St John the Baptist's church 81n, 81–2, 131
Dryslwyn 165
Dublin, St Audoen's church 100
duchy of Lancaster 44, 62, 66, 103, 104, 106, 108, 109, 116, 119, 125–8, 129, 145, 146
Dudley, Edmund 69
Duffield Frith (Derbyshire) 125, 126, 127
Dugdale, Sir William
    Book of Monuments 99
Dunham Massey (Cheshire) 112, 130

East Harling (Norfolk) 9
East Riding 101
Edgecote, battle of (1469) 68, 147, 148, 149–52, 154, 158, 159, 160, 165, 167, 175n, 178, 184
Edmund, earl of Lancaster 41
Edward I, king of England 40
Edward III, king of England 23, 39, 59
Edward IV, king of England 14, 15, 23, 26, 27, 29, 31, 34, 38, 40, 41, 42, 44, 58, 61, 65, 67, 68, 68n, 70, 72, 89, 92, 105, 109, 113, 120, 122, 123, 126, 128, 130, 134, 145, 147, 154, 155, 159, 161, 162, 163, 165, 166, 167, 168, 172, 175n, 176, 184, 184n
    coronation 155
    French expedition of 1475 112
    household ordinances 26, 44–5, 73
Edward of Lancaster, Prince of Wales 59, 62
Eleanor of Provence, queen of Henry III 40, 41
Ellen Gethin 172

Ellesmere, Edward 25
Elvaston (Derbyshire) 108, 145
Elwyck, Thomas 157
Emscote (Warwickshire), All Saints' church 99
enamel 7, 21n, 27, 162
enfeoffments 15, 109, 115, 117, 120, 125, 158
English Civil War 99
Epiphany Rising 19
Esdaile, Katherine A. 9
Etwall (Derbyshire) 111, 116, 124
Ewyas (Monmouthshire) 100, 157, 174
exchequer 22, 27, 111
Eylestone, John, sheriff and mayor of Lincoln 44
Eyre, family
    Ralph, son of Robert I 82, 131
    Robert I (d. 1459) 131
    Robert II (d. c. 1500) 131

Fastolf, Sir John 28
    collar 24, 28, 40
Felbrigg (Norfolk), St Margaret's church 23
Felbrigge, Sir Simon 23
Ferdinand II, king of Aragon 114
Ferrers, family 118, 120, 125
    Thomas 114
Fetherstone, Thomas 76n, 83
fetterlock 23, 40
fictive kinship 93–5, 151
Finch, Jonathan 10
FitzEustace, Sir Roland 100
Fitzharry, Thomas 164
Fitzherbert, family 81, 82, 90, 107, 108, 109, 112, 114, 115, 117, 118, 124, 125, 127, 140–1, 146, 163
    Anne 114
    Barbara 116
    Elizabeth 110, 124, 185
    Jane of Etwall 116, 124
    John (d. 1531) 110, 112, 114, 124, 125, 127, 128, 134, 135
    John of Etwall 111–12, 116
    John of Somersal 118
    Nicholas 83, 107, 108, 109, 110, 112, 116, 118, 127, 133, 134, 135, 144–5
    Nicholas of Somersal 118, 127
    Ralph 23, 82, 107, 108, 109, 112, 112n, 124, 127, 128, 129, 133, 134, 135, 144–5
    Robert 128
    Sir Anthony 114, 117, 128
    Walter of Somersal 127
    William of Somersal 118
Fladbury (Worcestershire), St John the Baptist's church 44
Flamborough (Yorkshire), St Oswald's church 68
Foljambe, family 123, 128
    Benedicta 140
    Henry (d. 1504) 140
    John 131
Foremark (Derbyshire) 117, 139
forget-me-not 21, 36
Fortescue, Sir John 13, 70
    Governance of England 70
Foston (Derbyshire) 109, 128
Fotherby, family
    Henry 33, 182
    John 33, 182
Fotheringhay, (Northamptonshire)
    castle 104
    collegiate church 42
Foulshurst, Sir Robert 103n
France 13, 35, 36, 60, 64, 72n, 157, 161, 163
Fraunceys, family 108, 110, 113, 115, 117, 118, 125, 126, 129
    Cicely 118
    Isabell 117
    Margaret 118
    John 127
    Richard of Ticknall 117
    Robert (d. c. 1463) 118, 135
    Sir Robert (d. 1420) 135
    Thomas (d. 1482) 81n, 107, 110, 112, 118, 138–9, 146
    Thomas of Ticknall 117
    William of Ticknall 117
Frecheville, family 123
    Peter (d. c. 1504) 131
Friar, Stephen 3
Froissart, Jean 35

Gam, Sir David 158
Gardner, Arthur 9
Gascoigne, family
    Sir William (d. 1419) 81
    Sir William (d. 1461–65) 26, 184
Gaynesford, family
    Margaret (d. 1503) 46
    Nicholas (d. 1498) 46
Geertz, Clifford 5
Gesamtkunstwerk 9
gift theory 29–30
Glamorgan 153

Glastonbury Abbey 150
Gloucester Cathedral 161
Gloucestershire 23, 57n, 102, 163, 165
Golden Fleece, Order of the
  collars 34, 173, 184
goldsmiths 25–6, 28
Gonzaga, family 35
  Gianfrancesco 35
Gough, Richard 9, 170
Govely, Raulyn 19, 57
Gower, John 19, 54–5, 56, 69
  collar 45, 83
  Confessio Amantis 45, 54
  Cronica Tripertita 19
  tomb 45, 83
  Vox Clamantis 19
Great Wardrobe 25
Grene, Ralph (d. 1418) 21, 81
  tomb contract 81
Gresley, Sir John 120
Grey, Edmund, Lord Grey of Ruthin 79
Grey, Henry, Lord Grey of Codnor 108, 114, 115, 120
Grey, Sir Anthony 105
greyhound 20, 52–3, 56
Greystoke, Lord 65
Griffith, family
  Henry 160
  Jane 160
  Joan 160
  William (d. c. 1483) 149, 160, 166, 174
Grimston, Edward 20, 52n
Grove (Herefordshire) 165
guilds 44n, 86, 123
  Corpus Christi 85
Guinigi, family
  Ladislas 35–6
  Paolo 35–6
Guto'r Glyn 148, 163, 167
Gutyn Owain 148
Gwladus Ddu, daughter of Sir David Gam 158, 160
  tomb 152

Haddon Hall (Derbyshire) 89, 122–3
Hall, Edward 12, 41
Hall, John 26
Hampstall Ridware (Staffordshire) 114
Hampton, W.E. 11
Harcourt, Sir Robert 23, 31
Harewell, Roger 65

Harewood (West Yorkshire), All Saints' church 26, 81, 82n, 184
Harlech Castle (Gwynedd) 156, 157
Harling, Anne 9
Harpur, Henry, mason 132, 139–40
Hastings, William Lord (d. 1483) 15, 65, 105, 106, 110, 117, 126, 127, 128–30, 144, 146, 168, 175
  collar 28
Hatfield, family 103
  Robert (d. 1417) 103
Hathersage (Derbyshire), St Michael's and All Angels' church 82, 131
Havard, family of Brecon 151
Haverfordwest (Pembrokeshire) 156, 157, 159, 160, 164
Hawtmount, Robert of Watlington (Oxfordshire) 55
Heage (Derbyshire) 113
  chapel of St Mary 125
Henderson, Virginia 41
Henry Bolingbroke, earl of Derby, afterwards Henry IV 19, 20, 21, 46, 52, 53, 57n, 59
  collars 19, 21, 46, 67, 79
  fox's brush device 52
  greyhound device 20, 56
Henry I, king of England 120
Henry III, king of England 40
Henry IV, king of England 19, 20, 21, 22, 27, 30, 34, 35, 36, 39, 40, 41, 45, 56–7, 59, 103, 108, 120, 126
  motto 28, 36
Henry V, king of England 22, 23, 24, 35, 66, 99, 103, 108, 126, 158
Henry VI, king of England 13, 22n, 35, 60, 65, 67, 71, 83, 108, 126, 129, 167, 182
  portrait 2, 22
  Readeption 33n, 120, 182
Henry VII, king of England 2, 13, 24n, 40, 41, 44, 58, 68, 74, 76, 80, 99, 119, 122, 123, 127, 130, 135, 142, 143, 147, 155, 156, 161, 162, 166, 168, 176
  collars 24, 25, 33, 100, 102, 106
  red dragon 175
Henry VIII, king of England 20, 25, 41, 172
  inventory of goods 26
Henry, Prince of Wales, afterwards Henry V
  collars 57
Henry the Impotent, king of Castile 63
heraldry 6, 11, 12
heralds 2

Herbert, family 68, 151, 157, 158–9, 160, 162, 165, 166, 172, 175, 184
    Anne 152n, 155, 168–9
    Edward, Lord Herbert of Cherbury 172
    John 150, 158, 163–4
    Margaret, wife of Sir Richard Herbert (d. 1469) 170
    mottos 155
    Richard of Ewyas (d. 1510) 100, 174
    Richard, bastard son of William Herbert, 1st earl of Pembroke (d. 1469) 150
    Sir Richard (d. 1469) 82, 100, 148, 150, 151, 152, 154, 155, 156, 158, 162, 164–5, 166–8, 170–1
    Sir Richard (d. c. 1470–80) 148, 172
    Sir Richard (d. 1539) 172
    Sir Walter 160, 162, 169n, 176
    Sir William (d. c. 1518) 160, 164
    Thomas (d. 1469) 150, 152, 159, 162, 163
    Thomas, son of Thomas (d. 1469) 162
    William, earl of Pembroke (d. 1469) 147, 148, 148n, 149, 150, 152–8, 160, 162–3, 166–8, 168–70, 172, 176, 182
    William, 2nd earl of Pembroke and earl of Huntingdon (d. 1491) 157–8, 169n
    William, half-brother of William Herbert, earl of Pembroke 150, 162, 164
    wyvern crest 172
Herbertorum Prosapia 148n, 169
Hereford 152
hermeneutics 4
Hexham, battle of (1464) 89
Heydon, John 65
High Peak (Derbyshire)
honour 122, 125, 127
    lead mine 128
    steward 127, 128
Higham Ferrers (Northamptonshire) 104
Hilton (Derbyshire) 112
Hitchin (Hertfordshire) 105
Hoccleve, Thomas 69
    Regement of Princes 90, 179
Holbrook (Suffolk), All Saint's church 105
Holland, family
    John, duke of Exeter (d. 1447) 60n
    Margaret, duchess of Clarence (d. 1439) 8, 45–6
    Thomas, earl of Kent 36
Hollar, Wenceslaus 8
Holme Pierrepont (Nottinghamshire), St Edmund's church 73, 103, 105n, 107, 124, 135, 143

Holt Castle 28
Holy Trinity
    images 6, 33
House of Lancaster 40, 103, 119, 120, 181
House of York 23, 40, 41, 42, 61, 75, 103, 112, 113, 115, 135, 139, 147, 148, 152, 154, 157, 161, 163, 166, 168, 172, 181
Howard, family
    collar 31
    John, duke of Norfolk (d. 1483) 31, 64
    Margaret, wife of John, duke of Norfolk 31
Hugford, family 99
Hulland Ward (Derbyshire) 127
Humphrey, duke of Gloucester 60n, 115, 159, 163
    collars 25–6
Hungerford, Robert Lord 23

Ieuan Deulwyn 166
Ingoldesthorpe, Sir Edmund 27
Inyn, chief justice 87
Ireland 28, 76, 100
Isabella I, queen of Castile 114
Isabella of Valois, queen of Richard II 36
Italy 2, 92, 100

jewellery 3, 20, 23, 25–6, 28, 33, 38, 46, 57, 90
    inventories 25, 26, 40
Joan of Navarre, queen of Henry IV 28
John of Gaunt, duke of Lancaster 35, 40, 50, 51, 52, 53, 54, 63, 125–6
    arms 20, 51
    collar 20, 21, 34–5, 50, 79, 88
    retainers 20, 52, 54, 103, 104
    Savoy 51
John of Wales 85
John, duke of Bedford (d. 1435) 37, 60n, 64, 83
    collar 35–6
John, duke of Brittany 57n
Johnys, family
    Maud 176n
    Sir Hugh (d. c. 1485) 176n
judiciary 2, 24, 46

Katherine of Aragon 24
Kedleston (Derbyshire), All Saints' church 24, 81n, 107, 114, 131, 132, 140, 141
Keen, Maurice 89
Kennington 51
Kent, Thomas, ambassador 163
Kidwelly (Carmarthenshire) 103, 151, 154n
Killingworth, Henry, abbot of Darley 131

King, Pamela 11
King's Bench, court of 27
King's Newton (Derbyshire) 120
Kington (Herefordshire), St Mary's church 149, 172–3, 176
Knaresborough (North Yorkshire) 103, 104
knight of the Bath 30, 113, 122, 143
knight of the Garter 23, 31, 34, 35, 143, 156
Knightly, family
 Edmund 104n
 Sir Richard 104n
Kniveton (Derbyshire) 121
Kniveton, family 119, 121–2, 124, 126
 Anne 76n, 123, 124 *see also* Bradbourne, Anne
 John 114n, 121, 124
 Nicholas (d. *c.* 1494) 121–2
 Nicholas (d. 1500) 82, 83, 107, 120, 121–2, 128, 129, 141–2, 146
 Thomas 121
Knyvet, William 111

Lancaster, duchy of 44, 62, 66, 103, 104, 104n, 106, 108, 109, 115, 119, 125–8, 129, 145, 146
Lancastrians 11, 22, 23, 24, 30, 35, 46, 52, 55, 59, 60, 60n, 62, 66, 71, 75, 84, 103–4, 105, 106, 108, 109, 110, 113, 115, 119, 121, 122, 124, 126, 138, 144, 145, 149, 154, 155, 156, 157, 165, 168, 180, 181, 182
 affinity 62, 103, 183
Langland, William 52
 Piers Plowman 7, 51
Langley, Elizabeth 130
Langton, Euphemia 26n, 33
Laundey, Thomas, curate 26
lawyers 11, 64, 72, 91, 110, 119
Leicester 103, 153
Leicestershire 14, 81, 106, 133, 140
Leventhorpe, John 44
Lévi-Strauss, Claude 29
Lewis Glyn Cothi 148, 154, 162–3, 165, 166, 167, 173
Lillingstone Lovell (Buckinghamshire), St Mary's church 83
Lingfield (Surrey), St Peter's and St Paul's church 8
literary studies 4
literature 3, 12, 29, 59–60, 69, 85, 89–90, 180
Little Chart (Kent), St Mary's church 83
Little Easton (Essex), St Mary's church 104
Little Longstone (Derbyshire) 115–16

liturgy 7
livery
 and maintenance 2, 49, 50, 54, 61, 62
 badges 1, 22, 27, 28, 57, 58 *see also* badges
 caps/hats 1, 21, 54
 legislation 1, 2 *see also* livery collar, legislation
 ordinances 1, 26, 49
 petitions against 1, 54
 robes 1, 21, 27, 49, 55, 62, 64, 75, 79n, 87
 royal/king's 2, 28, 36, 44–5, 58, 61, 68n, 73, 76, 79–80, 87, 95, 182
livery collar
 and diplomacy 28–36, 44, 93, 183
 and dog collars 20, 50, 52
 and king's dignity 16, 73, 79, 80, 87, 179, 183
 antiquarian interest 3, 15, 170–1, 173
 bequests 27, 31–4, 46, 76, 83, 123, 182, 184
 boar pendant 23, 113, 130, 133, 182, 184n
 broken 29
 broomcod 35, 35n, 55, 57, 88
 cross pendant 1, 172
 depictions in stained glass 9, 20, 34, 80, 102
 distribution of 2, 22, 28, 44, 67
 falcon and fetterlock 23
 gifts 19, 27, 28–36, 44, 46, 72, 183
 gold 1, 8, 21, 25n, 26, 27, 28, 29n, 31, 33, 35, 37, 52, 53, 57, 79, 83n, 93, 123, 162, 170, 184
 Golden Fleece 34, 173, 184–5
 heirlooms 27, 32
 king of France's 35
 leather 1, 20, 46, 93
 legislation 44, 54–61, 97, 179, 183
 lion pendant 23, 27, 34, 46, 130, 133, 137, 138–9, 172, 173, 184n
 Lord Mayor of London's 9, 32
 mermaids 57n
 of hearts 99
 of the duke of Norfolk 57
 park palings 57n
 political significance 21, 36, 147, 181–2, 184
 portcullis pendant 24, 33, 122, 141–2
 ragged staffs 57n
 roses 24, 143, 173, 176n
 silver 1, 8, 22, 22n, 26, 33, 35, 46, 67, 79, 93
 silver-gilt 1, 8, 22, 22n, 26, 35, 67, 79, 93
 SS 2, 3, 8, 9, 13, 14, 19, 20, 21, 22, 23, 25, 25n, 26, 27, 28, 30, 31, 31n, 33, 35, 36–7, 44, 45, 45n, 50, 50n, 67, 68, 72n, 80–1, 83, 93, 100, 102–4, 104n, 107, 114, 116, 122, 123, 128, 140, 141, 142, 143, 144, 152, 155, 161, 175, 176n, 182, 183

suns and roses/Yorkist 2, 3, 9, 12, 13, 14,
    20n, 23, 26, 27, 31, 34, 37–43, 46, 83n, 99,
    100, 102, 104–5, 107, 108–9, 111, 113, 115, 116,
    124, 129–30, 133, 135, 136, 137, 138, 139, 143,
    148, 151, 155, 161, 161n, 170, 172, 173, 174,
    176, 182, 184
  swan pendant 23, 35, 45, 57
  Tudor rose pendant 24, 33, 114
  value 8, 16, 20, 25, 29, 31, 33, 91, 93
  velvet 1, 20
  white roses and mascles 40
Llandaff 153
  Cathedral 26, 82, 174
Llandegai (Gwynedd), St Tegai's church 149,
    174
Llewellyn, Nigel 10, 11
Llywellyn the Great 148
London 4, 50–1, 52, 53, 65, 101, 111, 136, 141,
    148, 157
  Blackheath 34
  Museum of London 2
  National Portrait Gallery 22
  Old St Paul's Cathedral 20, 21, 51
  Tower 25, 26, 153
  Victoria and Albert Museum 2
Longford, family 108
  Alfred 115
  Sir Ralph 114
Louis, duke of Orleans (d. 1407) 20
  porcupine collar 20–1
Lovell, family
  Francis, Viscount Lovell 143
  William, Lord Lovell 24
Lowick (Northamptonshire), St Peter's
    church 21, 68, 81, 83
Ludford Bridge, battle of (1459) 108
Ludlow Castle 104
Lullingstone (Kent), St Botolphs' church 44
Lusk (County Dublin), Church of Ireland 100
Luton, Henry, goldsmith 25
Lutterworth (Leicestershire), St Mary's
    church 81
Lydgate, John 69
  Troy Book 154–5, 176
Lytton, Robert 131

Macclesfield (Cheshire), St Michael's
    church 100, 107, 135, 143
Machen (South Wales) 155
Mainwearing, family 103n
Malory, Sir Thomas
  Le Morte Darthur 72, 90

Mansion House, London 30
Mantua 35
  church of S. Maria delle Grazie 100
  Palazzo Ducale 35
manuscript illumination 1, 20–1, 34, 37, 38,
    38n, 41, 57n, 154–5, 176
Marcus Aurelius Antoninus 40
Margaret of Anjou, queen of Henry VI 25, 31,
    40, 59, 72, 113, 149
Markenfield, Thomas 75n
Marmion, Sir John 104
Marshall, John of Upton 133
Marston Montgomery (Derbyshire) 118
Martorell, Joanot
  Tirant lo Blanc 37
Mathew, family 26, 82
  Christopher (d. *c*. 1531) 174
  David (d. before 1470) 174, 175n
  Sir William (d. 1528) 174
Mauleverer, Joan 141
Maures, Marcellus, goldsmith 25
Mauss, Marcel 29
McFarlane, K.B. 13
Mead, George H. 84
Melbourne (Derbyshire) 127
Melbury Sampford (Dorset), St Mary's
    church 105, 137
Memling, Hans 2, 46
Mercaston (Derbyshire) 121
merchants 1, 6, 11, 31, 93
Metcalfe, family 15
Methley (West Yorkshire), St Oswald's
    church 45, 103
Methley, Joan 24
Meverell, Sir Sampson (d. 1462) 64, 131
Meycok, John 120
Middleham (North Yorkshire) 15, 65, 66
Milan, church of St Eustorgio 100
Minster Lovell (Oxfordshire), St Kenelm's
    church 24
misericords 6
Montagu, family 64, 132
Montgomery, family 107, 108, 109, 118–9, 121,
    125, 126, 128, 143, 139n
  Isabel 118
  Joan 121
  John (d. 1513) 119, 139
  Margery 124
  Nicholas (d. 1465) 81n, 107, 108, 118, 139–40,
    146
  Roger 118
  Sir Nicholas (d. 1435) 118

Sir Nicholas (d. 1494) 119, 124, 126, 127, 129, 132, 139–40
Montgomery 157, 172
 Lymore chapel 172
 St Nicholas's church 148, 172
Monumental brasses 3, 5, 6, 7, 12, 20, 20n, 23, 34, 34n, 38, 44, 46, 57, 57n, 59, 68, 73, 74, 80, 82, 83, 90, 91, 99, 100, 101, 102, 103, 104, 105, 111, 113, 116, 122, 130, 131, 136, 140, 141, 145, 146, 176n, 180
 workshops 101, 101n
Moorecock, William, mason 132, 139–40
More, Sir Thomas 12, 24–5
Morgan, family 151
 Sir John (d. 1493) 174
Morgan, Lewis H. 29
Morley (Derbyshire), St Matthew's church 74, 82, 130
Morley, family
 arms 131
Mortimer, family 40, 147, 148, 167
 Anne 104
 estates 104, 105, 147
Mortimer's Cross, battle of (1461) 38, 148, 154, 159
Moton, Elizabeth, daughter of Reginald Moton 140
Mottram in Longendale (Greater Manchester), St Michael's and All Angels' church 103n
Mountford, Sir Edmund 83
Mowbray, John, duke of Norfolk 60n, 64
Mugginton (Derbyshire), All Saints' church 82, 83, 107, 119, 121, 141–2

Namier, Lewis 68
Neath Abbey 165
necklace 1, 33, 39, 51, 52n, 151
 cockleshells 114
Needwood Chase (Derbyshire) 125
Nero, Emperor 40
Netherton (Derbyshire) 114
Neville, family 15, 57, 60, 62, 65, 113, 154, 182
 Cecily, duchess of York (d. 1495) 42, 64
 George, Lord Latimer (d. 1469) 150n
 Isabel 113 see also Bothe, Isabel
 Joan, countess of Arundel (d. 1462) 8n
 John, Lord Neville 65
 Ralph, 2nd earl of Westmorland 23, 161n, 182
 Ralph, 3rd earl of Westmorland 113
 Richard, earl of Salisbury 12

Richard, earl of Warwick 14, 15, 60, 108, 149
 Sir Henry 150
 Sir William 151
Newport 155, 159, 164
 St Woolos Cathedral 174
Newton, family
 Emmota 102
 Isabel 102
 Sir John (d. 1488) 102
 Sir Richard (d. 1449) 102
Nibley Green, battle of (1470) 160–1
nobility 6, 13, 15, 29, 44, 69, 87, 88, 89, 90
Norbury (Derbyshire)
 hall 109, 117
 St Mary's and St Barlok's church 23, 81n, 82, 83, 107, 111, 112, 113, 132, 133–6, 141
Northampton 150, 169
 battle of (1460) 108, 154
Norwich 101
 Cathedral 33
Nottingham 132, 143, 149, 161
Nottinghamshire 14, 63, 68, 74, 82, 106, 110, 121, 123, 135, 143

Offer, A. 30
Okeover, family 116
Order of Granada 114
Order of the Garter 35, 42, 100, 157
Ormskirk (Lancashire) 103
Osmaston (Derbyshire) 109
Over Peover (Cheshire), St Lawrence's church 103n
Ovid 56
Owain Glyndŵr 167
Owen, George 173
Owston (South Yorkshire), All Saint's church 103
Oxford
 Merton College 20
 St John's College 37
 Sarum Breviary 37
Oxnead (Norfolk) 66
oyer and *terminer*, commissions of 88, 164

Paestum 39
painting 4, 9, 20, 22, 38, 92, 184
Pampynge, John 73
Panofsky, Erwin 10
parhelion 39
Paris
 St Denis 6

parliament 19, 25, 34, 50, 54, 67, 89, 107, 115, 118, 180
  ('Bad', 1377) 51, 52
  ('Good', 1376) 52
  see also livery, legislation; livery collar, legislation
Paston, family 63, 95
  John II 61, 90
  John III 59, 65
  Margaret 65–6
Paynell, Richard 115
Peak forest 126
Peasants' Revolt 52
Pecche, Sir William 44
Peirce, Charles Sanders 78
Pembroke Castle 156, 159
Penrhyn (Gwynedd) 174
Percy, family 15
  Henry, 4th earl of Northumberland 65
  Henry, marshal of England 51
  Thomas, Lord Egremont 62
Peryent, Joan (d. 1415) 59
petitions 1, 54, 58, 71, 79
Philip the Good, duke of Burgundy 34
Pickering (North Yorkshire), St Peter's and St Paul's church 103
Pierrepont, Sir Henry (d. 1499) 74, 103, 106n, 107, 122, 123–4, 123n, 135, 143
Pinxton (Derbyshire) 124
Pisan, Christine de 20
Plantagenet, family
  Cecily, duchess of York see Neville, Cecily
  Edward, earl of March, afterwards Edward IV 40, 105, 148, 154, 164
  Edward, earl of Warwick 34
  Edward of Middleham, Prince of Wales 59
  Edward, Prince of Wales, afterwards Edward V 29, 55, 113, 163, 164
  Elizabeth of York 13, 41, 46, 135
  George, duke of Clarence 42–3, 61, 62, 64, 65, 70, 71, 110, 115, 117, 122, 128, 130, 144, 145, 149
  Isabel, sister of Richard, duke of York 104n
  Katherine, illegitimate daughter of Richard III 157
  Richard, duke of Gloucester, afterwards Richard III 15, 60, 63, 64, 65, 66, 113, 182
  Richard, duke of York (d. 1460) 24, 28, 40, 58, 62, 64, 66, 71, 104, 105, 108, 114, 147–8, 152, 153, 154, 158, 163, 164, 165, 176
Pliny 39

Plummer, Charles 13, 61
poetry 19, 41, 60, 168, 170
  Richard the Redeless 56
Pole, family of Radbourne 114, 120, 121, 125, 126, 128, 134
  German 120
  Jane 140 see also Fitzherbert, Jane of Etwall
  John of Hartington 120
  John, son of Ralph (d. 1492) 124, 140
  Peter 107, 119
  Ralph (d. c. 1460) 107, 119, 120
  Ralph (d. 1492) 81n, 107, 114, 119, 129, 140–1, 146
Pole, family
  John de la, 2nd duke of Suffolk 12n
  William de la, 1st duke of Suffolk 65
Polesworth (Warwickshire) 137
political culture 16, 49
  flags 78
Pollard, Anthony 14, 15
polychromy 7, 26
Pontefract (West Yorkshire) 60, 66, 103
  castle 36, 103
Pooley (Warwickshire) 137
Porter, Thomas 64
portraiture 2, 20, 22, 24, 26, 31, 36, 40, 52n, 183, 184
Postern (Derbyshire) 127
Powtrell, Thomas 110, 118
prayer beads 42
Prentys, Thomas, mason 81, 132
Prince Fee (Derbyshire) 111, 163
propaganda 12, 22, 38, 41, 61, 76
Puleston, Roger 154
Purbeck marble 136
purgatory 6

Raby Castle 113
Radbourne (Derbyshire) 107, 114, 119–20, 121, 124, 134
  chapel of St Nicholas 140
  St Andrew's church 81n, 107, 114, 132, 140–1
Raglan (Monmouthshire) 68, 160
  castle 156, 158, 160–1, 162, 168, 170
Ravensdale (Derbyshire) 122
Reames, James 83
Redesdale, Robin of 71, 149
Redman, Edward 82n
regalia 5, 22, 34
religion 38, 85
Repton (Derbyshire), St Wystan's church 81n, 107, 110, 132, 138–9

Reresbie, family 184
   Lionel 33
   Thomas 33
Resumption, Act of 162
retainers/retinues 20, 21, 22, 34, 35, 50, 52, 53, 54, 55, 56, 57, 58, 59, 60, 62, 63, 64, 65, 66, 67, 79, 86, 87, 88, 93, 94, 108, 114, 115, 120, 126, 128, 129, 130, 144, 158, 159, 163, 166, 175
Reynolds, Susan 86
Rhys ap Thomas, Sir 147
Richard II, king of England 13, 21, 23, 24, 30, 36, 52, 53–4, 56, 58
   badges 39, 54, 55, 56
   Cheshire affinity 55, 73
   collars 30, 34–5, 88
   tomb 55
   white hart badge 53, 55, 57n
   Wilton Diptych 88
Richard III, king of England 23, 24, 27, 40, 59, 68, 74, 113, 119, 122, 130, 132, 135, 157, 161, 164–5, 166, 182, 184n *see also* badges, white boar
Richmond (North Yorkshire) 15, 24n, 66, 75
Ripon Cathedral 57n
Rodsley (Derbyshire) 118
Rolleston, John (d. 1482) 81n, 82, 131
Rome 39
   emperor 39
Roos, family
   Sir Henry 33
   Sir Richard 33
rosary 42
   Langdale 42
rose 2, 24, 26, 27, 38, 39, 40, 42, 47, 61, 136, 137, 139, 140, 143, 173, 174, 176n
   chaplets 39, 42
   gold 40, 41
   red 33, 39, 40, 41, 42, 61
   red and white/Tudor 24, 40, 41, 80, 114, 139, 140, 141
   Rosalia 39–40
   tree 41
   white 23, 24, 28, 38, 40, 40n, 41, 42, 60, 61, 154
   wreaths 39, 42
rose-en-soleil 2, 23, 38, 39, 40, 41, 85, 136
Rouen 40
Rous Roll 42
Rowcliffe, family
   Margaret 103
   Sir David (d. 1407) 103
   Sir Richard 103

royal household 2, 26, 30, 31, 36, 43, 44, 45, 46, 52, 57, 61, 72, 73, 84, 87, 103, 105, 119, 122, 145, 155, 162, 163, 165, 166, 183
   king's esquires 26, 27, 44, 45, 57, 73, 87, 113, 120, 122, 154, 154n, 162, 163, 164
   king's knights 26–7, 45, 56, 57, 61, 68, 73, 156, 162
   sergeant of the kitchen 87
   yeomen of the crown 61, 73, 79, 162
Roydon (Essex), St Peter's church 44, 104
Rozmital, Leo of 26
Rugeley (Staffordshire) 120
Russell, John, bishop of Lincoln 70
Ryde, Colin 81

Sacheverell, family 130
   John (d. 1485) 74, 130
sacred monogram 139
saints 6, 33, 41–2, 46, 141
   relics 80
   St Anne 42
   St Antony 135, 141
   St Katherine 38
   St Margaret 38
   St Sitha/Zitha 140, 141
Salisbury Cathedral 33
Sandal Castle 104
Santiago de Compostela 114
Saul, Nigel 11, 12
Saussure, Ferdinand de 78
Savage, family 100, 124
   Sir John IV (d. 1495) 107, 122, 124, 127, 128, 135, 143
   Sir John V (d. 1492) 128–9, 143
Saville, Sir John (d. 1481) 104, 105, 174, 184
Sawbridgeworth (Hertfordshire), St Mary's church 44
Sawley (Derbyshire), All Saints' church 82, 106, 107, 112, 113, 136
Say, Sir John 104, 105
Scarborough (North Yorkshire) 122
Scolton Manor museum 149, 173–4
Scotland 99
Scrope, Thomas, Lord Scrope of Masham 63, 65
skull cap 141
sculpture 1, 4, 22, 31–2, 33, 83, 85, 92, 100, 168, 180
   Decorated 9
   Gothic 9
   Romanesque 9
seals 37, 79

of Richard, duke of York 40
Secreta Secretorum 90
semiotics 16, 78–9, 80
Sherburn-in-Elmet (North Yorkshire), All Saint's church 33
sheriffs 2, 44, 72, 107, 110, 116, 119, 120, 121, 130, 153n, 155
Shirley, family 116, 143
Shottle (Derbyshire) 122
Shrewsbury (Salop) 115
    battle of (1403) 103, 108
    St Mary's church 116
Sigismund of Luxembourg, Holy Roman Emperor 35
sign, semiotics concept 56, 78–9, 80
signets 20, 58
Skinner, Quentin 49, 71
Skipwith, Sir William 64
Skydmore, Sir John 156, 164–5
Slebech (Pembrokeshire), Commandery church 173
Smith, C.E.J. 3
Smith, Jankyn/John 104, 105
Smithfield
    St Bartholomew's church 111
    tournament (1390) 55
Snelston (Derbyshire) 109, 118
Somersal Herbert (Derbyshire) 118, 127
Somerset 102, 105
Sorell, John 112
Southworth, Nicholas 72
Spain 21, 114, 163
Spratton (Northamptonshire), St Andrew' church 50n, 100
St Albans
    Cathedral 105
    first battle of (1455) 12, 62, 64
St David's Cathedral 175
St Lowe, Elizabeth 130
Stafford, family of Shrewsbury
    Johanna 115
    John 115
    Nicholas (d. 1471) 115–16
Stafford, family 159
    Edward, earl of Wiltshire (d. 1499) 68, 76n, 83
    Henry, duke of Buckingham (d. 1483) 129, 159, 164, 165, 166, 175
    Humphrey, duke of Buckingham (d. 1460) 59, 108, 114, 120
    Humphrey, earl of Devon (d. 1469) 149, 150
    Sir Humphrey (d. 1450) 23

stained glass 1, 8, 9, 20, 30, 34, 38, 38n, 43, 49, 72, 80, 90, 95, 100, 102, 106, 115, 125, 134, 175, 183
Stainsby (Derbyshire) 124
Stallworth, Simon 129
Stanhope, Margaret 130
Stanley, family
    Catherine 143
    George, Lord Strange 64
    Sir Edward 62
    Sir William (d. 1495) 28–9
    Thomas, earl of Derby 103, 143
Stanton (Derbyshire) 117
Stathum, family
    Henry (d. 1480) 130, 131
    John (d. 1454) 130
    Nicholas 131
    Sir Thomas (d. 1469) 130, 131
Staunton, Thomas (d. c. 1486) 106n
Staveley (Derbyshire), St John the Baptist's church 131
Stenton, Lady 62
Stoke (Derbyshire) 115
Stone, Lawrence 9
Stonor, family
    Sir William 64, 129
    Thomas 64
Stothard, Charles Alfred 9, 23n
Strelley (Nottinghamshire), All Saints' church 82, 143
Strelley, Sir John (d. 1501) 82, 143
Sudbury (Derbyshire) 118
sumptuary legislation 91
sun 2, 8, 23, 24, 38, 39, 40, 41, 42, 47, 134, 176n
    Sol Invictus 39
sunburst 39, 41, 60
sundial 39
Sutton Bonington (Nottinghamshire), St Anne's church 106n
Sutton Scarsdale (Derbyshire), St Mary's church 131
Sutton, Robert, mason 81, 132
swan 23, 35, 36, 45, 52, 57, 59, 60, 60n *see also* livery collar, swan pendant
Swansea, St Mary' church 176
Swarkestone (Derbyshire), St James's church 25, 81–2, 131
Swayne, family
    Henry 33
    William 33
Swinton, Sir Thomas 50, 52, 75
Swynford, family

Sir John 50n, 100
symbol, semiotics concept 5, 10, 77–80
Symonds, Richard 8, 26, 170

Tabowre, Edmund 31
Talbot, family 60, 123
    Anne, wife of Sir Henry Vernon (d. 1515) 142
    John, 1st earl of Shrewsbury (d. 1453) 123
    John, 2nd earl of Shrewsbury (d. 1460) 108
    Sir Gilbert 122
    Thomas, Viscount Lisle 161
Tapton, John, retainer of George, duke of Clarence 65
Taster, Peter, ambassador 163
Tenby (Pembrokeshire)
    St Mary's church 176n
    St Anne's chapel 176n
Tetzel, Gabriel 26
Tewkesbury, battle of (1471) 70, 157, 165
The Descryuyng of Mannes Membres 69
Thomas ap Griffith 170
Thornhill (West Yorkshire), St Michael's and All Angels' church 104, 105, 174, 184
Thorplandclose (Northamptonshire) 79
Throckmorton, John 44
Thwaytes, Thomas, chancellor of the exchequer 111
Tickhill (South Yorkshire) 103
    steward 122, 128
Ticknall (Derbyshire) 117
Tideswell (Derbyshire), St John the Baptist's church 64, 131
Tildesley, Christopher, goldsmith 28
Tintern Abbey 148, 168–9, 169n
Tissington (Derbyshire) 118
tombs
    angel motif 6, 81–2, 81n, 133, 137, 139, 141
    cadaver 11, 31
    canopies 7, 10
    contracts 81, 83, 132, 140, 181
    Greek 10
    inscriptions 6, 46, 64, 68, 86, 111, 112, 121, 133–4, 134n, 136, 137, 139n, 141, 169, 173
    lion motif 133, 173
    mural 137
    oil gilding 8
    sandstone 143
    sketches of 82, 169–70, 170–1, 173
    sleeping bedesman motif 82, 82n
    weepers 83

Tong (Salop), St Bartholomew's church 23, 24, 67, 107, 122, 123, 142–3, 144, 145
Tournai, siege of 116
Towton, battle of (1461) 40, 67, 71, 175n
Tremayl, Thomas 126
Tresham, family
    Sir Thomas 67
    William 79, 80
Tretower (Powys) 156, 158
Trevisa, John 89
Trueblode, John 157
Trussell, Sir William 120
Tuddenham, Sir Thomas 65
Tudor, family
    Arthur, Prince of Wales 24, 122, 123
    Edmund, earl of Richmond 152
    Jasper, duke of Bedford 83, 147, 154, 155, 156, 157, 165, 166
Tutbury (Staffordshire)
    castle and honour 65, 66, 103, 106, 108, 109, 125–8, 129, 132, 145, 146, 184
    deputy steward 110, 127
    constable 126
    priory 109, 112
    steward 126, 127, 129
Tyrell, Ann 104

Upton (Northamptonshire), St Michael's church 104
Upton, Nicholas 1
Usk (Monmouthshire) 152, 156, 157, 158

van Delf, John, goldsmith 25
Vaughan, family 148, 152, 154n, 155, 156, 159, 160, 162, 166, 168, 176
    John 158
    John, chaplain 160
    Philip 154
    Sir Roger of Bredwardine 152, 158, 176
    Sir Roger of Tretower (d. 1471) 154, 156, 157, 158, 162, 164, 165
    Thomas (d. 1469) 149, 150, 153, 158, 159, 162, 166, 172–3, 176
    Thomas, (d. 1493) 162, 165
    Thomas, son of Watkin Vaughan (d. 1456) 162
    Thomas, yeoman of the crown 162
    Watkin (d. 1456) 159
    Watkin (d. 1504) 166
    Watkin, son of Sir Roger Vaughan of Tretower 152, 165
    William of Clifford 158

Vaux, Nicholas 24
Vegetius Renatus, Publius Flavius 90
Venus 39
Vere, family
    John de, earl of Oxford 60
Vernon, family 67, 89, 108, 113, 117, 122–3, 124, 127, 128, 143, 145
    Agnes 117
    Benedicta 23, 144
    John 110, 117
    Richard (d. 1517) 24, 123
    Roger 110, 125
    Sir Henry (d. 1515) 70, 107, 117, 122, 123, 124, 129, 142–3, 144
    Sir Richard (d. 1451) 23, 107, 114, 123, 137, 144
    Sir William (d. 1467) 122, 145
    Thomas 117
Virgin 38, 39, 41, 43
    alabaster figure 33
    Ave Maria 42
    figure at Norwich Cathedral 33
    Our Lady's Psalter 42
    statue 33, 80
    symbolism 41–2
Visconti, Gian Galeazzo 39

Wakefield (West Yorkshire) 104, 105
    battle of (1460) 154
Walker Bynum, Caroline 80
Warbeck, Perkin 28
Warburg Institute 4, 10
Warkworth, John 150
Warwickshire 14, 20, 64, 67, 99, 137
Waterton, Robert (d. 1424) 27, 27n, 45, 83, 103
Weever, John 7, 9, 72
Welle, Eleanor 57
Welles, family 117
    John 111
Wenlock, John Lord 60
Wentloog (Newport) 155
West Tanfield (North Yorkshire), St Nicholas's church 104
Westminster 154
    Abbey 6, 24, 55, 59, 99
    jewel house 25, 26
Weston Underwood (Derbyshire) 120
Wethersfield (Essex), St Mary Magdalene's and St Mary the Virgin's church 104
Whitchurch (Salop), St Alkmund's church 123
White, family
    John 176n
    Thomas 176n
Wighton, Edmund 82
William ap Thomas, Sir 152, 158, 159, 160–1, 163, 173
    tomb 81, 100, 176n
Willoughby, family
    Henry 14
    Richard 68, 83
wills 15, 26, 26n, 27, 31–2, 42, 44n, 72, 76, 82, 83, 85, 109, 110–11, 112, 120, 123, 123n, 124, 125, 128, 130–1, 134, 135, 150, 151, 154n, 158, 168–9, 170, 182
Windsor Castle 153, 154
    Poor Knights of 176n
Wingerworth (Derbyshire) 120
Wingfield (Derbyshire) 89
Wingfield (Suffolk), St Andrew's church 12n
Wingfield, Sir Robert 9
Wirksworth (Derbyshire)
    lead mines 128
Wiston (Pembrokeshire) 148, 160, 173
Wogan, family 148, 156, 158
    Elizabeth 159
    Henry of Boulston 160
    Margaret 173
    Sir Henry 149, 151, 159–60, 163, 173–4
    Sir John 151
Wollaton (Nottinghamshire), St Leonard's church 68, 83
Woodville, family 150
    Anthony, Lord Scales and Earl Rivers 149
    Elizabeth, queen of Edward IV 46
    Mary 149
    Richard, Earl Rivers 149
Wotton-under-Edge (Gloucestershire), St Mary's church 57n
Worcester, William 87, 154
workshops 77, 80–4, 101, 101n, 102, 132, 143, 174, 180, 181
Wright, Susan 107, 145
Writhe's Garter Book 41
Wyclif, John 51
Wymondham, John 73

Yatton (Somerset), St Mary's church 102
Year books 87
York 101, 132
    Minster 22, 31
Youlgreave (Derbyshire), All Saints' church 81, 106, 107, 116, 117, 132, 137–8, 144